Inherent Human Rights

Pennsylvania Studies in Human Rights
Bert B. Lockwood, Jr., Series Editor
A complete list of books in the series is available from the publisher.

Inherent Human Rights
Philosophical Roots of the Universal Declaration

Johannes Morsink

PENN

University of Pennsylvania Press

Philadelphia

Published by
University of Pennsylvania Press
Philadelphia, Pennsylvania 19104-4112

Printed in the United States of America on acid-free paper

10 9 8 7 6 5 4 3 2 1

Library of Congress Cataloging-in-Publication Data

Morsink, Johannes.
   Inherent human rights : philosophical roots of the Universal Declaration / Johannes Morsink.
       p.   cm. — (Pennsylvania Studies in Human Rights
   ISBN 978-0-8122-4162-4 (alk. paper)
   Includes bibliographical references and index.
       1. Human rights—History—20th century. I. Title
JC571.M837   2009
323.01—dc22   2008041884

For Nancy

Contents

Introduction: The Need to Think Beyond the Political

During the sixty years since its adoption by the Third UN General Assembly in December 1948, the Universal Declaration of Human Rights has become a remarkable success story. When one buys the document in bulk from the UN it costs only seventy-five cents, measures four by five inches, and can be readily put in one's hip pocket or purse. Yet within this little blue and white booklet one finds articulated the moral lingua franca of our age. This booklet has been the inspirational source for millions of persecuted and oppressed individuals around the world. It has been translated into even more languages than has the Bible. It became the platform for thousands of domestic and international nongovernmental organizations (NGOs) and served as a model for the bills of rights in the constitutions of dozens of countries that have been liberated from colonial yokes and crumbling empires. It is the ultimate source of almost any human rights reference that my reader may run across in the media, and it lies at the heart of most accusations that some government or other has grossly abused the human rights of its own or other peoples. For all these reasons it makes sense for us to scrutinize the Declaration and to lay bare and explain the philosophical roots of the rights it proclaims.

Most great movements of history have had their texts to carry around with them. For religious movements, it may be a version of the Bible, the Qur'an, the Bhagavad Gita, or another sacred text. Believers can be seen reading and getting in touch with their source of inspiration while standing in line or sitting on a bench. For those not religiously inclined, the text could be Confucius's *Analects*, Marx's *Communist Manifesto*, or Mao's Little Red Book. To understand any of these religious or secular movements and engage in dialogue with their members, others would do well to follow their example and study these inspirational texts. They are canonical and serve as catechisms for their members, who study them to learn the basics of their religious or secular faith. If we wish to succeed in our dialogues with adherents of these ideologies, we must familiarize ourselves with their texts, for it is on these texts that they take their stand and from them that they draw their inspiration. The document that is the subject of this study performs this kind of canonical function for the enormous human rights movement that has sprung up since the end of World War II and that has covered the globe, so that now there is not a single nation on earth that is not caught up in the moral web woven by the articles of this document.

The seminal texts that feed some of history's great movements make their impact and then take on a life of their own, without the movement members always taking the time to see what precisely their sacred text says or does not say, or how it was written and by whom and for what reasons. It was this kind of problem that in the 1980s led me to an investigation of how the Universal Declaration came to be written and its text negotiated in the drafting chambers of the early, heady days of the United Nations.[1] Being a philosopher and political theorist by training and teaching courses in these fields, I could not help but notice the intellectual challenges that this booklet threw up to contemporary theorizing about human rights while the movement grew to its present humongous proportions. Because the language and substance of human rights worked its way into international legal structures and into the discourse of diplomats and statesmen on all continents, theorists noted the movement's spread and began to theorize about it. From their different perspectives in political science, philosophy, anthropology, international law, psychology, and literature, they made theoretical observations about what a human right is, how many there are, and about what might justify our belief in them. Because these theoreticians hail from different corners of the academic world, the literature on human rights is not tied together by any single theme or by an easily managed single body of data. This is not necessarily a bad thing, for, as I said, these seminal texts do take on a life of their own that separates them from their drafting and founding periods. These are living documents that are animated by the vision of those who wrote them under certain specific conditions, documents whose original vision may require adjustments in a later day and age.

The history of the human rights movement in the second half of the twentieth century is not unlike that of the French and American experiences at the end of the eighteenth century. As Lynn Hunt points out in her book on those two revolutions, when in the 1790s the French General Assembly set out to write a new constitution and to revamp its legal system, "the supposedly metaphysical nature of the [1789] Declaration of the Rights of Man and of the Citizen proved to be a very positive asset."[2] In the ensuing legislative discussions "The virtue of beginning with the general became apparent once the specific came into question," which it did as soon as Protestants, Jews, women, those who owned no property, slaves, and actors heard or read about the abstract rights the French Assembly had declared (151). "In other words," says Hunt, "the abstract universalism of the declaration was now coming home to roost" (153). Speaking of the abolition of slavery by the 1794 French Assembly, she reiterates that "Once again the potent combination of theory (declaring rights) and practice (in this case outright revolt and rebellion) forced the hand of the legislators" (164).

The same thing happened in the second half of the twentieth century. Practitioners of human rights counted on and used the metaphysical abstractions of the 1948 Universal Declaration to place the burden of proof on those who sought to hold back on the implementation of these rights. After the abstractions of the Declaration were further elaborated in the International Covenants of the 1960s, diplomats, domestic constitution writers, and parliamentarians around the world have been "forced" into taking the next implementation step, whatever that was. For once the genie is out of the bottle, there is no way of getting it back in. Even a pragmatic thinker like Machiavelli understood this.[3] The difference between these eighteenth° and twentieth-century installments of the movement is that to illumine the metaphysics used in the eighteenth century, scholars needed to analyze the debates of domestic legislatures, as Hunt and Elston have done,[4] whereas contemporary research must spread itself out over any number of global assemblies and conferences, organized by the United Nations and its various affiliated institutions, as well as numerous regional human rights organizations. My first book on the Declaration, the findings of which I use throughout the present volume, serves as an example of this global kind of research.[5] There exist today some 200 human rights implementation instruments that cover most of the rights in the Universal Declaration, and this number is still growing. What we see at work in these varied expansions and elaborations of abstract declarations is the same "bulldozer force of the revolutionary logic of rights" (Hunt, 160). This is the logic of the Enlightenment claim that there exists a "sameness of human nature across cultures and classes" (86), one that in this book I recast as the doctrine of simple inherence. Hunt's bulldozer metaphor helps us see that metaphysical thinking is an essential component of the fight against conditions of oppression and suppression around the globe.

This book addresses the enormous proliferation of human rights interpretations in various disciplinary discussions by offering a unified theory that is openly based on a close study of the intellectual implications of the UDHR for our present-day theorizing about the concept and scope of human rights. Just as it makes a great deal of sense for moral, political, and legal theorists to make a close study of a country's founding document or constitution, so it makes sense for us to make a close study of the theoretical implications of the UDHR as the founding document of the human rights movement. While it is not at all a world constitution and does not even pretend to recommend a world government, this small booklet has ended up being the mother of more than 200 regional and international human rights instruments that divide themselves into declaratory, promotional, and enforcement regimes that cover all persons, groups, and peoples or nations on earth. It has therefore had a profound moral impact on our world and stands as a moral (and increasingly legal) beacon in the midst of the horrors of the twentieth and twenty-first centuries. I make no apologies for the obvious connections that the theory I here develop has with Enlightenment ways of thinking about morality and politics. That suits my desire to hold contemporary human rights theorists accountable to their founding document. It just so happens that respecting that heritage also has numerous theoretical benefits. The great majority of the drafters of the blue booklet believed that just as a scientist in a California research lab can make a discovery that is valid the world over, so the rights in this booklet (written up in the late 1940s) are possessed by all people everywhere. And just as 2 plus 2 made 4 before there ever were man-made states, so it has always been wrong to torture people or deny them the basics of health care.

The theory of inherent human rights that I present and defend in this book came to me as a result of my joint study of the contents of the blue booklet and my simultaneous discovery that what I found there often conflicted with what human rights theorists in various disciplines were writing (or not writing) about the booklet or its articles. I often felt that certain authors strayed too far from what I understood the booklet to be saying about what a human right is, or how many of them there are. Over the years this joint effort in both history and human rights theorizing led to the confrontation that this book places before the reader. The point of the present book is to warn the international human rights community—and especially its theorists—not to ignore this connection between metaphysical thinking and the forces of rebellion. By ignoring the philosophical roots of the founding text of their movement, many human rights theorists are weakening those forces and making them fight with one hand behind their back.

I find an example of such handicapped fighting in Michael Ignatieff's 1999 Tanner Lectures. These Lectures demonstrate to me the need for human rights theorists to think beyond the political and to return to the metaphysical thoughts that informed the birth of the movement. We must not let the notion of human rights be imprisoned in the domain of the political and juridical, which is what will happen if thinkers like

Ignatieff have their way. For that reason I lay out in this book the philosophical roots of the founding text of the human rights movement. The idea is to give activists a place to gather philosophical strength when someone asks them for an argument that explains and defends the universality of human rights. As I take issue in the rest of this introduction with Ignatieff's much too pragmatic approach to our belief in human rights, the reader will get a preview of what I argue in each of the book's chapters.

In Chapters 1 and 2, I set before us the doctrine of inherent human rights that I claim to find in the Universal Declaration. That doctrine is made up two universality theses. According to the first thesis, discussed in "The Metaphysics of Inherence" (Chapter 1), we have our human rights by virtue of our humanity alone and not by any executive, legislative, or judicial procedures or decisions. Most theorists agree that to have human rights means we have them by virtue of our humanity. But many of them do not mean this literally, thinking instead that we get these supposedly "inherent" rights through the activity of diplomats, legislators, and international lawyers who write the treaties that make up the system of international human rights law. At the end of Chapter 1 we charge these theorists with committing the fallacy of implementation, which fallacy we define as the pulling of the measures of implementation into the very definition of what a human right is. Our account differs from this majority view in that we argue that most drafters of the blue booklet meant the inherence claim literally and not just symbolically or rhetorically. By thinking of these rights as moral birth rights, they separated them from the numerous legal rights that accrue to us later in life and that we possess as a result of the various roles we play within the domestic legal systems of the countries in which we live.

According to the second universality thesis, defended in "Obeying the Conscience of Humanity" (Chapter 2), we also know by virtue of our humanity alone that we have these moral birth rights. We have no need for any kind of experts (though we do need good nurturers) to tell us what our moral birth rights are. I defend the thesis that we discover the existence of human rights by encountering gross injustices done to ourselves or others, or even to complete strangers. The great wrongs that enraged and engaged the Declaration's drafters were the events of the Holocaust. With remarkable unanimity they drew up their list of rights from this list of Holocaust wrongs. They thought of themselves as articulating what the "conscience of mankind" was saying when faced with the Nazi gas chambers and related events. They codified, if you will, their reactions into a set of rules or moral rights. I also argue that this same idea of the conscience of humanity can be found in the decisions of the military tribunals of most civilized nations and in the Statutes of the International

Tribunals set up since World War II. At the end of this second chapter, I place all this legal history within the framework of classical moral intuitionism. This theory is not popular with philosophers, but it seems to me to make most sense of the 1940s drafting of the blue booklet and of subsequent developments in international criminal law.

In his Tanner Lectures, Ignatieff addresses the world mood of the late 1940s, when the human rights movement was born and the UDHR was written.[6] He notes the "global infusion" of human rights language into all manner of discourse and believes that this infusion is a mark of real progress. His approach is similar to that indicated by the title of William F. Schulz's *In Our Own Best Interest: How Defending Human Rights Benefits Us All.*[7] Schulz's point is that realists in the American foreign policy establishment have been shortsighted because they have ignored the benefits that would accrue to Americans if only their government would take a more pragmatic approach to human rights questions. Our leaders should unabashedly say: "Support human rights! They are good for us!" (34). Schulz's pragmatism came from his being executive director of Amnesty International USA and from wanting to increase American membership in his organization. Ignatieff's pragmatism is fed by his interpretation of what history since the end of World War II teaches us. He places the writing of the Universal Declaration in the context of the larger juridical, advocacy, and enforcement revolutions that have swept the world since the middle of the twentieth century and have led to a "global infusion" of human rights language into any number of diverse international conversations. He wants us to see this infusion as progress, but not of a philosophical or metaphysical kind. The ground for calling it progress is for him decidedly "pragmatic and historical" (Ignatieff, 4). We agree with much of what he says, but take exception to his main thesis that human rights must be understood "as a language, not for the proclamation and enactment of eternal verities, but as a discourse for adjudication of conflict" (20).

Ignatieff's view amounts to a rejection of metaphysical thinking as (supposedly) sapping the energy that human rights activists need for their "practical responsibilities" in resolving conflicts around the world. "It may be tempting," Ignatieff says, "to relate the idea of human rights to propositions like the following: that human beings have an innate or natural dignity, that they have a natural or intrinsic self-worth, that they are sacred" (54). He warns us against buying into these kinds of metaphysical propositions "Because these ideas about dignity, worth and human sacredness appear to confuse what is with what ought to be, they are likely to fragment commitments to practical responsibilities entailed by human rights" and "because each version of them must make metaphysical claims about human nature that are intrinsically contestable"

(54). There is some truth to the idea that foundational claims like these cannot be resolved "in the way humans usually resolve their arguments by means of discussion and compromise." But we do not follow Ignatieff at all when he urges us "to forgo these kinds of foundational arguments altogether and seek to build support for human rights on the basis of what such rights actually *do* for human beings" (54; emphasis original). There is nothing wrong with philosophical explorations of what human rights *are*, even if we need them to *do* a great many things. In fact, such philosophical scrutiny may help us understand better why these rights do what they do. Ignatieff's advice keeps human rights discourse imprisoned in the realm of the political, where negotiations take place and compromises are routinely made. It also blurs the distinction between human rights and ordinary legal rights that often are needed to implement human rights.

Throughout his well-received Tanner Lectures, Ignatieff replaces philosophical reasons for a commitment to human rights with prudential and pragmatic ones, as if the latter could do their work without making use of the former. At first he says that when the Declaration is read against the disastrous heritage of European collectivism, it is "a studied attempt to reinvent the European natural law tradition in order to safeguard individual agency against the totalitarian state" (66). That suggests that quite a lot of metaphysical thinking was done at the time of drafting. He is right, and our exposition of the doctrine of inherence in Chapters 1 and 2 supports that supposition. But later in the same Lectures he tells us that "Article 1 of the Universal Declaration cuts short all justification and simply asserts" what it states. Again, "The Universal Declaration asserts rights; it does not explain why people have them" (77) and "The Universal Declaration simply takes the existence of [human] rights for granted and proceeds to their elaboration" (78). These later statements suggest a nonmetaphysical reading to which we take exception. They are a misreading of the historical record. Article 1 tells us that human rights accrue to us as birth rights, which same rights the First Recital calls "inalienable" and "inherent." The alleged "silence" on ultimate metaphysical questions, of which Ignatieff makes a great deal, conflicts with the repeated appeal to inherence on which we report in Chapter 1 of this study. It also stands in contrast with the numerous references to inherent human dignity and inherent human rights that one finds in contemporary international human rights instruments.

Reflecting on these metaphysical anchors or roots is for Ignatieff a waste of energy. For him, "universality properly means consistency," by which he means the consistency involved in diplomatic maneuvering, where "the West is obliged to practice what it preaches. This puts the West, no less than the rest of the world on permanent trial" (92). The upshot is that the same conflicts that Ignatieff analyzes in political terms are to us loaded with philosophical implications that need to be drawn out if these more practical conflicts are to be satisfactorily resolved. In an answer to two of his respondents Ignatieff admits that they made him realize that "you cannot do without some notion of *intrinsic* dignity to sustain belief in human rights" (164; emphasis added). That is exactly the point we make in this book, by defending the inherence of human rights in the human person. In Chapter 1 we give an initial historical and metaphysical exposition of this idea, which in Chapter 4 is fleshed out into a full fledged moral and species wide cosmopolitanism that is based on an adoption of the capabilities approach to human rights as it has been worked out by philosopher Martha Nussbaum. We also explain in Chapter 4 how patriotism and multiculturalism fit into this wider cosmopolitan human rights commitment.

Ignatieff's realm of the prudential and the pragmatic cannot be sustained without a great deal of philosophical thinking. He is far too quick to conclude that the vision of "moral equality" that comes with a commitment to human rights is simply one of "a world of conflict, deliberation, argument and contention" (95). It was not so for the drafters of the Universal Declaration, and it is not so for us. An entire philosophical world is packed into the word "basis" when he recommends that we "stop thinking of human rights as trumps and begin thinking of them as a language that creates the *basis* for deliberation" (95; emphasis added). What, for instance, is the difference between human rights being the *basis for* or *result of* deliberation? For what kinds of deliberations are human rights the basis—for all or just some? And why is that? What does it mean to say that human rights are "the shared vocabulary from which our arguments can begin and the bare minimum from which differing ideas of human flourishing can take root" (95)? What is that bare minimum, how is it established, and by whom? And what does "flourishing" mean or entail? What kinds of roots are those? Clearly, these questions drive us beyond the political and into the philosophical in ways Ignatieff's own statements suggest. Let me now summarize some further ways in which our defense of human rights leads us to think beyond the political and juridical.

In his discussion of the relationship between the birth of human rights and the Holocaust Ignatieff mixes two universality theses (the metaphysical one and the epistemological one) into a single, unhelpful one. He believes that the horrors of the Holocaust taught us "not to build foundations on human nature but on human history, on what we know is likely to happen when human beings do not have the protection of [human] rights" (80). A few pages later he tells us that "All that can be said about human rights is that they are necessary to protect individuals from violence and abuse, and if it is asked why, the only possible answer is historical" (83). By "historical" he means the political liberation struggles of individuals caught in traps sprung by tyrannical governments, especially the Third Reich, but also by oppressive families, churches, and tribal communities. But the relationship between history and human rights is far more complicated than Ignatieff makes it seem. In Chapter 2 we defend a moral psychology for belief in human rights that draws the metaphysics of inherence out of the gross violations that the Holocaust and history generally present to us.

Ignatieff cites Isaiah Berlin's observation that "Because these rules of natural law were flaunted [then], we have been forced to become conscious of them" (80–81). True enough, but this awareness goes much deeper than the mere "prudential necessity" that Ignatieff takes from it. Our take on the doctrine of inherence interprets this awareness of transcendent values in terms of a moral epistemology of rights, where a gross violation itself becomes the occasion for learning the metaphysical lesson that each human being has inalienable dignity. Ignatieff sidesteps the metaphysical part of this history lesson with the (correct) observation that the Holocaust also teaches us the "ultimate fragility" of human rights. To his two human rights lessons from the Holocaust (prudential necessity and ultimate fragility) we would add a third one called metaphysical solidarity. For when morally healthy people see or are told about gross human rights violations—whether from the Holocaust or some other abomination—they cringe and are repulsed. It is at that moment of revulsion that the awareness Berlin speaks of is born in the human psyche. If they are not blocked by a sick ideology, a brain tumor, or some other cause, our consciences are woken up. At that moment, to borrow from Camus, solidarity becomes metaphysical.

Ignatieff is of the opinion that "The Universal Declaration set out to reestablish the idea of human rights at the precise historical moment in which they had been shown to have had no foundation whatever in natural human attributes" (80). The truth of this claim depends on what attributes of the human being one has in mind. If we think of an attribute like inherent dignity we *can* "defend human rights as moral universals." But if we think of the human propensity to hate and brand outsiders as non-humans, then we cannot. In that case, we must learn to defend the moral universals of the Declaration "in full awareness that they must counteract rather than reflect natural human propensities" for hatred and exclusivity. Since history is populated by all sorts of human agents, we can, if we want to do so, focus on the Nazi guards and say that there is no natural propensity toward decency and solidarity in the human species. In that case Ignatieff's conclusion that "we cannot build a foundation for human rights on natural human pity or solidarity" would seem to follow (80). But we can also focus on the rescuers of Jews and say that human beings do have a moral conscience (which the Nazi guards blocked out with alcohol and a sick, racist ideology), which alerts them to the difference between good and evil acts and policies. Ignatieff's Lectures take the first tack and our book takes the second approach. Ignatieff agrees that "we all possess a conscience" (89), but he does not explore what is involved in the horror-induced wake-up calls that take center stage in his Lectures.

We ourselves engage in that kind of analysis when in Chapter 2 we place both the adoption debates for the Declaration and the international legal doctrine of manifest illegality within the context of the theory of classical moral intuitionism. We defend that theory as the best available epistemological framework for the historical findings of this second chapter. It is not a very popular theory, but it seems to us to fit better than the rationalist approaches of Gewirth, Rawls, and Habermas that we reject in Chapters 3 and 6. The Golden Rule or the principle of reciprocity does not adequately explain our reaction to what was done by the Nazis. We therefore cannot justify our belief in human rights simply by reference to that rule as, in Ignatieff's words, a "secular defense of human rights" (88, 95). In Chapter 3 we laud that rule as a handmaiden to our moral intuitions, but criticize its shortcomings when it is allowed to operate on its own.

It would seem that Ignatieff does not shun all metaphysics, for he repeatedly asserts that the purpose of human rights is to defend human agency. Our objection is that he construes this agency far too narrowly and primarily as a political agency to rebel against and liberate oneself from tyrannical governments and oppressive groups, such as one's family, church, or tribe. While we agree that human rights spell out "the minimum conditions for any kind of life at all" (56), the implications of that claim go far beyond Isaiah Berlin's idea of negative liberty. Writes Ignatieff: "Human rights matter because they help people to help themselves. They protect their agency." He then adds this libertarian explanation: "By agency I mean more or less what Isaiah Berlin meant by 'negative liberty,' the capacity of each individual to achieve rational intentions without let or hindrance" (57). Berlin described negative liberty as the "area within which a man can act unobstructed by others. If I am prevented by others from doing what I could otherwise do, I am to that degree unfree; and if this area is contracted by other men beyond a certain minimum, I can be described as being coerced, or, it may be, enslaved."[8] To see what is involved here philosophically and how this might be used to justify belief in human rights, we need to ask what is involved in Ignatieff's crucial admission that a "human rights abuse is something more than an inconvenience, and seeking human rights redress is distinct from seeking recognition. It's about protecting an essential exercise of human agency" (57). In Chapter 3, section A, we point out that Alan Gewirth has outlined just such a theory of human agency. And while Ignatieff maintains a narrow political conception, Gewirth has linked his theory of agency to the full range of human rights in the Universal Declaration of Human Rights, its civil and political rights as well as its social, economic, and cultural ones. We adopt Gewirth's full scope, though not his method, when we argue (in Chapters 4 and 5) that social, economic, and cultural rights are just as inherent in the human person as are the first generation civil and political rights. The arguments of these chapters combat the famous Cranston attack on second generation human rights as unrealistic and "utopian." Ignatieff echoes this (to us) mistaken reading when he tells us that "Human rights is morally universal because it says that all human beings need certain specific freedoms 'from'; it does not go on to define what their freedom 'to' should consist in" (76). We very much beg to differ. Many of the rights in the Declaration are rights *to* various kinds of goods.

In Chapter 4's exposition of the cosmopolitanism of human rights we support Ignatieff's vigorous defense of the Declaration's moral individualism, and help him face up to the postmodern challenge of there being, as he puts it, a "plethora of world cultures that do not actually share the West's conception of individuality, selfhood, agency or freedom" (62). By blending contemporary emphases on patriotic sentiment and the simultaneous spread of multiculturalism into a wider cosmopolitanism, we acknowledge the complications of intercultural dialogue. We introduce three concentric circles of commitment: a wider cosmopolitan one, within which we place a narrower patriotic circle, and within that one an even narrower one of multicultural attachments. We do not agree with Ignatieff that "all cultures participate as equals" (63). Instead, we agree with Diane's Orentlicher's objections to Ignatieff's use of the victim's consent test, where cultural practices that seem damaging to human dignity can "be abandoned *only* when the whole community decides to do so" (145; emphasis added). She is right to point out that Ignatieff does not go far enough in his search for "a principled basis" on which to settle these disagreements (146). A test like this fails to condemn and eradicate female genital mutilation, trial by ordeal, the caste system, slavery or bondage, and any number of other assaults on human dignity by traditions where the victims have been silenced or brainwashed into submission.

If Ignatieff admits to there being such a thing as intrinsic (his word) or inherent (my word) dignity, then he owes us an explanation of what the content of that dignity is. He cannot convincingly just link it to a minimalist conception of human agency, for the notion of agency itself begs for an elaboration that goes beyond the political. His push for the equal status of cultural traditions leads Ignatieff to overlook the wide scope of the Declaration when he says that the UDHR drafters "explicitly constructed their task . . . as an attempt to define a limited range of moral universals from within their very different religious, political, ethnic, and philosophic backgrounds" (64). While he is right about the great diversity of perspectives that the drafters brought to the sessions, it does not follow that they for that reason settled on a short list of human rights. The thirty articles of the Declaration show that they did not. And the presence of the social, economic, and cultural rights is testimony to the document's deep communitarian and cosmopolitan roots.[9] Our argument is that these two root systems do not have to fight each other.

By presenting the notion of human rights as primarily a political and juridical invention in world affairs since the Second World War, many of the theorists I take issue with in this book have helped foster the misconception that the human rights movement is one of opposition between the West and the rest. The worldwide acceptance of the Universal Declaration ever since it was written by representatives from all over the world and adopted by their consensus tells a far different story. From the start, the commitment to human rights has involved a worldwide moral and individual cosmopolitanism with metaphysical and epistemological underpinnings. And the great majority of those involved understood these underpinnings to go far beyond the political and juridical. So we do not follow Ignatieff when he construes the various international "conflicts" about human rights as primarily of a political character. In Chapters 5 and 6 we discuss how nations lower the abstractions of the Universal Declaration and its offspring into place in an enormous variety of different cultural contexts. Sometimes politicians (like Malaysian president Lee Kuan Yew) turn these differences into political "conflicts," but that is not how the various international and regional human rights Committees, Courts, and Commissions look at their tasks. The international civil servants who staff these posts—and who labor in the shadow of their more visible diplomatic colleagues—do not look at the construction of human rights thresholds as "conflicts" between different traditions. It is for them more a question of what a right that has already been formulated in the abstract in one or another international treaty or convention means concretely in different domestic settings. Presently, the movement of thought in these underfunded committees and courts that oversee this process of human rights implementation is not so much a horizontal one between clashing values of different world regions as it is a vertical one between an already accepted and codified international norm and a national or domestic application of that norm.

It is true that we find a reflection of Ignatieff's pragmatic and prudential calculations in the Preamble of the Universal Declaration. But those calculations stand in a certain tension with the idea of these rights as being inherent in the human person. We see this tension when we read the recitals of the Preamble as no more than a wish list of things the drafters wanted, and to which ends observance of human rights serves as the means. In each of the recitals they tell us that *if* we want something else badly enough, *then* we must want to respect and observe human rights: "freedom, justice and peace in the world" (First Recital); "the highest aspirations of the common people" (Second Recital); the avoidance of "rebellion and tyranny" (Third); gaining "friendly relations between nations" (Fourth); fulfilling our UN charter pledges (Fifth, Sixth, and Seventh). In short, *if* the nations of the world want justice and peace, and *if* they want to fulfill the highest aspirations of their own peoples, and *if* they want to avoid having their peoples fall into anarchy and rebellion, and *if* they want to keep their UN pledges, *then* they should respect the rights proclaimed in this document. Whether human rights are good for their own sake, can, so goes this argument, be left to the side, for the consequences of the mere supposition of their existence are enormous and worth pursuing.

Structurally, this consequentialist approach asks us to look at the Universal Declaration the way some theorists have looked at the American Bill of Rights.[10] In 1789, thirteen American colonies united into one nation "to form a more perfect union, establish justice, insure domestic tranquility, provide for the common defense, promote the general welfare and secure the blessings of liberty to ourselves and our posterity." Collapsing these several goals into just one, such theorists might argue that the goal of the American Revolution was the welfare of the American people. Then, three years later, the colonists decided that it would be helpful for the sake of that same general welfare to add a bill of rights to their constitution, which they did by adding various amendments at later dates when they had come to a joint realization that strict adherence to such a bill would be a very good way to achieve their stated goal of domestic tranquility. On this reading, the Bill of Rights serves the larger aim of domestic tranquility, never mind questions of inalienability and inherence. Analogously, one could hold that international peace and security are the stated goals of the United Nations Organization that was founded in San Francisco in 1945. Then, so goes the argument, three years later, working in New York, Geneva, and Paris, the Third General Assembly proclaimed the Universal Declaration of Human Rights because it had come to the realization that strict adherence to such an International Bill of Rights would be good for international tranquility. Certain institutional calculations are made about what it takes to secure domestic or international peace, and on that basis, national or international bills of rights are adopted by the appropriate authorities.

The problem with this approach is that it is too crude and therefore very dangerous. We can see this if we think of how a dictator like Hitler calculated the general welfare of the German people. He figured that the greatest happiness of the greatest number of Germans would be best served by the extermination of Jews, gypsies, and homosexuals. For that reason, *merely* calculating cannot be the key move in the justification of our belief in human rights. Too much depends on who does the calculating and on what the scope of the general welfare is taken to be. This pragmatic approach overlooks the main thesis of this book, which is that human rights are *inherent* in all human beings, who have or possess them from birth. The dignity of the persons who have these rights should be respected because these are their moral birth right and not merely (though that may be the case as well) because of certain rough calculations concerning general welfare. While such calculations are very important, human rights are not derived from them or based on them, not if the arguments of this book withstand scrutiny. To have our possession of human rights based on calculations of the general welfare leaves open the possibility that should—God forbid—the calculations turn out some other way, then some unfortunate individual or group may no longer be protected and instead be killed, tortured, or oppressed. That method of justifying human rights flies in the face of the idea of inherent possession.

Besides Hitler's, Stalin's, and Mao's sick real world calculations of what was supposed to enhance the welfare of the German, Russian, and Chinese peoples, philosophers exploring this kind of problem use the example of an innocent person being lynched to appease an angry mob, or of a surgeon taking body parts from five terminally ill patients (without their consent) to restore life to a sixth patient. While such acts are supposedly done for the sake of the general welfare, they all seem to us profoundly immoral and in violation of the inherent right to life, no matter what calculations dictators, police sergeants, or surgeons might make. As Glaucon intimates to Socrates in Plato's *Republic*, ultimately calculations about justice (as the Greeks put it) and human rights (as we put it) must start with the recognition that these rights are good in and of themselves, that is, as inherent in the human person, without regard for the extra benefits one gets from observing and respecting them.

> Tell me [asked Glaucon]; do you think there is a kind of good which we welcome not because we desire its consequences but for its own sake: joy, for example, and all the harmless pleasures which have no further consequences beyond the joy which one finds in them?
>
> Certainly, said I [Socrates], I think there is such a good.
>
> Further, there is the good which we welcome for its own sake and also for its consequences, knowledge for example and sight and health. Such things we somehow welcome on both counts.
>
> Yes, said I.

Are you also aware of a third kind, he asked, such as physical training, being treated when ill, the practice of medicine, and other ways of making money? We should say that these are wearisome but beneficial to us; we should not want them for their own sake, but because of the rewards and other benefits which result from them.

There is certainly such a third kind, I said, but why do you ask?

Under which of these headings do you put justice? he asked.

I would myself put it in the finest class, I said, that which is to be welcomed both for itself and for its consequences by any man who is to be blessed with happiness.

That is not the opinion of the many, he said; they would put it in the wearisome class, to be pursued for the rewards and popularity which come form a good reputation, but to be avoided in itself as being difficult.[11]

The conversation continues with Glaucon and Adeimantus pressing Socrates to first defend justice for its own sake or as inherent before the pay offs of living a just life get discussed.

Citing Plato like this, I do not mean to suggest that the theory of inherent human rights here presented is an entire theory of justice, whether domestic or global. It is no such thing. That would have required entertaining far more questions in traditional political theory than we have considered in this volume. That said, it would seem that no contemporary theory of justice could be thought complete if it did not include an account of human rights. And if these rights are inherent in the human person—as we maintain in this book—then we must conclude that there is something deeply wrong with much contemporary political theorizing. What Emil Fackenheim said of the great theologians of the latter half of the twentieth century may well be true of some of the great Anglo-American political theorists also writing at that time. Fackenheim accused these theologians of passing by the gates of Auschwitz in silence, and averting their theoretical gaze as they constructed their pristine theological systems. He said they did not help us mend "the total rupture" of our world that the Holocaust had presented.[12] Looking at what the theorists have said about human rights, we reluctantly conclude that they, too, seem to have passed by Auschwitz with an averted theoretical gaze. For I do not see how their almost exclusively procedural accounts of justice and their consistent denial of inherence help us mend the total and partial ruptures of our moral and political worlds. As in the case of Ignatieff, it is not that these theorists deny that the Holocaust happened or that they have averted their personal gaze. This book argues that there is a deep philosophical connection between the Holocaust and the Universal Declaration. Our objection is that human rights theorists have learned too few theoretical lessons from what went on in the camps. To the extent that their accounts ignore this metaphysical connection, they have weakened the human rights movement and its ability to mend our world.

Chapter 1
The Metaphysics of Inherence

Right in its opening clauses the Universal Declaration presents us with a very important philosophical challenge. There the drafters reach back to the eighteenth century and present us with what I shall refer to in this book as the doctrine of inherent human rights. This doctrine consists of two complementary theses about the universality of human rights, some key Enlightenment terms of which I have italicized in the citations that follow. The first universality thesis is a metaphysical one about the way the world is. It states that people everywhere and at all times have rights that are not man-made, but inherent in the human person from the moment of birth. This metaphysical universality thesis is found in the First Recital and in the first sentence of Article 1. The drafters there tell us that "The recognition of the *inherent* dignity and of the equal and *inalienable* rights of all members of the human family is the foundation of freedom, justice and peace in the world" (First Recital) and that "All human beings are *born free and equal in dignity and rights*" (Article 1).

The second universality thesis is a matching epistemological one which tells us that ordinary people in any of the world's villages or cities can come to know in a natural manner—unaided by experts—that people everywhere have the moral birthrights spoken of in the first universality thesis. We find this matching epistemic or knowledge-focused equivalent in the Second Recital of the Preamble and in the second sentence of Article 1. In the Second Recital the drafters share with their readers the observation that "disregard and contempt for human rights have resulted in barbarous acts which have outraged the *conscience of mankind*," and in the second sentence of Article 1 they add "reason" to this route of conscience with the claim that all people "are endowed with *reason and conscience* and should act toward one another in a spirit of brotherhood."

These two theses belong together. For it would have made no sense for the drafters to proclaim a list of universally possessed, inherent human rights and then let the discovery of this fact rest on the availability of, let us say, religious or legal experts prepared to awaken humankind to a knowledge of its moral birthrights. Morality is not like biology, where our deep DNA structure has been discovered and related to us by experts. If there are universal moral truths, then it does not make a great deal of sense to say that ordinary human beings must await the arrival of experts to tell them about truths like those found in the Universal Declaration, which is the mother of all human rights norms. If there is such a thing as universal possession of moral rights (by virtue of our humanity alone) then we should be able (by virtue of our humanity alone) to come to know that this is so. Indeed, human experience confirms that those whose human rights are being violated almost always know that they are being wronged in some gross way, even if fear of more pain prevents them from saying so.

The first two chapters of this book are devoted to an explanation and defense of this doctrine of inherent human rights, while the other chapters extend this argument. In section A ("Enlightenment Precedents") of this chapter, I show how the drafters of the Universal Declaration stood on the shoulders of their eighteenth-century predecessors and took over from them the idea that human rights are inherent in the human person and not simply the result of social, legal or political processes. In section B ("From Natural to Human Rights") I discuss the key link of inherence that the drafters of the Universal Declaration sought to preserve between their own ideas and those of the eighteenth century. The retention of this idea of human rights as genuinely (and not merely rhetorically) inherent in the human person puts the Declaration at odds with a good many contemporary accounts of human rights. I explore these errant definitions in section C, "Duties and the Fallacy of Implementation."

The conclusion of this first chapter is that we face a gap between what the Declaration—which has been the inspiration for most international human rights texts—says a human right is, and what political and legal theorists tell us it is. While the founding text of the movement affirms the idea of inherence, later theorists have ignored this foundational and definitional element. By pointing to this gap I hope to lessen the alienation I see between theorists of the human rights movement and that movement's founding document.

A. Enlightenment Precedents

The Universal Declaration was adopted by the Third General Assembly of the United Nations, which met in the fall of 1948 in Paris, France. The document had been drafted by a commission and subcommittee of which the chief U.S. delegate, Eleanor Roosevelt (widow of President Franklin Roosevelt) had been the chairperson. So both the place of adoption (Paris) and the very prominent role that Eleanor Roosevelt had played in the drafting process were highly symbolic. They linked adoption of the Universal Declaration to its two most important precedents: the proclamation of the rights of man by the American colonists in their state constitutions and in their 1776 Declaration of Independence, and the 1789 French Declaration of the Rights of Man and of the Citizen.

In their speeches the drafters of the 1948 Declaration proudly dwelled on these connections. Jorge Carrera Andrade, the delegate from Ecuador, was optimistic that the delegates to the Third Committee, which met in the fall of 1948 in Paris, would come up with a "true charter of human rights." He said he was delighted that the meetings were being held in Paris, for France was "the birthplace of the rights of man."[1] Peng Chung Chang, the Chinese representative, also thought it proper that the final formulation should take place in France, "the birthplace of modern ideas of freedom," and he explained to his colleagues that translations of Chinese philosophical classics had inspired such thinkers as Quesnay and Diderot "in their humanistic revolt against feudalistic conceptions" that led to the 1789 French Declaration (48). Partly because he wanted it to be seen as "a tribute to France," Henry Carton de Wiart, the representative from Belgium, hoped that the General Assembly would adopt the Declaration in Paris that winter (49).

These sentiments were repeated on the day of adoption itself, December 10, which has for that reason come to be celebrated as International Human Rights Day. Émile Saint-Lot, rapporteur of the Third Committee and delegate from Haiti, began his report by "proclaim[ing] his satisfaction that, by coincidence the declaration had come into being in Paris, the capital of liberty and that the Commission of Human Rights which was mainly responsible for it had been presided over by the apostle of fundamental human rights and liberties," by which he meant Eleanor Roosevelt (GAOR, 854). A few moments later Roosevelt herself rose to announce "that [the Declaration's] proclamation by the General Assembly would be of an importance comparable to the 1789 proclamation of the Declaration of the Rights of Man, the proclamation of the rights of man in the Declaration of Independence of the USA and similar declarations made in other countries" (862). Hernán Santa Cruz of Chile "emphasized that the presence of Mrs. Roosevelt and the proximity of the place where a century and half before the 1789 Declaration of the Rights of Man had been born would make the proclamation a solemn occasion" (863). Not all comparisons with those earlier declarations were totally in favor of the UN Declaration. For Juliusz Katz-Suchy, the Polish delegate who abstained in the final vote, the Universal Declaration "in reality represented a step backward if compared with the Declaration. . . . which had been produced during the French Revolution" (904). The UDHR drafters clearly saw themselves as standing on the shoulders of these

eighteenth-century predecessors and as making huge improvements on
the work begun earlier. They felt a kinship with the American and French
revolutionaries, for they felt they had just cut their own international bill
of rights from the same moral and philosophical cloth.

The American colonists—as well as millions of people all over the world
today— believed "these truths to be self-evident, that all men are created
equal, that they are endowed by their Creator with certain unalienable
Rights, that among these are Life, Liberty and the pursuit of Happiness."
It was to secure these "certain unalienable Rights" that they believed
"Governments are instituted among men." When a despotic government
does not protect, or, worse yet, abuses these (other) unalienable rights,
then and only then is it the people's "right and their duty, to throw off
such a Government and to provide new guards for their security."[2] The
right to rebel is based on the possession of a whole set of even more basic
"unalienable rights" (such as the ones to Life, Liberty, and the pursuit of
Happiness) which it is the purpose of governments to protect. The word
"unalienable" (or "inalienable") comes from "to alienate," and it means
that these rights cannot be taken away; not even by—or especially not
by—despots such as King George and his British Parliament, which had
taxed the colonists without representation. These rights cannot either
be taken away by any modern government or agency—even by a single
torturer, who can violate but not take away a person's inherent moral
right not to be tortured.

This famous (federal) American sentence expressing the self-evident
character of the moral truth of unalienable rights was based on an earlier
Declaration of Rights issued a month before by the colony of Virginia.
That document is more direct about the secular and natural foundation
of these same rights, for it states that "all men are *by nature* equally free
and independent, and have certain *inherent* rights, of which, when they
enter into society, they cannot, by any compact, deprive or divert their
posterity; among which are the enjoyment of life and liberty, with the
means of acquiring and possessing property, and pursuing and obtaining happiness and safety" (Melden, 135). The rest of the bill lists more
of these inherent rights. These rights are inherent *because* people have
them by nature. It is only a matter of word choice that kept the phrase
"natural rights" out of this Virginia bill and so out of the 1776 American
Declaration of Independence. If the federal American drafters had used
the Pennsylvania draft Constitution (instead of the Virginia one) as their
model, they might have used the phrase "natural rights." The Pennsylvania Constitution was adopted in the same month as the Declaration
of Independence, and it does state that "all men . . . have certain natural, inherent and inalienable rights, amongst which are . . ."—and then
comes the list.[3] Here we have all three key terms—natural, inherent,

and inalienable—in one place. The logic of the situation is that all men have inherent and inalienable rights *because* these rights are *natural* ones, meaning that people have them by nature, or by their own nature, and not—and this is the revolutionary point—as the result of social custom, judicial announcement, or act of some parliament, whether British or one of those created in the American colonies. We find this language of natural rights in numerous late eighteenth-century revolutionary documents on both sides of the Atlantic.

Jean-Jacques Rousseau, the philosopher of the French revolution, basically recognized only one natural right, namely the one to equality, which equality finds its expression in the General Will of the people. It is to this General Will that the French at first looked for the content of their natural rights. In the Natural Law entry for his 1755 *Encyclopedia*, Diderot goes back to Rousseau's idea of the General Will, from which he believes the natural rights of man are derived. He asks his readers to consult this Will and reminds them: "Tell yourself often: I am a man, and I have no other true, inalienable *natural rights* than those of humanity."[4] In his 1763 *Treatise on Toleration* Voltaire gives us a secularized echo of Aquinas when he asserts that "Human law must in every case be based on natural law. All over the earth the great principle of both is: Do not unto others what you would that they do not unto you" (Hunt, 39–40). In 1787, just two years before the French Revolution, Louis XVI decided that Calvinists finally should have civil (though not political) rights, on the grounds that "a rather long experience has shown that harsh ordeals are insufficient to convert them" to Catholicism. So the king decided that the laws should no longer "depriv[e] them of the rights that nature constantly claims for them" (41). A pastor in the city of Nîmes responded that it would have been better if Louis' edict had not mentioned the topic of natural rights. The pastor wrote, "we know today what *natural rights* are, and they certainly give to men more than the edict accords to Protestants. . . . The time has come when it is no longer acceptable for a law to overtly overrule the *rights of humanity* that are very well known all over the world" (46).[5]

Indeed they were. But vehicles for the spread of that knowledge are needed, and the French cause was greatly helped when in 1783 the duke de la Rochefoucauld d'Enville, with the help of Ben Franklin, translated and published many of the American colonial constitutions from which I quoted above, under the title *Constitutions des treize États-Unis de l'Amérique*.[6] A book like this—and the travels between the two countries of people like the Marquis de la Fayette, Benjamin Franklin, Thomas Jefferson, John Adams, and Thomas Paine—helped fill in the blank left by Rousseau's vague appeal to the General Will. This American assist gave the French people several examples of bills of the natural rights of man.

La Fayette, an aide to George Washington, had an unfinished copy of the Declaration of Independence hanging in his house and was a deputy to the French General Assembly. On July 11 this nobleman introduced his version of a bill of rights to his fellow French deputies and gave them two reasons for adopting a bill before they had even finished their new French constitution. If they adopted a bill—as they did on August 26, 1789—without having finished writing their constitution, they would be undercutting the priority of Rousseau's General Will. For this Will could only operate after it had organized itself under a constitution, within which framework it could then be decided which rights citizens were to have.

The early adoption of the French bill was in keeping with the habit of American colonists, who usually placed their bills of rights at the start and not at the end of their constitutions. This order supports the idea of inherent rights because the rights come before the framework of government is spelled out in the rest of the constitution. If the rights were listed at the end of a constitution, the mistaken belief might arise that these rights were somehow the result of this governmental framework. The revolutionary point, however, is that the purpose of government is the protection of these preexisting and inherent rights. This point lies at the heart of my rejection of procedural accounts of justice in Chapters 3 and 6 of this book. These rights are not the result of any kind of legislative process, not even a basic or a founding one. The natural rights of citizens were not to be derived from the framework (not even the constitutional framework) of government. Rather, governments must be attentive to these preexisting, prepolitical and prejuridical inherent-in-the-people rights and implement them by adopting them in their constitutions and by codifying them further in the legal framework that is and flows out of the constitution.

La Fayette argued that prior adoption of a bill would "recall the sentiments that nature has engraved on the heart of every individual" and that, its being an expression "of the moral truths from which all institutions should be derived," such a bill would "become, in the labors of the representatives of the nation, a loyal guide that always leads them back to the source of natural and social right" (72). A month later Duke Mathieu de Montmorency reiterated what La Fayette had said, namely, that "It was important to declare the rights of man before the constitution, because the constitution is only the continuation, the conclusion of this declaration. This is a truth that the examples of America and of many other peoples . . . have made tangible" (73–74). The duke clearly saw the universalistic implications of a bill of inherent natural rights. He declared that the "rights of man in society are eternal [and] that no sanction is needed to recognize them." This made him dare hope that the French declaration would "be within the reach of those who would be least able to comprehend it." Such a bill would not just be applicable to the common man in America and France. It would be applicable to all people everywhere. Echoing the American supposition of "self-evident truths" the duke declared that "There are no doubt some truths which are in all hearts," and he pleaded with his fellow deputies to "follow the example of the United States: they have set a great example in the new hemisphere; let us give one to the universe, let us offer a model worthy of admiration" (74).

Pierre Victor Malouet objected. He saw great danger in the proclamation of a list of abstract rights that outstripped the legal system then in force. He pointed out "that American society, newly formed, is composed in its totality of landowners already accustomed to equality, foreigners to luxury as well as to poverty, barely acquainted with the yoke of taxes or the prejudices that dominate us, having found on the land that they cultivate no trace of feudalism" (Hunt, 75). "But we, Sirs," he went on to compare, "have for fellow citizens an immense multitude of men without property who expect above all their subsistence from an assured labor, right regulation, and continual protection, they become angry sometimes, not without just cause, at the spectacle of luxury and opulence." Perhaps, he said, the Americans could afford to take "man from the bosom of nature and presen[t] him to the universe in all his primitive sovereignty" (75). The faction that wanted to follow the American model won out, and on August 26 the French people adopted the Declaration of the Rights of Man and of the Citizen. Its representatives resolved "to set forth in a solemn declaration, *these natural, inalienable, and sacred rights of man*" (77). After that follow seventeen articles spelling out what these rights are. Article 1 repeats the common Enlightenment theme that "Men are born and remain free and equal in rights." (78). Article 2 is molded after the American precedents from which I quoted above: "The purpose of all political association is the preservation of the *natural and imprescriptible rights* of men. These rights are liberty, property, security, and resistance to oppression" (78). In Article 4 the French deputies tell us that the "exercise of the *natural rights* of every man, has no other limit than those which are necessary to secure to every other man the free exercise of the same rights" (78).

It is quite clear that these Enlightenment precedents share with our contemporary idiom the idea that human rights are inherent in the human person. This explains why the drafters of the Universal Declaration saw no problem and were even proud to model their list of rights on a conception that goes back to this period of Western history. The citations at the start of this chapter support this contention. But the 1948 drafters did not slavishly follow these precedents and in numerous ways

adapted their own conception to twentieth-century conditions. I begin
with reasons why the 1948 drafters turned away from the language of
natural rights to that of simple inherence.

B. From Natural to Human Rights

Paul Lauren and more recently Lynn Hunt have given us fine accounts
of how our own talk of human rights evolved out of these natural rights
precedents of the Enlightenment.[7] However, both of them write as if
the history and evolution of human rights out of the natural rights of
that period can be read as a seamless web without significant intellectual
bumps in the road. They acknowledge that there obviously were practical, political, and obstructionist blocks of all kinds. But neither author
investigates the possible anachronism involved in writing about *human*
rights in the eighteenth century. That does present a slight problem,
for in our brief survey we did not run across many references to plain
"human rights." Only Paine regularly used the phrase "rights of man,"
and the pastor from Nîmes used the phrase "rights of humanity."[8] The
problem is not a huge one, for in this section I defend these authors'
assumption that our own talk of human rights shares at least one crucial
feature with the natural rights language of the eighteenth century. That
is the idea that these moral rights are inherent in the human person.

Some human rights theorists do not think the transition is quite as smooth
as our view of shared inherence suggests it is. Thomas Pogge, for instance,
has given us a thumbnail sketch of the historical transition from the natural rights discourse surveyed above to what he sees as our own much less
cumbersome talk of human rights. While we accept most of the benefits
that Pogge says come with our contemporary shift to the simpler discourse
of human rights, I do want to discuss Pogge's dismissal of all metaphysics
from the notion of a human right. To be blunt, it is our contention that
Pogge, and many of the other thinkers discussed in this chapter, has thrown
out the baby of inherence with the bathwater of natural rights. They have
turned their theoretical backs on the single most important characteristic
that our own notion of human rights has in common with the natural rights
discourse of the Enlightenment: the belief that human rights (for us) and
natural rights (for them) are inherent in the people that have them.

Pogge begins his sketch with some helpful comments about the earlier
shift in ethics away from the natural law tradition of the Middle Ages,
where we find Stoic and Catholic strands, to the one of natural rights
in the modern era. In the case of the former, the emperor or king felt
obligated to obey the natural law because it was (in those days) seen as
the imprint of the almighty God. That law could be and no doubt frequently was obeyed without the subjects of the ruler being cared for at

all. The point was to please God, the author of that natural law, and to avoid His wrath. We find this system of law expounded in a very clear way in the writings of Thomas Aquinas, for whom natural law is a reflection of God's eternal law. With the shift to modern natural rights in thinkers like Locke, Paine, and the American Founding Fathers, the source of a ruler's obligation shifted away from God to the human person, who had the natural rights that it was the purpose of the state to protect. Now the human person had natural rights by virtue of his or her own nature and not necessarily by virtue of a transcendent system of natural law that was linked to God's eternal law from which it got its authority. It was therefore easier to be an atheist or agnostic and still honor human dignity as expressed by adherence to these inherent natural rights. People benefited because the duties that correlate with natural rights were no longer directly owed to God but to themselves as the possessors of these rights and as the subjects of their ruler. Instead of being a triadic relationship with God as the mediator between ruler and ruled, morality became a bilateral relation between one human being and another. Ordinary people and aristocrats felt emboldened, and out of their courage came the great revolutions and bills of rights of the late eighteenth century.

Pogge sees our own shift to human rights talk as another step in this secularization process, for he holds that our notion of human rights "manifestly detaches the idea of moral rights from its historical antecedents in the medieval Christian tradition, thereby underscoring the secularization implicit in the language of laws to that of rights."[9] The suggestion here is that the adjective "human" is even more pedestrian and has even fewer transcendent attachments than does the concept of natural rights, which already represented a step down from the notion of natural law. Because the language of "natural rights" caries more philosophical baggage than does that of "human rights," Pogge believes that the shift in our own day from the former to the latter "serves the continued maintenance of broad sharability" of the moral demands being made (57). By broad sharability Pogge means what I have called the epistemic universality thesis that matches the metaphysics of simple inherence. We both agree that ordinary people from all walks of life in a great variety of different cultures have access to the moral truths of human rights. Where we disagree is on how much or how little metaphysics is involved in the accession of these truths. Pogge follows his mentor Rawls's adage that the principles for democracy are "political, not metaphysical." He interprets the contemporary shift to human rights as a license for total metaphysical liberty, much the way Rawls does.[10] I quote Pogge on this:

The adjective "human"—unlike "natural"—does not suggest an ontological status independent of any and all human efforts, decisions, (re)cognition. It does not rule out such status either. Rather it avoids these metaphysical and metaethical issues implying nothing about them one way or the other. The potential appeal of the select moral demands is thereby further broadened in that these demands are made accessible also to those who reject all variants of moral realism—who believe, for instance that the special moral status of all human beings rests on nothing more than our own profound moral commitment and determination that human beings ought to have this status. (57)

If we cut all metaphysics out of the notion of human rights, *then* the epistemic doors are indeed thrown wide open. But what people come to know may not be what most of us mean when we talk about human rights. I think we mean that people have these rights *by virtue of their humanity*, and we say that not because experts or theoreticians of human rights told us what the phrase "human rights" means, but because of the kind of creatures we know human beings to be.

Pogge's willingness to open up the definition of what a human right is to all sorts of philosophical positions seems to us to be no real benefit. It opens the door to philosophical free-riders who want the benefits of human rights talk without making the ontological commitment our theory considers necessary for a clear understanding of what a human right is. A commitment to inherence can be of enormous help in various implementation battles where computations of the public welfare are matched against the notion of inherent rights, which is a point I often make in this book. Another benefit that Pogge sees in the language of human rights is that it shows how human rights attach to "all and only human beings" (57). I agree that that is a benefit and would add that *human* rights differ from the rights other animals have because our human capacities differ in both nature and scope from the capacities they have. As for the benefits that our human rights talk explains more clearly that "all human beings have exactly the same human rights" and that "the moral significance . . . of human-rights violations does not vary with whose human rights are at stake," it is our contention that these two benefits get a better grounding with the metaphysics of inherence than without it.

The Text of the UDHR. So as to set the stage for the survey of errant definitions that do not match the doctrine of inherence, I devote the rest of this section to a brief exegesis of the Enlightenment terminology in the First Recital ("Whereas recognition of the inherent dignity and of the equal and inalienable rights of all members of the human family is the foundation of freedom, justice and peace in the world") and in the first sentence of Article 1 ("All human beings are born free and equal in dignity and rights"). Placing that later survey against the background of these Enlightenment anchors in the text of the Declaration will reveal the gap between what many theoreticians say a human right is and what the foundational text of the movement tells us it is.

The officers of the Commission of Human Rights, Eleanor Roosevelt of the United States (chair), Peng Chung Chang of China (vice chair), René Cassin of France (vice chair), and Charles Malik of Lebanon (rapporteur or executive secretary) had been constituted into a Committee on the Preamble. All four of these delegations accepted the inherence view of human rights as birth rights of every person in the world, so it is no surprise that this Committee selected the text we have from half a dozen proposals. The language we have is almost identical to that proposed by the Lebanese (E/CN.4/132) and the U.S. (E/CN.4/119) delegations, except that the Preamble Committee substituted "of all members of the human family" where these proposals had "of all persons."

While it is not surprising that the members of this Preamble Committee opted to start the Preamble with such clear borrowings from Enlightenment discourse, it *is* surprising that this most philosophical of recitals caused the least bit of controversy. The Third Session adopted it "by 11 votes to none, with 5 abstentions" (AC.1/SR.75/5), which means that even the communist delegations from the USSR, UKSSR, and Yugoslavia (all of whom were present that day) abstained but did not overtly reject this kind of language. In explaining his abstention in the vote on the second recital, Joza Vilfan, delegate from Yugoslavia, passed up a chance to directly object to the Enlightenment phraseology of the First Recital. "Since the first paragraph spoke of observing the respect due to all members of the human family and their equal and inalienable rights, one naturally expected," he said, "the second paragraph which spoke of the war to say that the Second World War had imperiled the value and existence of those rights and freedoms" (SR.75/12). He here expressed the connection between inalienable moral rights and their violations during the War which the majority of delegates saw as the main reason for proclaiming the rights in the Declaration. In short, the Enlightenment language in the First Recital was not objected to, and it was "unanimously" adopted by the thirty-eight delegates present and voting in the Third Committee that day (786).

When the Drafting Sub-Committee asked René Cassin to streamline the first rough draft that had been done by John Humphrey, director of the Secretariat's Division on Human Rights, he submitted this version of Article 1: "All men are brothers. Being endowed with reason, members of one family, they are free and possess equal dignity and rights" (E/CN.4/AC.1/W.2/Rev.2). Cassin had reached back to the 1789 French Declaration for a suitable opening philosophical statement. He explained to his colleagues that "his text alluded to the three fundamental questions of liberty, equality, and fraternity because during the war, these great fundamental principles of mankind had been forgotten. The text was trying to convey the idea that the most humble of the most different races have among them the particular spark that distinguishes them from animals, and at the same time obligates them to more grandeur and to more duties than any other beings on earth" (AC.1/SR.8/2). On the whole the reactions were positive. The Chinese delegate, Chung Chang, thought that there should be added to the idea of "reason," the idea which in literal translation from Chinese would be "two-man-mindedness," which suggestion led to the insertion of the word "conscience" into the article (AC.1/SR8/2 and SR.13/5). Professor Vladimir Koretsky, USSR delegate to the First Drafting Session, observed that Cassin's language was sexist and that the phrase "all men" "should be modified" (SR.13/6). But he did not object to the Enlightenment implications of the Cassin text. With the help of the Commission on the Status of Women a correction was made, which gave us the final wording "All human beings." Two other votes taken in the Third Committee relate in a specific way to the idea of inherence. One was the retention of the word "born" in the first sentence, and the other the deletion of the phrase "by nature" from the second sentence. I discuss them in this order.

Together with the words "inherent" and "inalienable" of the First Recital, the word "born" in the first sentence of Article 1 anchors the doctrine of inherence explicitly in the text of the Declaration. Even the rationales offered for the deletion of this word support this view. Its presence was not questioned until in the Third Committee both the Lebanese and the Chinese delegations proposed its deletion (see A/C.3/235 and A/C.3/326). Yet both of these delegations supported the doctrine of inherence. In a later discussion of the article on asylum, Karim Azkoul, the Lebanese representative, called this right "part of the birthright of man" and one of those that was "inherent in the human person" (335). The rationale for the deletion of the word "born" given by Azkoul was that "There should be no implication that people, though born equal, might loose that equality for any reason," which is an observation aimed at establishing inherence (GAOR Third, 98). While Azkoul worried that the word "born" might suggests that people's freedom and dignity could at some future point be taken away, other delegations worried that that had already happened in numerous instances and that the word sounded unrealistic against the background of evident gross inequalities in the world. However, most delegates realized that the claim that people "are born free and equal in dignity and rights" was in no way meant to deny that gross inequalities existed everywhere. On the contrary, against the background of those inequalities they wanted to assert the rights that were inherent in the human person. The word "born" did just that. Abdul Rahman Kayala, delegate from Syria, for instance, wanted to retain the word "born" "as it would exclude the idea of hereditary slavery" (118). In the Third Committee, A. M. Newlands, delegate from New Zealand, said she wanted the word retained, but gave no reasons. In later General Assembly debates, she did say that "human rights were rooted in the nature of man himself, as well as in the structure and needs of the modern world" (GAOR, 887). Apparently she also took the word "born" to be a reference to inherence. Salomon Grumbach, from whose French delegation the first sentence of Article 1 had originated, said it "meant that the right to freedom and equality was inherent from the moment of birth." He then pointed out that the drafters of the French bill of 1789 had also known that there were inequalities everywhere, but they had "wanted to affirm their belief in man's inherent right to equality and freedom" (GAOR Third, 116). This sentiment prevailed in a vote of 20 for, 12 against, with 5 abstentions (GAOR Third, 124).[11]

Right after the Committee had voted to retain the word "born," Chang, the Chinese representative, proposed to add to it the words "and remain," making the sentence look even more like its French counterpart of 1789: "men are born, and always continue, free and equal in respect of their rights" (Melden, 140). If the motivation for the proposal to delete the word "born" had been to get way from the eighteenth-century implication of inherence, Chung Chang would never have made this proposal. His idea was rejected in a vote of 23 to 14, with 4 abstentions (124), and the word "born" was left standing by itself as an intentional reminder that human moral rights are rights people have simply by virtue of being human beings. The Third General Assembly adopted Article 1 by 45 votes, with 9 abstentions (933).

The extensive Third Committee discussions and votes connected with the occurrence of the word "born" show us that the idea of human rights as birthrights of every man, woman, and child was not an afterthought or a lightly considered proposition on the part of just a few drafters. Most of the drafters felt that the physical or biological birth of a person is accompanied by a moral birth into the realm of rights-bearers. They did not agree as to when this moral rider attached itself to the biological process,[12] but they rejected the idea that the only rights people have are legal ones that accrue to them because they inhabit territories covered by positive legal systems. The point of the retention of the word "born" was precisely the fact that people are born with moral rights that cut across frontiers, categories, and classes created by various local customs or domestic legal systems. Since these rights are inherent in people and not the result of history or circumstance, they can be used according to the Declaration's operative paragraph "as a common standard of achievement for all peoples and all nations." Positive legal systems that fall short of the standards set by the Declaration must be held up—as is done by any number of human rights organizations—to the standard and made to conform. So the significance of the first sentence of Article 1 is difficult to overestimate. Amendments to move the Article to what their sponsors thought was the less important Preamble failed. Together with the words "inherent" and "inalienable" of the First Recital, the phrase "born free and equal in dignity and rights" of Article 1 constitutes a clear statement of the doctrine of inherent moral rights that I am imputing to the great majority of the drafters.

The deletion by the Third Committee of the phrase "by nature" from the second sentence of Article 1 is a good reason for us not to assign to the drafters a traditional deductive natural rights approach. But we also must not overdramatize the significance of this deletion. Lindholm does that when on the basis of this deletion he concludes that the drafters excluded the idea that "human beings have human rights solely on the basis of their human nature or in virtue of Nature's endowment" (*Comm.*, 53). He here denies the very doctrine of inherent human rights that he seems to affirm in the following citation: "Christians, Muslims, atheists, Buddhists, Marxists, and so on, may from their own normative heartland come up with full-fledged justificatory doctrines of globally binding human rights, none of which need to be compatible with any of the others, if only each of them provides the proper kind of support to the principle of inherent freedom and equal dignity for every human being" (*Cross.*, 388–89). The proviso that subscribers to the Declaration must adhere to this principle limits the metaphysical openness that Lindholm wants to ascribe to the drafters. He argues that the drafters did not want to base their system of human rights on "any [specific] conception of Human Nature" (*Comm.*, 47). This is only correct if we insert the term "specific," as I just did. It may well be true that people with "fundamentally different" and "antagonistic" theories on human rights can agree on the rights in the Declaration (*Comm.*, 37), but if they want to be true to the document's original intent they must subscribe to the metaphysics of inherence. The metaphysical openness of the document starts *after* the assertion of inherence has been made.

Lindholm suggests that two drafters, Carton de Wiart from Belgium and Chung Chang from China, "wanted to drop 'by nature' so as to avoid interminable, and specifically Western, debates about either God or Nature or Human Nature" (*Comm.*, 47). That is true. Carton de Wiart defended the deletion of "by nature" because he felt that the clause "might be ambiguous and lead to long, philosophical arguments, and certain proposed amendments to them, such as the Brazilian proposal [containing a theistic reference] were of a particularly delicate character. The Belgian delegation *therefore* proposed to simplify the text by deleting the words 'by nature'" (GAOR Third, 96–97; italics added). But this proposal cannot be used to undercut the doctrine of inherence, which both Belgium and Brazil supported.[13] I already made reference to Chung Chang's observation "that the basic text of article 1 . . . would be acceptable to the Committee if it were understood on the basis of eighteenth-century philosophy" (GAOR Third, 113). That view, he said, could accommodate both the Belgian amendment to delete the clause (A/C.3/234) and the Lebanese one to replace it with the phrase "by their nature" (A/C.3/235). He then urged the Committee not to "debate the question of the nature of man again but [to] build on the work of the eighteenth-century philosophers" (114). Long before, Chang had reminded his colleagues of "the historical background of human rights, particularly the emphasis placed on human values by the 16th-century thinkers" (E/CN.4/SR.7/4). The Lebanese proposal to replace "by nature" with the phrase "by their nature" seems to represent the position of most of the drafters. Unfortunately, it was swept away by the above-mentioned bargain to avoid a reference to the deity in the document.

Since the Latin American delegations did not want to offend the Brazilian delegation, which wanted to see human rights grounded in religion, they voted to delete the offending phrase "by nature" together with the Lebanese substitute "by their nature." Yet, twenty-one Latin American nations (plus the United States) had just that April (1948) voted for the "American Declaration of the Rights and Duties of Man" That document speaks of the "essential rights of man" and of "the fundamental attributes of the individual" (E/CN.4/122/1) And its first recital reads just like Article 1 of the Universal Declaration, except that it does say that people are "by nature endowed with reason and conscience" (2). If the phrase "by nature" was unobjectionable in April in Bogota, then it still must have been acceptable in Paris that fall, except, of course, if its deletion could forestall an embarrassing vote on the question of God. The Uruguayan delegation is a good case in point. Even though its delegate, Eduardo Jiménez de Aréchaga, voted to delete "by nature" from the Universal Declaration, he did think that human "rights were derived from the nature of man and not from the acts of states" (GAOR Third, 101), which is clear support for the inherence doctrine.

This doctrine of inherence reverberated throughout the adoption debates on the Declaration and from time to time broke through to the surface. Chung Chang, the Chinese representative, defended freedom of thought and religion as one of the "most important principles in the Declaration" because "From the eighteenth century, when the idea of human rights was born in Western Europe, freedom of thought had figured among the essential human freedoms" (GAOR Third, 397). Enrique Armand Ugon told the Third General Assembly that his Uruguayan delegation "warmly supported" the draft of the Universal Declaration because "the inherent rights and freedoms of the human being should be internationally protected and guarded" (GAOR 887). Eduardo Anze Matienzo, a colleague from Bolivia in the Third Committee, defended the right to a nationality in Article 15 as "an unalienable human right" (GAOR Third, 35). The draft of a bill submitted by the Indian delegation in the form of a General Assembly Resolution began by "Recognizing the fact that the United Nations was established for the specific purpose of enthroning the natural rights of man" (E/CN.4/11). In the Third Committee the Egyptian delegation proposed a recital which stated that "the fundamental rights of man are not derived from his status as a national of a particular state, but constitute inherent attributes of his person" (A/C.3/264). When the Third Committee started its deliberations, Shaista Ikramullah, the delegate from Pakistan, expressed her hope "that the declaration would mark a turning point in history of no less importance than the work of Tom Paine and the American Declaration of Independence" (GAOR Third, 37).

Guilt by Association. I support the drafters' replacement of natural rights language with human rights language because I think that many contemporary theorists have burdened the notion of a human right unfairly with the notion of a human essence. These theorists associate this idea of human essences with the classical natural rights tradition in which natural rights were deduced from an identifiable human essence. To them the metaphysical universality of human rights that I say comes with simple inherence is derived from this shared human essence that all members of our species have. Historically, that essence was usually thought to be our capacity to reason, and if not reason, then some other single property that is essential to any creature's being a human being. In Chapter 4, I myself will also link human rights to human nature, but not in this essentialist kind of way, neither through a single property nor through a closed, disjunctive list of properties. In my argument, the link between human capabilities and human rights will be built from the empirical ground up rather than based on deductive argumentation of the type found in the Western rationalist tradition. My point here is that some very influential contemporary theorists, among them Alasdair MacIntyre and Richard Rorty, have construed the connection between human rights and human nature in just this Western rationalist and essentialist way. This has made them reject the thesis of metaphysical universality for unsound reasons, and I see their lack of support for inherence as a classic case of guilt by association. Before I discuss these two thinkers' views, I want to make the point that this virus of essentialism is not just theoretically bothersome, it is also practically dangerous. For when the idea of essences falls into the hands of demagogic leaders, it can also have devastating practical consequences. While I agree with MacIntyre, Rorty, and others in welcoming the passing of belief in human essences, I disagree on what the consequences of that happy passing are.

In his book *Act and Idea in the Nazi Genocide*, Berel Lang suggests that the Kantian Enlightenment bears some responsibility for the Holocaust, because the structure of Kantian ethics and the genocidal mentality are similar in one crucial respect. Odd as it sounds, they both treat human beings as ends in themselves. Both are essentialist, and Lang speculates that the Nazis could have learned from Enlightenment thinkers how to play with the idea of an ahistorical essence. For Kant, a person's claim to moral status has to do with that person's ahistorical, transcendent, and noumenal self, the self where the will and the rational capacity are located. In this way, says Lang, Kantian "human beings are alike in their essential nature. Any differences that foster apparent distinctions among human beings are thus at best morally irrelevant; at worst in so far as they may obstruct the process of universalization, they are moral liabilities" (175). If moral rights and duties accrue to human beings because they have this kind of an ahistorical essence, then—so goes the implication—any creature that does not have this kind of an essence does not need to be treated the way human beings deserve to be treated, which in Kant's terminology means that they do not need to be treated as ends in themselves. Vladimir Koretsky, USSR representative to the First Session of the Human Rights Commission, caught this point very well when he argued against making reason a prerequisite for possession of the rights to be proclaimed. That line of thinking, he said, could "be interpreted as justification of the fascist destruction of feeble-minded people on the grounds that they were not reasonable beings" (SR.13/6). Lang shows us how that might be done.

He points out that the Nazis replaced Kant's rational human essence with a racist human essence and drew the "logical" consequence that anyone who did not have that racial essence need not have been treated as humans ought to be treated. In both cases the essentialism of the approach leaves the concrete individual of flesh and blood out of the moral picture. What counts is the having or the not having of a particular essence. Thus it is not all that far of an intellectual journey from Kant's categorical imperative to the Nuremberg laws of 1935 when, says Lang, "the Jews were formally excluded from the body politic on the grounds that *by their nature* they did not qualify for the rights of citizenship" (188, emphasis original). In the genocidal mentality the "individual is attacked not for anything he himself is or does, but for his relation to a group, a relation over which he has no control; the reason for the attack is not personal interest, gain or inclination, but the membership in the group itself suffices to exclude him from the domain of humanity" (19). This fits the Nazi theme, already stated in *Mein Kampf*, that the Jews were parasites on the human race, a virus that was trying to destroy the healthy human organism and therefore had to be excised. Says Lang, "The agent of genocide does not treat his victims as means; he attacks them as ends in themselves and on the grounds of principle, rather than inclination. There is no use that the agent wishes to make of this victim, nothing he requires or wants of the latter except to deprive him of all claims to self-hood" (18–19). Lacking the required essence, in genocide "the victim is no longer, except in an accidental physical sense, a person at all" (20).

We can see how the essentialism of Kant's great moral philosophy and that of the Nazi genocidal mentality are in this way similar. Whenever and wherever human beings are said to have an essence, room is created for gross discrimination. People who are thought not to possess that essence are read right out of the human race and persecuted, dispossessed, or destroyed. Since for many theorists the language of natural rights is tied to this kind of essentialism, it is advisable that we drop that language. The doctrine of inherence takes that hint, and has the further advantage that it more clearly suggests that human rights inhere in each historical, individual human being. The "birth" in the first sentence of UDHR Article 1 is a real, historical, and biological birth that all humans go through. Inherent in that unique birth lies our own individual dignity, as do the rights that express this dignity. My rights inhere in me and not in any essence I may or may not have. I cannot give them away and they cannot be taken away (except to protect the like rights of others) because they inhere in me, the concrete person that I am, Jew, Gypsy, Muslim, Serb, Tutsi, Hutu, Kurd, or whatever. The doctrine of inherence stresses the historical, human individual and thereby avoids the essentialism which has turned critics against the idea of human rights and which has at times been used as a foil for the very violations the Declaration is meant to condemn.

Alasdair MacIntyre and Richard Rorty have used the idea of a human essence to cast doubt on the concept of inherent human rights. As communitarian thinkers, they emphasize community over individuality and charge that liberalism has worked with an unrealistic view of human beings and of citizens as atomic and abstract individuals. They believe that liberal theory has torn human beings and citizens from the communal soil in which duties come before rights instead of—as the Declaration seems to suggest—rights before duties.

For MacIntyre the Universal Declaration is a child of modernity and therefore born of confusion and incoherence. In his now-classic 1981 book *After Virtue*, MacIntyre made a road cut through the intellectual terrain of modernity. He uncovered what he claims are incompatible and conflicting moral traditions in our intellectual landscape. Just as deep faults lie hidden below our smooth freeways, so too are believers in human rights fooled by the apparent universal acceptance of their discourse. What to human rights believers feels like an intellectually smooth ride through modernity is in reality a treacherous journey over great divisions and separations that have barely been covered over. MacIntyre sees these hidden fault lines coming to the surface in the seemingly interminable discussions Americans have over the death penalty, just wars, abortion, affirmative action, and welfare programs. Such public moral disputes are geysers of disagreement caused by conflicts between different fragments of our intellectual history. While I contend that the ideology of human rights can serve as an intellectual umbrella for people who do indeed have very different intellectual backgrounds, MacIntyre sees no chance of that happening.

He regards the opening philosophical clauses of the Universal Declaration—from which I have drawn the doctrine of inherent rights—not as possible grounds for a common morality, but as inchoate fragments of a failed Enlightenment tradition. The philosophers of the Enlightenment made two mistakes in a row. First, they threw out the teleological framework they had inherited from the Greeks. Then they compounded this rejection of Greek teleology by nevertheless insisting on deriving the sources of morality from this truncated (because lacking final causes) view of human nature. MacIntyre dubs this attempt to find a universal and secular moral code "the Enlightenment Project," and he is of the opinion that it failed miserably. The flow of his attack on the idea of human rights goes from failed eighteenth-century deductions that relied on the misguided idea of human essences (or essential characteristics) to equally defective contemporary efforts, and from there to a free-floating and, to him, indefensible discourse of human rights.

The supposed problem with the Enlightenment thinkers is that they took away these built-in (Greek) universal human purposes but still wanted a universal morality. Enlightenment writers all shared "in the project of constructing valid arguments which will move from premises concerning human nature as they understand it to be to conclusions about the authority of moral rules and precepts."[14] But once you take away the idea that human beings have built-in purposes, you forfeit an easy way of arriving at the rules of morality. What are we to do with a lyre, if we have not yet figured out that it was meant to make music? If you take away those inborn (ancient Greek or medieval divine) purposes from us human beings, you deprive yourself of any objectivity in moral guidance. So goes the argument. When we (in Chapter 4) adopt the capabilities approach to human rights, I do not argue that those capabilities are built-in "purposes" of human beings. But I do claim that human beings share most of those species-wide capabilities and that positive or negative steps to block their development are violations of the victims' right to develop such capabilities. We reject MacIntyre's overreliance on deductive argument as the only viable epistemic route into the domain of human rights.

MacIntyre realizes that the expression "human rights" is now commoner than eighteenth-century expressions of natural rights. "But however named, they are supposed to attach equally to all individuals, whatever their sex, race, religion, talents or deserts, and to provide a ground for a variety of particular moral stances" (69). He thinks that the emergence of a proof that human beings have rights "simply *qua* human beings" would be a "surprise" because of the fact that "the concept [of a human right] lacks any means of expression in Hebrew, Greek, Latin or Arabic, classical or medieval, before about 1400, let alone in Old English, or in Japanese as late as the mid-nineteenth century" (69). I call this the language test for the existence of human rights and respond to it in the discussion of Jack Donnelly's constructivism at the end of Chapter 3, section B. In Chapter 2 I respond to MacIntyre's claim that "The best reason for asserting so bluntly that there are no such rights is indeed of precisely the same type as the best reason which we possess for asserting that there are no witches and the best reason for asserting that there are no unicorns: every attempt to give good reasons for believing that there *are* such rights have failed" (69). I argue that there is such a thing as the conscience of humanity and that it speaks through the moral sentiments of millions of people, some in and some outside the human rights movement.

A cofounder with MacIntyre of the communitarian school of thought, Richard Rorty is not as critical of the language of human rights as is MacIntyre. In his 1993 Amnesty Lecture, Rorty is very supportive of the movement as a political movement, but he in no way supports the metaphysics of inherence. Rorty does not trace the promise of the American nation back to the rights (and the rhetoric) of its Founding Fathers. This omission is not simply because this alternative would not appeal to the members of the cultural Left whom Rorty is seeking to recruit. A deeper reason for Rorty's omission of the rights tradition as a way of unifying liberal thinking in America is that he himself does not really believe in it. He does not accept the difference (which I am defending in this chapter) between earlier natural rights that became burdened by essences and a human rights culture that has done away with essences while keeping inherence. He dismisses Enlightenment appeals to the human conscience, of which we give an exposition in the next chapter, as an "ahistorical essence of the human soul" that contemporary intellectuals can easily do without.[15] Metaphysically speaking, human rights activists (mostly Eurocentrics in Rorty's account) are no better than the perpetrators of human rights violations because everyone draws a line that divides the human family into two species, the "us" and the "them" groups.

After he shares with his readers some of Philip Rieff's stories about the most gruesome human rights violations perpetrated by Serbs against Muslims, Rorty concludes that "the moral to be drawn from Rieff's stories is that Serbian murderers and rapists do not think of themselves as violating human rights. For they are not doing these things to fellow human beings, but to Muslims. They are not being inhuman but rather are discriminating between true humans and pseudo-humans. They are making the same sort of distinction as the Crusaders made between humans and infidel dogs, and the Black Muslims make between humans and blue-eyed devils" (112). He points out that Jefferson drew a similar line between himself and his black slaves who, he felt, were more like animals "participating more of sensation than of reflection" (112). Like Aristotle before him, Jefferson felt that black people lacked the essence of rationality. As Rorty sees it, "we" Eurocentric intellectuals are prone to draw the same kind of immoral line between "us"—believers in the human rights culture—and the Serbian torturers and rapists. We think about "the Serbs and Nazis as animals because ravenous beasts of prey are animals. We think of the Muslims or Jews as being herded into concentration camps as animals because cattle are animals. Neither sort of animal is very much like us, and there seems to be no point in human beings getting involved in quarrels between animals" (113).

The essentialist virus has reared its head again, this time to explain why the West was so slow in getting involved in Bosnia, Kosovo, and Africa. The reason Rorty thinks we draw this line between us (the activists) and them (the perpetrators) is that we, too, tend to pick a single characteristic as a sign of humanity. We use this characteristic (being educable, being male, or being white) as *the* trait that constitutes the essence of being human. Rorty reports that "Philosophers have tried to clear up this mess by spelling out what all and only the featherless bipeds have in common, thereby explaining what is essential to being human" (114). But they have not been successful, and Rorty is pleased to discover that the waning of belief in these essences has freed us up to adopt a far more flexible view of our humanity. At this point we want to inject the idea of inalienable and inherent rights *without*—and this is important—attaching them to any single characteristic.

But Rorty's preoccupation with the virus speeds him on his way to a completely constructivist view of human nature: "We are coming to think of ourselves as flexible, protean, self-shaping, animals, rather than as the [Platonic] rational animal or the [Nietzschean] cruel animal." He thinks it is nice that "one of the shapes we have recently assumed is that of a human rights culture" (115). It is a waste of time to find a foundation for this newly adopted human rights culture, for, like all culture, it is self-made. It is not clear to him why "respect for human dignity—our sense that the differences between Serb and Muslim, Christian and infidel, gay and straight, male and female should not matter—must presuppose the existence of any such *attribute*" (116; emphasis added). The answer I give in Chapter 4 is that human rights need not be deduced from one single attribute, but instead may be normatively associated with an open-ended list of capabilities. I maintain in Chapter 2 that we come to know about this moral supervenience not by reason, but by moral intuitions. To look for just one attribute, as Rorty does here, is to construct the relationship between human nature and human rights deductively and also much too narrowly. Ever since the Greeks floated the idea of a human essence, this approach has had its pernicious side effects, and Rorty is right to applaud its demise. But that does not mean that human rights are man-made, and that the culture of human rights has no foundations or attachments to the world outside itself. Rorty's linking of "us" Eurocentric intellectuals with foundationalist philosophers like Plato, Aquinas, and Kant is a gross oversimplification. There is no need to dismiss "trans-cultural universals" (120) together with Platonic Forms, Transcendental Subjects, and human essences. We ought to keep the first and let go of the rest. What about transcultural species-wide capabilities normally inherent in human beings? The doctrine of simple (as over against essentialist) inherence aims to take a middle position between the full-blown essentialism Rorty rightly rejects and the total constructivism he ends up recommending when he tells us that "If we work together, we can make ourselves into whatever we are clever and courageous enough to imagine ourselves becoming" (121). I take aim at this kind of constructivism in Chapter 3, section B, where we reject John Rawls's constructivism, which is a far sturdier structure than is either Rorty's or Jack Donnelly's, which I also discuss at that time.

C. Duties and the Fallacy of Implementation

Some current definitions of what a human right is make for a good fit with the metaphysics of inherence that we have seen in the text of the Declaration. Alan Gewirth has defined human rights as "moral rights which all persons equally have simply because they are human."[16] He adds the explanation that a human right is a claim right, which means that the "claim right of one person entails a correlative duty of some person or persons to act or refrain from acting in various ways required for the first person's having that to which he has a right" (12). That to which one has a right is called the "substance" of the right, and it could be any number of things: life, freedom of speech, a job, or any of the rights listed in the Declaration, the full scope of which Gewirth defends in his writings, and the main argument for which I discuss in Chapter 3.

Judith Jarvis Thomson also believes that "we do think of ourselves born with claims—claims that others not murder or imprison us," which claims are the same thing as our having or being born with "the rights to life and liberty."[17] She refers to these rights as "inalienable," by which she means that no other person "can make us cease to have" them (283). She connects these moral (or human) rights to people having what she calls "inherently individual interests" (222), which is language that echoes the UDHR text. Thomson also believes that my having a human right means that I, as person x, have a claim against person or institution y, such that "other things being equal, y ought not let the such and such fail to be the case," where the "such and such" refers to my getting the substance of the right in question, be it freedom of movement, access to education, to health care, or to a fair trial (214).

My having a human right entails that others (be they persons or institutions) have duties to make sure that I have whatever the right in question spells out that I ought to have, but the Gewirth and Thomson definitions do not say that these other people actually do their duties or are even aware of having them. All that matters definitionally is that my human right to food, for instance, is matched by other people's duties to feed me, should I be a child, be disabled, or be caught, as UDHR 25 puts it, without some "other lack of livelihood in circumstances beyond [my] control." Should it happen that, for whatever reason, these duty-bearers do not do their duties, in that case it is still true of me that I have the human right to food; I can still claim it, or others can claim it on my behalf. This holds true whether these duty-bearers are private individuals, governmental agencies, or international aid organizations. That there *are* duty-bearers is part of the Gewirth/Thomson definition of what a human right is, but it is not part of their definition that these duties are recognized by, or actually being performed by, the persons or institutions that have those duties. Their definition separates the morality of the situation from the legal and social practices in just the way the Universal Declaration as a list of moral rights is separated from the later-adopted, legally binding international covenants that implement the birthrights of the Declaration.

This separation of moral rights from legal and social systems of implementation brings with it the priority of rights over duties and the related asymmetry of the two. For someone to have a moral right, there must at least be one other (even if as yet unknown) person that has the correlative duty. In this limited but important sense, rights and duties are on the same plane ontologically. The drafters admit this in Article 29, where they tell us that "Everyone has duties to the community in which alone the free and full development of his personality is possible." But that does not mean that the flow can go either way. In the Universal Declaration and in the Gewirth/Thomson definition the flow goes from my having a right to others having a corresponding duty, and not in the reverse direction. Also, my having a human right does not require that the corresponding duty-bearers be immediately identifiable. Since my having, for instance, the right to food depends only on my own humanity and since that presumably is not in question, I have that right even if it is not immediately clear who—among a range of possible duty-bearers—has the moral duty to actually feed me. That is why the drafters of the Declaration felt no need to be as clear about the precise location of the duties of Article 29 as they were about the rights being inherent and inalienable in every human being. They did not think that they needed to know the map of the land of moral duties before they could publish the text on rights, so they published it first.

The Asymmetry of Rights and Duties. Of the thirty articles in the Declaration, only one, Article 29, is devoted to duties, and that one comes toward the end. This creates an asymmetry between rights and duties that is distinctive to the notion of human rights and has gone underappreciated by legal theorists. In my previous commentary on this pivotal Article 29, I explained how in the early drafting stages, duties to our fellow human beings, to society, even to the state and to the United Nations, used to be up front in four articles that were collapsed into two articles, Article 1 remaining up front and the rest of the ideas being put into what became our Article 29.[18] Even after being moved to the end, Article 29 is still a formidable article with a first paragraph devoted to duties to the community "in which alone the free and full development of [our] personality is possible," and a second one to the limitations placed on the exercise of our rights "by law solely for the purpose of securing due recognition and respect for the rights and freedoms of others and of meeting the just requirements of morality, public order, and the general welfare in a democratic society." The third one tells us that in the exercise of our rights and freedoms we should not contravene the "purposes and principles of the United Nations." Between them, Article 1 (especially its second sentence: "They are endowed with reason and conscience and should act toward one another in a spirit of brotherhood") and Article 29 represent a strong communitarian and cosmopolitan strand that is present throughout the Declaration and that I discuss in some detail in Chapter 4. Here I draw out the definitional problems that we face as a result of the asymmetry between rights and duties.

When we leave the confines of the Declaration and look at the domain of international human rights law as it has developed since the Declaration was adopted, we find that this asymmetry has deepened significantly. In the postwar human rights system the burdens of having these correlative duties are almost exclusively placed on the state parties that create international instruments. Moments before the Third Committee adopted the Universal Declaration, it wanted to make sure that the duties states have to implement these rights (which duties they did not mention in the Declaration) would not be ignored. To that end the Committee adopted an Egyptian motion stating "that the declaration of human rights shall be limited to the formulation of principles relating to human rights which presuppose the existence of corresponding duties on the part of States and defers the formulation of principles relating to the duties of States for incorporation to an appropriate instrument" (GAOR Third, 81). The appropriate instrument turned out to be the two international covenants that were adopted in 1966 and that came into force in 1976. States that ratify these instruments take on obligations to deliver the substance of human rights to the people living under their jurisdiction. These two instruments lie at the center of a large and still-growing domain of international human rights law. This entire system is a man-made one; it therefore has difficulty embracing the inherent character of the human rights that, according to the Declaration, accrue to us automatically at birth without the intervention of anything made or done by humans other than the acts of (natural or artificial) conception that bring us into the world. This new emphasis on the duties of states has deepened the asymmetry between inherent human rights and their correlative duties, for while the right-holders are still individual human beings, in this new international system the primary duty-bearers are still mostly, though not exclusively, states and their agencies rather than individual human beings. We have a correlation between holders of inherent rights that are not man-made and state duty-bearers that are man-made and therefore contingent. This hybrid of inherent moral rights matched with mostly contingent, man-made state duties has created puzzlement and discomfort among theoreticians of human rights.

Onora O'Neill, for instance, has bemoaned the fact that in contemporary discussions of justice almost nothing is said about the "agents of justice," by which she means states and a plurality of other duty-bearers. "Nowhere is this more evident," she says, "than in the text of the Universal Declaration of 1948."[19] She speculates that the drafters were so "cavalier about identifying agents of justice" because working in the late 1940s they incorrectly assumed that these duty-bearing agents were all nation-states. They did not foresee the enormous plurality of agents that have popped up since they wrote, which is why they did us a great disservice by not spelling out the duty end of the spectrum more precisely. They

focused on "recipience and rights rather than on actions and obligation" (191). O'Neill ignores the asymmetry that the drafters saw between
inherent human rights and their correlative duties, not just the ones
states have, but also those of a host of other duty-bearers like parents,
school boards, government agencies, multinational corporations, and
the readers of this book, to name a few. The drafters did not overlook
this "enormous plurality" of duty-bearers and were not "cavalier" about
them. They felt they could agree far more readily on a list of inherent
rights than on a list of duties that would shift with the circumstances of
time and place. While the rights they wanted to proclaim had a steady
and inherent location in every human person and could therefore be
captured by a repetition of the words "everyone" and "all" in the articles
of the Declaration, the correlative duties that go with these rights depend on which of various possible duty-bearers are nearest in the moral
countdown. The duty-bearer could be a victim's family, an international
corporation in the vicinity, or perhaps some official in the state bureau-
cracy, each of which would—if it were the culprit—probably have its duty
delineated in a different way.

This plurality of agents of justice, whose task it is to deliver the substance of human rights, varies enormously from individuals to states, and
to the numerous domestic and international organizations that fill the
civic space between these two end points. The word "everyone" in UDHR
Article 29 does not have a narrower scope than it has in the other articles of the Declaration: "everyone has duties to the community in which
alone the free and full development of his personality is possible." The
second paragraph tells us that these duties arise because in the exercise
of our own rights "due recognition and respect" must be had for the
"rights and freedoms of others." No adult human being can escape the
moral pull that comes from the direction of other people's rights and
from the communities in which they are nurtured from childhood on.
The American Declaration of the Rights and Duties of Man, which was
adopted in April 1948 and the writing of which overlapped significantly
with that of the Declaration, tells us outright in its title that all individuals
have duties to others that match their human rights.[20] The Preamble of
this Bogotá Declaration explains that these are not "Duties of a juridical
nature" but "others of a moral nature which support them in principle
and constitute their basis"). Chapter 2 contains articles on the duties of
individuals to society, to their children, their parents, their community,
and their nation, as well as to pay taxes, work, and not engage in political activities in other countries. The African Charter on Human and
Peoples' Rights also has a separate chapter devoted to the duties of individuals that correlate with the proclamation of these universal rights.[21]
Article 27 of what is also called the Banjul Charter gives us this overview:

"Every individual shall have duties towards his family and society, the State and other legally recognized communities and the international community." These documents lend support to the thesis that inherent human rights are matched with universal duties that accrue to individuals in the course of their lives as parents, citizens, and fellow members of the human race. We have human rights "against the whole world" because the whole world is full of duty-bearers who, through their linkages in a host of intermediate organizations (family, village, nation, state, and global networks), must work to deliver the substance of our rights to us, just as we ourselves have the duty to work through such networks to deliver the substance of their rights to them.

Regarding the sparse treatment of duties in the Universal Declaration, O'Neill feels betrayed by the "scandal" of our not knowing "whether these universal rights are matched and secured by universal obligations or by obligations held by some but not by all agents and agencies" ("Agents of Justice," 191). It is for her "a matter of deep regret that the Declaration is so opaque about allocating the obligations of justice" (193). While O'Neill overlooks the asymmetry issue, she is right to point us to the disarray in contemporary discussions about the duties that correlate with human rights. With the proliferation of human rights instruments, a plurality of duty-bearers has indeed sprung up, and different theoreticians capture all or only some of those duty-bearers in their definitions of what a human right is. When states sign and ratify any international human rights instrument, they are just as eager as any other duty-bearer to know precisely what it is that they commit themselves to doing. While it took only two years (January 1947–December 1948) to agree on a list of rights for the Declaration, it took the UN twenty more years to adopt the matching list of obligations of states in the two International Covenants. That was not simply because the Cold War intervened, although it did. The enormous differences between the ideologies and circumstances of states made it difficult to find the right level of abstraction for these shared correlative duties.

After that, the international community has even been slower to spell out the duties that non-state or nongovernmental actors have to implement the human rights that have been spelled out in various international bills of rights, the Declaration foremost among them. These non-state actors include businesses, international corporations, and international organizations like the IMF, World Bank, WTO, and ILO.[22] Martha Nussbaum makes the point against O'Neill "that so far as definiteness goes, the shoe is squarely on the other foot: we can give a pretty clear and definite account of what all the world's citizens should have, what their human dignity entitles them to, prior to and to some extent independently of solving the difficult problem of assigning the duties—

although obviously there must be a generality level in our account of entitlements."[23] Nussbaum's list of capabilities is based on "the [same] concept of a life worthy of human dignity" as is the Declaration's list of human rights. We agree with her that, given "the multiplicity of institutional and individual actors" both domestically and internationally, it is "much easier" to draw up a list of "species entitlements" (Nussbaum, *Frontiers of Justice*, 278) or of human rights (our terminology) than it is to draw up a list of duties. The drafters foresaw this when they adopted the above-mentioned Egyptian motion and postponed spelling out the correlative duties in Covenants that were to be adopted later.

As an individual human being, each one of us is located at the center of a whole series of concentric circles of duty-bearers that surround us from the moment of birth. These circles extend from our families and next of kin to our local communities with their school boards and the like, to regional and state affiliations, and from there to states and international organizations like the United Nations, all the way until we reach the human family. It all depends on the example one picks as to who or what organization has the correlative duty to deliver the substance of the right in question. For the great majority of my readers, the duty to feed them when they were young fell on their parents and next of kin. For anyone born in a refugee camp or orphaned soon after birth, that duty may have fallen on the International Red Cross. For someone living below the poverty line in a city in the United States, that duty might fall on the city, county, or private volunteer agency set up to shelter and feed the homeless of that particular city. Since we have a human right by virtue of our humanity, the fact that we have it is immediately clear. But in certain circumstances it may take a day, a year, or a decade for the rest of the world to decide who the duty-bearers in a particular case are and in what order they should step up to the plate, whether it is our parents, the village elders, government agencies, international aid organizations, or individual citizens of nations. This is why it is so important that the developing world have a thriving civil society containing numerous duty-bearers that keep government agencies from being overwhelmed by the delivery of the substance of even the most basic human rights. Realizing that some of these other duty-bearers are "dragging their heels" or otherwise not in a position to deliver the substance of a right, it often happens that individual citizens of one nation will help the victims of oppression or famine in another nation. They give this help not just to make themselves feel good, but also and sometimes only because the rights that are being violated are held, to use Feinberg's phrase again, "against the whole world."[24]

To have human rights "against the whole world" means that the concentric circles of duty-bearers with which right-bearers are surrounded must coordinate their activities to make sure that people receive the substance of their birthrights. This feature of the general rather than the specific location of the correlative duties follows from the doctrine of inherence. As Richard Wasserstrom explains it, "because they are rights that are not possessed in virtue of any contingent status or relationship, [human rights] . . . are rights that can be claimed equally against any and every other human being."[25] People who help others in need often see themselves as part of this larger, worldwide network of duty-bearers. The great tragedy of the modern world is that, in spite of our increased affluence, millions of victims of human rights violations fall (for a variety of reasons, but mostly because of corruption and ignorance) between the cracks of the system of duty-bearers. Initially and in adulthood the main duty-bearer involved is the healthy adult who has the right and is perfectly able (because not prevented by internal or external forces) to look after his or her own affairs. But as babies and children, and frequently as adults, we cannot deliver the substance of a right by ourselves to ourselves, and it falls on those located on the concentric circles of duties to help make that delivery. Sometimes those other duty-bearers do not just help us, but they make the entire delivery. That happens every time a mother puts a baby to her breast and when prisoners of conscience are let out of prison because thousands of people wrote letters to the minister of justice of the country involved.

A fair number of international human rights instruments do mention the fact that the rights they codify are inherent in their possessors. The instruments do this in spite of the fact that they stress and spell out the obligations of the states that ratify them. For convenience's sake I have added italics where appropriate. In its first recital the 1956 Supplementary Convention on the Abolition of Slavery speaks of "freedom [as] the *birthright* of every human being."[26] The 1965 International Convention on the Elimination of All Forms of Racial Discrimination begins with the consideration that "the Charter of the United Nations is based on the principles of the dignity and equality *inherent* in all human beings,"[27] which is also how the General Assembly begins its Preamble to the 1981 Declaration on the Elimination of All Forms of Intolerance and of Discrimination Based on Religion or Belief.[28] Each of the two 1966 International Covenants that came out of the Universal Declaration say in their second recitals that the rights they seek to protect "derive from the *inherent dignity* of the human person."[29] The Civil and Political Covenant asserts in Article 6 that "every human being has the *inherent right* to life" and in Article 10 that "all persons deprived of their liberty shall be treated with humanity and with respect for the *inherent dignity* of the person," which exact phraseology is also used in Article 17 of the 1990 International Convention on the Protection of the Rights of All Migrant Workers and Members of their Families.[30] The 1993 Vienna Declaration and Programme of Action tell us that "human rights and fundamental freedoms are the *birthright* of all human beings."[31] The States Parties to the 1989 Convention on the Rights of the Child begin their Preamble with the recognition that "the *inherent dignity* and the equal and *inalienable rights* of all members of the human family is the foundation of freedom, justice and peace in the world" (430), which language they took from the First Recital of the Universal Declaration. They also tell us in their sixth article that "every child has the *inherent right* to life." In 1988 the General Assembly made a resolution regarding treatment of "all persons under any form of detention or imprisonment," Principle 1 of which states that that all such persons "shall be treated in a humane manner and with respect for the *inherent dignity* of the human person."[32] It repeated this concern in its 1990 Resolution that "all prisoners shall be treated with the respect due to their *inherent dignity* and value as human beings."[33]

We would expect to find the metaphysics of inherence prominently displayed in the 1984 Convention Against Torture and Other Cruel, Inhuman or Degrading Treatment and Punishment, for it is very difficult to conceive of any pragmatic rationale for that kind of convention.[34] Indeed, the Convention borrows the Universal Declaration's First Recital when its own Preamble espouses the "recognition of the equal and *inalienable rights* of all members of the human family [a]s the foundation of freedom, justice and peace in the world." This is also the First Recital of the 1992 General Assembly Declaration on the Protection of all Persons from Enforced Disappearance (127). In its Second Recital, the Torture Convention also repeats the claim that these rights "derive from the *inherent dignity* of the human person." In 1998, UNESCO adopted the Universal Declaration on the Human Genome and Human Rights, Article 1 of which gives us the biological basis of the UD First Recital that other declarations and conventions have also copied. It states that "the human genome underlies the fundamental unity of all members of the human family, as well as the recognition of their *inherent dignity* and diversity."[35] The 1985 Declaration on the Human Rights of Individuals Who Are Not Nationals of the Country in Which They Live "encourages universal respect for and observance of human rights and fundamental freedoms" in part because "the Universal Declaration proclaims that all human beings are *born free and equal* in dignity and rights and that everyone is entitled to all the rights and freedoms set forth in that Declaration without distinction of any kind. . . .", all of which my readers will recognize as taken from Articles 1 and 2 of the Declaration.[36]

The Fallacy of Implementation. In what follows I discuss some current definitions and expositions by international legal scholars of what a human right is. My thesis is that many of these contemporary definitions do not fit the outlook of the Declaration because they start with duties that are located at the other end of the spectrum from rights. Given that international human rights and humanitarian law have evolved mostly around the articulation of states' duties, this definitional focus on duties is understandable. But as definitions of what a human right is, these do not fit well with the outlook of the Declaration, which, as we just saw, has been the midwife for numerous regional and international legal human rights instruments. If we place rights and duties on a correlation continuum, then some theoreticians start with rights and work their way toward the duties at the other end. This is the approach taken by Gewirth and Thompson in the definitions discussed at the start of this section. The definitions I now discuss come at the definition of human rights from the side of contingent duties, which makes them unfriendly toward the metaphysics of inherence. I therefore charge them with the fallacy of implementation.

Most of the important definitions that do not fit the outlook of the Declaration come from theorists who have taken their cue from Wesley Newcomb Hohfeld's analysis of legal rights.[37] Wanting to bring what they see as the abstractness of human rights down to earth, they seek to define what a human right is on the model of what most scholars say a legal right is. Being intentionally shy about making an ontological commitment to a realm of separate moral rights, these theorists define human rights in terms of extant practices of implementation, which is why I charge them with committing a corresponding fallacy. This fallacy does to human rights what functionalism and behaviorism in psychology did or still do to our mental states. These schools of thought in psychology translate mental states out of existence as irrelevant to the real business of science. Just as some doctors and neurologists only want to know about the bodily behavior and neurobiological condition of their patients, so some human rights theorists are only interested in the instruments of international human rights law. And just as their behaviorist counterparts tend, for all practical purposes, to ignore people's mental states, so purists in the legal human rights field ignore the metaphysics of inherence because they are only interested in how the international legal system works on a practical level.

In man-made systems of law, right-holders and duty-bearers are equally defined by and bound by the rules that constitute a system of positive law. This means that there is in principle a similar clarity of location for both the rights and the duties in such a system. Duty-bearers and right-holders are equally identified or identifiable. The one group is no more abstract or mysterious than the other, and no general priority is assigned between them. The drafters of the Declaration broke this legal mold when they published a detailed map of the realm of moral rights without giving us similar details about the realm of duties that correlate with these rights. They evidently felt no discomfort in doing so, which suggests that it may not be a good idea to define human rights on a precise analogy with legal rights. The two first Hohfeldian theorists I discuss here, Carl Wellman and Rex Martin, do not deny that we have human rights, but they do pull the machinery of implementation into their definitions of what such a right is. The third, Raymond Geuss, is a purist in that he denies that people actually have such independent human rights.

A legal right is created and maintained by actual, historical (legal) practices and systems that govern the behavior of the relevant group of people. Such social and historical practices and actual systems of positive law are the breathing space of legal rights and duties that are inextricably linked by the rules of the system that created them. Thus, a legal right is defined in terms of the system of institutionalized rules of which it forms a part. If a human right were to be real in the only way a legal right can be said to be real, it would from day one need to be embedded in, and so be dependent on, a minimum of such institutionalized practices. In that case, the right would not be inalienable and not be inherent in the newborn human being. To commit the fallacy of implementation is to say that without such (obviously desirable) practices and customs human rights do not exist. It is to ignore the ontological distinction between, on the one hand, the inherence of the rights proclaimed in the Declaration, and on the other, the international system that has been created to implement these rights. The Hohfeldian theorists see duty-bearers as markers for the presence of human rights. Such theorists reverse the flow between rights and duties, making it go from duties to rights instead of from rights to duties, as the drafters would have us do. Since these systems of positive law and customs are themselves man-made, the human rights defined by them also end up being man-made and not inherent in the human person. This kind of systems analysis of what a human right is does not do justice to the concept of human rights that informs the Declaration, for systems are not inherent in the people that voluntarily make them; they are a product of human deliberations. We find especially clear echoes of this Hohfeldian analysis of rights in Wellman's and Martin's definitions of what a human right is.

According to Wellman, a human right is "cluster of ethical liberties, claims, powers and immunities that together constitute a system of ethical autonomy possessed by an individual human being vis-à-vis the state."[38] Since the duty-bearers Wellman has in mind are the agents of the modern state, human rights cannot be said to exist at a time when those agents did not yet exist. This in turn means that human rights came into existence only when those duties of states were being spelled out for the first time. At the heart of this cluster of ethical liberties lies the idea of an ethical claim right, which "one party x . . . has against some second party y, that y perform some action A if and only if y has a duty to x to do A" (91). Since y is the modern state as duty-bearer, and since x can be said to have a certain ethical claim against y if and only if y has the corresponding duty, the flow goes from the duties of y to the rights in *x*, which is the reverse of what the Declaration teaches us.

Martin commits the same fallacy when he says that "the notion of a right contains the element of appropriate practices of recognition and maintenance within it."[39] He concludes that, in "a society which has no civil rights (e g , a caste society, in particular one with a slave caste) there are no human rights. They are not observed there" (83). This conception of human rights as nonexistent where they are not observed is alien to the Declaration. If there are no human rights in a society like that, to what are the slaves and untouchables going to appeal when they seek their freedom?[40] Martin's reversal of the flow from individual rights to states' duties can be clearly seen in the admission that his account is one in which "individual persons play only a derivative and sometimes incidental role."[41] This kind of ontologically subordinate and "derivative" status of the individual does not accord with the drafters' willingness to adopt a list of moral rights without any machinery of implementation.

Martin defines a human right not simply as a valid claim but as "the combination of a claim with what it takes to satisfy the claim" (*A System of Rights*, 84). Since it is the duty-holders that must satisfy the claim, this means that we must be able to locate the duties that go with the rights before we can really call rights "rights." Martin believes that the duties that correspond to human rights are primarily and in the first instance duties held by governmental agencies. It is these kinds of "appropriate" governmental duties he has in mind when he says that "the concept of a human right as moral right includes within it practices of recognition and promotion of some appropriate sort: these things are internal to the concept in that they are necessarily considered in determining whether any such right has been instantiated" (85). Here we need to make a distinction between the instantiation of a right and its implementation. With the adoption of the Declaration the drafters announced that human rights are (automatically) instantiated with the birth of each human being because they saw the rights they declared as being inherent (and thus instantiated) in all human beings. It is the burden of this chapter to make sense out of the claim that these instantiated rights are real in spite of the fact that they are frequently violated and often not implemented by those who have the correlative duties.

Martin and Wellman make the common mistake of thinking that— like most other international human rights documents—the Universal

Declaration was in the first instance addressed to governments. The real addressees of the Declaration, however, were the common people and educators in any of the world's villages and cities, and not (in the first instance) their governments or experts in the realm of law or religion. The second (epistemic) universality thesis I mentioned at the start of this chapter gainsays Martin's approach, for such epistemic universality means that ordinary people of all walks of life can come to know about these human rights with their natural epistemic equipment. Governments are mere vehicles—though still the most important ones—that deliver the substance of rights to people within their territories who already (inherently) possess these rights. Martin sees his analysis as giving us "a reason for the central place occupied by government in our concept of a human right" (92). This is not true of the conception the drafters used. They studiously ignored states and their governments and turned down all amendments that sought to introduce references to states. Still, Martin is right when he claims that the great human rights manifestos "were intended to impose restraints upon governments" (86–87). This lends plausibility to his further claim—and I add the italics—that "*insofar as* human rights claims are addressed to governments . . . *[t]o that degree* governmental practices are included within the notion of human rights" (87). Even then, we should hesitate to include these practices in the generalized "notion" or concept of what a human right is. The italicized phrases delineate the difference between the Declaration, which in the first stance was not addressed to governments or their agents, and other human rights instruments that are so addressed. Martin's analysis ignores this difference between the basic concept and later practices.

Martin believes that there are two aspects to any human right, a claim-to aspect and a claim-against aspect. As a claim to, for instance, food, a human right is truly universal because all people have a moral claim to food. But as a claim against someone, this right is not universal, but contingent and specifically tied to whoever or whatever it is that has the duty to deliver that food to the person in need of it. Since for Martin human rights documents are typically addressed to governments and their agencies, it is these agencies that typically have the specific duties that go with these universal moral claims. For him, the universality of the Universal Declaration is in a way fraudulent, as it is for O'Neill, because the list it contains is not really a list of moral *rights*; it is only one of moral claims, and claims (for Martin) are not themselves rights because they tell only half the story. The other half is that these universal moral claims are not rights until the agencies that have the corresponding duties are marked or markable. For Martin a human right is a "hybrid" made up of a morally valid claim backed up by appropriate government practices. And it is only the latter that turn such claims into rights. What "serves to constitute the [moral] claim a [human] right" is "the recognition in law and promotion by government" of the claims in question (97). We can see how in this passage Martin moves straightway from moral claims to legal acts of recognition and promotion, thus obliterating the very concept of an *inherent moral right*, as we find it in the Declaration. For him, there are only moral claims and legal rights, but no moral rights as such. While these legally recognized human rights "carry" their special "moral valid- ity" with them, this special backing does not in itself turn a moral claim into a human right (93). That conversion can only be accomplished by the machinery of implementation, that is, by "the recognition in law and promotion by government." It is this train of thought which leads Martin to say that the "existence [of legal civil rights] is a necessary element in a morally valid claim's being or becoming a human right," so much so that "If there are any human rights at all, it follows that there are civil rights in at least some countries" (97). Regardless of the historical accuracy of this claim, conceptually it places the cart of contingent duties before the horse of universal (because inherent) rights.

While we can compare Martin to the neurologist who ignores our mental states for purposes of scientific research only, Raymond Geuss, a respected Cambridge political philosopher of the analytic school, goes the extra step of denying outright that we have such things as human rights. He is an adherent of the legal positivist school of legal thinking. This theory is also often called the command theory of law, because it identifies a legal system with the expression of commands by a political sovereign (be that a king or a parliament) who, of course, backs up such orders with sanctions or punishments in case of disobedience. Accord- ing to this theory, there are no rights where there are no laws which tell us what these rights are, and there are no (real) laws where there are no sanctions to enforce those laws. Geuss's view is the contemporary equiv- alent of Jeremy Bentham's famous quip that (imprescriptible) natural (and now, human) rights are nothing but "nonsense on stilts." Since for Geuss the only real rights are local and domestic ones or international ones that have real sanctions attached to them, such as the enforcement of international trade law by the WTO Dispute Settlement Panels, he sees the entire realm of human rights (which we explore in this book) as nothing but a "ghostly analogue" of that other, man-made realm of real positive law.[42]

Geuss admits that the phrase "human rights" in the first instance is simply a right all humans possess. He derives the meaning of this phrase from the context of international politics, where he says it "refers in the first instance *not* to the source or grounds of validity of the purported right in question ('nature') but to the domain of its application ('to all human beings')" (140). I suspect that most people who use the phrase "human rights" mean precisely what Geuss rejects, namely, that these are rights that people have by virtue of their humanity or their "nature" or "human nature." At the time the drafters wrote the Declaration, the phrase "human rights" had hardly become current in international politics and law, so we must look for its meaning elsewhere. Geuss's answer to the question as to why these rights are universal differs from that of the drafters. They felt that these rights are, as they put it in the First Recital, "inalienable" and "inherent"; or, as Article 1 has it, that we are "born with" them. Geuss thinks that they are applicable to all people only if we make them so and attach enforceable sanctions to them, as we do with our domestic laws. For there to be a system of human or natural rights, he believes, there would have to be "some specifiable and more or less effective mechanism for enforcing them" (143). Since there was no such system in place in 1948, and Geuss doubts such exists even today, the title of the Declaration would express nothing but the wishful thinking of those who wrote it.

Actually, his criticism is stronger than this. He thinks that believers in human rights are walking around with an "incoherently vacuous conception" in their heads (144). For to "speak of 'human rights' is a 'kind of puffery or white magic'" (144). As with all magic, the human rights kind uses certain formulas which invoke "the names of the spirits involved ('rights,' the will of God, nature) and these formulas "matter less than that those on the receiving end *believe* in the reliable efficacy of whatever is invoked" (144; emphasis original). Or as someone (sitting next to me at a human rights dinner) once remarked by way of explaining his lack of philosophical interest in human rights questions: "it works, doesn't it?" Should it turn out that there is today some sort of enforcement system for human rights, as I submit there is, Geuss thinks that we would then still not have human or natural rights that are any different from the ordinary legal rights with which we are all familiar in our daily lives. Any kind of international enforcement system, if there is such, "would constitute not so much a vindication of the doctrine of human rights as a transformation of individual components of someone's moral beliefs into a system of positive rights. We would merely have begun to invent and impose on the nations of the world a new layer of positive (international) law" (144).

As Geuss sees things, "The question is not whether this [positive enforcement system] is possible or whether it would be a good thing, but whether such a development is the invention of a new set of positive 'rights' into a new international legal system or the emergence into visibility of a set of natural human rights that already existed" (145). I readily admit that the numerous measures of implementation that make up the enforcement system for human rights, such as it is, is an invention and the result of much hard work and diplomatic ingenuity. But Geuss for his part fails to see that these same measures do in fact also and at the same time reveal the step-by-step "emergence into visibility of a set of natural human rights that already existed" in people everywhere. Every December 10, we celebrate this emergence into visibility of what hitherto had been denied and covered up. On that day numerous individuals, groups, and even whole nations celebrate new visible chunks of the hitherto-submerged but now emergent field of human rights law. Geuss does not see that the international community is draining long submerged fields of human dignity and discovering an entirely new moral topography.

Geuss would presumably think that what I just said is incoherent. For "the point . . . of appeal to 'natural or human rights' was to be that they were not supposed to be something we made exist, but something we discovered which served as the grounds for judging actual legal rights and thus relative to which we could criticize some existing system of positive right. The only thing that can serve that purpose seems to be the flickering light of our variable moral beliefs" (146). These flickering lights of our individual human consciences, I argue, add up to a formidable beam or beacon that helped the drafters uncover or "recover" or, to use a verb from the UN Charter, "reiterate" respect for human rights. Geuss claims that human rights believers have talked themselves into adopting "an inconvenient fiction" (147) and that they try to press upon others an idea of natural or human rights that "is neither well formed nor well grounded" (150). He thinks that present efforts to develop an efficacious system of enforcement "combined with residues of religious beliefs" might give "our legal system further stability by *imagining* it as grounded in a system of pre-determined natural or human rights" (151, emphasis added); this "whole process can become a kind of self-reinforcing spiral with each turn making the notion of natural rights seem more and more intuitively unavoidable and substantial" (151). Although the human rights regimes that now cover the globe are becoming stronger and stronger, this fact need not be the result of people's powerful imaginations alone.

It can also be the result of the conscience of humanity stirring in people everywhere and prodding them to set up these regimes, as I argue in the next chapter and in the rest of this book. For Geuss, the whole approach of seeing "politics . . . through the lens of rights is one of the great illusions of our epoch." While some areas of public life may benefit from this rights approach, he is sure that others will not. Other parts, like "the doctrine of human rights, are, in [his] view, inherently confused" (156). My conclusion is entirely different: when it comes to the notion and practice of human rights there is a great need for metaphysical thinking. We must follow the lead of the Declaration's drafters and liberate the idea of human rights from the realm of the political and juridical, which is where contemporary theorists have imprisoned it. These theorists will respond to this call for metaphysical thinking with the counter-charge that the domain of the metaphysical that I have painted in this chapter is not reachable from where we, ordinary people and theorists alike, stand in this world of flux. The thesis of the next chapter is that here, too, the UD drafters have shown us the way.

Chapter 2
Obeying the Conscience of Humanity

As I noted at the start of Chapter 1, the doctrine of inherent human rights has two parts to it, a metaphysical part that says that all human beings have these rights inherently by virtue of their humanity, and an epistemic or knowledge-based part that says that all human beings can come to know that this is so by virtue of their own natural epistemic (or knowledge) equipment. I devoted that first chapter to an exposition of the idea of inherence as the best way to capture the *metaphysical universality* that we found embedded in the opening clauses of the Universal Declaration and that are often referred to in international human rights instruments constructed since 1948. The three sections of this chapter are devoted to the idea of *epistemic universality*, which comprises the second half of this doctrine of inherence. I pursue this second half in order to avoid having critics dismiss the universality of human rights as so much philosophical or metaphysical spinning of wheels. Just as one might interrupt a description of an exotic island somewhere on earth with the question how one might travel to that enchanted place, so critics of human rights frequently overlook the metaphysical descriptions of inherence and inalienability in the Declaration because they believe that that enchanted metaphysical domain is not really accessible to ordinary human beings like you and me. You can't get there from here, they say.

In fact, the drafters pointed us in the direction of two epistemic routes into the metaphysical domain of human rights. Both routes are named in the second sentence of the first article of the Declaration, where we are told that all human beings "are endowed with reason and conscience and should [therefore] act toward one another in a spirit of brotherhood." On the suggestion of Peng Chung Chang, Chinese representative, the route of what he called "two-man-mindedness"—which his colleagues translated into "conscience"—was without opposition added to the route of reason. This second route of conscience is also mentioned in the second recital of the Preamble with its suppressed reference to the Nazi horrors: "Whereas disregard and contempt for human rights have resulted in barbarous acts that have outraged the conscience of mankind." The two routes work in tandem. We can say that reason (or its most popular embodiment, the Golden Rule) supplies the framework for our moral intuitions, or we can say that our conscience (or moral intuitions) supplies the necessary background for a correct use of the Golden Rule. Different theorists stress different parts of this tandem arrangement. Alan Gewirth, John Rawls, and Jürgen Habermas, with whom we take issue in Chapters 3 and 6, have stressed the route of reason at the expense of conscience. They in turn would probably charge our account with a gross neglect of reason as the preferred route into the territory of human rights.

Epistemic universality is the idea that the people (who have these human rights) must by their own powers know, or be able to come to know, that they have them. While in the exact sciences metaphysical and epistemic universality need not and usually do not go together, in morality and law they cannot be separated. Here there is at least the presumption of their togetherness. The expositions I give here of our moral sense and of the Golden Rule (in Chapter 3) are to the human rights in the Universal Declaration what the idea of promulgation is to the rights and duties in positive legal systems: a law is not a just law unless (among other things) it is somehow made known to those to whom it is addressed. Usually, this is done by printing the new legal ordinances in the Congressional Record (in the United States) or in a town's local paper. Analogously, it would have made no sense for the drafters of the Declaration to assert that every human being has the rights they list, and yet for there to be no normal or natural way the human beings who have these rights could come to know that they have them. Since having these rights requires nothing other than that one be a human being, so knowing that one has them must be just as easy or natural. The first kind of universality implies and requires the second.

This is why the authors of the Declaration did not address their document to jurists, scholars, international lawyers, diplomats, or any other kind of expert. They were not even thinking of intellectuals in general. Throughout their deliberations their intended audience consisted of ordinary men and women in the streets of any of the world's cities or villages. Whenever they worried about their text becoming too long, they would cut it back because, as Hansa Mehta, the Indian delegate, said, "it was to be understood by the common man" (E/CN.4/SR.50/ 8). At one point the French delegate proposed that certain articles be merged because he felt the time had come for the Drafting Committee to "shorten and clarify the Draft Declaration" (ECN.4/AC.1/SR.35/2). This was not a desire for brevity's own sake, but to make sure the masses would understand the document. Peng Chung Chang, the Chinese delegate, agreed that the Declaration "should be as simple as possible and in a form which was easy to grasp" (AC.1/SR.50/7). Michael Klekovkin, their colleague from the UKSSR, had also been worried that the document had become too long, "with the result that it would be difficult for the ordinary people to understand it" (SR.41/7). More than once, Eleanor Roosevelt, as chair, felt it necessary to remind "the representatives of [the need for] a clear, brief text, which could be readily understood by the ordinary man and woman" (SR.41/9). The Declaration, she often said, "was not intended for philosophers and jurists but for the ordinary people" (GAOR Third, 138, 609). In the midst of some troublesome discussions on Article 1, Luis Alfonso de Alba, the Mexican representative, did not want it to be "forgotten that the declaration was intended primarily for the common man and for that reason it was important that it should be as clear as possible" (GAOR Third, 162). Most of these comments were made in the debates of the Third Committee early in the fall of 1948. Similar ones were made in the General Assembly debates that December.[1]

An important title change of the document fits well with this supposition of epistemic universality. Because it was being referred to as an International Bill of Rights, the Haitian delegation got the Third Committee to adopt a resolution affirming "the universal character of the Declaration of Human Rights" (A/C.3/373). This led to a French proposal that the title of the document be changed to read "Universal Declaration of Human Rights" (GAOR Third, 775). This change (from "international" to "universal") shifted the attention from the international delegations that did the proclaiming to the peoples of the world being addressed. As a result, the term "universal" in the title of the document captures both the metaphysical and the epistemological universalities that make up the doctrine of inherence. In his defense of the title change, René Cassin, the French delegate, noted that "the chief novelty of the declaration was its universality. Because it was universal, the declaration could have a broader scope than national declarations and draw up the regulations that were essential to good international order. It was for states to conclude conventions between themselves for the preservation of that order; otherwise it would establish itself over their heads, for men could not be indefinitely deprived of the necessary protection of their rights" (866). Cassin repeated this theme of universality in many of his later essays and speeches because he was of the opinion that the Declaration was "the first document about moral value adopted by an assembly of the human community." On the tenth anniversary of the Declaration he wrote that it formed "the basis for a list of minimal, common right[s] and offer[ed] a common moral code to each member of the human community."[2]

The three sections of this chapter spell out what I take to be the moral epistemology of human rights that underlies these citations form the UD adoption debates. That epistemology is captured in the snappy title of Alan Dershowitz's recent book *Rights from Wrongs*, where he argues that we learn what rights are from the wrongs we encounter.[3] While we object to Dershowitz's rejection of the idea that basic rights are even minimally or inherently grounded in human nature, we do support his contention that our experiences of great moral wrongs like the Holocaust (which he mentions frequently) are "the source" of human rights. We have shown elsewhere how clauses and even whole articles of the Declaration were adopted simply because the drafters agreed that this would prevent another Holocaust.[4] In answer to the question as to what might justify belief in human rights, Dershowitz gives us the "bottom-up" answer that rights are to be read off from our experience of injustices. In his discussion of how Franklin Roosevelt sought to convince the American people that the time had come to add to their rather narrow bill of mostly civil and political rights, Cass Sunstein makes the same "bottom-up" argument for our belief in social and economic human rights.[5] This is important, for it means that the linkage between occurrences of gross violations and recognition of the rights enunciated in the Universal Declaration works not just for a few selected rights, but for the whole range of the Declaration. These linkages also help us answer possible charges of Western ethnocentrism, for delegates from all over the world were equally repelled by the horrors the Nazis had perpetrated and wanted to forestall a repeat of that kind of abuse of state power.

We can look at this idea of epistemic universality from the point of view of our *discovery* (alone or in groups) of human rights, or from the point of view of the later *justification* of this belief to others after we have made our discovery. Using examples from the debates and votes on the articles of the Declaration and by citing court cases and statutes from twentieth-century legal history, I argue that every normally healthy human individual has the epistemic equipment to *discover* that we all have human rights. This theme of discovery sets my argument apart from the justificatory approach of theorists like Rawls and Habermas, whose views we discuss in Chapters 3 and 6 respectively.[6] Because our conscience or moral sentiment is enraged and engaged by the evils we encounter, our theory holds that there is a difference between the initial discovery of human rights and any later justification of that discovery to others in the court of reason. Justificatory liberals argue like scientists who, on realizing that the existence of certain infinitesimally small entities is demanded by their calculations, declare by fiat that those (theoretically postulated) entities do indeed exist. As long as the calculations are confirmed by their colleagues, there is in these specialized cases no need for an independent corroboration by telescope, microscope, or otherwise. Whatever its merit in those highly specialized fields of science, we object to this kind of reductionism (or constructivism) in political theory. It ignores the huge difference that we hold exists between ordinary legal rights and universal human rights. The experience of radical evil with its attendant discovery of human rights cannot, we maintain, be reduced to or be fully explained by contemporary theories of procedural justice. Since it is through their moral sentiments that people discover the metaphysical universality of human rights, these other theorists end up denying the *real* presence of human rights in the human person. They offer us a *factitious* or manmade (that is, constructed or invented) presence, or even a merely symbolic or rhetorical presence. Compare this to the disagreements among theologians in the days of the Reformation when they argued about the way "the body of Christ" could be said to be present in the host at communion. When it comes to human rights, we maintain the thesis of the real presence, even though we admit that human rights are "invisible" in the sense that they are obviously not physically observable.

This difference between discovery and justification explains why we take exception to the title of Lynn Hunt's *Inventing Human Rights: A History*.[7] To us the language of "invention" suggests that human rights are man-made instead of being inherent in the human person. Hunt may well be right when she points out that the widespread reading of novels together with the campaigns for the abolition of torture expanded and strengthened interior human sentiments in the eighteenth century. But, since the thesis of epistemic universality holds that people everywhere have known all along (especially in situations of gross abuse and violation) about inherently existing human rights, the invention of these rights should not be ascribed to just one historical period or one region of the world. This does not mean that different cultures at different times have not used different terminology to describe their experiences of abuse and domination. What is most helpful about Hunt's history is that she shows us how the idea of natural (or human) rights became a political and juridical item in the consciousness of whole peoples and was for that reason written into the domestic constitutions of their time. In the second half of the eighteenth century there definitely was among the bulk of civilized peoples an increase in their awareness of the moral rights of human beings regardless of class, culture, race, and (eventually) sex. And this awareness had political consequences.

The thinking of the second half of the twentieth century resembles Enlightenment thinking more than just in the metaphysics we borrowed when we took over their language of "inherent rights," as I argued in Chapter 1. Also, our own epistemic moral equipment has been stirred in similar ways. The Holocaust shocked the moral consciousness of all civilized peoples into an increased awareness of the inherent dignity of every human being. The use of the phrase "the conscience of mankind" in the second recital of the UDHR Preamble reflects the general view in the late 1940s that the horrors of the war were an affront to the human conscience. The 1946 UN General Assembly condemned the crime of genocide because the "denial of the right to existence of entire human groups . . . shocks the conscience of mankind . . . and is contrary to moral law."[8] This "moral law" is not the moral code of any one particular group, nation, or state, but a universal moral law that informs the conscience of mankind. One of the UDHR drafters, Jorge Carrera Andrade from Ecuador, spoke for many of his colleagues when he said that the Declaration "was the most important document of the century, and indeed . . . a major expression of the human conscience" (GAOR Third, 36). Ever since, friends of the Declaration have described it this way.

Our media have on a regular basis been flooded with images of massacres and incredible suffering all over the globe. These images draw on an ever expanding range of our moral sentiments; this expansion, in turn, has made the human rights movement into the mass movement it has become. This movement is fed and sustained by millions of people who find their moral sentiments enraged and engaged by their discovery of one or several rights as enunciated in the Universal Declaration. Their consciences might be triggered by images that call to mind the abolition of "slavery or servitude . . . in all their forms" (Article 4), the "right to a nationality" (Article 15), "the right to peaceful assembly and association" (Article 20), or the right "to a social and international order in which the rights and freedoms set forth in this Declaration can be fully realized" (Article 28). Since there are thirty articles, many of which enunciate more than one right, the international order envisioned by the drafters is a highly complex one. This book offers the reader a theoretical framework that ties together the disparate parts of this complex order and shows how the pieces can be seen making a unified whole.

In section A of this chapter, "Rights from the Wrongs of the Holocaust," I argue that this idea of a shared or common human conscience on which individual human beings can and do draw lies behind the adoption of the Universal Declaration. I use it to rebut charges that the Declaration is a Western ethnocentric document because the membership of the UN has since then almost quadrupled or because eight nations abstained in the final vote. It is my contention that the moral epistemology of human rights (that recognition of rights comes from the wrongs we encounter) answers the charge of ethnocentrism and that the shared revulsion the drafters felt amply makes up for the fact that in the 1940s the UN had a much smaller membership. To know that genocidal crimes and other gross human rights violations are always and everywhere radically wrong, one needs to witness or hear about only one of those abominations, if that. In section

B, "The Doctrine of Manifest Illegality," I connect the drafters' appeal to "the conscience of mankind" with the theme of "the conscience of humanity" that runs through recent histories of military and international law. I defend the thesis that this notion of the conscience of humanity is embedded in the doctrine of "manifest illegality" that is used in various domestic military manuals and courts-martial and in the international criminal tribunals that have been established after World War II. I trace this embeddedness from Nuremberg to Abu Ghraib, with stopovers in Vietnam (for the Calley trial), Jerusalem (for the Eichmann trial), the Hague (for the Yugoslav and Rwanda statutes and cases) and Rome (for the International Criminal Court statutes). My point will be that these contemporary repeats of Nazi genocidal crimes do not lead morally sensitive people to question or doubt their commitment to human rights. Rather, these atrocities strengthen that commitment because they make us aware of how terribly defective the machinery for implementing human rights still is. Their wrongs being so obvious and the violated rights *therefore* so clear, contemporary abominations lead us to clamor for justice and accountability much in the way the visionaries in the late 1940s did. In section C, "The Framework of Moral Intuitionism," I interpret both the adoption of the Declaration and these later appeals to the conscience of humanity with the help of the theory of classical moral intuitionism. This is not a popular theory, but it explains better than most the shared moral revulsion we experience when we—like the UDHR drafters and the members of the tribunals I survey—are asked to judge acts of radical evil.

A. Rights from the Wrongs of the Holocaust

The Charge of Western Ethnocentrism. At the time the Universal Declaration was being drafted—between January 1947 and December 1948—the membership of the UN was about a fourth of that in 2008, close to 200. Philippe de la Chapelle has estimated that of the 56 nations that participated in drafting the Declaration, "North and South America with 21 countries represented 36 percent of the total, Europe with 16 countries 27 percent, Asia with 14 countries 24 percent, Africa with 4 countries a mere 6 percent and the South Sea Islands with 3 countries 5 percent."[9] Only four of the now more than fifty African nations voted on its articles. It is obvious that Africa and Asia were grossly underrepresented in this process. From Africa only Egypt, Ethiopia, Liberia, and South Africa were represented, and only the Egyptian and South African delegations played an active role. India, China (with the Chiang Kai-shek regime still clinging to power), and Siam (today's Thailand) represented the peoples on the Asian continent, with the Siamese delegation totally inactive.

These facts can be used to launch an attack on the alleged universality of the Declaration, and—since this document is the moral backbone of the movement—on the idea of human rights generally. From this perspective the title of the document seems a misnomer, for it is hard to see how any international document can lay a claim to universal applicability if it was adopted before the collapse of the colonial empires of the 1950s and 1960s. The People's Republics of China and Indonesia, born in 1949, and Laos, Cambodia, and Vietnam, which gained independence from France in 1954, were not represented in the meetings that hammered out the text of the Declaration. It is hard not to assume that the thirty-seven nations of Western Europe and the Americas (which had 63 percent of the votes) imposed their own value system on the Declaration.

Before the drafting was even finished, the American Anthropological Association (AAA) warned the Human Rights Commission in 1947 that its "primary task" would be to come up with a declaration that was not "a statement of the rights conceived only in terms of values prevalent in the countries of Western Europe and America."[10] The anthropologists' key contention was that "standards and values are relative to the culture from which they derive so that any attempt to formulate postulates that grow out of the beliefs or moral codes of one culture must to that extent detract from the applicability of any Declaration of Human Rights to mankind as a whole" (119). They had their doubts that the drafting team gathered by the UN was inclusive enough of the world's different cultural, religious, linguistic, and economic traditions to avoid the imposition of values from Western Europe and America. They reminded the Commission of the devastating effects of the history of colonialism, with its twin powers of economic expansion and missionary zeal; they spoke of the "white man's burden" and the "civilizing mission" that ascribes to non-Western peoples a "cultural inferiority" and a "primitive mentality" that "justified their being held in tutelage of their superiors" (118). The anthropologists pointed out that the classical declarations of the eighteenth century had been so much easier to write because they had been addressed to the citizens of a single society and therefore were not really bills with a universal intent. But the 1940s were different: "Today the problem is complicated by the fact that the Declaration must be of world-wide applicability. It must embrace and recognize the validity of many different ways of life. It will not be convincing to the Indonesian, the African, the Indian, the Chinese, if it lies on the same plane as like documents of an earlier period. The rights of Man in the twentieth century cannot be circumscribed by the standards of any single culture or be dictated by the aspirations of any single people. Such a document will lead to frustration, not realization of the personalities of vast numbers of human beings" (119).

A number of critics believe that these worries of the AAA were in fact justified and that the 1948 Declaration is weakened or even crippled by a Western ethnocentric perspective. They argue that the lack of sufficient representation from the Asian and African continents means that, from the procedural point of view, the Declaration does not really deserve the adjective "universal" in its title. They believe that the flawed representational character of the proceedings damaged the substance of the product. Abdullahi Ahmed An-Na'im, for instance, is a defender of the Declaration in the world of Islam. He probably had the above-cited percentages in mind when he wrote that "given the historical context within which the present standards [of international human rights] have been formulated, it was unavoidable that they were initially based on Western cultural and philosophical assumptions."[11] Because they see the Declaration as "an articulation and reinforcement of political values that had prior existence" in Western Europe and the United States, Adamantia Pollis and Peter Schwab at one time felt that "efforts to impose the Declaration as it currently stands not only reflect a moral chauvinism and ethnocentric bias, but are also bound to fail."[12] Alison Dundes Renteln also believes "that the Declaration bears a Western imprint," because the few representatives from non-Western cultures could not or did not resist the ethnocentric encroachments of Western-oriented delegations. "Consequently, the promulgation of the UDHR appears to many countries as the imposition of an alien values system."[13] According to African human rights scholar Asmarom Legesse, Western liberal democracies ended up writing "most of their values and code of ethics into the Universal Declaration."[14] And former judge of the Yugoslav UN Tribunal Antonio Cassese has wondered how it could be that "the West succeed[ed] in imposing its philosophy of human rights" on the Universal Declaration.[15] The literature on human rights is replete with comments like these.

My response to this charge is that the Declaration is the result of a genuinely international effort that drew on far more than just Western perspectives. The delegations came from nations with very different political, cultural, religious, ethnic, economic, and legal traditions. What this shows is that when atrocities or gross violations are clear enough, moral outrage against them will also be clearly shared. The horrors of the Nazi camps had been brought to the attention of the Allies long before the war ended, and they had made respect for universal human rights a goal of the peace negotiations and of the later tasks given to the Human Rights Commission that was to draw up the International Bill.

At the first meeting of the Drafting Committee in early 1946, Geoffrey Wilson, the UK delegate, reminded his colleagues "of the historical situation in which the Committee met. It was one he said where Germany and other enemy countries during the war had completely ignored what mankind had regarded as fundamental human rights and freedoms. The Committee met as a first step toward providing the maximum possible safeguard against that sort of thing in the future" (E/CN.4/AC.1/ SR.7/5). Two years later, in the fall of 1948, that view had shaped a consensus on thirty articles. Lakshmi Menon from India told the assembly that the Declaration had been "born from the need to reaffirm those rights after their violation during the war" (GAOR, 893). Henry Carton de Wiart from Belgium thought that "the essential merit of the Declaration was to emphasize the high dignity of the human person after the outrages to which men and women had been exposed during the recent war" (879). Ernest Davies, another UK delegate, sounded a note of warning that the title of this section ("Rights from the Wrongs of the Holocaust") seeks to heed: "It should not be forgotten that the war by its total disregard of the most fundamental rights was responsible for the Declaration, for previous declarations had lived in history long after the wars and disputes which had given rise to them" had been forgotten (883). This shared, humanity-wide revulsion helps explain why the criticisms leveled at the Declaration as a Western ethnocentric document are shortsighted and often plain wrong, for that revulsion affected all the delegations and not just those from around the North Atlantic. All morally healthy people are repulsed by what the Nazis did to their victims. This explains how a human rights consensus could and did develop among delegations from a great variety of cultural, economic, and religious traditions. The obvious wrongs of the camps elicited from the delegates a moral reaction that transcended local cultural and ideological frameworks, and made them declare a list of rights that they looked on as equally transcendent and universal. I support these claims with three separate but related responses.

Response 1: Adopting the Text of the Declaration. The first draft of the second recital ("Whereas disregard and contempt for human rights have resulted in barbarous acts that have outraged the conscience of mankind. . . .") came from the pen of René Cassin, the French delegate, who had had a Nazi arrest warrant posted on his Paris apartment door. We can therefore appreciate the fact that Cassin's first draft of this recital was far more explicit than what we have in the final text. He wrote that "ignorance and contempt of human rights have been among the principal causes of the suffering of humanity and of the massacres and barbarities which have outraged the conscience of mankind before and especially during the last world war" (AC.1/Add.3). After witnessing genocides in Cambodia, Bosnia, Rwanda, and now the Sudan, we understand Cassin's straightforward reference to the "massacres and barbarities . . . of the last war" or explicit references to Nazi and fascist ideologies for which he was rebuffed by his colleagues. But when the Third Committee met later that fall and the Berlin Airlift was back in place, explicit references to World War II and to the Holocaust became points of contention. Two amendments were offered that went in opposite directions. The French delegation wanted the Second Recital to read: "Whereas ignorance and contempt for human rights are one of the essential causes of human suffering; whereas particularly during the Second World War, Nazism and racialism engendered countless acts of barbarism which outraged the conscience of mankind" (A/C.3/339). This version added the enemy's ideology of Nazism and racialism to the mention of the war. An Australian proposal went the other way in that it weakened the connection between the Declaration and World War II. It deleted from the Commission's text the phrase "before and during the Second World War," leaving only the general claim that "disregard and contempt for human rights [have] resulted in barbarous acts which have outraged the conscience of mankind" (A/C.3/314/Rev.1, A/C.3/257). The time and place of the outrage are left unspecified.

In defense of the French proposal Cassin argued that "when dealing with the body of the declaration he had always advocated the removal of any controversial wording; but in the preamble it was absolutely essential to set down a protest against the horrors which had taken place before and during the Second World War" (GAOR Third, 760). The references to Nazism and racialism were "controversial" because in the rhetoric of the Cold War the Allies felt that the communists were seeking to co-opt the meaning of words like "democracy" by redefining it as "people's democracy" and of fascism by claiming that it was an extreme form of capitalism, the economic system most North Atlantic nations had adopted in one form or another. The Soviet delegation was faced with a difficult choice. Alexandre Bogomolov applauded the references to the War and the Nazis, but "did not consider the explanation given of the barbarous acts committed by exponents of Nazism and racialism a valid one" (775). For pure Marxists, World War II was caused not by gross violations of international human rights standards but by "the internal upheaval of a segment of capitalism" in its extreme fascist sector. By linking Nazi Germany so directly to capitalism and by extension to market-driven liberal democracies, Bogomolov's observation made Western bells ring and increased the appeal of the Australian proposal.

Alan S. Watt, the Australian delegate, defended the deletion of all references to the war "because the Declaration ought to contain immutable principles" and should not "give the impression that it was prompted by the ideas of one epoch" (756). Carrera Andrade, the representative from Ecuador, agreed that "it would be undesirable to include matter which referred to conflict rather than facts of common assent. Thus, the allusion to the Second World War should be deleted" (757). The Belgian delegate, Carton de Wiart, thought it was "logical" to delete all historical references "because quite as many barbarous acts had been committed in the First World War." "In any case, it would be better to exclude controversial matter from the preamble. That argument also applied to the mention of Nazism and racialism by the French amendment." He also wondered "why allusions to fascism had been omitted" (761). That omission could, of course, have been fixed by adding "fascism" to the French amendment, which is why the Philippine delegation argued that "it was necessary to include a reference to the Second World War" in the Declaration (766). Unfortunately, the matter never came up for a vote because the French and Australian delegations submitted the "compromise" proposal that is our text and which was adopted by 32 votes to 0, with 5 abstentions (787).

Before leaving the text of the Declaration, I should report on one vote that goes to the heart of the concept of epistemic universality. The Second Recital now begins with a reference to "disregard and contempt for human rights." In the Third Committee the word "disregard" was put in and the word "ignorance" taken out. Before that, in the Third Session of the Commission, the British delegate asked that the word "of" be inserted after the word "ignorance" because he wanted it to be clear that it had been ignorance of human rights and not a more general kind of ignorance that had led to these barbarous acts (E/CN.4/SR.78/5). This suggestion made the delegates realize that the word "ignorance" was not at all the right word. Alexei Pavlov, the USSR representative, said that "the retention of the word 'ignorance' would give the impression that the acts of the Germans and of the Japanese were being excused because they did not know they were violating human rights. This was, he said, "the most serious error in the whole paragraph. . . . There had been no ignorance on the part of the aggressors, but a natural development of a system which had led to war. Public opinion had been shocked by the measures which the Fascists had taken, first in their own countries and later during the war in occupied countries" (7).

Peng Chung Chang of China agreed. He thought that "it was true that the Germans and the Japanese were to blame for their contempt of human rights, but it could not be said that they had been ignorant of those rights" (E/CN.4/SR.78/7). Since military discipline in both nations was notoriously strict and even cruel and, as the war progressed, involved increasingly younger soldiers, this is a remarkable statement. In line with more recent developments in international law on which I report below, Chang apparently felt that though these Germans and Japanese had no doubt acted under "higher orders," that fact did not exculpate them. A member of the French delegation pointed out that the word "disregard" fit much better with the French word "méconnaissance," which carried the meaning of "intentional ignorance" (7). Considerations like these led to the change from "ignorance" to "disregard," the vote being 10 for, 1 against, with 5 abstentions.

A vote like this supports my thesis that the drafters of the Declaration worked with the idea that (unless blocked) human beings have an operative moral conscience that tells them when they are about to engage in a gross violation of human dignity or when others have done so or are about to do so. This conscience puts us in touch with a realm of moral values and inherent rights which the drafters articulated in the articles they drafted. This realm is an objective one in that ordinary people from all walks of life and from any of the world's cultural milieus can (unless blocked) enter it with their own unaided epistemic equipment. If the systems of military discipline of the German and Japanese armies were not thought strong enough to wipe these truths from the hearts and minds of their young soldiers, the same can be said about the perpetrators of gross human rights violations before and since that time. Even though the final text makes no specific reference to the horrors of World War II, or to the Holocaust by name, or to the ideologies that fed into that abomination, the *travaux* I cited make it clear that it was the outraged consciences of the peoples they represented more than anything else that gave the drafters a common platform. They were so confident in their own reactions and so sure of how the persons and peoples they represented felt that they generalized these feelings of outrage when they used the phrase "the conscience of mankind" in their Second Recital. It is this moral confidence that makes their document such a powerful beacon in our world. When I show my classes tapes of the liberation of the Nazi death camps my students invariably share the reactions of the drafters. They cry or are stunned into silence. The same thing happens when we see a CBS video of the Rwanda massacres or a film on the Cambodian Killing Fields. It is true that these images need to be put into an interpretive framework, and I give one below. But, if Susan Sontag has it right, we need not worry that these iconic images will dull us into insensitivity. As a rule they do not. We do, however, need to guard against viewing them in settings that are not respectful of the moral outrage the images elicit. To create such settings is part of the task of human rights educators and of the creators and presenters of these images.[16]

Response 2: The "West" and the Colonies. Under this heading I will address two related issues that can lead to confusion if they are conflated. The first is the claim that in the 1940s the peoples living in what were then colonies of the metropolitan powers were not represented around the table where the Declaration was drafted. That claim I grant has merit.

The second is the charge that (because of this underrepresentation) the West kept the colonies out of the Declaration and (by implication) from having human rights. I argue that that does not follow. So, I will grant that the colonies were underrepresented, but also respond that the damage is not nearly as large as those who level this charge think it is.

According to Pollis and Schwab, "to argue that human rights has a standing which is universal in character is to contradict [the] historical reality" that millions of people had no direct representation, there being only four nations from Africa and only three from Asia. They are right to claim that "the Universal Declaration was adopted at a time when most Third World countries were still under colonial rule."[17] But whether this historical fact robs the idea of human rights of its universal character is an entirely different question that I want to answer in the negative. While the authors are correct in claiming that the Declaration represents "only one particular value system" out of many, and that large parts of it had "prior existence in Western Europe and the US" (7), those facts *by themselves* do not uphold the charge of Western ethnocentrism. This charge of ethnocentrism cannot be validated by the mere fact that millions of colonial peoples were not themselves sitting around the drafting table. As Socrates taught us, numbers by themselves are not indicators of the truth of things.

To these numbers of absent peoples must be added the additional contention, which the above critics also make, that the Declaration is an excessively individualistic document and for that very reason does not fit with the communal ways of thinking that are said to govern traditional life and politics on the Asian and African continents. Ethnocentrism is not simply a belief in the superiority of one's own numbers. It is far more the belief that one's own *way of life* is superior to all other ways. Pollis and Schwab find in the Declaration certain "democratic and libertarian" values that they say are based on a Western view of "atomized individuals possessed of inalienable rights in nature" (17). They believe that the strong individualist and anticommunitarian "Western bias" of the document gives it "limited applicability" and will make attempts to enforce the document globally "bound to fail" (4). Part of our response is that this alleged individualist bias is belied by the strong showing of the social and economic rights in the Declaration, which we discuss in Chapter 5. Also, the process of drafting the Declaration was a great deal more inclusive of non-Western perspectives than critics generally think it was.

It is not true, as the charge of Western ethnocentrism suggests, that Western delegations imposed their ideological perspectives on non-Western delegates and peoples. Our discussion of the adoption of the text shows that during the drafting years there emerged what one reviewer of my previous book felicitously described as a "universality by consensus."[18] The disagreements among the delegations were as big within regional blocks as they were between regions. The largest block was the 36 percent of the votes made up by the twenty-one representatives from North and South America. However, these countries had quite different views on the scope of human rights. While the U.S. delegation swung back and forth between wanting and not wanting social, economic, and cultural rights in the Declaration, the Latin American nations consistently fought for the inclusion of these rights. There was nothing libertarian or conservative about the Latin position, since it was heavily influenced by the socialist and Catholic traditions of Central and South America. Franklin Roosevelt's famous four freedoms (to which the drafters make reference in the Second Recital) did not keep the United States from being extremely reluctant about accepting second generation human rights into the UDHR. The Canadians generally stayed out of these debates, which placed the United States closer to some of its European allies.[19]

But the Europeans also did not speak with one voice. The French delegation was frequently rebuffed in its desire to give the new UN organization a prominent place in the Declaration.[20] Since human rights belong to persons on account of their humanity and not on account of their place of birth or residence, it made sense to have the UN involved in the implementation of these rights. The UK was not successful in its continued lobbying to have its own version of the draft Declaration (which was in the form of a convention) adopted as the main basis for discussion. And it was the Belgian and French delegations that finally in the Third Session undercut the British (and Australian) approach for an all (a declaration *and* a convention) or nothing approach.[21] The Dutch delegation (in cooperation with the delegation from Brazil) was not able to garner sufficient votes for a religious reference in the document.[22] Through its representation on the Commission on the Status of Women, the Danish delegation had enormous positive influence on the shape of the Declaration, cleansing it of most of its sexist language. In doing so it frequently clashed with the U.S. delegation (headed by Eleanor Roosevelt) and with some of its European neighbors. This women's lobby cut across blocks of votes and imposed an agenda that drew on delegations from Latin American (especially Bolivia) and Asia (especially India).[23] All these disputes cut across the Western 63 percent block of votes and presented deep intellectual challenges that are still with us today.

It therefore makes no sense to say, as some critics have done, that the Western powers imposed their own view of human rights on the rest of the delegations. There was no such thing as *the* Western position on either the main structure of the document or many of its details. Most of the structure as well as the details had to be thrashed out in numerous meetings and hundreds of votes, in almost none of which Western votes "simply" overruled the views of non-Western delegations.[24]

There were, of course, the usual diplomatic alliances of the kind that John Humphrey, the first director of the Secretariat's Division on Human Rights, describes in his memoirs.[25] But there was no preset plan to impose a Western agenda. Humphrey was asked to write the first draft, which was then streamlined by a small group of drafters headed by René Cassin, the French delegate. Humphrey was a UN employee and used as the raw material for his first draft numerous proposals and a collation of relevant articles drawn from all of the then-extant domestic constitutions. The shared revulsion against Hitler's horrors provided the energy to both Humphrey and the delegates he served to chisel a crisp bill of rights out of the material he had gathered for them. Other than the numbers I already cited there was nothing particularly Western about this process. The Declaration was born out of a genuine international give and take with the usual political alliances but with no single individual or delegation as its main author. None of the disagreements I mentioned can be labeled a case of the West versus the rest. Since there was a strong moral consensus on the wrongs of the Holocaust, the supposition that the Enlightenment idea of inherent rights needed to be updated (and expanded) was not a bone of contention. What took most of the negotiating time was to find the right formulations.

I now want to point out that regardless of this issue of representation, it does not at all follow that the peoples in the colonies were left out of the text of the Declaration and (by implication) deprived of their human rights. I begin by making the point that the very last clause of the operative paragraph of the Declaration ("and among the peoples of the territories under their jurisdiction") was expressly put in to draw the peoples of the colonies into the protective web of the Declaration. The same holds for the second paragraph of Article 2, behind the adoption of which lies a fierce battle that shows us just how defensive the metropolitan powers were about keeping their "possessions" out of the text of the Declaration and how much the rhetoric of the Cold War intruded on what had until then been a remarkably transcendent debate.[26]

In the fall of 1948 this tension rose to a pitch when the Third Committee adopted by a vote of 16 to 14, with 7 abstentions (746), a Yugoslav-inspired article that extended the rights of the Declaration to the Non-Self-Governing Territories, understood to be a euphemism for the colonies held by Western metropolitan powers. Speaking up for the colonies were the delegations from BSSR, Czechoslovakia, Ethiopia, Haiti, India, Iran, New Zealand, Pakistan, Peru, Poland, Saudi Arabia, Syria, UKSSR, USSR, Yemen, and Yugoslavia (746). Abstaining were the delegations from Argentina, Brazil, Denmark, Ecuador, Greece, Uruguay, and Venezuela. All those who voted against a separate article on the colonies either themselves had authority over non-self-governing territories or were close allies of those that did: Australia, Belgium, Canada, Chile, (Cheng Kai-shek's) China, Costa Rica, Dominican Republic, France, Honduras, Netherlands, Paraguay, Sweden, UK, and the United States. Belgian delegate Fernand Dehousse saw in the Yugoslavian proposal "an implicit reproach against certain Member States" (742). He was vigorously supported by Ernest Davies from the UK. Davies, who saw "no necessity to single out such [colonial] territories for mention," thought that the peoples living there were adequately covered by the first paragraph of Article 2 (744).

When the Third General Assembly convened on Thursday, December 9, to consider the Declaration, only two of the fifty-six member nations had submitted amendments to change the text at this very late moment. The UK proposed (A/778/Rev.1) to turn the independent Yugoslav Article 3 (applying the Declaration to the colonies) into the second paragraph of our Article 2. Juliusz Katz-Suchy, the Polish delegate, stoked the fires of the debate with his observation that his colleagues from capitalist countries were "not willing to admit that the capitalist regime permitted discrimination and that millions of people were victims of it at the present time, in the colonies and Non-Self-Governing Territories and even in certain sovereign States such as the United States of America" (GAOR, 907). "He pointed out that the most ardent defenders of human rights forgot those rights when dealing with the colonial question. When it was a question of applying progressive measures to the colonies, they invoked local legislatures and the need to abide by the wishes of the populations" (908). He asked the UK representative if he was "not aware that the British colonies were a gigantic enterprise for the exploitation of cheap labor? That was sufficiently evident from the reports submitted to the Trusteeship Council by the Non-Self-Governing Territories, each page of which showed that oppression, slavery and exploitation of labour, to a hitherto unknown degree, were the characteristic features of colonial administration" (909). "In the opinion of the Yugoslav delegation, the colonial world was, in general, under a rule of cruel inequality and such an explicit statement was necessary," said Ljuba Radovanovic (918).

USSR delegate Andrei Vyshinski tipped off the Western powers on how the Soviets might interpret a reference to the colonies when he stated that Article 3 should "contain a reference to the highly important question of the right of all nations to self-determination" (926). This not-so-hidden reference to the independence movements that the Soviet Union had started to sponsor all across Asia and Africa doomed the independent status of the Yugoslav Article 3. The UK amendment (which demoted the colonies from having their own article to being mentioned in a paragraph of another) was adopted by 29 votes to 17, with 10 abstentions (932).[27]

When we add Western fears about these liberation movements, in Indonesia for instance, to the heated exchanges from which I just quoted, we can guess that many delegations found a false safety in the British proposal to demote the issue of the colonies to the status of a paragraph. But even there the Declaration is as clear as a bell in its pronouncement that "no distinction shall be made on the basis of the political, jurisdictional, or international status of the country or territory to which a person belongs, whether it be independent, trust, non-self-governing or under any other limitation of sovereignty." In other words, persons have human rights regardless of the political arrangements under which they are born and in which they live their lives. This is a ringing endorsement of the idea of human rights as inherent in the human person and of their not being the result of any kind of political or jurisprudential procedures.

Response 3: The Eight Abstentions. It should now be clear that the disagreements that existed among Western delegations created ample room for non-Western contributions to be made. With this question in mind, let us take a look at the eight nations (South Africa, USSR, UKSSR, BSSR, Czechoslovakia, Yugoslavia, Poland, and Saudi Arabia) that abstained in the final vote of 48 for and 0 against that was taken on December 10, 1948.

The South African Abstention. In 1946 the Union of South Africa was asked by the General Assembly to bring its treatment of Indians—about which India had complained—"in conformity with . . . the relevant [human rights] provisions of the Charter."[28] South Africa was the first member to be censored by the General Assembly because it refused to place its South-West Africa territory under UN trusteeship. During the drafting procedures South Africa took a conservative stance, one that is quite respectable, except that it sought to pay for it with racist coin. Appealing to the UN Charter, E. H. Louw, the country's delegate to the Third Committee, argued that by "fundamental rights and freedoms" the Charter had meant only those rights that were connected to human dignity and that were "indispensable for physical and mental existence as a human being." True enough, but then he added that he did not see "how that dignity would be impaired if a person were told that he could not live in a particular area" (GAOR Third, 39). As he made this observation his country was in the process of establishing its infamous system of apartheid, with separate homelands for black workers and their families. His government's view was that "What the Charter envisages is the protection of that minimum of rights and freedoms which the conscience of the world feels to be essential, if life is not to be made intolerable at the whim of an unscrupulous government" (E/CN.4/82/Add.4/25).

In its Second Recital the Declaration also appeals to the "conscience of mankind," but that appeal covered a great deal more than South Africa's short list of the "freedom of religion and speech, the liberty of the person and property and free access to courts of impartial justice" (GAOR Third, 40).

The lack of integrity of the South Africa abstention comes not from its defense of a short list of rights but from the weak rationale it gave for that list. Human dignity *is* affected when people are discriminated against in their government's housing policy. Louw admitted the racism of his country's position when he argued that the right to freedom of movement in Article 13 "would destroy the whole basis of the multiracial structure of the Union of South Africa and would certainly not be in the interest of the less advanced indigenous population" (GAOR Third, 39). In its written reaction to the draft Declaration, the South African government explained the need for these "homelands" as arising from the requirements of "good government," which involved preventing "the influx of large numbers of unskilled workers into urban areas" and requiring "individuals . . . to work in specified industries" (E/CN.4/82/Add.4/15). No other government had bothered to comment on the right to freedom of movement. Louw also argued that the right to take part in the government of one's country (Article 21) "was not universal; it was conditioned not only by nationality and country, but also by the qualifications of franchise" (GAOR Third, 39). These qualifications could, of course, be tinkered with, which the Union's Constitution in force at that time did by openly stating that "only a person of European descent" could have a seat in the House of Assembly or the Senate" (E/CN.4/82/Add.4/43). The race factor was also woven into the observation that sometimes "the inability of convicts, aliens, and in some cases absentee voters" in homelands kept them from participating in elections. Nor could any person vote "who cannot comply with property and literacy or educational qualifications where such . . . are in vogue" (23). Like the Jim Crow laws in the United States, these measures effectively barred the black population from participation in government. The right to freedom of association was similarly gutted when South Africa gave its minister of justice the prerogative to "prohibit a public gathering if . . . the gathering will engender feelings of hostility between European inhabitants of the Union on the one hand and any other section of the inhabitants of the Union on the other hand" (19). We conclude that this abstention lacked integrity.

The Six Communist Abstentions. The six communist delegations struggled with the idea of transcendent and inherent rights. Since according to Marxist doctrine morality is an epiphenomenal reflection of whatever social group happens to be in possession of the modes and means of production in a given society, there can be no such things as *inherent* human rights that are not the result of social or legal practices. This philosophical stance probably should have made them vote against the document. But just as moral relativists can change their minds when brought face to face with Nazi ovens, Bosnian woods, Cambodian Killing Fields, or Rwandan courtyards, so delegates to international conferences can ignore party doctrine and vote their own and their nations' consciences instead. This is what I think happened with the communist delegations. The communist delegations (USSR, Czechoslovakia, Poland, Byelorussia, Ukraine, and Yugoslavia) could have safely voted against the Declaration and not have lost any money, for the opportunity to participate in the Truman Doctrine had already passed. For them, too, there was too much at stake that went beyond politics as usual. They were just as eager as any other delegation to formally condemn what the Nazis had done. In spite of their party doctrine, they were tempted by an international code of ethics that would openly and objectively condemn the Nazi atrocities. To that end they had insisted on the adoption of very strong antidiscrimination language in the document,[29] they attended all the meetings, and they submitted (unsuccessful) amendments that would have kept freedom of association and free speech rights from Nazi groups.[30] In short, they wanted to join the rest of the world in its formal condemnation of Nazi atrocities, from which they themselves had suffered a great deal, quite likely more so than their allies who were now in the forefront of drawing up this universal moral code.

The communists' desire to condemn gross violations of human rights overruled their theoretical scruples. Their delegates did what we ourselves constantly do when we let our emotions overrule more or less abstract doctrines we have been taught and to which we tend to cling, against the better intelligence of our emotions. I will return to this point below when I present the theory of classical intuitionism as a moral framework for the Declaration. That theory relies on people's desires to stop radical evil when they see it perpetrated. I am not suggesting that Marxist ideology is compatible with the theory of human rights set forth in this book, for it probably is not. My point is that the communist delegations cooperated from the start and stuck with the project to the end because their desire to condemn the Nazis in the court of world opinion was stronger than their theoretical objections, which fits the pattern of what Martha Nussbaum has described as "upheavals of thought" that are caused by the independently operating intelligence of our emotions.[31] Jonathan Glover reports that in 1941 Himmler, Hitler's right-hand man, "watched a hundred people being shot at Minsk. He seemed nervous and during every folly he looked to the ground. When two women did not die he yelled to the police sergeant not to torture them."[32] Similar testimony to the power of conscience to overrule ideological commitments comes from the willingness of communist delegations to work on the "practical application" of human rights while theoretical differences were being debated. As I argued in Chapter 1, we must not interpret this to mean that there is no metaphysics involved at all in a commitment to human rights. In 1989, millions of communist hearts woke up to the transcendent truths of the Declaration when they judged their regimes to fall short of human rights norms that had for the first time been openly allowed behind the Iron Curtain when the Helsinki Agreements were signed in 1975. Since then all the post-communist states in Eastern Europe and in Eurasia have joined the UN and in that act of joining have consented to being judged by the human rights standards of the Declaration and its offspring. Many of them have enshrined human rights norms in new constitutions. With seeming prescience, the communist delegations forgot to abstain (as was their custom) when the First Recital (containing the phrases "inherent dignity" and "inalienable rights") was adopted "unanimously" in the Third Committee (786).

The Saudi Arabia Abstention. In the late 1940s there were ten UN member nations that had been significantly shaped by the religion of Islam: Afghanistan, Egypt, Iran, Iraq, Lebanon, Pakistan, Saudi Arabia, Syria, Turkey, and Yemen. Nine of these voted for the final draft; just one, Saudi Arabia, abstained. Of these ten Arab delegations only Egypt and Lebanon had been members of the Commission that oversaw the drafting of the text, and only Lebanon had been a member of the much smaller eight-member drafting Sub-Committee. Procedurally, this is a very weak representation for the Islamic perspective, especially since the main Lebanese representative, Charles Malik, was a Christian and a Thomist. However, all ten Arab delegations had a chance to make their views heard in what have come to be called "the great debates" in the Third (humanitarian, social, and cultural) Committee of the General Assembly. The Saudi delegation took the lead in representing the Islamic objections to the text that had come down from the Human Rights Commission to the Third Committee. These objections focused on the texts of Articles 14 (on asylum), 16 (on marriage), and 18 (on the right to change one's religion). On the question of asylum the Saudi delegation led a successful effort to have the right to "be granted" asylum deleted from the text so that it now says only that one has a right to ask for it and to enjoy it once it has been given. This unfortunate success was followed by two setbacks involving the secular character of the document, and for that reason caused the abstention.

The ten Arab delegations were split between wanting to see Shar'ia (the Islamic religious law that governs the lives of all Muslims) prevail over international human rights and taking a more liberal approach that felt no deep contradiction between the two systems. This conflict still has not been resolved, but with this difference: in the late 1940s nine of the ten votes were of the accommodationist kind, while today that tally might go in the other direction. The two points of view were set out at the start of the Third Committee debates. Jamil Baroody, the Lebanese-born Saudi delegate, "called attention to the fact that the Declaration was based largely on Western patterns of culture, which were frequently at variance with patterns of culture of Eastern states. That did not mean, however, that the Declaration went counter to the latter, even if it did not conform to them" (GAOR Third, 49). This was a smart reading of the text, for as it then stood it did not literally (though it did by implication) conflict with stipulations of Islamic law. For that reason the Saudi delegation could leave the door open for a positive vote on the document. However, during the course of the debates that followed, these implications were made explicit, and the Saudi delegation abstained in the final, crucial vote.

The more liberal Islamic position was articulated for the Arab delegations by Pakistani delegate Shaista Ikramullah. She "said that her delegation fully supported the adoption of the declaration because it believed in the dignity and worth of man. It was imperative that the peoples of the world should recognize the existence of a code of civilized behavior that would apply not only in international relations but also in domestic affairs. It was her hope that the declaration would mark a turning-point in history of no less importance than the works of Tom Paine and the American Declaration of Independence" (GAOR Third, 37). The other nine (more or less) Islamicist delegations, though they were equally offended in the ensuing debates, did not change their initial positive stance and voted for the Declaration in that final vote. The 1948 vote of these nine delegations confirms our thesis that the Declaration was adopted by a remarkable consensus among delegations from a wide variety of cultural, religious, and economic traditions. Susan Walz has shown that active Arabo-Muslim support for internationally accepted human rights continued at least through the 1960s and 1970s when the two International Covenants were written and adopted by the UN membership.[33] That means that the Islamic fundamentalist challenge we read so much about today did not rear its head till long after the international bill was well on its way to universal acceptance.

Conclusion. I take it as established that there existed in the late 1940s a strong consensus for the universality of human rights as possessed by every human being. The above survey of debates on the adoption of the text of the Declaration reveals that the drafters shared a moral revulsion to the horrors of the Holocaust, and they broadened their approach to cover the human race when (in the Second Recital) they used the expression "the conscience of mankind." With that phrase the drafters captured the moral epistemology of human rights, according to which basic human rights are discovered from the obvious wrongs we encounter in our experience. Their wrongs were the ones of the Holocaust, while ours include those we have encountered since, such as the genocides in Bosnia, Cambodia, Rwanda, and (as I write) Darfur, to name just four. It was the experience of radical evil that made the drafters agree on a list of rights that belong to people as their birthrights and not as the result of any kind of judicial, governmental, or legislative procedures, whether these be on a domestic or international level. I showed how the various ideological stands of different delegations and their abstentions in the final vote do not negate or undercut this idea of epistemic universality. Because they all had encountered the radical evil of the Holocaust, no delegation voted against the document. The wrongs having been so obvious, they had no doubts about the rights they articulated. In the words of the Preamble of the UN Charter, they set about to "reaffirm [their] faith in fundamental human rights" and "in the dignity and worth of the human person." The thirty articles of the Declaration are the authoritative interpretation of the seven human rights references in the UN Charter, and just as the Charter is not usually thought of as a Western ethnocentric document, so too we should not look on the Declaration as being that sort of thing. Right after World War II there was a remarkable consensus on a list of radical wrongs that came to light with the discovery of what had gone on in the concentration camps. These recognized gross moral wrongs gave birth to a list of human rights that would be hard for us, even more than sixty years later, to improve on.

B. The Doctrine of Manifest Illegality

I now expand on this historical sketch of the Declaration's adoption to the military law of most civilized nations and to statutes of the Nuremberg Trials and of the international criminal courts that have been set up in our own time. These statutes make use of the doctrine of "manifest illegality," which I claim makes no sense unless the defendants involved are thought of as having a functioning conscience about good and evil acts that reflects what, in the language of the International Criminal Court, is called "the conscience of humanity."

There being such a thing as a human conscience about good and evil has come to be a fundamental proposition in the international law of war, in international humanitarian law, and in international human rights law. This supposition is the international analogue of a situation with which many of my readers are familiar from their own domestic legal systems, which presupposes that defendants on trial could have done something other than what they did. With some rare exceptions (due to brain tumors, severe disorders or diseases, and so on) defendants are held individually responsible for what they did, and, if found guilty, punished accordingly. These domestic systems run on the assumption that human beings (usually) have choices and it holds them responsible for these choices. While some philosophers design theories about behavior that make punishment and blame compatible with the determinist thesis that every event or action has to happen because of the circumstances that precede it, the world at large operates on the assumption of human freedom. This domestic presumption of freedom also plays a role in international criminal law and informs the doctrine and test of manifest illegality. After I discuss the use of the test in Nuremberg and Vietnam, I give examples of it in the military law of other civilized nations and in the statutes of international tribunals after Nuremberg.

My thesis is that the epistemic universality that helps ground the Declaration is also the empirical backbone of this universally accepted test about ordinary people's ability to tell the difference between good and evil. I use the last section to place all of these findings within the framework of classical moral intuitionism. Should my critics find fault with that epistemic theoretical framework, they will owe us an alternative explanation of the data I here present. Any theoretical framework will need to cast its net wide enough to cover both the variety of domestic uses of the manifest illegality test as well as its incorporation in the statutes of international tribunals.

Nuremberg and Vietnam. Article 7 of the Nuremberg statutes disallows defendants the defense of "superior orders." The Nazi officials in the docket were not allowed the defense that they acted on orders given by their superiors and that they therefore could not be held responsible for the crimes they were supposed to have committed. The Article presumes that in certain specified conditions defendants can and should act against the orders of their superiors. (The Nuremberg rules did, however, allow the appeal to superior orders to count as a mitigating circumstance.) This denial of the defense of superior orders supposes: (1) that the defendant could have done otherwise than the act with which he or she is charged, (2) that the defendant must have good reasons to disobey the orders received from his or her superior so as to avoid being charged with these gross violations, (3) that these reasons for disobedience cannot be very complicated since more often than not such orders are received in the heat of battle, and (4) that these reasons are either clear cases of violations of the international law of war, or (5) that they are clear cases of violations of international humanitarian law. The International Law Commission that summarized the international legal rules that emerged from the Nuremberg Trials formulated the principle that those acting pursuant to the order of a government or superior cannot relieve themselves from responsibility under international law, "provided a moral choice was in fact possible" to them.[34] According to the Commission, the upshot from Nuremberg is that "individuals have international duties which transcend the national obligations of obedience imposed by the individual State."[35] The reason is that other individuals have inherent rights to life and limb that also transcend national prerogatives. The Nuremberg legal reflections on the Holocaust drove home this two-pronged transcendence (of both rights and duties) over systems of domestic law and raised the individual human person to the status of being a subject of international law.

Critics of the Nuremberg Trials use this feature of individual responsibility to argue that the judgments are based on odious retroactive law-making: since, prior to Nuremberg, only states were held collectively accountable and liable for breaches of international law, to suddenly hold individuals and natural persons criminally responsible is unjust to the defendants. The drafters of the Declaration carefully considered this issue and stepped around it with their pronouncement in Article 11(2) that "No one shall be held guilty of any penal offence on account of any act or omission which did not constitute a penal offence, under national or international law, at the time it was committed."[36] Since we are focusing on the role of conscience in these guilty verdicts, Hans Kelsen's response to the critics of the Nuremberg rulings is worth quoting here: "Since the internationally illegal acts for which the London Agreement [that contains the Nuremberg Charter] established individual criminal responsibility were certainly also morally most objectionable, and the persons who committed these acts were certainly aware of their immoral character, the retroactivity of the law applied to them can hardly be considered as absolutely incompatible with justice."[37]

As we have learned from the 2004 Abu Ghraib prison scandal in U.S.-occupied Iraq, violations of the law of war have to do, among other things, with the treatment of prisoners of war and of civilian populations in occupied territories. It is understood that no army can operate without the strictest discipline and that almost all military activity (except that at the highest level of policy making) can be defended as being done on "superior orders." Almost all acts—but not quite all—can be defended in this way. This "not quite all" is the space inhabited by the test of manifest illegality. Some kinds of acts are so obviously immoral that in terms of military law they are called "manifestly illegal" or "obviously immoral." These kinds of acts are not permissible even when one is ordered to do them by one's superior officer, for they are self-evidently immoral. People with an ordinary functioning moral conscience can pick out these obvious wrongs and would know not do them for that very reason, even when ordered to do so by their superiors. For example, First Lieutenant Calley shot and killed at least twenty-two infants, women, and old men, all unarmed, in a village in Vietnam where his forces had not encountered any enemy fire or other resistance. In his defense he said that he was ignorant of the laws of war and that he did not know that the order "to kill everyone in the village" was "palpably illegal." Judge Quinn of the U.S. Military Court of Appeals disagreed. Two other soldiers, James J. Dursi and Robert E. Maples, had refused similar orders that same day in the same village, where U.S. forces killed some three hundred Vietnamese. Also, Hugh Thompson, a twenty-five-year-old helicopter pilot, incredibly "ordered his [U.S.] crew to use their machine-gun against the American troops if they fired on the villagers." He told two nearby gunships that his machine gunner would fire on the infantry if they fired on the civilians. So the other helicopters went away and Thompson and his crew saved two men, two women, and five or six children."[38] The judge instructed the Calley panel as follows: "If you find beyond a reasonable doubt, on the basis of all the evidence [education, training, IQ] that Lieutenant Calley actually knew the order under which he asserts he operated was unlawful, the fact that the order was given operates as no defense" for him.[39]

In another Vietnam case the U.S. Army Field Manual was cited to explain that the only time a soldier could deviate from the rule of obedience was "in the case of orders so manifestly beyond the legal power of discretion of the commander as to admit of no rational doubt of their unlawfulness."[40] Consistent with these rules of engagement, we read in that manual that a military inferior would be justified in disobeying a military superior if the order required "something to be done which is palpably a breach of law and a crime or an injury to a third person, or is of serious character . . . and if done would not be susceptible of being righted" (Blakesley, 1306). Sergeant Walter Griffin was found guilty of homicide because "the killing of a docile prisoner taken during military operations is not justifiable homicide." Similar crimes are winding their way through courts-martial in U.S.-occupied Iraq in the first decade of the twenty-first century.

If Calley had forgotten what he was told during his training, then how could he have known not to follow this particular order? The answer is that this particular part of his training is so elementary that any normally functioning person is thought of as already having knowledge of it by virtue of his or her humanity. We are, of course, faced with a broad spectrum of cases from clearly immoral acts to clearly legal acts. In their military training soldiers need to be, and are, trained to suppress their ordinary instinct and revulsion against shooting other human beings. For that reason (among others) Mark Osiel points out that the manifest illegality test "turns out to fail, in many situations, precisely because it relies on unrealistic assumptions about the strength and universality of 'humanitarian' moral sentiments."[41] He wants to individualize the test and replace it with the question as to "whether the defendant's protessed error about the legality of his order was reasonable all things considered" (136). That would make room for exculpatory decisions both by soldiers who are smarter than the average as well as by those of less than normal intelligence. However, Osiel undercuts his own proposal by the admission that "To be sure, superior orders calling for manifestly illegal acts can often be distinguished from other combat orders on the basis of the unique revulsion they are likely to awaken in recipients" (114). That is precisely my point in this discussion, namely, that there is a level of gruesomeness below which a soldier with an ordinary moral sense may not fall. The shared human revulsion I trace in the cases below is the same moral outrage the drafters speak of in the Second Recital of the Declaration when they talk about "barbarous acts which have outraged the conscience of mankind."

Osiel is right when he says that modern technology has greatly complicated the use of the manifest illegality test, for it is easy to see that shooting innocent children to death in a ditch or a cave in front of oneself cannot possibly be a legitimate tactic in warfare, while killing them in a naval blockade or from on high is less obviously immoral because the causal connections between one's own actions and the deaths of innocents are less obvious. Here all sorts of distinctions involving causation and individual responsibility both on the level of policy making and in field operations must be made. My point is that military courts, for some time, and international tribunals since the end of World War II, have made these distinctions and have not abolished the manifest illegality test. The panel members that found Calley guilty looked at him (even in the circumstances described) as someone with an ordinarily functioning moral conscience of the kind the UDHR drafters used when they condemned the Nazi atrocities. As I said, two other soldiers had disobeyed their orders—one even refused to lend Calley his rifle—and instead honored the right to life of the innocent villagers huddled before them. In his obedience to higher orders Calley made the wrong choice and violated his victims' right to life. He allowed his hatred for the enemy to wipe out all moral and legal distinctions between enemy combatants and innocent civilians of any age. The presumption that he had the moral choice and willpower not to let that happen runs throughout the military law of most civilized nations.

Examples from Other Countries. In the 1921 *Llandovery Castle* case the German Reichsgericht ruled that "killing of survivors in life-boats was clearly illegal."[42] It therefore would not let two German seamen of the U-boat that sank the British hospital ship use the defense of superior orders in their killing of the survivors of the *Llandovery Castle* in their lifeboats. In October 1945 a British military court, sitting in Hamburg, Germany, made a similar ruling when it had to pass judgment on U-boat commander Heinz-Wilhelm Eck, who had torpedoed another British hospital ship, the *Peleus*. To wipe out all traces of the enemy Eck had ordered the defendants to shoot and kill members of the *Peleus* who had gotten into their lifeboats. The British court ruled that "members of the armed forces are bound to obey lawful orders only, and that they cannot therefore escape liability if in obedience to a command they commit acts which both violate unchallenged rules of warfare and outrage the general sentiment of humanity" (Blakesley, 1282). In 1967 an Austrian defendant was convicted of murdering Jewish and Polish inmates in a Nazi labor camp during the war. The defendant claimed that he was "unable, owing to his limited intelligence, to realize the criminal nature of the execution of an illegal order."[43] Citing the Austrian Penal Code at the time, the court ruled that "orders to kill without previous proceedings, in respect of individuals or groups of inmates of this labor camp, could not even as a matter of form have any legal justification" and "were clearly recognizable by anybody as illegal." The "anybody" here refers to ordinary people with a functioning conscience. In 1994 the Supreme Court of Canada held in the *Finta* case that "military orders can and must be obeyed unless they are manifestly unlawful," by which the Court meant that it "must be an order which is obviously and flagrantly wrong."[44]

The 1960–61 Israeli trial of Adolph Eichmann, the committed Nazi who helped organize the killing of millions of Jews, provides us with a transition from the national cases I have been citing to the international tribunals I cite in a moment. Yoram Dinstein cites a particularly explicit statement of the manifest illegality test from the judgment rendered by the Israeli District Military Court of Appeal in the *Kafr Kassem* case. I quote it in full because it was later used in Eichmann's Jerusalem trial. It reads:

The distinguishing mark of a "manifestly unlawful" order should be displayed like a black flag over the order given, as a warning reading "Prohibited!" Not formal unlawfulness, hidden or half-hidden, not unlawfulness which is discernible only to the eyes of legal experts is important here, but a conspicuous and flagrant breach of the law, a certain imperative unlawfulness appearing on the face of the order itself, a clearly criminal character of the order or of the acts ordered, an unlawfulness which pierces the eye and revolts the heart if the eye is not blind and the heart not obtuse or corrupted— that is the extent of "manifest" unlawfulness required to override the duty of obedience of a soldier, and to charge him with criminal responsibility for his acts.[45]

Eichmann maintained that he had never personally killed a Jew or anyone else. He admitted no responsibility for what he had done because he said he acted under superior orders when he organized the trains to the concentration camps, knowing full well that he was sending millions to their gruesome deaths. Citing the above statement of the manifest illegality test, the court overruled all Eichmann's legal defenses by claiming that his crimes against humanity made his case one of universal jurisdiction. That principle allows a third state (where the crime did not occur and of which the defendant is not a citizen) which has possession of the defendant to act "as the organ and agent of the international community and [to] mete out punishment to the offender for his breach of the prohibition imposed by the law of nations" (Blakesley, 1379). The court ruled that "the harmful and murderous effects" of Eichmann's crimes "were so embracing and widespread as to shake the international community to its very foundations." That is why the state of Israel had the right to try him, even though Israel did not exist at the time Eichmann committed his crimes, the statue under which he was tried was not written until 1950, and so on. When it kidnapped Eichmann and brought him to Jerusalem to stand trial, Israel acted as a "guardian of international law and an agent for its enforcement." The tribunals on which I report in a moment do the same thing. That is a good development because unlike Israel, which had a particular interest in pursuing crimes against the Jewish people, some states (like Argentina and Cambodia) are not strong enough to try their own violators of manifest illegality, and some (like the United States) are so strong that the world community finds it difficult to hold them accountable for violations of the test.

In the aftermath of the Argentine "dirty war," violators of human rights in that country were brought to trial during the presidential term of Raúl Alfonsín (1983–89), but were pardoned by his successor Carlos Menem. At the time of Alfonsín's election in December 1983, Article 154 of Argentina's military code stated that "when [a] crime was committed in order of service, [the] superior who gave [the] order will be [the] sole responsible person, and [a] subordinate will only be considered [an] accomplice when he has exceeded in fulfillment of that order."[46] As it reads, this would only expose the very highest policy makers in the junta and leave those who did the actual killing by, for instance, pushing sedated prisoners out of planes above the Atlantic Ocean, untried and unpunished. To clear even the superiors that had given the orders for the disappearances, acts of torture, and extrajudicial killings, the military had passed a general amnesty law. Alfonsín had come to office on a human rights platform and immediately sought changes in the military code. During the debate an exception for those who "committed abhorrent or atrocious acts" was built into the due obedience clause of the above-cited article with Alfonsín's support.[47]

This exception matched the manifest illegality test. It supposed that, contrary to the way Argentina's military code was written, all servicemen were capable of moral choice and that those who had committed "abhorrent or atrocious acts" certainly knew their acts were flagrantly immoral, and so had to be illegal, regardless of the reigning military ethos that justified "the sacrifice of innocent individuals and the complete disrespect for the Constitución and for the rule of law as a necessary means for preserving the National Being"[48] The adoption of this exception threatened a great number of lower ranking military personnel with being put on trial for the torture, murder, and rape they committed on orders of the junta in its war against terrorism, the excesses of which were blared out to the wider world in the 1984 best-selling book *Nunca Más*.[49] Unfortunately, to avoid a "near mutiny" by the armed forces and the courts, Alfonsín compromised and allowed the exception to be removed from the code, which reduced the number of those facing trial from hundreds to between twenty-five and thirty. But in July 2005 the Argentine Supreme Court declared the two ("full-stop" and "due obedience") Amnesty Laws of the 1980s unconstitutional. This ruling does not wipe out the more than 400 pardons granted to senior officials, but it does revive hundreds of cases against lower-level torturers.[50]

Similar domestic complications at first delayed the operation of the "Extraordinary Chambers" set up to bring "to trial senior members of Democratic Kampuchea and those who were most responsible for the crimes and serious violations of Cambodian penal law, international humanitarian law and custom, and international conventions recognized by Cambodia, that were committed during the period from 17 April 1975 to 6 January 1979."[51] Ratner and Abrams report that the Khmer Rouge killed about 20 percent of the April 1975 Cambodian population of around 7.5 million people.[52] That makes 1.5 million deaths. Article 3 of the Law on the Amendments to Articles of the Cambodian Constitution—that implements this Extraordinary Chambers Agreement with the UN—states outright that these Chambers "shall have the power to bring to trial all Suspects who committed any of these crimes set forth in the 1956 Penal Code" of Cambodia and which were committed in the above-mentioned time period. The crimes in the code and the international norms that were added in the Chambers Agreement are much the same as the lists of crimes in the Yugoslav and Rwanda tribunals. Article 29 adds that "The fact that a Suspect acted pursuant to an order of the Government of Democratic Kumpuchea or of a superior shall not relieve the Suspect of criminal responsibility."[53] Once again the supposition is that subordinates and minors would know when not to obey a manifestly illegal order. While Ratner and Abrams think that the cadres who committed "lesser offenses" might draw on the fact that they followed orders as a possible defense, they also are of the opinion that "some crimes are so patently atrocious that such ignorance is never an excuse" (298). The film *The Killing Fields* drives that point home in a poignant manner.

In a later book on the Argentine trials, *Radical Evil on Trial,* Carlos Santiago Nino analyzes them from a moral and legal perspective that also fits the Cambodian delay in the execution of its agreement with the UN. Nino concludes that Alfonsín's compromise on the issue of manifest illegality had "serious negative side effects" in that it "converted moral persons from autonomous, inviolable, and dignified human beings to machines who will abuse fellow human beings without regard to their own moral and legal responsibility" (180).[54] He ends his discourse by making a plea for "international law to recognize the right of the world community to punish human rights violations in an international forum" instead of putting the whole burden on often "fragile new governments." Such governments are often too weak to take full advantage of the increased moral power of global norms.

Abu Ghraib. Having started this survey of the Nuremberg legacy with the U.S. Calley case, I end it by teasing the manifest illegality text out of the official army report on the allegations of "abuse" by U.S. military intelligence personnel in the Abu Ghraib prison during the early years of the U.S. occupation of Iraq. In June 2004 Lieutenant General Anthony R. Jones and Major General George R. Fay of the U.S. army investigated allegations that the 205th Military Intelligence Brigade had grossly abused and tortured prisoners at the Abu Ghraib prison. Their report (known as the Fay-Jones Report) defined "abuse as treatment of detainees that violated U.S. criminal law (including the Uniform Code of Military Justice [UMCJ] or international law, or treatment that was inhumane or coercive without lawful justification."[55] The report divided the Abu Ghraib cases into two kinds, "first intentional, violent or sexual abuses and, second, actions taken based on misinterpretation of or confusion about law or policy." The second kind have dominated news reports since the scandal broke because this and other reports indicated that many of these less serious "abuses" have "occurred due to the proliferation of guidance and information from other theaters of operation; individual interrogator experiences in other theaters; and, the failure to distinguish between permitted interrogation techniques in other theater environments and Iraq" (424). The lines between these two kinds of "incidents" may of course have blurred, but we catch a glimmer of the manifest illegality doctrine in the report's definition of the first kind of cases as those "of physical and sexual abuse . . . serious enough that no Soldier or contractor believed the conduct was based on official policy or guidance" (423–24). That is to say, the act could not have been legitimately ordered because it was blatantly immoral.

While the U.S. army manual is being rewritten as we write, the doctrine of manifest illegality is made to struggle for its survival in U.S. interrogations practices.[56] Part of the public outcry over the Abu Ghraib treatment of detainees has come from the U.S. government's attempt to rewrite the internationally understood content of that doctrine and test. Both houses of Congress voted to stop the Bush administration's weakening of the international torture ban with the adoption of an amendment stating that the United States "would not use cruel, inhuman or degrading treatment" at home or abroad, the phraseology of which can also be found in the Convention Against Torture. The new law commits the United States to continued use of the manifest illegality test and also bars the second kind of incident, which the Fay-Jones Report says might have been the result of confusion and lack of guidance rather than outright criminality. However, President Bush threatened to veto this law because the restrictions the new Military Manual requires interrogators to observe are seen as too burdensome.[57] Also, on June 29, 2006, in *Hamdan v. Rumsfeld*, the U.S. Supreme Court rejected the U.S. government plan to try detainees in "military commissions" that the Court ruled did not meet the requirements of Article 3 of the 1949 Geneva Conventions. Said the Court: "We need not decide the merits of this argument [about the type of conflict the United States has with Al Qaeda] because there is at least one provision of the Geneva Conventions that applies here even if the relevant conflict is not one between signatories."[58] The Court then quoted Article 3 of those Conventions, which provides that in a conflict "not of an international character occurring in the territory of one of the high contracting parties, each party to the conflict shall be bound to apply, as a minimum, 'certain provisions protecting 'Persons taking no active part in the hostilities, including members of armed forces who have laid down their arms and those placed hors de combat by . . . detention."

The Court went on to point out that one such provision prohibits "the passing of sentences and the carrying out of executions without previous judgment pronounced by a regularly constituted court affording all the judicial guarantees which are recognized as indispensable by civilized peoples." The military commissions the United States government had been planning on using to try detainees in various locations do not meet the requirements that civilized peoples have agreed are needed to assure a fair trial for civilians caught in armed conflict and for soldiers that have put down their arms, which covers almost all those held in detention by the United States. It goes without saying that these minimal provisions include adherence to the international standards embodied in the manifest illegality test that the Bush administration has been trying to "domesticate" in its justification of these illegal military commissions and interrogation practices. The House vote, which was nonbinding, and the June 2006 ruling by the Supreme Court, which is binding, have set back these attempts of the U.S. government to "domesticate" standards that were agreed on by civilized nations at the end of World War II because the German treatment of civilians and detainees had, as the Declaration puts it, "outraged the conscience of mankind."

The manifest illegality doctrine shines through in the Fay-Jones Report's observation that the more serious incidents were "*clearly* in violation of law, policy and doctrine and contrary to Army values."[59] The word "clearly" is a poor substitute for the more elaborate versions of the doctrine that I have cited from the Vietnam era and from foreign cases. The official version of the Army Manual (before the more recent rewrites) states that "The fact that the law of war has been violated even if on the order of a superior authority, whether military or civil, does not change the act in question of its character as a war crime. It does *not* constitute a defense in the trial of an accused individual unless he did *not* know and could not reasonably have been expected to know that the act was unlawful."[60] Since two negatives make a positive, soldiers are here told that superior orders may not be a valid defense if the military judges find, as they did in the Calley and Griffin cases, and may well find in some of the cases coming out of Abu Ghraib, that the defendant had an operative conscience and functioning reasoning powers that should have made him refuse the order that led to the act in question. It goes without saying that the same act when done without orders is ipso facto a breach of army rules, not just because it violates the values of the U.S. army, but also because it violates the conscience of humanity.

While humanity's voice speaks through the U.S. army's doctrine of manifest illegality, it speaks far more clearly through the international legal texts on the basis of which the army could (but chooses not to)[61] prosecute defendants implicated in the Abu Ghraib and other "abuse" scandals. These other texts include the Convention Against Torture (CAT) and the International Covenant on Civil and Political Rights (ICCPR), both of which the United States has ratified, and for the first of which it has adopted the required implementing legislation, albeit with strong reservations that domesticate the meaning of the key terms used.[62] The CAT categorically prohibits "torture"[63] and provides "No exceptional circumstances whatsoever, whether a state of war or a threat of war, internal political instability or any other public emergency" that might be invoked by way of justifying acts of torture" (Article 2 (2)). It also forbids "other acts of cruel, inhuman or degrading treatment or punishment which do not amount to torture" (Article 16). These two prohibitions cover most of the "incidents" reported to have taken place in the Abu Ghraib prison, which is why the army chooses to prosecute under its own vaguer UCMJ.[64]

International Tribunals. This U.S. attempt to give a specific U.S. content to the barring of torture as part of the manifest illegality test shows us how important it is to internationalize and globalize the domestic statutes and rulings I surveyed. While these domestic examples show that there are limits to what can constitute the (military) law of the land in most places, a word of caution is needed here. Unless the crimes involved are spelled out in some detail and the nations involved dialogue with each other about what is understood by "manifestly illegal" and "clearly immoral," these phrases can be subverted and stood on their heads. We may doubt, for instance, that Josef Goebbels, Hitler's propaganda minister, saw a "despicable crime" the way the drafters of the Universal Declaration saw it, or that he meant by the phrase "all human morality" what they meant by "the conscience of mankind" in the Second Recital. Writing in 1944 in the *Völkischer Beobachter*, the Nazi paper, Goebbels argued that "It is not provided in any military law that a soldier in the case of a despicable crime is exempt from punishment because he passes the responsibility to his superior, especially if the orders of the latter are in evident con- tradiction to all human morality and every international usage of war- fare" (Blakesley, 1286). To prevent the manifest illegality clause from being abused or gutted in this way it is crucial that the content of the clause be internationalized and codified through specific examples on a regional and global scale. The Nuremberg statutes and guilty verdicts I cited above were the first step in that direction. So is the principle of universal jurisdiction that Israel used in the Eichmann trial. The interna- tional statutes that I cite below do the same thing in our own day. They help fix the content of the manifest illegality clause and so help further establish the thesis of epistemic universality that is part of the doctrine of inherent human rights.

In 1993 the UN Security Council established the International Tribu- nal for the Prosecution of Persons Responsible for Serious Violations of International Humanitarian Law Committed in the Territory of the Former Yugoslavia (ICTY). This tribunal is charged with prosecuting persons who have committed four broad categories of crimes.[65] The long list of crimes listed in the ICTY statute shows us the wide reach of epistemic universality. Article 6 stipulates an interesting and important limitation on the authority of the Tribunal in that it limits that authority to the prosecution of "natural persons" only. It forbids the prosecution of other kinds of legal persons, such as political parties, organizations, and governments. The international community holds natural persons, like you and me, responsible for their behavior, even to the point of refusing to follow orders when that is the morally right thing to do. Article 7 explains that the "official position" of any of these natural persons "shall not relieve such a person of criminal responsibility nor mitigate punishment."[66] Like the top Nazis in Nuremberg, ICTY defendants had a choice about the grossly immoral plans they made and about the manifestly illegal orders they gave. Anyone reading an account of the massacre at Srebrenica immediately knows that what the Serbian forces did there was an abomination and obviously immoral.[67] Nothing at all can make that kind of genocidal act legal or part of the acceptable rules of war. We are faced with a continuum here from the Srebrenica extreme on the one hand to the legal memos exchanged among top U.S. civilian and military officials on the other. Anyone reading these memos cannot help but wonder about the scope of "command responsibility," both on the part of the policy makers and by the superior officers in the field.[68] Similar questions must be raised about the U.S. practice of "extraordinary rendition," where detainees were sent to other countries to be allegedly interrogated under torture.[69]

As for those taking instead of giving orders, Article 8 of the ICTY statute states that anyone committing an act "pursuant to an order of a Government or of a superior shall not relieve him of criminal responsibility, but may be considered in mitigation of punishment if the International Tribunal determines that justice so requires." To overrule one's superior in this way when one is under great peer pressure to go along is a strong indication that the Security Council (which drew up this charter) must have believed that all persons in the area of former Yugoslavia had the epistemic equipment (whether their reason or their conscience) to know that the acts under discussion were so immoral that they could not possibly have been legal under any circumstances. I cite three examples, two where the moral choice was clear and one where it was ambiguous.

The Trial Chamber in the Yugoslav Tribunal's Celebici Camp case stressed that the four defendants' (Delalic, Mucic, Delic, Landzo) "exercise of moral choice" had not been eclipsed by the chaotic conditions under which the camp in which they "worked" operated (Blakesley, 1348). Finding that Delic "displayed a singular brutality in causing the deaths of two men detained in Celebici prison camp and a calculated cruelty in the torture and mistreatment of many others" the Tribunal sentenced him to twenty years imprisonment (1347). In the Rape Camps case, the Tribunal found three defendants (Kunarac, Kovac, and Kukovoc) guilty of raping, torturing, and enslaving Muslim women, one of whom was a twelve-year-old child "that had not been heard of since she was sold by one of the accused" (1351). The Trial Chamber took note of the fact that even if the defendants had been following orders (which was not clear) "the evidence [still] show[ed] free will on their part" (1385). This question of free will is crucial in the matter of obedience to the voice of conscience. For example, in the trial of the Einsatzgruppen who had massacred thousands of Jews in the Ukraine, a U.S. military court noted that the "obedience of a soldier is not the obedience of an automaton. A soldier is a reasoning agent. He does not respond, and is not expected to respond, like a piece of machinery. It is a fallacy of widespread consumption that a soldier is required to do everything his superior officer orders him to do" (1287).

The third case I cite from the Yugoslav Tribunal shows how difficult it can be to decide whether a defendant charged with participating in an all-day massacre could have and therefore should have refused to obey the order of his superior commander.[70] As a member of the 10th Sabotage Unit, Drazen Erdemovic participated on or about July 16, 1995, in "the shooting and killing of [hundreds of] unarmed Bosnian Muslim men at the Pilica collective farm" outside Zvornik, not far from the town of Srebrenica where thousands of Muslim men, women, and children had surrendered to Bosnian forces after their town had been overrun. Erdemovic confessed that on that July day on the Pilica farm he himself shot and killed between 70 and 100 unarmed innocent Muslim men. None of the other cases in my short survey involved defendants who claimed that if they had not followed their superior's order to kill innocents they themselves would have been instantly killed, which is what Erdemovic argued his predicament was. "Your honor," he told the Court, "I had to do this. If I had refused, I would have been killed together with the victims. When I refused, they told me: 'If you are sorry for them, stand up, line up with them and we will kill you too.' I am not sorry for myself but for my family and son who then had nine months, and I could not refuse because they would have killed me."[71] The Erdemovic case makes us realize that we cannot always do what our conscience bids us to do, to preserve the lives of innocent victims at all cost. It is a good thing then that the epistemic route into the realm of human rights is a two lane road with reason and conscience supporting and supplementing each other.

There are four conditions that must be met for a defense of duress to succeed and for one's conscience to be legitimately (legally) overridden. Because Erdemovic pleaded guilty, he never did have to prove that (i) "the act charged was done under immediate threat of severe and irreparable harm to life or limb," that (ii) "there was no adequate means of averting such evil," that (iii) "the crime committed was not disproportionate to the evil threatened," and that (iv) "the situation leading to duress must not have been voluntarily brought about by the person coerced."[72]

In his Appeals Chamber dissent Judge Cassese argued that Erdemovic should be given a "real" trial in which he could plead not guilty and in which he could seek to establish conditions (i) through (iv), after which the Trial Court could then either rule that he was not guilty because he had not had a moral choice, or could reduce his sentence. However, the majority of the judges in all three chambers (Trial I, Appeals, and Trial II) accepted the following rule: "duress does not afford a complete defense to a soldier charged with a crime against humanity and/or war crime involving the killing of innocent human beings: it is admissible in mitigation" only.[73] The fact that duress could not by definition (no matter what the circumstances) be a "complete" defense meant that (given the agreed-on facts) the verdict could never be "not guilty as charged," because a complete defense adds up to a justification of the deed done. The majority of the judges were of the opinion that our consciences can never be wiped clean and that there never can be a justification or full defense for committing the kinds of crimes the Tribunal was asked to judge.

Judge Cassese felt that at least in theory there could be such a defense and that the Tribunal should be open to that possibility by seeing how far Erdemovic could make his case for having been under extreme, meaning exculpatory, duress. After a survey of international case law pertaining to this issue, Cassese drew on earlier proceedings from the Tribunal to draw out the following example: "An inmate of a concentration camp, starved and beaten for months, is then told after a savage beating, that if he does not kill another inmate, who has already been beaten with metal bars and will certainly be beaten to death before long, then his eyes will, then and there, be gouged out. He kills the other inmate as a result" (Cassese, §47). We might hesitate about whether the first inmate should have been willing to be shot so as to avoid killing the second inmate. What then about Cassese's question whether he "should have allowed his eyes to be gouged out" to avoid killing the second inmate, and whether "he is a criminal for not having done so?" Comments Cassese: "Any answer to the question of duress has to be able to cope with such examples which the war in Yugoslavia—and war throughout the world—have generated and, regretfully, will continue to generate." I quote him again: "Law is based on what society can reasonably expect of its members. It should not set *intractable* standards of behavior which require mankind to perform acts of martyrdom and brand as criminal any behavior falling below these standards" (emphasis original).

The Erdemovic case invites us to consider the proposition that to be given a superior order to do a manifestly immoral act does not *all by itself* lead to the conclusion that such an order should be disobeyed. While it almost always does mean this, it can happen that the evil to be averted by the disobedience (the killing of the hundreds of innocent Muslim men *plus* one's own death after having one's eyes poked out) is greater than the evil caused by obedience (the killing of hundreds of innocent Muslim men). When the evil is bound to happen in any case, the test of proportionality (condition (iii) above) comes—so argued Cassese and Stephens—to naught. This is a very dangerous proposition because it injects utilitarian considerations into what should be a strictly criminal procedure. The Trial Chamber sent the case back for a second look, but the majority of three did not agree with Cassese's point of view. By three votes to two his colleagues found that "duress does not afford a complete defence to a soldier charged with a crime against humanity and/or war crime involving the killing of innocent human beings and that, consequently, the guilty plea entered by the Appellant before Trial Chamber I was not equivocal"[74] (IV,4/10/11). In other words, there can never be a full justification or defense for committing one of these crimes, and anyone who commits such a crime is bound to be guilty. All that can be done is to add up the mitigating factors. The judges in Trial Chamber II followed this line of thinking when they reduced Erdemovic's sentence from ten to seven years instead of granting him a new trial.

Concerned that acts of genocide had taken place in Rwanda in 1994, and responding to a request by the new government of Rwanda, in 1995 the UN Security Council created the International Tribunal for Rwanda (ICTR). This tribunal was given authority to prosecute persons for Crimes against Genocide (Article 2), Crimes against Humanity (Article 3), and for Violations of Article 3 common to the Geneva Conventions and of Additional Protocol II (Article 4). The crimes against genocide are the same ones as those stated in the Yugoslav tribunal's charter. They are also the same as the list of crimes against humanity, except that the introduction to this list is different. Again, "natural persons" (like you and me) rather than groups, organizations, or governments are singled out for attention (Article 5). Article 6 repeats that superiors will be held responsible for those serving under their command and defendants cannot plead the defense of acting "pursuant to orders from a Government or a superior," though this fact may serve as a mitigating factor, should the Tribunal so decide.[75]

Since the gruesome acts committed were not done in the context of normal warlike combat, the Rwanda defendants are not likely to plead "higher orders."[76] Because the killings were done with "guns, grenades, pangas, machetes, spears, cudgels and other weapons" in an atmosphere of slaughter and mayhem, the defendants frequently plead an alibi instead of absurdly arguing that they did not know that butchering Tutsis to death was immoral and therefore manifestly illegal. They knew the immorality and illegality of their acts, which is why they plead having been elsewhere when the killings took place. It then falls on the Tribunal to hear the witnesses who place the defendants at the scene of the massacre and to weigh the evidence for and against the defendants. Having done this, the Tribunal did not believe Clement Kayishema and Obed Ruzindana when they claimed "that they were not at the sites when any of the massacres occurred" (§232). Both defendants had and have a functioning moral conscience and good enough reasoning powers to know an evil (genocidal) act of murder and mutilation when they do one or see one done.[77]

The First Amended Indictment of these two men lists four massacre sites.[78] In the case of Kayishema "most witnesses had either not seen him at all during the period in question . . . or had seen him for very short periods of time on isolated occasions" (§247). In the case of Ruzindana, most of the twenty-one witnesses "did not give a comprehensive account of Ruzindana's whereabouts during the period when massacres were known to have occurred in the Bisesero region" (§§258, 263). In each case those killed were primarily Tutsis who had come to these sites for protection against Hutu attacks. They were prevented from leaving the sites when they realized that they were going to be killed by members of the communal police and armed civilians "with guns, grenades, machetes, spears, cudgels," and other tools of genocide. The two accused ordered and personally participated in these killings. They did not stop the genocidal acts when they could have and should have and made no attempt to punish any of the perpetrators. The Tribunal rejected the alibis that the defendants gave and found both of them guilty of genocide (Counts 1, 19; VIII, 235).[79]

Jean-Paul Akayesu was born in the Taba commune, where in his youth he was on the local football team and where he became a teacher and primary school inspector. He was a very popular substitute teacher. The indictment tells us that "the Accused was a well known and popular figure in the local community" (1.5§51).[80] Evidently, the accused had a functioning conscience and good reasoning capacities, for he "was considered a man of high morals, intelligence, and integrity, possessing the qualities of a leader, who appeared to have the trust of the local community" (§53). During the time that the worst atrocities took place, April–June 1994, the accused was the bourgmestre (mayor) of his commune, which gave him the authority and duty to keep law and order in his district and which made him someone whose orders the police and the ordinary citizens would automatically follow, much as they might have followed a chief's orders in precolonial times (§73). The tribunal's main charge against Akayesu was that, given his official position as bourgmestre, he must have known about the roughly 2,000 Tutsis who were killed during his tenure, for those killings "were openly committed and . . . widespread." "Although he had the authority and responsibility to do so, Jean-Paul Akayesu never attempted to prevent the killings of Tutsis in the commune in any way or called for assistance for regional or national authorities to quell the violence" (1.2§12). The indictment contains page after page detailing acts of murder, rape, torture, and beatings that resulted in death that were committed in the presence of and on the direct order of the accused. Many of the crimes were committed in and around the Bureau Communal or city hall. Because of the causal connections between his position and his presence at most of the scenes, the Tribunal found the accused "individually criminally responsible" for the acts by subordinates who listened to him and followed his orders (7.8§707). It is estimated that some 2,000 Tutsis were killed in Taba on his authority and under his supervision.

For our purposes we need not sort out the intricacies of international law (such as the partial overlap of genocide charges with crimes against humanity) and the different types of responsibility (command, criminal, direct or indirect, intended or negligent) that can and do arise in cases like these. The Tribunal did not rubber stamp the charges leveled by the prosecutor; not infrequently the indictment notes that "the Prosecutor failed to satisfy the Chamber that [the charges] were proven beyond a reasonable doubt" (7.8§§713, 708). It did find, though, that "there was a causal relationship between Akayesu's speeches at the gathering of April 19, 1994, and the ensuing widespread massacres of Tutsi in Taba" (7.5§665/vii). From the speeches he gave and the effects he knew they would have the Tribunal judged that the accused "had the intent to directly create a particular state of mind in his audience necessary to lead to the destruction of the Tutsi group, as such" (7.5§674). That is the definition of genocide, and the Tribunal found that Akayesu was "successful" in that his speeches did in fact lead "to the destruction of a great number of Tutsi in the commune of Taba (7.5§675).

Conclusion. Critics of my epistemic universality thesis might want to suggest that the conscience of the world is awake only where these kinds of trials take place and that it lies dormant or is nonexistent where there are no international trials going on or where truth commissions hold no sessions. But human epistemic equipment is not that spotty. In these regional tribunals for the former Yugoslavia and Rwanda the defendants were not simply found guilty of acting contrary to local domestic rules, mores, customs, or even legal statutes. Nor were they found guilty of violating the prevailing moral codes found in Eastern Europe or Central Africa in the last quarter of the twentieth century. The statutes I cited and under which these defendants were found guilty were drawn up under the auspices of the UN and are seen as a codification and distillation of the conscience of humanity. Still, the Yugoslav and Rwanda Tribunals were aimed at specific conflicts and bound by a time frame. However, the crimes with which they dealt do not stand alone. They are only a very few of a long list of horrors we have witnessed in the twentieth century. In his sweeping survey of these horrors, Jonathan Glover has described how the naval blockade of Germany in World War I prepared the way for the World War II fire bombings of cities in which thousands of people died and were asphyxiated.[81] That in turn allowed us to drop atomic bombs on two Japanese cities, which was itself just another example of bombing from on high without seeing any of the horrors that take place on the ground, as we did to great "effect" in Vietnam and Cambodia. Glover reminds us of the 20 million deaths incurred by the utopian dream of communism under Joseph Stalin, of Mao's blind reconstruction of Chinese society that led to between 20 and 30 million unnecessary deaths, and of how that crazy vision nevertheless became a model for the Khmer Rouge in Cambodia to "overturn the basket" and kill off all those not handpicked for survival in the totally new society inhabited by totally new people. Glover ends with an account of Hitler's madness and the Nazi horrors that inspired the Universal Declaration. The list of horrors and unnecessary deaths in the twentieth century is truly astounding. And these millions upon millions of deaths are not ones that resulted from natural disasters. They resulted from human decisions, from the behavior of natural persons who could and should have chosen to do otherwise than they did.

Looking back at this litany of horrors the UN membership decided in 1998 that the time had finally come to establish a permanent International Criminal Court (ICC) with universal jurisdiction. As if they had just read Glover's survey, they state in their preamble of the statute that in establishing this court the state parties were "mindful that during this century millions of children, women and men have been victims of unimaginable atrocities that deeply shocked the conscience of humanity." This is a less sexist reference to the same barbarous acts that the drafters of the Declaration referred to in the Second Recital, except that this time the horrors are spread out over the entire century instead of just the first half of it. This time, instead of what in the late 1940s was still a nonbinding declaration of inherent moral rights, the reference to "the conscience of humanity" comes at the head of a working legal document under which criminals from all over the world can be, and hopefully infrequently will be, charged. The statute of the ICC presumes, as did the Declaration in 1948, that this "conscience of humanity" is present and operating in all "natural persons" (Article 25) in all the world's cultures, regions, and corners. As did the two regional tribunals, this ICC statute "shall apply equally to all persons without any distinction based on official capacity." This pulls heads of state, government officials, and military commanders within reach of the statute. And also as before, if a crime is committed "pursuant to an order of a Government or of a superior, whether military or civilian, [that fact] shall not relieve that person of criminal responsibility" (Article 33). This pulls in all those who do the dirty work for those higher up in the chain of military or civil command.

The scope of the crimes brought under the jurisdiction of this Court, with its worldwide jurisdiction, is very much the same as that of the regional tribunals I surveyed above. There are four categories: the crime of genocide, crimes against humanity, war crimes, and the crime of aggression. The first three categories are repeats of the Yugoslav and Rwanda statutes, though a number of details have been added to the last two. The fourth category is not further defined in the statute as adopted and awaits action on Articles 121 and 123 of the statute. Article 7 goes far beyond the already detailed lists of crimes against humanity in the Yugoslav and Rwanda statutes. It covers not just rape but "sexual slavery, enforced prostitution, forced pregnancy, enforced sterilization, or any other form of sexual violence of comparable gravity" (7(g)). Words like "extermination," "enslavement," "deportation," "torture," "forced pregnancy," "persecution," and "enforced disappearance of persons" are defined. The definition of "torture" is, for instance, taken from the Convention by that name and defined as "the intentional infliction of severe pain or suffering, whether physical or mental, on a person in the custody or under the control of the accused; except that torture shall not include pain or suffering arising only from, inherent in or incidental to, lawful sanctions" (e). Any reader who peruses these "most serious crimes of international concern" (Article 1) and these "most serious crimes of concern to the international community as a whole" (Article 5) will immediately see that the international community has come out in full support of our own moral intuitions (whoever we are), which were repulsed as we watched on television images of the scenes of these kinds of crimes or read reports about them. Some of my readers may even have personally experienced one or several of these crimes as a victim or a direct witness. When the sixty necessary ratifications were reached in July 2003, the statute came into force and has started to operate. As of spring 2008, 105 nations from all continents had joined this International Criminal Court. The United States is (still) not among them. The court's first case is likely to be an investigation of international crimes committed in the Darfur region of Sudan.

Article 33 of the ICC statute deals with the question of whether someone who commits one of these gross violations of human dignity "pursuant to an order of a Government or of a superior, whether military or civilian" can use that as a defense. The answer is that such a supe-rior order will "not relieve that person of criminal responsibility" unless several conditions hold, the last one being that "(c) The order was not manifestly unlawful." An order can be illegal, but not manifestly so. This can happen, for instance, when an order is given to storm and destroy a building which the superior knows is used as a hospital for women and children, but the defendant does not know the purpose of the building. In that case—as happens all too often in warfare—the defendant acts on good faith that the order is a legal one, though in actual fact his superior is violating the Geneva Conventions, which state that hospitals should not be made targets. But some orders are so obviously immoral that it does not matter who gives them, whether an imposter or the defendant's legal superior. The ICC presumes that if a defendant is asked to do any of the acts in our survey of courts-martial and tribunals, the order can-not be a legal order and should not be obeyed because it violates the conscience of humanity as well as that of the defendant. When it comes to the outer limits of warfare, the dictates of morality govern what can and cannot be legal. At these junctures in domestic and international military law something transcendent lingers and rubs against positivistic interpretations of legal theory.

To make sure that there is no confusion about defendants having a functioning conscience, the second paragraph of Article 33 of the ICC states that "orders to commit genocide or crimes against humanity are manifestly unlawful." In the case of these kinds of crimes no gray is al-lowed. They are one and all "unlawful" or "illegal" on the face of it. The only way the international community can make a claim like this and cover all natural persons in a great diversity of cultural settings is if it operates with the presumption that people have a moral sense or a con-science which immediately tells them when they are faced with one of these kinds of crimes. This conscience (or inner voice, or moral intu-ition, faculty, or sense) tells them that the act they are about to commit is "manifestly illegal," which it can only be if it is obviously immoral. In short, at the heart of all these domestic and international tribunals and statutes we find an appeal to a moral conscience or sense of good and evil that all natural persons are presumed to have. The category "crimes against humanity" has become an accepted part of international criminal law and has been written into the statutes of the international courts that are operating in the Hague, the Netherlands, and in Arusha, Tanzania. Any ordinary person is presumed to know what does and does not count as a gross violation of human rights. Since the trials I have been discussing do follow strict legal procedures of due process, these tribunals do investigate any claim on the part of the defendant that his or her conscience was blocked. But the presumption is that his or her conscience exists and was functioning at the time the gross violations were committed.

C. The Framework of Moral Intuitionism

Let me now place a theoretical framework around this worldwide appeal to the conscience of humanity that we have found in the widespread use of the doctrine of manifest illegality. My readers' shared reactions of moral outrage when we see or hear about gross human rights violations have been written into the international legal statutes I have quoted, for these are a codification of that conscience. Both our reactions and these statutes of condemnation lie at the heart of the theory of (classical) moral intuitionism, the four main propositions which I will now set out and defend as constituting the main epistemic route into the domain of basic human rights. When, in section B of the next chapter, we come to discuss John Rawls's use of the principle of reciprocity as the key step in our justification of human rights beliefs, we will see that he takes this theory of classical moral intuitionism as his main bugbear. It is therefore important for us to apply this theory clearly to the writing of the Declaration since we will use this application to a real life document to reject Rawls's dismissal of intuitionism as too philosophical for the give and take of diplomatic maneuverings. Our response will be that Rawls "ignores" or plays down the moral facts that play such a big role in the theory we here embrace.

The four tenets of this school of thought are (1) that there exists in the world a realm of objective moral values; (2) that we can enter that realm through our shared moral sense, faculty, or conscience; (3) that as far as the basics are concerned we have a remarkable certitude about these matters; and (4) that this certitude is often prereflective and precedes formal intellectual contributions.[82] Together these tenets add up to a defense of the idea of epistemic universality, which provides most of the knowledge half of our doctrine of inherence. These four propositions add up to a good bit of philosophy in and beneath the text of the Declaration. They put our account of the role of the human conscience at odds with the one Michael Ignatieff has given.

The appeal to human conscience of a theorist like Ignatieff lacks depth because he collapses that appeal into "the idea of moral reciprocity: that we judge human actions by the simple test of whether we would wish to be on the receiving end."[83] Ignatieff has reduced the drafters' two routes of conscience and reason (UDHR, Article 1) into just one, the reasoned route of reciprocity. Ignatieff makes the puzzling observation that "that conscience is free" (89). Instead of using the conscience of humanity as a background check on any sick use of the Golden Rule, as we argue should be done, he uses the rule to expound on the content of this supposedly free moral conscience. There is for him only one route, that of reason or the Golden Rule, into the domain of human rights. Since that route is "free" and open for all to travel as they see fit, there really are no such things as universal values that exist independently of human choice. There is for him no realm of values that this freely roaming conscience can violate, for it creates its own values when it gives its own reading to what the Golden Rule demands in any particular case. Having reduced the voice of conscience to the dictates of formal reason *without remainder*, Ignatieff has robbed our rational capacities of their independent helpmate and watchdog. In this section I object to this kind of epistemic reductionism.

The four propositions that follow are not meant to be final. I discuss them to place international appeals to the "conscience of humanity" in a theoretical framework and to make these propositions part of the theory of human rights set out in this book. I make no claim that all or most of the drafters consciously held all four of these propositions as I present them here, but I do think that by voting and writing the way they did, they are implicitly committed to these general propositions in some form or other. Also, I wish to avoid any suggestion that this ability of ours to detect and condemn cases of radical evil is linked to any particular physical organ we have. While a particular area of the brain seems to be the base for our moral sensitivity, no modern intuitionist makes a more specific physiological connection, which is not to say that none may ever be found.

Proposition I: Moral Truth and Falsehood. The phrase "the conscience of humanity"— the nonsexist version of "the conscience of mankind" that I have been using—suggests that there exists in the world a realm of moral values to which this conscience gains us entry. The implication is that there are values that cut across time and place and are accessible to a generalized conscience that people of all ages and cultures share, which is why these values are thought of as constituting an external and objective realm. The values to which this conscience gains us access are not thought of as resulting from local or regional decisions made at any one particular time, place, or culture. It does not tell you that you should eat with your fork in your left and your knife in your right hand, or that you must drive on the right-hand side of the road. But is does tell you that torturing little children for pleasure, or shooting innocent civilians in a cave or ditch, or gouging out another defendant's eyes is always and everywhere wrong, and that there are no exceptions to the prohibition against racial discrimination. Classical moral intuitionists think of these values not as man-made, but as discovered by the shared moral sense and further elaborated by various social customs and governmental programs, including military codes and international statutes. Belief in such a realm sets the ideology of human rights apart from more procedurally based theories of justice, such as those of Rawls (discussed in Chapter 3) and Habermas (discussed in Chapter 6).

Classical moral intuitionists agree that there are such things as moral facts that ordinary people can come to know. Many of these theorists think that this knowledge comes in the form of moral truths that are indigenous to the realm of morality, much in the way the truths of mathematics are indigenous to the realm of mathematics. Sir David Ross, a well-known British intuitionist, believed that "one of the most evident facts of our moral consciousness is the sense which we have of the sanctity of promises." He argued that just "as we come to see that it is of the nature of two and two to make four . . . , [so] we see the prima facie rightness of an act which would be the fulfillment of a particular promise."[84] This analogy between ethics and mathematics is a strong theme in at least one branch of intuitionist literature, its most famous proponent being Plato. It makes basic moral truths independent of all other kinds of truths, such as those of psychology or theology. And it explains why people are so certain about these truths. Since these basic moral truths stand on their own two feet, Thomas Jefferson was right to point out that one does not really need to have much education to be able to lay hold of them: "State a moral case to a ploughman and a professor. The former will decide it as well, and often better than the latter, because he has not been led astray by artificial rules."[85] This became an issue in the U.S. Vietnam trial of First Lieutenant Calley with which I began the preceding section. Calley's appellate defense counsel argued that because of his lack of education and training and because of his low IQ, Calley could not have known that the order to shoot numerous innocent women, children, and old men was "palpably illegal." To the conern that in his instructions to the jury Calley's trial judge should have used as standard what a person of "*commonest* understanding" (that is, lowest IQ) in the army could grasp and not what any man of "*ordinary* sense and understanding" could grasp, Judge Quinn of the Appeals Court responded that this fine tuning made no difference in a case like this: "whether Lieutenant Calley was the most ignorant person in the U.S. army in Vietnam, or the most intelligent, he must be presumed to know that he could not kill the people involved here" (Blakesley 1301; emphasis added). In cases like these the dictum that ignorance of the law is no excuse translates into a call to obey one's indwelling conscience of humanity. No details of poor training or poor command communications can wipe out this kind of moral knowledge in someone who has a functioning moral conscience. It is the universal sharing of this kind of basic moral knowledge that allowed the drafters to aim their Declaration at ordinary men, women, and children at all levels of development in any of the world's cultural settings, and why it has been worthwhile to translate the Declaration into all the main languages of our world.

I have called this the *realm* of moral rights and not a *system* of rights, for the word "realm" conveys an objectivity that the word "system" lacks. This is a main difference between the treatment of moral rights in such different volumes as Judith Jarvis Thomson's *The Realm of Rights* and Rex Martin's *A System of Rights*, whose definitions we took (in Chapter 1) as good and bad examples of how to define what a human right is.[86] The difference between the definite article ("the") in Thomson's title and the indefinite one ("a") in Martin's suggests that there is only one realm of rights that Thomson plans to explore, while for Martin there can in principle be a plurality of systems of rights. Thomson starts with the assertion that all theorizing begins with a body of data, and her data, she says, "will throughout be moral judgments that I think you would take to be clear moral truths" (33). The entire discussion of her *Realm of Rights* is based on the supposition that her readers believe that there is indeed a realm of clear moral "truths" or "facts" or "data" (4). Thomson uses these moral facts to make positive and negative judgments about moral theories. For instance, a theory that would in principle allow a surgeon to carve up one unfortunate patient to save the lives of five others would conflict with the basic right to life of that one patient and would therefore be rejected as inadequate. Just so the drafters of the Declaration rejected fascist racism as an inadequate moral theory because it conflicted with the moral facts they set forth in their Declaration. For the same reason the Yugoslav tribunal rejected Serbian dreams of a "cleansed" greater Serbia, the Rwanda tribunal rejected the Hutu view of Tutsis as "dispensable," and Calley's judges rejected his beliefs that the Viet Cong and their sympathizers were not really human beings.[87] All these twisted views conflict with the moral facts of life. The phrase "conscience of humanity" does not lend itself to a multiplicity of man-made systems of rights. It implies that there is only one such system for the whole world and that we discover it and bump into it when we are faced with gross violations of human dignity. This does not take away the fact that the implementation of these abstract moral truths can lead to quite different local and regional legal systems and to diverse social and cultural customs.

Some moral intuitionists, call them contextual intuitionists, do not believe that there is this objective realm of morality to which our shared conscience gains us access. They do not see our conscience or our moral intuitions as a universal piece of epistemic equipment with which all of us are born. They instead hold that people's moral intuitions are mostly or even totally shaped by the cultural milieu in which they were raised, without there in addition being a transcendent element that would allow for and even sanction the kind of cross-cultural judgments that the drafters of the Declaration made when they condemned the Nazi and Japanese horrors, and that the judges in the international tribunals make when they hand down guilty verdicts of the kind I have cited in section B above. From the perspective of human rights, these other intuitionists are "bad" ones, for their theories destroy the kind of transcendence on which these transcultural judgments depend.[88] When it comes to choosing between a theory (even an intuitionist one) and our most basic moral insights, we must stay with the insights of the moment and put these other intuitionist theories on the side. In our favor speaks the fact that when their own dignity is violated in some gross way, ordinary people frequently exhibit just the kind of transcendence that these contextual intuitionists hold not legitimate or declare unsubstantiated. Those of us who live in modern, civilized, or, as Rawls would say, "nearly just" societies do not need to give much thought to the realm of human rights because our own domestic legal systems closely echo the moral realm described in the Declaration. As a matter of positive law and practice they forbid murder, assault and battery, torture, the breaking of contracts, rape, starvation, and (except for the United States) medical neglect. Classical moral intuitionists gather up these stirrings of the conscience of humanity that break through the surfaces of history and of our own personal lives and construct them into a *theory* about morality.

This moral truth-is-objective feature explains why the Declaration was intellectually out of sync with the time of its birth. For example, Margaret MacDonald, a leading analytic philosopher at the time when the Declaration was being written, held that "assertions about natural [or human] rights . . . are assertions of what ought to be as the result of human choice."[89] These choices are based on feelings and emotional reactions to experiences in the world that we record in statements like "Freedom is better than slavery" or "All men are of equal worth." Such statements do not record a fact, but announce where the speaker takes his or her stand. Each of the articles of the Declaration is thought to record a *decision* on the part of the drafters as to where they stood vis-à-vis Hitler's atrocities (that is, that they abhorred them) and not an *observation* of moral wrongs as facts to be noted. MacDonald sees the drafters as "more like artists who use material with results which impress and convince but do not *prove.* There is no conceivable method of *proving* that Keats is a better poet than Crabbe or that freedom is better than slavery. For assertions of value cannot be subjected to demonstrative or inductive methods. It is for this reason that such assertions have been regarded as simple expressions of feeling or emotion like cries of pain and anger" (59). Again: "There are no certainties in the field of values. For there are no true and false beliefs about values, but only better or worse decisions and choices" (60). Classical moral intuitionists hold that that our moral sentiments *do* help us discover truths and *do* yield knowledge of the world.

MacDonald makes light of Rousseau's statement that "man is born free and everywhere he is in chains" because Rousseau clearly did not "observe ten or ten million babies after birth and record when the infant limbs were manacled." But I have already quoted the debates about UDHR Article 1 that show that the great majority of the drafters were not simply reacting or taking a stand; they were also and at the same time making a truth claim about a moral rider on the biological process of birth. MacDonald's question "How can facts about nature be discovered which have never been observed or confirmed by observation?" (44) reveals her adherence to the dictum of logical positivism that only those statements that have been verified by science and observation can be said to have a truth value. That dictum has been widely found wanting and does not support the truth of its own pronouncement. From this limiting theory of meaning MacDonald moves straightway to a legal positivist interpretation of rights that we have argued (at the end of Chapter 1) commits the fallacy of implementation. She thinks that it makes no sense to say of the slaves in the antebellum American South that they had a "right" to their freedom because no statutes to that effect existed there (51–52). Intuitionists respond that unless their consciences were warped or blocked (by a sick ideology or prolonged oppression) people in antebellum America *did* know that what UDHR Article 4 says is true, namely, that "No one shall be held in slavery or servitude; slavery and the slave trade shall be prohibited in all their forms." The drafters voted to include this truth after they discussed the more recent practices of slavery in the work factories located next to the Nazi concentration camps.

Classical moral intuitionists hold that moral truths or falsehoods are true or false not by virtue of what people decide but because of the way the world is. These truths are what they are by virtue of some state of affairs outside the mind or feelings of the knower or feeler. The truths of the Declaration, for example, are not what they are because of the emotional state of the drafters in the 1940s or our own personal preferences and feelings today. They are truths because of the kinds of creatures that human beings are, namely, ones with inherent moral rights. Contextual intuitionists place the cart before the horse. They think that people have human rights because our consciences get outraged, while classical intuitionists think that our consciences get outraged because people have human rights. Should anyone wonder where in the world he or she might find that objective realm of moral rights, the answer is that this realm is to be found wherever and whenever there are people, which is pretty much everywhere.

Proposition II: The Conscience of Humanity Gains Us Entry. The second proposition holds that when our moral intuitions are operating normally they bring us into contact with this objective—that is, existing externally to our own intuitions or moral perceptions of it—realm of universal values. We do not gain this epistemic entry at the moment of our birth, and we do not gain it without pedagogical midwives at various points along the way. The most influential of these midwives are those in our immediate family circle, our teachers, and, not least, our own experiences. While all human beings do possess all the inherent rights of the Declaration from the moment of their births, they do not come to enjoy the active exercise of those rights at one and the same time. In situations where capitalist entrepreneurs have not yet set foot, the moral truth about the right to unionize (Article 23(4)) is still dormant and not crucial, since the conditions that would bring it to the surface are not yet present. Children do not have the right to work, but when they grow up they do (Article 23). Young people do not yet have the right to "marry and to found a family," but when they are "of full age" they do (Article 16). When, precisely, "full age" kicks in awaits the determination of specific regional or national legal systems. But such waiting must not be interpreted to mean that the truths as stated do not exist or have no significance in the abstract.

There are two ways to state the truths embedded in each of the Declaration's articles, a positive way and a negative way. When we pick the positive route we introduce a right with the phrase "It is true that. . . .", and when we introduce that same right negatively we use the phrase "It is wrong to. . . ." Using the right to work from Article 23 as an example, we can claim positively (quoting the text) that it is true that "Everyone has the right to work, to free choice of employment, to just and favourable conditions of work, and to protection against unemployment." Or (and the last clause of the text already helps us do this) we can state the same right negatively by saying that it is wrong not to be upset by the ravages of unemployment on the lives of capable and willing adults. Philosophers generally agree that the concepts of truth and knowledge are intimately connected. We can therefore even introduce the negative way of stating a right with a truth claim. In that case the opening clause ("It is true that it is wrong to . . .") introduces some gross human rights violation. I have found that the best way to defend the positive claim of a human right is to draw out examples of the negative claim and see what reactions I get. This leads us again to the importance of this second proposition's appeal to the conscience of humanity, for it is that very conscience that is stirred when the negative image of a gross human rights violation is visually or verbally drawn out.

In *The Rebel* Albert Camus explored this experience of moral rebellion and based it on the experience of solidarity within the human family, a phenomenon we explore in Chapter 4 under the theme of human rights cosmopolitanism. As Camus sees it, there is a universal metaphysical element that is built right into the experience of rebellion. This means that an analysis of proposition (ii) leads us back to proposition (i) of the theory of classical moral intuitionism. *Pace* Ignatieff, Camus holds that our own consciences are not free because they are embedded in the conscience of humanity with its realm of values that exists externally to our own powers of feeling and reason. No doubt this conscience must be woken up and activated to operate effectively in our lives, and for that we need good nurturers and role models that help us develop healthy emotions.[90] But once it is woken up, it speaks in a universal voice. Henry Sidgwick also thought that a moral truth apprehended by our moral faculty "must be intrinsically universal, though particular in our first apprehension of it."[91]

We can read *The Rebel* as a philosophical prelude to the Declaration, for the drafters were very much rebels in his sense of that word. Camus tells us that a rebel is "a man who says no, but whose refusal does not imply a renunciation."[92] He or she is someone who "affirms the existence of a borderline" and who wishes to "preserve certain things on this side" of that line (15). By drawing that kind of a line, a rebel "implicitly brings into play a standard of value" and so makes the "transition from facts to rights" (16). And though these values are still very "indeterminate," the rebel feels they "are common to himself and to all men." It is not necessary that the rebel himself or herself be a victim of oppression. "The mere spectacle of oppression of which someone else is the victim" can turn bystanders and observers into becoming [moral] rebels (16). While some of the drafters had personally been sought by the Nazis, most were bystanders to the Holocaust and heard about the horrors of the camps later. They also read about them in UN reports especially prepared for them. According to Camus, there is a universal element in this act of moral rebellion that we all experience when we draw this line between good and evil. This is not some personal reaction that we happen to have. To the contrary, "when he rebels a man identifies himself with other men and so surpasses himself and from this point of view human solidarity is metaphysical" (19).

In the act of rebellion there comes an Archimedean point of leverage in which a person transcends himself and his or her own background and cultural milieu and identifies with all members of the human family. In her poignant discourse on the pain of others published just before her death, Susan Sontag asks, "What does it mean to protest suffering, as distinct from acknowledging it?"[93] The difference lies in the metaphysical element spoken of by Camus and echoed by Sontag in a speech she gave for the presentation of the Oscar Romero Award to Ishai Menuchin, chairman of Yesh Gvul ("There Is a Limit"), the Israeli soldiers' movement for selective refusal to serve in the occupied territories.[94] She told those present that "At the center of our moral life and our moral imagination are the great models of resistance: the great stories of those who said no." The Yesh Gvul banner of the Israeli refuseniks perfectly captures Camus's description of rebellion as drawing a line around the principle on which the resister stands, but which is drawn on behalf of others and not just for himself.[95] "You don't do it," said Sontag, "just to be in the right, or to appease your own conscience; much less because you are confident your action will achieve its aim. You resist as an act of solidarity" (13).

A critic of this appeal to our moral sense or intuitions might well object that our approach works for the rights not to be subjected to slavery or torture, but surely not for all the rights that are listed in the Declaration. We respond that when the details of particular and specific human rights violations are drawn starkly enough, then it often becomes clear that some deep, universal moral truth is at stake. This holds for both the civil and political rights in the first half of the Declaration, as well as for the economic, social, and cultural ones in the second half. We should therefore not back down too quickly when we are asked how we know that it is true that it is wrong not to help willing and capable adult human beings find jobs (Article 23), or to deny a child its right to an education (Article 26) or to participation in culture (Article 27). Jeremy Waldron has, for instance, constructed a rebellious situation for UDHR Article 24 ("Everyone has the right to rest and leisure, including reasonable limitation of working hours and periodic holidays with pay"), which he expands into an argument for labor rights generally. This book defends an inherence view of social, economic, and cultural human rights, first with the adoption of the capabilities approach in Chapter 4 and then further in Chapter 5, where in section C I discuss Waldron's construction. Throughout we employ the intuitionist approach to questions of inherence. We argue there (just as we did in the case of international criminal law) that it is through seeing gross deprivations that we know that people have inherent rights to the goods they need to live a minimally dignified human life. The Declaration was written to protect human beings against the perpetration of fundamental wrongs against their personhood. Its drafters took most (though not all) of their examples of fundamental wrongs from what they had seen done to people during World War II. We can support the same rights they enunciated so succinctly, but take our fundamental wrongs from the massacres in Rwanda or Srebrenica, or the labor conditions in the factories along Mexico's border with the United States, or the lack of health insurance for millions of Americans.

What matters for a defense of the doctrine of inherence is the connection between the experience or observation of gross injustice or wrongs done and the discovery of inherently possessed human rights. I maintain that this connection lies behind most of the articles and rights in the Declaration.

I have found frequently in conversation with those who have doubts about the existence of human rights or even with outright critics of the idea, that when I ask them point blank to condemn a specific gross human rights violation, that they suddenly become pensive and more often than not *do* want to condemn that violation. I then take that condemnation as a point for a further discussion of the ethical theory here under discussion. When such a condemnation is not forthcoming, I admit to being puzzled. If the withholding is done to see where things will lead, I ask my discussion partner(s) to be as seriously engaged as I am, warts and all. When that still fails to produce a condemnation, I admit to being worried, for then the implication is that for this interlocutor, in that particular time and place, the particular piece of evil behavior under discussion might have been okay. This exception destroys the solidarity of the human family. Things are not morally well with someone who cannot bring him or herself to condemn gross violations of human rights when presented with them visually, orally, or in print. This brings us to the next of the four propositions of our moral framework.

Proposition III: The Limitations of Reason. At the start of this section I mentioned how Ignatieff seemed to collapse his appeal to the human conscience into an appeal to the Golden Rule or the principle of reciprocity. A collapse like that results from a failure to keep the two routes into the domain of human rights sufficiently separated. Equally puzzling is Alan Dershowitz's failure to identify the epistemic faculty (reason, conscience, or something else) that we use when we recoil from Nazi and other horrors. He is very explicit in defining "rights [as] those great fundamental preferences that experience and history—especially of great injustices—have taught are so essential that the citizenry should be persuaded to entrench them and not make them subject to easy change by shifting majorities" (*Rights from Wrongs*, 81). He refers to these experiences of gross injustice as entirely "untheoretical" ones, but he does not follow that criticism of reason with an exposition of the role of conscience or of our moral emotions, though that is probably part of what he has in mind.

I frequently find that those who cannot bring themselves to openly condemn gross human rights violations are struggling with a conflict between their rational capacities and their emotions. Their emotions tell them to condemn the atrocities, but they are puzzled because they feel they cannot defend that condemnation in the court of reason and so must hold back. By exhibiting an open distrust of the powers of reason as the basic or main barometer of moral health and sickness, this third proposition of classical of intuitionism takes sides in this conflict between reason and our emotions. In the next chapter, I support this moral intuitionist contention that the wings of the Golden Rule cannot deliver a justification of belief in human rights all by themselves. This is also why the drafters supplemented the "reason" of Article 1 (second sentence) with the Chinese proposal of "two-man-mindedness" that became the text's "conscience." Their use of the phrase "the conscience of mankind" in the Second Recital underscores this need to complement the powers of reason. Intuitionists view the fundamentals of morality as operating before reason kicks in to help with the implementation of the moral intuitions arrived at on a prereflective and (depending on the details of the theory) possibly precognitive level.

Intuitionists are not worried about the failure of the Western rationalist tradition to produce a knockdown argument for the existence of human rights. For the drafters of the Declaration, the Enlightenment project of finding a universal moral code does not stand or fall with our ability (or inability) to offer an argument with premises and human rights conclusions, such as the one Gewirth constructs, and which in the next chapter we will criticize as inadequate. Nor did that project depend on philosophical agreement of the kind a UNESCO survey had hoped to find among the world's leading intellectuals when it asked them what the philosophical foundations of human rights might be. The editors who interpreted the survey's answers reported to the Human Rights Commission their conviction "that the philosophical problem involved in a declaration of human rights is not to achieve doctrinal consensus, but rather to achieve agreement concerning rights and also concerning action in the realization and defense of rights, which may be justified on highly divergent doctrinal grounds."[96] The Commission did not pay much attention to this report on UNESCO's survey, and were a bit miffed that the survey had been done at all. They evidently felt no need for it, which I interpret as a sign of their confidence in the other route of conscience into their domain of moral rights. [97]

We should read UDHR Article 1 as a generalization of what the drafters discovered when they started to reflect on and react to the Nazi horrors. The refusal to accept oppression, to echo Camus again, "opened up" for the drafters "the way to a morality which, far from obeying abstract principles, discovers them only in the heat of battle" (283). Each basic human right has its own justification, one that is discovered when that particular right is violated in some gross way. This link with experience explains why so many delegates from so many different social, cultural, political, religious, and economic systems could nevertheless agree on a list of rights. They had all witnessed or heard about the same horrors and therefore were able and willing to proclaim the same rights. When morally healthy people—regardless of their ideological or religious affiliations—witness or hear about a gross human rights violation, they recoil and want to rebel in the name of the value being violated. That is how inherent rights are discovered and why World War II gave birth to the Universal Declaration. The phrases "the conscience of mankind" and "the conscience of humanity" capture this phenomenon and also apply to other horrors witnessed by other peoples in other times and places.

Stuart Hampshire has used the Nazi experience much in the way the drafters used it, as a negative entry into our concept of justice and to legitimize cross-cultural moral judgments that we make before the reflections of reason help us with the details of how to do what we think we ought to do. And like Camus and the drafters, he sees a universal element that transcends every immediate situation. He believes that

There is nothing mysterious or "subjective" or culture-bound in the great evils of human experience, re-affirmed in every age and in every written history and in every tragedy and fiction: murder and the destruction of life, imprisonment, enslavement, starvation, poverty, physical pain and torture, homelessness, friendlessness. That these evils are to be averted is the constant presupposition of moral arguments at all times and in all places . . .—these are some of constancies of human experience and feeling presupposed as the background to moral judgments and arguments.[98]

Hampshire implies that all normal, morally healthy human beings intuitively accept these "presuppositions" or "constancies" as the "background to moral judgments and arguments." And he believes that universal acceptance occurs "for reasons that are independent of any reflective thought" (106). I take this to be a reference to the conscience of humanity that is the subject of this chapter. I am inclined to give the same reading to Alexander Solzhenitsyn's remark that people would actually start to feel physically "sick" with revulsion when asked to enter the NKDV police schools, which he thought was prompted by an "inner intuition, not founded on rational argument."[99]

Writing long before Hampshire and Solzhenitsyn, and before either of the two world wars, Richard Pritchard argued much the same point in his celebrated paper "Does Moral Philosophy Rest on a Mistake?" He felt that it was a mistake to think that people's moral knowledge is based on argumentation and on the offering of proofs. Rather, argued Pritchard, "the sense that we ought to do certain things arises in our unreflective consciousness, being an activity of moral thinking occasioned by the various situations in which we find ourselves."[100] This is what happened to the drafters of the Declaration and what should have happened to the defendants before the above-mentioned military and international tribunals. It is not that reason never enters in or does not make any kind of contribution to our moral decisions. It does, but it does not enter on the ground floor where the fundamentals dwell. According to Sir David Ross, on that ground floor we find "the main moral convictions of the plain man," and he felt it was not for philosophy to prove or disprove such convictions but instead should take them as "knowledge from the start" (21). As in all disciplines, so in moral philosophy the questioning and doubting must come to an end sooner or later. Why then not, asks William Gass, "call a halt . . . early and [let] the evident, the obvious, the axiomatic, the indemonstrable, the intrinsic, or whatever one wants to name it, be deemed those clear cases of moral goodness, badness, obligation or wrong, which no theory can cloud, and for which men are prepared to fight to the last ditch"[101]

Proposition IV: Transparent and Immediate Certainty. This leads me to briefly mention a fourth tenet of classical intuitionism that I see in the writing of the Declaration and in the rulings of the tribunals. These moments of transcendence, in which our sense of morality makes itself heard over the clamor of fear, indoctrination, and custom, are generally not moments of confusion about the right course of action. Usually it is "simply" a question of doing or not doing what we know to be the right thing. This is the moral analogue of Descartes's notion of "clear and distinct" ideas which we grasp with indubitable certitude and on which we build the edifice of knowledge. Intuitionists think that our knowledge of these ground-level moral truths is remarkably uncluttered. Americans call them "self-evident" truths in their Declaration of Independence. By that they mean that these basic moral truths are not derived or deduced from other ones that are more basic. It does not mean that everyone knows these truths in their early years or that they are never hindered. We must first be introduced to them by someone or some situation (such as a gross violation of human dignity), but once that introduction has taken place, our moral sense often speaks with a single and clear voice.

David Little is one of the few scholars who have used the theory of intuitionism to justify belief in human rights. He argues that people have certain "primary intuitions" that inform them of certain "taboos," which spell out some of what he calls "the unalterable and universal foundations of human life."[102] He believes, for instance, that the "moral authority of the prohibition against torture rests finally and exclusively on an intuition or recognition of the transparent wrongness of at least certain forms of torture" (83). Article 5 of the Declaration ("No one shall be subjected to torture or to cruel, inhuman or degrading treatment or punishment") supposes that there are indeed clear cases of torture and other forms of inhuman treatment that both victims and perpetrators immediately know to be violations of this universal taboo. Unless, of course, either or both have had their normal conscience blocked or overridden by external or internal deformities. Most of the articles of the Declaration presuppose a clear grasp of one or several basic moral truths. When the drafters voted for everyone's right to an education they did so against the background knowledge that the Nazis had warped the minds of pupils with a sick kind of racism that was bound to undercut every child's right to a full and healthy development of its personality. The delegates did not debate or argue these fundamental truths but treated them as self-evident. Many of the articles and clauses were adopted because the drafters had witnessed or heard about "barbarous acts" which they immediately saw to be "transparently wrong" or "bad in themselves."[103] Intuitionists stress this direct and immediate (meaning nondeductive) character of big chunks of our moral knowledge. Sidgwick might have said that the drafters saw "the wrongness" of what the Nazis did "by simply looking at the actions themselves without considering their [further] consequences."[104]

It is amazing how rescuers uniformly report that they knew beyond the shadow of a doubt that they were doing the right thing when they decided to rescue Jews or other endangered persons from the Nazis. Research has consistently supported the claim that—no matter what their ideological colorings—these rescuers acted with great clarity and certainty of conscience, even if through their actions they exposed themselves and their families to great dangers.[105] The debates about the Declaration reflect this same moral clarity and certainty. The drafters never doubted or argued about whether they should condemn the Nazi acts that inform most of the articles they drafted. Even the communists, who had theoretical doubts about the language of "inherent" rights, in practice joined the enterprise wholeheartedly and made the condemnation a unanimous one. They attended meetings, made proposals, and at times even voted in spite of having made a policy to abstain in formal votes. In short, there was, to use Gass's phrase again, a "moral transparency" and immediacy to what the drafters were doing. This lifted them up beyond the intellectual climate of their day and allowed them to place into world affairs a moral beacon that has inspired the creation of some two hundred international human rights instruments that can be used by an ever-growing movement of human rights activists in all walks of life, in all corners of the world.

Chapter 3
The Shortcomings of the Golden Rule

Having considered the route of conscience into the domain of human rights, we now embark on an investigation of the route of reason that is yoked with conscience in Article 1 of the Declaration. People are frequently torn between these two routes and experience a kind of moral schizophrenia. While their emotions tell them the horrors they witness or learn about are evil and must be stopped and absolutely forbidden, they feel awkward about defending that point of view in the court of reason. While their consciences support the epistemic half of the doctrine of inherence (that all people possess human rights by virtue of their humanity), rationally they are not so sure. When nevertheless pressed to reason things out a bit further my students often fall back on the famous Golden Rule that most of us have been taught in our childhoods: "Do unto others as you would have them do unto you." In this chapter, I explore two uses of that rule, a micro use of it—when it is used by individual human beings—and a macro use of it—when this same rule is used collectively by whole peoples and governments in the shaping of their relations with each other. For the individual use I take the philosopher Alan Gewirth as our guide, and for the collective use I refer to the philosopher John Rawls.

In several of his essays the Islamic scholar Abdullahi Ahmed An-Na'im has argued that the Golden Rule can and should be used to argue for a universal cultural legitimacy of human rights. The rule ("that one should concede to the other whatever one claims for oneself") can be used both to defend human rights internally in particular cultural communities, and "in the cross-cultural search for the content and necessary implications of the inherent dignity and integrity of human beings."[1] Viewed both internally and externally, "human rights are those that a person would claim for herself or himself and must therefore be conceded to all human beings" (366). In this way An-Na'im believes that "the full range of human rights can gain cultural legitimacy everywhere in the world" (367). This is an appealing solution to the challenge of Western ethnocentrism that is so often lodged against the Declaration. A less lofty incarnation of the Enlightenment Goddess of Reason, this rule of reason is thought to have the power of kindling belief in human rights in hamlets of even the remotest corners of the globe. Because the rule already lives in the hearts and minds of people everywhere, it can function like a Trojan horse. All we need to do is draw out the implications of its presence. To someone who says he or she lives or intends to live by this popular rule, we simply need to point out the consequences of that admission. When looked at uncritically, it does indeed seem reasonable to suppose that over time any rights based on this rule will find eventual acceptance in the public playgrounds and hidden torture chambers of any culture or nation whatsoever.

Unfortunately, there are serious difficulties attached to the use of the Golden Rule as a vehicle for the spread of human rights, and in the end I conclude that we should be hesitant about using the rule as the *main* gateway into the metaphysical domain of human rights. When allowed to operate all by itself, without the input of healthy moral sentiments, the rule fails us.

A. Micro: Gewirth's Rationalization

In his writings on the Golden Rule, Alan Gewirth has given us a philosophical rationale for the full scope of all the rights in the Universal Declaration. Gewirth does not link his rationalization program to any specific part of the Declaration's text. However, Norwegian scholar Tore Lindholm does make those connections. Lindholm believes that in UDHR Article 1 the drafters used the Golden Rule (or the principle of reciprocity) as a first premise in an argument from which, together with the Preamble, the rest of the document's articles can be readily deduced. Lindholm reconstructs the drafters' thinking in this simple syllogism: "Only from [1] the normative principle of inherent freedom and equal dignity in conjunction with [2] the interpretation of the contemporary and prospective world situation does [3] a binding commitment to a global human rights system follow."[2] On his reading, the normative principle mentioned in step 1 has embedded within in it a commitment to the Golden Rule or the principle of reciprocity. In this way Lindholm connects the idea of Enlightenment rationality, captured in Article 1's principle of reciprocity, with the rest of the articles of the Declaration.

Whereas both Lindholm and Gewirth see the relationship between the rule and the rights in the Declaration as a deductive one, I see that connection as an inductive one. For Lindholm the flow of the argument goes from step 1, or the Golden Rule as a justificatory principle, combined with the details of the world situation supplied by step 2 and the

Preamble, to step 3 as our commitment to the system of human rights we see operative in the world today. When we ask what might have motivated the drafters to accept Lindholm's principle "of inherent freedom and equal dignity," we cannot answer that it was an awareness of the Nazi atrocities, because these atrocities do not enter the argument until step 2. For Article 1 to serve as the justificatory first principle in Lindholm's proto-argument it must have functioned as a justificatory first principle in the adoption arguments for the other articles in the Declaration, which is doubtful. Lindholm correctly notes that "Article 1 received more time and attention than almost any other [article]," and that the delegates "variously named it 'keystone,' 'basis,' 'foundation,' and 'framework of the rights enumerated in its various articles.'"[3] These comments were made in the Third Committee debate about moving Article 1 to the Preamble. While they underscore the importance of the article, they do not suggest a deductive reconstruction. Fatal to any overtly deductive reconstruction of the Declaration's philosophy is the fact that Article 1 was not discussed and adopted until after all the other articles had already received several coats of paint.

Speculative as any reconstruction will have to be, I find an inductive account of the relationship between Article 1 and the rest of the articles more plausible. Many of the articles and rights in the Declaration were adopted as a direct and immediate reaction to the horrors of the Holocaust. The adoption debates show us that more often than not the drafters went straight from having witnessed or heard about some gross human rights violation to the adoption of the right in question, without the intervention of the Golden Rule. From the medical experiments, they went straight to the right not to be tortured; from the slave labor camps attached to the ovens, straight to decent working conditions; from brainwashing in Nazi schools, straight to the right to development of one's personality without the interference of a sick state-sponsored ideology; from Jews being blocked from escaping Germany, straight to the right to freedom of movement across borders; and from the discriminatory Nuremberg marriage laws, straight to the right to marriage based on the consent of the parties, without state restrictions other than age. And so on. While most delegates probably subscribed to the Golden Rule, they do not seem to have used that rule as a justificatory principle from which they deduced the rights they list in the Declaration.

Even if there is no textual link between the Golden Rule and the justification of the rights in the Declaration, it could, of course, still be that a good case can be made for a purely philosophical reconstruction of a deductive kind. That is what Alan Gewirth's "rationalization" of the Golden Rule means to give us. Gewirth does not think that the rule, as ordinarily conceived, yields a proof of human rights, but that it does do so after he has fixed it. I will use An-Na'im's above-mentioned appeal to the rule to explain the defects Gewirth sees in that kind of use of the rule. After that, I will set out how Gewirth proposes to fix those defects and why I think the result is not good enough. Any application of the rule always involves at least two people, an agent and a recipient. Gewirth points out that both perspectives fail to justify belief in human rights.

If we look at the Golden Rule from the point of view of the agent (the one initiating a certain action), the rule states that I should treat others the way I would want them to treat me. Here the "I" is the person of the agent who needs to decide what standards to use in the treatment of other people. An-Na'im puts it this way: "Placing oneself in the position of the other person, one is able to see if he or she [the agent] would find the treatment to which the other person is subjected inhumane or seriously objectionable" ("Problems," 345). The Gewirth version goes like this: "One should act in relation to others *on the same principles or standards* that one would have them apply to oneself."[4] This version of the rule authorizes the agent to do to the other person whatever the agent wishes as long as he or she is consistent and willing to have that same standard applied to him- or herself. In An-Na'im's example a consistent Muslim would be justified in imposing the Shari'a on non-Muslims, as long as that Muslim is perfectly willing to say that that law should be imposed on himself should he (contrary to fact) turn out to be one of those unbelievers. This perspective would allow any theist to impose on all others a theocratic form of government. Or take Richard Rorty's example of a consistent Nazi. From the agent perspective of the Golden Rule, there would simply be "no way," says Rorty, "to 'refute' a sophisticated, consistent, passionate psychopath—for example, a Nazi who would favor his own elimination if he himself turned out to be Jewish."[5] Gewirth is right when he points out that this agent perspective on the use of the rule is much too restrictive on the life of the recipient. It would lead to grossly unfair and totally immoral situations.

But the recipient perspective fares no better. Here the point of view taken is that of the person to whom the act is being done: do unto others, as *they* would have you do unto them. As An-Na'im puts it, "In placing oneself in the position of the other, one should *not* impose one's own perceptions on the other's position. For example, it should *not* be open to a Muslim to say that since he accepts for himself to be subject to the application of Islamic law (Shari'a), he would conform with the principle of reciprocity in imposing Shari'a on non-Muslims" (345, emphasis added). Following Singer, Gewirth calls this the "inversion" of the Golden Rule, for now instead of all the say going to the agent, it all goes to the recipient. When faced with an application of the rule, we must ask ourselves not what we would like, but what they—the others at whom the action is aimed—want done; their perceptions of the situation should govern our action. If we carry this to its logical conclusion, we would never have any rest, for we would constantly be at the mercies of the wishes of our recipients. We would always be doing what other people want us to do, and our own desires and needs would go unmet.

So we cannot interpret the Golden Rule from the perspective of the agent, for then the recipient will (sometimes literally) have no life, nor can we interpret the rule from the perspective of the recipient, for then the agent will never have any time. Obviously, what the rule supposes— and what most people in most situations in fact do—is to strike a compromise between the needs of the agent and those of the recipient. One throws out the cases of the Nazi who is willing to have himself eliminated (should he turn out to be a Jew, a gypsy, or gay) and of the mother who runs herself ragged meeting the needs of her recipient children. The normal use of the rule supposes that in its application we use a good deal of (moral) common sense. Because of these difficulties, Gewirth claims that the Golden Rule needs to be fixed before it can be used as a foundation stone for our belief in human rights. His way of fixing the rule amounts to a "rationalization" of it, by which he means that the rule can only be used for belief in human rights if we build rational criteria into our use of it. It will then read: "Do unto others as you would rationally want them to do unto you" (Gewirth, "Golden Rule Revisited," 133). The "rationality" requirement refers to the "generic rights" that are the necessary conditions of human agency. Conflicts about the use of the rule will be settled once the two parties see which of the competing desires and wishes are the most rational ones. Those that are most necessary for rational human agency and thus the most generic will get priority, be they the rights of the agent, the recipient, or both. Depending on the situation, my right to life will take priority over your right to freedom of expression, while your right to freedom of expression may take priority over another person's right to freedom of association. And so on. Gewirth's argument for belief in human rights is a multistep argument to determine which desires and wishes meet that test of being necessary for rational human agency.

In most of his expositions Gewirth unpacks his argument in at least thirteen steps. I here give his own much shorter summary in just four steps:

First, every agent holds that the purposes for which he acts are good on whatever criterion (not necessarily a moral one) enters into his purposes. Second, every actual or prospective agent logically must therefore hold or accept that freedom and well-being are necessary goods for him because they are the necessary conditions of his acting for any purposes; hence he holds that he *must* have them. Third, he logically must therefore hold or accept that he has rights to freedom and well-being; for, if he were to deny this, he would have to accept that other persons may remove or interfere with his freedom or well-being, so that he *may not* have them; but this would contradict his belief that he *must* have them. Fourth, the sufficient reason on the basis of which each agent must claim these rights is that he is a prospective purposive agent, so that he logically must accept the conclusion that all prospective purposive agents, equally and as such, have [human] rights to freedom and well-being.[6]

Imagine, if you will, Socrates visiting one of the world's torture chambers and putting his usual dialectical screws on the torturer who works there. Socrates convinces the man to quit his prison job after he converts him to the human rights point of view. Whereas before Socrates' entry into his torture chamber, the torturer took pleasure in torturing people, after listening to Gewirth's argument (here given in summary form), he comes to believe that his way of making a living is totally unethical. He quits his job rather than live with the thought and the fact of contradicting himself and being irrational. Socrates puts the dialectical screws on him by making him see that he cannot claim rights to his own freedom and well-being (because he is a purposive agent and those things are necessary conditions for being such a human agent) and at the same time deny that his victim (who also is such a human agent and therefore can claim the same rights to freedom and well-being) has these same rights. To claim these rights for himself and deny that his victim also has them is to contradict himself. It is like the registrar of a college refusing to let one student with a C- average graduate while letting others walk across the platform when (we are supposing) a C- is the *only* requirement for graduation. The torturer and the registrar are both living lives of self-contradiction. Because he cannot stand to live with that feeling of self-contradiction, the torturer quits his job and the world is the better for it.

The torturer ends up accepting step 13 of the longer version of the argument, which has the same content as the fourth step in the summary: "All prospective purposive agents have rights to freedom and well-being." This admission follows from the fact that the torturer had been claiming that he himself has these rights *solely* on the basis of being a human agent. Any other creature that exhibits rational purposive behavior (or has the potential for it) has the same rights. His sister and his brother are also human agents with the same kind of rights derived from their own rational human agency. The torture victim on the bench before him had been engaged in the human act of voluntarily and intentionally distributing leaflets critical of the regime. But she was then, and still is, a purposive human agent and therefore also has the same rights to freedom and well-being as does our torturer. The word "all" in step 13 covers every member of the human race. It reminds us of the "everyone" or "all" or "no one" with which almost every article of the Declaration starts. Article 5, for instance, states that "No one shall be subjected to torture or to cruel, inhuman or degrading treatment or punishment." Gewirth holds that the first generation of civil and political rights (of the first half of the Declaration) can be derived from the human right to freedom, and the second generation of social, economic, and cultural rights (in the second half of the Declaration) from the human right to well-being.[7] Gewirth is perfectly aware of the fact that not all human beings are born with complete capacities for free and purposive behavior. They may be born severely handicapped, and because of that their human rights are tailored to the impaired state of their human agency, just as we have special provisions for handicapped access to buildings. Different legal systems do this in different ways.

The point before us is that our torturer, to avoid self-contradiction, has to include his victims in the scope of his admission that "All prospective and purposive agents have rights to freedom and well-being." This is not automatic at all, for the world includes a great many people who do not practice what they preach. There are millions of Muslims who do not give alms, communists who sidestep the will of the people, Christians who flaunt Jesus' Sermon on the Mount, Jews who break the Ten Commandments, and torturers who do not quit their jobs even after admitting to step 13. Let us suppose, though, that our imagined torturer does quit his job and walks out of the torture chamber simply because he does not want to contradict himself. He hands in his resignation and stops interfering with the freedom and well-being of his victims. The world rejoices, and a week later Socrates sees him at the grocery store where he works the cash register. He asks the man how he feels and is told that he feels great. He says that it was a more or less fair exchange of one pleasure for another one. He gave up the pleasure he received from torturing people in exchange for the pleasure he now feels when he realizes that he no longer lives a life of contradiction. He thanks Socrates for liberating him from his contradictory lifestyle and goes on his lunch break with a new bounce in his step.

Most students who read Gewirth's argument believe that the torturer has not really been converted to the ideology of human rights. While some of them catch a fine point like the (supposed) equivocation on the meaning of "ought" when the torturer is made to switch from claiming that he *must* have freedom and well-being to claiming that he has *rights* to these things, most of them think he still is the selfish man he was before Socrates engaged him in dialogue. Bernard Williams captures what most of my students want to say in response to Gewirth's argument. I suggest that we make the "I" and the "my" in this citation from Williams refer to the torturer: "The *I* that stands back in rational reflection from my desires is still the *I* that has those desires and will, empirically and concretely, act; and it is not, simply by standing back in reflection, converted into a being whose fundamental interest lies in the harmony of all interests. It cannot, just by taking this step, acquire the motivations of justice."[8] In other words, simply wanting to be rational is not what makes a human being a moral creature. That also requires a sincere interest in the well-being of other human beings, which the torturer lacks. It is helpful to look at our lives the way Robert Nozick does, as an interplay of forces of "moral push" and "moral pull." When the flow of moral energy goes from us *to* others Nozick calls it a case of moral push, and when it comes *from* others to us it is moral pull.[9] As I made clear during my discussion of errant human rights definitions in legal theory (Chapter 1, section C), in my theory of human rights the flow goes from the rights in others to the duties in us, which makes moral pull the dominant epistemic force. The question now is whether the torturer, whom Gewirth converted with his rationalized Golden Rule, quit because of moral push or moral pull.

As Williams and most of my students suspect, the torturer acts out of his own desire for rational consistency, which makes his conversion case primarily one of moral push. Our torturer is not morally pulled to quit out of respect for the inherent rights of his victim, who, we supposed, is a woman caught distributing antigovernment pamphlets and brought in for "questioning." The human rights perspective has built into it a respect for the inherent dignity of others that our torturer does not seem to have acquired when he was "converted" by the Gewirth-Socrates team. He acts out of rational push rather than moral pull, even though—this goes without saying—the world rejoiced when he quit. I conclude that Gewirth's argument for human rights does not deliver what it promises. Our torturer only postulated the rights in his victim after Socrates put the dialectical screws on him. But that kind of postulation conflicts with and even negates the idea of inherent rights that are already present in the victim, ready to awaken our consciences before we reach out for the rule.

The upshot is that reason left to work on its own has not (yet) delivered a knock-down argument for our belief in human rights. While the Golden Rule does capture what ordinary people (to whom the Declaration is addressed) think of as the embodiment of reason and is accepted worldwide, the rule needs to be supplemented and have its content safeguarded and possibly poured in from a deeper source. The rule in effect supposes that those who use it already have a rudimentary understanding of the basics of morality, which keeps them (if they are morally healthy people) from misapplying it, like Rorty's Nazi above, or deracinating it, like Gewirth's torturer. That is to say, the micro-users of the rule must have a healthy conscience and good moral intuitions to be able to use it properly. In the next section I argue that the same qualification holds for the rule's macro-users on an international level.

B. Macro: John Rawls's Ethnocentrism

I begin this second half of my discussion of the Golden Rule with an exploration of the rule's collective use as proposed by John Rawls in his 1999 book *The Law of Peoples*.[10] I defend the thesis that Rawls's late entry into the field of human rights theory does not help us answer the charge of Western ethnocentrism that has been leveled at the Declaration. More disappointing is the fact that he seems to be actually feeding that charge. This disappointment is the more painful because, more than most political theorists writing in the last half of the twentieth century, Rawls shared the drafters' Enlightenment views on the relationship between morality and politics. I trace this flaw to Rawls's reliance on the principle of reciprocity and his neglect of the Holocaust as a causal factor in the entry of human rights into international law. His use of this principle amounts to a macro-version of what I see Gewirth doing with our torturer. Once again it is a case of moral push over moral pull, this time on the grand scale of relations among whole nations and their peoples. Rawls's use of the rule as an international principle to defend and explain the popularity of human rights raises entirely new issues that live on the borderline between human rights and international legal developments since the end of World War II. After I give an exposition of Rawls's macro use of the rule, I will find it wanting because the principle of reciprocity does not do justice to the inherence feature of human rights that is embedded in international human rights law and that goes back to the Universal Declaration as the birthing ground for that system of law. Locating Rawls in this broader landscape of human rights matters a great deal, for he is by all accounts the most influential Anglo-American political theorist of the late twentieth century.

After I have explained what I see as the flawed ethnocentric approach Rawls takes in *The Law of Peoples*, we follow his own suggestion that we go back to the "political constructivism" he defends in his 1993 book *Political Liberalism*.[11] We need to go back there for two reasons. First, Rawls presents the philosophical underpinnings of his law of peoples as an "extension" of the domestic case he sets out in the earlier book. So we need to go there if we are to complete our investigation of the ethnocentric approach we see in his law of peoples. Second, the main competitor of the "political constructivism" Rawls defends in *Political Liberalism* is the theory of classical, rational (his terms), or moral (our term) intuitionism that I adopted at the end of the preceding chapter. I couch my response to Rawls's constructivism in terms of our disagreement about the role the Holocaust played in the development of international human rights law, and argue that in his justification of both domestic and international political orders, Rawls pushes aside or at least minimizes some obvious moral facts of our world. The drafters used the most salient of these facts to write the very Declaration which Rawls acknowledges is a key element in the construction of his Society of Well-Ordered Peoples. These moral facts need to be recognized if we are to have an adequate explanation for and justification of the entry of inherent human rights into the international legal system.

Now that he has branched out into international law, students of Rawls's political theory have to keep separate no less than three Original Positions, each with its own veil of ignorance. The first Original Position is the famous one in Rawls's path-breaking book *A Theory of Justice*. He there updated the social contract theories of the Enlightenment: representatives of heads of families in a modern liberal state are asked to step behind a veil of ignorance so that they may together adopt the principles of justice for the basic structure of their society. These representatives do not know how talented (rich, religious, athletic, and so on) they themselves and the persons they represent are. All they know are the laws of history, general science, and some basic facts about human nature in general. Not knowing any specifics about the households they represent, these representatives will be careful when they bargain about the principles of justice to be adopted. When the veil of ignorance lifts, they will be stuck with the principles they chose, so they will not select any kind of fundamentalist religious polity because they may find out that they (that is, the persons they represent) are atheists. And they will not adopt any kind of utilitarian principle because according to that philosophy the well-being of one individual can in a pinch be sacrificed to save the nation. The standard example is lynching an innocent person to prevent mob violence or civil war. Since one does not know when behind this imagined veil of ignorance whether one will be that particular innocent person, one will not vote for a principle of justice that will organize a society along the lines of calculations that may be detrimental to some individuals but end up benefiting the whole a great deal. To avoid such scenarios, Rawls argues in *A Theory of Justice* that the only two principles that will make it out of the Original Position (that is, emerge from behind the veil) and be unanimously accepted are his Principle of Equality and his Difference Principle. The first states that "each person is to have an equal right to the most extensive basic liberty compatible with similar liberty for others"; the second holds that "social and economic inequalities are to be arranged so that they are both (a) reasonably expected to be to everyone's advantage, and (b) attached to positions and offices open to all."[12]

The book was published in 1971, which means that while Rawls was working out his political theory the human rights movement was starting to take off internationally with the adoption of the two international covenants in 1966, their coming into force in 1977, and the coming on line of numerous other human rights instruments in this norm-setting period in the history of the UN. Yet human rights are not a topic in the index of Rawls's book. He designed his first Original Position with its own veil of ignorance for a domestic case of a liberal society. Many such societies are to be found around the North Atlantic and, as we saw in Chapter 2, section A, they had a strong hand in drawing up these international norms of human rights, but—if Rawls is right—that international task did not figure into their own internal justificatory operations.

In *Political Liberalism* Rawls reworked this first Original Position by historicizing the ideas in it and developing more keenly their political implications. Instead of approaching the contract idea with its veil of ignorance from an abstract philosophical perspective, he presented it foremost as part of a historical development toward an overlapping consensus among citizens who have very different comprehensive doctrines about the meaning of life. What came to preoccupy Rawls was the fact that citizens in today's modern nation-states (with so much immigration taking place) represent an enormous variety of divergent and often incompatible philosophical and religious views of life, views Rawls calls Comprehensive Doctrines (CDs). The same street in a modern democratic state or nation may have on it households that are Muslim, Christian, socialist, libertarian, and some with no deep ideological attachments who pick and choose as necessary. Rawls worried about how such great diversity of outlooks on life could ever be made to support fundamental principles of justice for the same liberal society. Without a solid consensus, modern multicultural nations could not be confident of a stable future, for at any moment they might be ripped apart at the seams by political fights about abortion, the death penalty, health insurance, the place of religion in public life, welfare provisions, and the like.

Rawls therefore constructed what he felt was the best possible case for a liberalism solidly grounded in *political* principles alone, without metaphysics, religion, philosophy, or deep cultural notions of any kind. Casting aside all such reflections, the representatives behind the veil of ignorance adopted the principles Rawls had defended in his earlier book. But this time their reasons for agreeing are drawn more from the realm of political, practical reason and the necessity for fair terms of cooperation than from the more theoretical considerations advanced in the first volume. The representatives are still only interested in the affairs of their own liberal state, and they still do not talk about human rights, which still does not appear in the index. However, they do talk a great deal about "basic liberties," which covers most of the international bill of rights that had been developing as Rawls did his theorizing. The theory of "political constructivism" Rawls expounds in *Political Liberalism* explains why these liberties are adopted as part of the basic structure of a liberal democracy. He opposes his constructivist route to the classical intuitionism I adopted in the preceding chapter as the moral epistemology of belief in human rights. If my own epistemic route into the domain of human rights is to be viable, I must analyze his construction.

Western Ethnocentrism and the Law of Peoples. A second veil of ignorance with two stages or parts to it brings us to the topic of human rights and to the Declaration specifically. This newly added international two-part veil is to be found in *The Law of Peoples*, which Rawls published shortly before his death in 2002. Whereas John Locke elaborated his theory of the social contract long *before* the American colonists used that theory to mount their colonial revolutions, and whereas Jean-Jacques Rousseau performed that same service *before* his compatriots stormed the Bastille, Rawls wrote *Law of Peoples* after the great shifts in international law had already taken place at the end of World War II—after the proverbial cow was out of the barn. He tells us that this is not a good objection to his theory because, like Locke and Rousseau, his interest is in the justification of certain moral considerations as part of political theory. But this caveat does not remove the fact that we can indeed judge Rawls's international veil and contract against the bargaining that I summarized in the opening sections of Chapters 1 and 2. Rawls's theorizing about the entry of human rights into international affairs ignores the consensus that was present in the United Nations in the late 1940s when the Declaration was written.

As Rawls sees it, there are five types of societies or peoples in the world: (1) reasonable liberal peoples, (2) decent hierarchical peoples, (3) outlaw states, (4) societies burdened by unfavorable circumstances, and (5) peoples under benevolent absolutist rulers. All of these types of peoples, with the exception of the outlawed societies of Japan, Italy, and Germany (who had lost the war) were represented at the founding of the UN and at the drafting of the norms set down in the Universal Declaration. They all helped shape the international law of peoples (with a built-in human rights component) as we now know it. However, Rawls's view is not historical in this straightforward sense. He is not so much interested in the historical origin of the eight principles I will cite in a moment as he is in their justification as the content of the law of peoples. From a justificatory point of view he thinks the story should go something like this. First, the liberal peoples of type 1 societies accept what they in their liberal club find to be the "familiar and traditional" eight principles of international law. Then, in the second phase of this international Original Position, this liberal club extends an invitation to the decent hierarchical societies of type 2. These societies accept the invitation to join the liberal club and agree to step behind the same kind of veil and to adopt the same eight principles. That makes for a much-enlarged society of well-ordered peoples, who hope to spread the virus of morality to the other types of peoples.

The representatives behind Rawls's international veil of ignorance—who do not know how big or small, how rich or poor, or how populated the nation they represent is—vouch to each other that as peoples they (1) are to be free and independent; (2) are to observe treaties and undertakings; (3) are to be equal and parties to the agreements that bind them; (4) are to observe the duty of nonintervention; (5) are to have the right to self-defense, but no right to wage aggressive war; (6)* are to honor human rights; (7) are to observe restrictions in the conditions of war; and finally (8)* have a duty to assist other peoples living under unfavorable conditions that prevent them having a just or decent political and social regime. I have starred numbers 6 and 8 because they have our human rights concerns in them and also because they seem to me anything but "familiar and traditional." The promise to honor the human rights, captured by principles 6 and 8, is familiar to us because since the end of World War II they have indeed become an accepted feature of international affairs and law, but they were hardly that in the late 1940s when the Declaration was written to work out the meaning of the seven human rights references in the UN Charter. And number 8 is not even a familiar or agreed-on item today, some sixty years later, though I do think that it should be part of the law of peoples. That leaves for our present focus the question of how number 6 got to be on this list of international legal principles and what the role of the Declaration is in that story.

These eight principles include two significant changes that took place in international law after the Second World War, both of which involve a limitation of what until then had been the almost limitless sovereignty of the nation-states that make up the international system. One was a limitation on the external sovereignty of these states, in that the new system forbade them to engage in wars of aggression, as Hitler had repeatedly done. The second limitation was on the internal sovereignty of states, telling states that they could no longer do to the people within their borders as they wished. Both limitations were written into the Charter of the UN and into the charges against the defendants at the International War Crimes Trials that were held after the war, in Nuremberg and Tokyo, as well as in the statutes of the international tribunals that we highlighted in Chapter 2, section B. The design of the international veil and contract is that the liberal club *first* adopts these eight principles and *then* extends an invitation to decent societies to join their club, in the hope that other not-yet-decent societies will transform themselves into well-ordered peoples and then also want to join the society of liberal and well-ordered, decent peoples. Let us for the moment suppose that the first phase of the international contract went very smoothly and that the club of liberal democratic nations (mostly) from around the North Atlantic had no problem coming to an agreement on the eight "familiar and traditional principles of justice among free and democratic peoples" (37). *If* the liberal peoples of the world got together to select the rules by which they would cooperate in their mutual affairs, *then*, so argues Rawls, they would select the eight principles he lists. These eight principles are now to constitute the content of the updated law of peoples. That having been done, let us take a brief look at the role of human rights in the invitation this club extends to decent peoples, and also at the ethnocentrism of the process involved.

Critics have noted that in a long note (*LP*, 80, n. 23) Rawls tells us that there are three sets of rights in the Universal Declaration. First there is the set of human rights "proper," which are to be found in Articles 3 through 18 of the document. While the implications of this "short" list of "proper" human rights might stretch farther than some critics allow,[13] it is important to note that Rawls cuts the list of proper rights just before those that are political in nature, namely Articles 19, 20, and especially Article 21 on equal participation in government. It is regrettable that when Rawls finally did take notice of the Universal Declaration, he did not see these democratic rights as part of a "proper" list of human rights. (We will return to this issue in Chapter 6.) Instead, he felt that "Articles 3 to 18 may all be put under this heading of human rights proper, pending certain questions of interpretation." The rights through Article 18 (to life; liberty; security of person; to a fair trial; to privacy; freedom of movement; asylum and citizenship; to be able to marry and have property; and to freedom of thought, conscience, and religion) are one and all thought "proper" human rights. We are not told what makes them "proper" and why the list should stop here. Before stopping at the end of Article 18 and the set of democratic rights, with Article 16's stipulation that there shall "no limitation due to race, nationality or religion" when it comes to marriage rights, Rawls has already offended the decent hierarchical societies to which the invitation to join the international club is being sent,.

That is not likely to sit well in his imaginary Kazanistan, or, for that matter, in the real Muslim nations of the late 1940s or even today. He has also put a thorn in the flesh of these Islamic nations by calling the rights in Article 18 "proper" ones. Perhaps this is where the "pending" questions of interpretation enter in, for many Muslim nations were greatly offended by everyone's right "to change his religion or belief." So much so that Saudi Arabia, which is as good a candidate as any for being one of Rawls's decent societies, abstained in the final vote on the adoption of the Declaration. Why then not go on and add the rights to freedom of expression (Article 19) and to freedom of peaceful assembly and associa-tion (Article 20) to the list of proper human rights? Why stop at Article 18? The reason is that the public authorities of the imagined decent society would not permit the kind of public dissent allowed for in Ar-ticles 19 and 20. Nor would they accept everyone's right to "take part in the government of his country" through "periodic elections, which shall by universal and equal suffrage and shall be held by secret vote or by equivalent free voting procedures." These stipulations of Article 21 spell out how the will of the people, which the article says "shall be the basis of the authority of government," is to be brought to expression. These demands do not fit and are not the equivalent of the consultation proce-dures Rawls has in mind as typical of the decent societies to be invited. These same elites also would not like everyone's right to "equal access to public service in his country" as required by 21(2). Whether by design or accident, Rawls has cut all specifically *political* human rights from the list of human rights proper. From the perspective of the drafters he has put the proverbial cart before the horse. Whereas they responded to the radical evil of Hitler's autocracy (which he began building when he suspended the rights in Articles 18–21) on a moral level, Rawls takes his point of departure from the political and foreign policy considerations of liberal democratic societies. I argue below that that is too narrow a point of departure.

The second class of rights found in the Declaration is an "obvious implication" of this first set and "covers the extreme cases described by special conventions on genocide (1948) and on apartheid (1973)." These two sets of rights, omitting Articles 18–21, are used by Rawls in his exposition of the common good conception of justice that allows Kazanistan into the society of well-ordered peoples. I discuss this ad-mission below. In addition to this short set (with its implications), the Declaration includes a third class of human rights that is, says Rawls, "more aptly described as stating liberal aspirations, such as Article 1 of the Universal Declaration of Human Rights of 1948," which he then quotes. He goes on: "Others appear to presuppose specific kinds of institutions, such as the right to social security, in Article 22, and the right to equal pay for equal work, in Article 23." Rawls does not include these social, economic, and cultural rights of the Declaration among the human rights "proper" of his short list, though at several points he does include the item of personal property. I defend their inclusion in Chapter 3 and comment on Rawls's dismissal of Articles 1 and 2 in the text below. While most commentators have criticized Rawls's short list and have sought to reconstruct how he might have arrived at his short-ened version of the usual longer liberal list,[14] our discussion asks how the sixth principle to honor human rights came to be on Rawls's list of eight international law principles. We agree that Rawls's list is too short, but add the criticism that it is wrongly arrived at.

Two criteria will be used for the invitation that is extended to decent societies. The first is that they may not threaten other peoples with war. The second one has three parts to it, all having to do with the kind of legal system that is operative in decent societies. Such a legal system "se-cures for all members of the people what have come to be called human rights" (*LP*, 65). It views all the persons within a given territory "as re-sponsible and cooperating members of their respective groups . . . in ac-cordance with their moral duties and obligations as members of these groups" (*LP*, 66). That law must be guided by "the common good idea of justice which assigns rights to all members of a people," which means that the judges and other officials of this system will not tolerate systematic violations of these legally assigned rights. There is in this society a certain reciprocity between ruler and ruled. We should note that in these decent societies, human rights are not seen as inherent in the individual citizen; they instead accrue to citizens *as* members of certain groups. This conflicts with our claim that a human right is inherent in a person because of his or her humanity.[15] Since Rawls does not hold this view of inherence, it does not bother him that a decent society may have Hegel's view of per-sons as "first" belonging "to estates, corporations, and associations—that is, groups," from which group membership they derive their basic rights and duties (*LP*, 73). Aside from this crucial qualification, the list of rights that decent societies are asked to embrace is fairly extensive: "the right to life (to the means of subsistence and security); to liberty (to freedom from slavery, serfdom, and forced occupation, and to a sufficient mea-sure of liberty of conscience to ensure freedom of religion and thought); to property (personal property); and to equality as expressed by the rules of natural justice (that is, that similar cases be treated similarly)" (65). But it does not include Article 2's long list of nondiscrimination items, which means that there can be widespread discrimination in de-cent societies. "Human rights, as thus understood," Rawls adds, "cannot be rejected as peculiarly liberal or special to the Western tradition. They are not politically parochial" (65). Rawls is aware that the challenge of ethnocentrism is hanging over his procedure, and my point in this sec-tion is that he does not meet it successfully.

One way of meeting it would be to adopt a large enough concept of what a human right is, so that it can accommodate different concep-tions of the idea. It is evident that human rights are not seen by Rawls as rights that belong to a person as an unqualified birthright, for then he would have had theoretical objections to a decent society's corporatist way of distributing these rights and liberties. And he would not have dismissed Article 1 of the Universal Declaration as merely "stating liberal aspirations" that have no place in a purely political (as over against a philosophical) rationale for human rights.[16] His institutional approach to human rights makes him define these rights as "intrinsic to the Law of Peoples" (*LP*, 80). So he sees their universality not in terms of the metaphysics of inherence, but because their "political (moral) force extends to all societies, and [because] they are binding on all peoples and societies, including outlaw states" (80–81). The universality of human rights is being read off from the fact that any violations of these rights may make violators liable to sanctions from the international community. It is the universal threat of these international sanctions that makes these rights everywhere binding and therefore universal on our globe, and not the fact of their inherence in the human person.[17] This puts Rawls in the group of theorists (discussed in Chapter 1) who commit the fallacy of implementation because they pull the measures of implementation into the very definition of what a human right is. The role of human rights in his law of peoples is to "set a necessary, though not sufficient, standard for the decency of domestic political and social institutions. In doing so they limit admissible domestic law of societies in good standing in a reasonably just Society of Peoples" (80). The question we will come to shortly is how the international community came to decide on that particular "standard for . . . decency." To reveal the importance of that question I will first need to draw out more of the ethnocentric character of the liberal club's invitation. For the sake of argument we are granting Rawls the first stage of the international veiled situation and will suppose that the liberal societies had no trouble agreeing on the eight principles that are to constitute the Law of Peoples.

It is already clear that this is a profoundly ethnocentric scenario. The parties of the liberal club "select from among the different formulations and interpretations of the 8 principles of the Law of Peoples, as illustrated by the reasons mentioned for the restrictions of the two [external and internal] powers of sovereignty" (40). These eight principles express "what we would accept as fair—you and I here and now, in specifying the basic terms of cooperation" (33), and the representatives of the liberal club "simply reflect on the advantage of these principles among people and see no reason to depart from them or to propose alternatives" (41). This meeting behind the veil is nothing but a foreign policy workshop. The representatives ask themselves "What kind of political norms do liberal peoples, given their fundamental interests, hope to establish to govern mutual relations among themselves and with non-liberal peoples?

Or what moral climate and political atmosphere do they wish to see in a reasonably just Society of well-ordered Peoples? In view of their fundamental interests, liberal peoples limit a state's right to engage in war to wars of self-defense . . . and their concern for human rights leads them to limit a state's right of internal sovereignty" (42). This Rawlsian scenario suggests that the world's interest in the protection of human rights originates with this liberal democratic subgroup of all those peoples who are or might be members of the Society of Well-Ordered Peoples.[18] "The Law of Peoples proceeds from the international political world as we [liberals] see it, and concerns what the foreign policy of a reasonable just people should be" (83). If we wanted to know why any one of the members of this liberal democratic club had acquired an interest in the protection of human rights, Rawls refers us back to his exposition of that topic in his *Political Liberalism*. We will go there in a moment, but I first want to push on to phase two of this international Original Position. We need to see how Rawls proposes to meet the ethnocentric challenge that he has now built in to his procedural approach to international justice.

The real challenge for the liberal club is to spread their consensus on human rights to the other four types of societies. They begin with an invitation to the second type of society, which comprises what Rawls calls decent hierarchical societies and for which he draws us a portrait of his imaginary Kazanistan (*LP*, para. 9.3). The veil of ignorance which bars philosophical and metaphysical considerations is still in place, and the invitation to other societies is not based on any of these CDs, which is why the corporatist view of human rights is allowed in as a bona fide conception of what a human right is. The decent hierarchical societies which are being asked to embrace the eight principles do so because they see or trust that the liberal peoples are actually willing to live by the principle of reciprocity, which is the principle of equal respect for peoples that is embodied in the Law of Peoples. The liberal peoples have no compunction about offering these principles to others because "These fair terms are those that a people sincerely believes other equal peoples might accept also; and should they do so, a people will honor the terms it has proposed even in those cases where that people might profit by violating them. . . . Thus, the criterion of reciprocity applies to the law of peoples in the same way it does to the principles of justice for a [domestic] constitutional regime" (35).[19] For Rawls the "peculiar evil of Nazism" did not first of all lie in the abomination that is the Holocaust, but in the "characteristic of Hitler that he recognized no possibility at all of a political relationship with his enemies" (99). This foreign policy perspective fails to explain the entry into international law of the two human rights principles that are included in the eight cited principles. It ignores the specific role that the Holocaust played in the writing of the Declaration and in the development of the worldwide consensus described in Chapter 2, section A. What made the representatives of the forty-eight nations (and the eight abstentions) commit their countries "to honor human rights" had very little to do with the principle of reciprocity and a great deal with the specific horrors of the Holocaust.

Rawls presents the argument in his *Law of Peoples* as "an *extension* of the liberal conception of political justice in democratic societies" (85; emphasis added). He says: "It is important to understand that the Law of Peoples is developed within liberalism. This beginning point means that the Law of Peoples is an extension of a liberal conception of justice for a domestic regime to a Society of Peoples" (56). He aptly observes that this shift from the local liberal to the more inclusive law of peoples is not "necessarily ethnocentric." Not necessarily, but it might be, and we should ask what prevents it from being just that. Rawls answers that "Whether it is so turns on the content of the Law of Peoples that liberal societies embrace. The objectivity of that law surely depends not on its time and place or culture of origin, but on whether it satisfies the criterion of reciprocity" (121). This is a key point in our disagreement. For our theory the time and the place, namely, the UN in the 1940s, do matter a great deal, for they help us understand the objectivity of the human rights plank far more than does the principle of reciprocity. We already saw that the nations that wrote the UN Charter and immediately thereafter the Universal Declaration were by no means a club of liberal democratic societies that "ask[ed] of other societies only what they can reasonably grant without submitting to a position of inferiority or domination." (121) The variety of polities, religious, economic, legal, and cultural traditions represented around the drafting tables was far too varied to make Rawls's reconstruction plausible. As I explained them in the first section of Chapter 2, even the eight abstentions were not really the result of a rejection of the idea of human rights. They were all based on fairly specific objections to particular features of the document. What the drafters discussed most is what rights they needed to list in order to protect individual human beings from abuses of state power such as Hitler had perpetrated. Political motives do now and admittedly did then play a role in the negotiations between peoples and their governments, but it is quite clear from the *travaux préparatoires* that documents like the Genocide Convention and the Universal Declaration hail from about as pure a moral ground as we are ever likely to get in international affairs and law.

Rawls believes that what "enabled the law [of peoples] to be universal in its reach" was that "The principle [of reciprocity] asks of other societies only what they can reasonably endorse once they are prepared to stand in a relation of fair equality with all other societies. They cannot argue that being in a relation of equality with other peoples is a western idea. In what other relation can a people and its regime reasonably expect to stand?" (122). I do not think that the principle of reciprocity is in this way basic to the entry of the human rights principle into international law, though it is no doubt crucial in other areas of public international law. When one government breaks a bilateral treaty on, let us say, the use of certain fishing grounds, the other is likely to say that it too will no longer honor the agreed-on limits. In this way reciprocity can be seen as the major glue for public diplomatic, commercial, and other areas of international law. But this is not true of human rights treaties and conventions. Take, for instance, the 1948 Genocide Convention. It makes no sense for people A (or their government) to say that if the dictator of nation B commits crimes of genocide, people A will also no longer respect the lives of whichever minority or majority is the hated one within their territory. Commenting on the motivation that states have for adhering to this convention, the International Court of Justice has pointed out that "In such a Convention States do not have any interests of their own, they merely have, one and all, a common interest, namely, the accomplishment of the high purposes which are the raison d'être of the Convention. Consequently in a convention of this type one cannot speak of individual advantages or disadvantages to the States, or the maintenance of a perfect contractual balance between rights and duties."[20] The same is true of the bulk of the two hundred human rights instruments now extant. The individual human person (and not just the state) has gained a standing in international law precisely because questions of international reciprocity were downplayed or filtered out at this crucial moment in history.

Rawls does not ignore the impact of the Holocaust on developments of international law. Two things motivated the emergence of his law of peoples. "The first is that the great evils of human history—unjust war, oppression, religious persecution, slavery and the rest—result from political injustice, with it cruelties and callousness. The second is that once political injustice has been eliminated by following just (or at least decent) social policies and establishing just (or at least decent) basic institutions, these great evils will eventually disappear" (126). For Rawls the connection between history and morality is a general, pragmatic, and diplomatic one: "The fact of the Holocaust and our now knowing that human society admits this demonic possibility, however, should not affect our hopes as expressed by the idea of a realistic utopia and Kant's *foedus pacificum*. Dreadful evils have long persisted. . . . Were these evils greater or lesser than the Holocaust? We need not make such comparative judgments. Great evils are sufficient unto themselves" (21–22). "Yet we must not allow these great evils of the past and present to undermine our hope for the future of our society as belonging to a Society of liberal and decent peoples around the world" (22). That is true, but we can go much further than that and say that something good, an international bill of rights, came out of this abomination. What Rawls's account ignores is the fact that the *particular evils* of the Holocaust shaped the *particular entry* into international law of numerous clauses and articles in the Universal Declaration.

When it comes to the emergence of human rights in international law and affairs, Rawls puts the cart before the horse. For him the duties of peoples and states regarding human rights are derived from the law of peoples (which itself is the result of reciprocal thinking), while in my theory those same duties derive from preexistent (inherent) human rights. While he follows Rousseau and places the contract before the recognition of human rights, I follow Locke and place the rights before the contract. Here I see Rawls putting the cart up front: "It is significant that peoples' rights and duties in regard to their so-called sovereignty derive from the law of peoples itself, to which they would agree along with other peoples in suitable circumstances. As just or decent peoples, the reasons for their conduct accord with the corresponding principles. They are not moved [as states might be] solely by their prudent or rational interests, the so-called reasons of state" (27). True enough, there may well be an important difference between peoples and states. But these peoples in their collectivities must somehow act and make their collective wills known. To do that, they must act through the governments they set up, as they did, for instance, in the late 1940s, by sending delegates to New York and Paris to draft an international bill of rights. While they were gathered in the drafting chamber they looked out, saw the horrors of the Holocaust, and were shocked into an awareness of the preexisting sacred dignity of individual human beings. This made them inject principle 6 (and plausibly 8) into Rawls's list for his law of peoples.

The principle of reciprocity cannot carry the weight of this human rights validation all by itself. What the Nazis did to the Jews, and the Hutus to the Tutsis, is not *in the first instance* a question of political justice between peoples, as such. What ties states and their peoples together in their commitment to fight the crime of genocide and human rights violations generally are "the high purposes" that bring them together when they draft treaties to effectuate that shared commitment. René Provost has made a comparative study of human rights law and humanitarian law on their respective use of the principle of reciprocity as a motivating force. He concludes his section on reciprocity and human rights law with the observation that "the nature and purpose of customary human rights norms a fortiori indicates minimal relevance for reciprocity in their creation."[21] A problem with Rawls's description of his "law of peoples" is that he does not break up that large domain of international law into several sections, one of which would then be human rights law. While reciprocity plays a crucial role in the creation and maintenance of big chunks of public international law, this is not true of the origin of international human rights law and fits only slightly better with that of international humanitarian law. Provost cites the European Commission telling Austria and Italy that the purpose of the European Convention of Human Rights "was not to create reciprocal obligations and rights, but rather to establish a common public order" that respects the human rights of individuals (*International Human Rights*, 134). And he cites the Inter-American Court of Human Rights as holding that the point of the American Convention on Human Rights is not "the reciprocal exchange of state [and peoples'] rights and obligations" but that it constitutes "a series of parallel unilateral undertakings by states to abide by certain human rights standards" (135). The "beneficiaries" of the "new legal order" so created "are not states [or peoples] but individuals."

If reciprocity had played a large role in the creation of international human rights norms, states would far more frequently ring the alarm bell about other states not fulfilling their obligations under the various treaties they have signed and ratified. But inter-state human rights complaints are very infrequent. Most of the time we find out that some government or other is violating human rights through any one of the thousands of domestic or international NGOs like Amnesty International, Human Rights Watch, Oxfam, or Doctors Without Borders. In part because states are not usually the ones to complain when other states in the system grossly violate human rights, several human rights conventions have attached to them complaint procedures for individuals. In these cases an individual can (when his or her state has signed this feature and when the individual has exhausted all domestic avenues of redress) lodge a complaint with an international Human Rights Committee (as is the case with the ICCPR and Torture Convention) or with a regional Human Rights Commission (as in Latin America and recently in Africa) or with a regional Human Rights Court (as in Europe and recently in Africa). None of these individual complaint procedures fit well with Rawls's reciprocity motif.

Political Constructivism and Moral Intuitionism. For the remainder of our discussion of Rawls's views I want to tie together two loose ends so as to explicitly defend the theory of classical moral intuitionism as an epistemic route into the domain of human rights. We have seen that Rawls presents his law of peoples as an "extension" of the domestic case for liberal democratic theory. This calls for an evaluation of the "political constructivism" Rawls offers in *Political Liberalism* and which he says is superior to the moral intuitionism I have adopted for my theory. Our disagreement will hinge on my claim that Rawls overlooks some crucial moral facts that are lying around on the floor of his constructivist workshop and whose importance he underestimates.

In *Political Liberalism,* Rawls is very much focused on the phenomenon of multiculturalism in liberal societies and on ways citizens with very different comprehensive doctrines about the meaning of life and society can reasonably agree on the guidelines for the basic structure of their society.[22] Given the multiplicity of CDs, Rawls believes that his theory of "political constructivism" (which sees no need for any extrapolitical metaphysical, religious, moral, or cultural philosophizing) is the only reasonable approach to take to the adoption of the two principles of justice that he carried over from *A Theory of Justice.* Constructivism's main competitor is the theory of classical or rational intuitionism, which holds that there is an independent realm of moral values and facts that people can come to know and then use to establish the principles of justice and the basic liberties that are the hallmark of liberal democratic societies. Rawls offers three possibilities for grounding the terms of cooperation. The representatives of the citizens behind the veil of ignorance can (1) think of these terms as laid down "by God's law"; or (2) they can, as did the Declaration drafters, come to accept them "as fair in view of their knowledge of an independent moral order"; or (3) they can see them, as Rawls proposes that they do, as "established by an undertaking among these persons themselves in view of what they regard as their reciprocal advantage" (*PL,* 97). Rawls believes that the fact of pluralism in our modern world prevents citizens from agreeing "on any moral authority, whether a sacred text, or institution. Nor do they agree about the order of moral values, or the dictates of what some regard as natural law." "Thus, it is only by affirming a constructivist conception—one which is political and not metaphysical—that citizens generally can expect to find principles that all can accept" (97). This phenomenon of multiple and conflicting CDs keeps the first two approaches from being adopted behind the veil. This leaves reciprocity once again as the motivating force for the political order being constructed, this time a domestic one that we already saw Rawls extend into an international one. (It also suffers the defects of Gewirth's micro (domestic) use of Golden Rule explored in the previous section.)

Using the drafting chambers of New York and Paris as a foil for Rawls's (international or domestic) Original Position, I have argued that the drafters accepted an order of values they saw as independent of themselves and as true of the world in which they lived. Rawls objects that when intuitionism accepts moral first principles and judgments as correct and sees them "as true statements about an independent order, this order does not depend on, nor is it to be explained by, the activity of any (actual) human minds, including the activity of reason" (91). This is correct, if Rawls means that intuitionists claim that the *existence* of human rights as moral facts does not depend on the operation of any actual human mind. The language and metaphysics of "inalienable," "inherent," and "born with" express this belief in an independent moral order. But, of course, there is a dependence on the activity of the human mind as to how human beings *might come to know* about these moral rights, for people need to engage the cognitive capacities of their reason or conscience (served by memory) to get access to this realm of inalienable and inherent rights. To use our perceptual or cognitive capacities to come into contact with the independent world of the physical objects around us does not mean that that world is somehow dependent for its existence on our use of those capacities for discovery. Our gaining access in this way does not negate that world's independence. Intuitionists hold the same to be true of the realm of moral values. Rawls explains that political liberalism "does not however, as rational intuitionism does, use (or deny) the concept of truth; nor does it question that conception. . . . Rather, within itself the political conception does without the concept of truth . . . the idea of the reasonable makes an overlapping consensus possible in ways the concept of truth may not" (94). Again "In any case, it is up to each comprehensive doctrine to say how its idea of the reasonable connects with its concept of truth, should it have one." Rawls would have us think that while each individual drafting delegate might have affirmed the rights in the Declaration as true (depending on his or her personal CD), the document as a whole should not be read this way. That I doubt. The reaction to the Holocaust was too uniform for us not to think that *as entire delegations* nations' votes confirmed these rights as truly attaching to or being inherent in every human being.

When it comes to the alleged objectivity of any principles of justice that are chosen behind the veil (like the Principle of Equality and the Difference Principle cited above), Rawls says that one "may conceive of correct judgments in the familiar way as true of an independent order of values, as in rational intuitionism; or, as in political constructivism, it may see correct judgments as reasonable: that is as supported by the preponderance of reasons specified by the principles of right and justice issuing from a procedure that correctly formulates the principles of practical reason in union with appropriate conceptions of society and persons" (*PL*, 111). The entry of human rights (as basic liberties) into the political order is here portrayed as the result of representatives following certain *correct procedures* instead of their looking out of the windows of the drafting chamber, being outraged by the killing fields they see, and *for that reason* stipulating that any political order (whether domestic or international) must protect human rights. On Rawls's account human rights result when delegates to conferences follow procedures of practical reason (like the principle of reciprocity or the Rawlsian Principles of Equality and Difference). Our theory offers a more inductive approach that is closer to historical reality.

Rawls compounds the problem when he injects the notion of an expert into his account of what makes his principles of justice objective. A conception of objectivity "must distinguish the objective point of view—as given by the point of view of certain appropriately defined reasonable and rational agents—from the point of view of any particular agents, individual or corporate, or of any particular group of agents, at any particular time" (*PL*, 112). All along, my point has been that the Declaration—though written by very well-educated people—was addressed to the average citizen, alien, or refugee on any of the world's highways or byways. According to Rawls, the account of agreement among reasonable agents "may say, as in intuitionism, that reasonable agents have the intellectual and moral powers that enable them to know the independent order of values and to examine adjust and coordinate their judgments concerning it by discussion and reflection; or . . . it may see reasonable persons as able to learn the concepts and principles of practical reason" (*PL*, 112). Siding with the intuitionist option, I have presented the drafters as reasonable agents who had the intellectual and moral powers to make the judgment that what had been done in the camps conflicted with "an independent order of values."

What makes the claims of rights in the document objective is not that experts vouched for them on the basis of certain shared "concepts and principles of practical reason," but that they recognized these rights in response to the wrongs they had witnessed. While both intuitionist and constructivists make reasonable judgments, Rawls "accuses" intuitionists of "add[ing] that a reasonable judgment is true, or probably true (depending on the strength of reasons), of an independent order of values—political constructivism would neither assert or deny that. For its aims . . . the concept of reasonable suffices" (*PL*, 113). We see here that Rawls bars the concept of truth from the domain of public political and moral discussions, a very counterintuitive move. Rawls is right when he tells us that intuitionists object that his nonmetaphysical "constructivism lacks a proper conception of the truth of moral judgments, one that views moral principles as being true or false of an independent order of values. Political constructivism does not use this idea of truth" (*PL*, 114).

These citations draw out the sharp contrasts between the realist intuitionist theory I have used to explain the birth of the Universal Declaration and Rawls's constructivist explanation of how human rights came

to be part of international law. Classical intuitionists hold that most ordinary people, and a good many theorists as well, engage in political
debates to ascertain what the truth is about various social and political
values. If there is no truth to be found there, why do so many people
argue so heatedly about public policies? If there were no truths at stake,
why did the debates in the Third Committee, of which we make so much
use in this book, come to called "the Great Debates"? By dropping the
truth claims made by the drafters and turning the drafters into reasonable diplomats motivated by the principle of reciprocity, Rawls's reconstruction of what happened leaves out the crucial moral facts that are the
real facts of the case. I call these the "moral facts" because the human
rights movement took off specifically in response to the moral wrongs of
the Holocaust, which is not to say that similar wrongs at other times or
places could not have elicited similar responses. The bargaining when
human rights entered international law was nothing like the ordinary
bargaining that takes place between equal parties on the basis of reciprocity. It was bargaining about how to state succinctly the truths they
pretty much all accepted and held dear, such as the ones that everyone
has a right to health care, to an education, to meaningful work, and not
to be tortured or blocked in freedom of movement.

When I said above that the Declaration's drafters were horrified when
they looked out of their drafting chamber, I was admitting that events
in the world caused them to be confirmed in the beliefs they enshrined
in their document, such as that "all human beings are born free and
equal in dignity and rights." In the realm of the political, Rawls's theory
rejects this kind of causal connection between what we see and what
we are justified in believing: "Constructivism holds that the objectivity
of practical reason is independent of the causal theory of knowledge."
There are "different conceptions of objectivity appropriate for theoretical and practical reason." In the former case it has to do with "knowledge
of a given object" and in the latter case with "knowledge of produced
objects." We must "suitably construct the principles of right and justice
that specify the conception of those objects we are to produce and in this
way guide our public conduct by practical reason" (*PL*, 117). For Rawls
human rights are man-made objects of production and construction;
they are not objects that we find inherent in human beings. They are not
inalienable, for what legislators (or representatives behind a veil) make
and produce, they can also take away. For Rawls, "political convictions
(which are, also, of course, moral convictions) are objective—actually
grounded on an order of reasons—if reasonable and rational persons
who are sufficiently intelligent and conscientious in exercising their
powers of practical reason, and whose reasoning exhibits none of the familiar defects of reasoning, would eventually endorse those convictions,

or significantly narrow their differences about them, provided that these persons know *the relevant facts* and have sufficiently surveyed the grounds that bear on the matter under conditions favorable to due reflection" (*PL*, 119, emphasis added).

This long and complicated proposition is Rawls's substitute for the much crisper and truer (to what happened) Second Recital of the Declaration, where we are told that the Third UN General Assembly was motivated by the "disregard and contempt for human rights [that] ha[d] resulted in barbarous acts which have outraged the conscience of mankind." Rawls postulates success in a meeting of the minds, and says of it that there is here "no defect in reasons of right and justice that needs to be made good by connecting them with a causal process" (*PL*, 119). Why then is it necessary (as the long citation above demands) for the representatives of the people to know and reflect on "the relevant facts"? Might they be the facts of the moral wrongness of what the Nazis did in the camps, or what the Khmer Rouge did in their killing fields, or the Hutus in their school yards, or the rebels in the Darfur villages? Why this ambivalence here between the "order of reasons" and what ordinary people with a functioning conscience know to be the obvious moral wrongs of our world?

The answer is that political constructivism deals in two kinds of facts. "One kind is cited in giving reasons why an action or institution is, say, right or wrong or just or unjust. These facts are the so-called right-and-wrong-making characteristics. The other kind is about the content of justice or the nature of the virtues, or the political conception itself. . . . They are given by the nature of the constructivist procedure" (*PL*, 121–22). I fail to see why it is that certain "right-and-wrong-making-characteristics" do not at certain times, as when bills of rights are drawn up, constitute the "content of justice." Rawls uses the example of slavery to explain the difference.

To illustrate the first fact, to argue that slavery is unjust we appeal to the [moral] fact that it allows some persons to own others as their property and thus to control and own the product of their labor. To appeal to the second kind of fact we may appeal straightway to the fact that the principles of justice as fairness condemn slavery as unjust. So there is a fairly close relationship between these [moral] facts and the principles that are the content of the constructivist procedure. *Not the fact that slavery is wrong is constructed,* but the principle that casts additional light on that fact. The constructivist procedure is framed to yield the principles and criteria that specify which facts about actions, institutions, persons and the social world generally, are relevant in political deliberations. (*PL*, 122; emphasis added)

I suggest a reversal of the moral facts (for example, that slavery is wrong) and the principles drawn from the constructivist procedure. Historically, the representatives who drew up the UN Charter, the Genocide Convention, and the Universal Declaration were one and all appalled by the horrors of the Holocaust. The moral wrongs perpetrated by the Nazis were present and visible to them. It was the sight of those wrongs that made these representatives first put the seven human rights references into the UN Charter and afterward follow them up with the Genocide Convention and Universal Declaration, all within three years after the conclusion of the War. These documents do include numerous explicit and implicit international rules and regulations. But it was not the existence or creation of these rules and regulations that enabled the representatives to see which facts would help them construct a better world and which facts they could just let be. Rather, the particular moral wrongs of the Holocaust screamed at them and made them realize that certain principles and regulations needed to be put in place to protect the dignity of the human person and to make the world a safer place for individuals and nations to carry on their affairs. In short, recognition of the moral facts came before drawing up a set of principles. On Rawls's reading, certain political principles confirm moral facts as relevant to political decision making; in my theory, recognition of the moral facts outside the drafting chambers of international organizations is a sine qua non for drawing up the right kind of rules. The drafters came up with a host of such facts before they ever had the benefit of Rawls's or anyone else's theorizing.

But Rawls's position about these alleged "moral facts" is difficult to ascertain. I believe I was justified in inserting the adjective "moral" before "fact" in the long paragraph I quoted because in the italicized phrase Rawls admitted that it was not a constructed fact. What then could it be other than a nonconstructed moral fact of the kind intuitionists claim they see and bump into? To further underline this difference between our views, I also inserted certain moral adjectives in the citations of this and the next paragraph. Rawls admits that there is "a fact" about slavery— that it "allows some people to [wrongfully] own others as their property [t]hat is . . . already there, so to speak, and independent of the principles of justice. The idea of constructing [moral] facts seems incoherent. In contrast, the idea of a constructivist procedure yielding principles and precepts to identify which [moral] facts are to count as reasons is quite clear" (*PL*, 122). Rawls consistently leaves out the adjective "moral" before "facts" in sentences like these. He must want to give the impression that it is only after these "facts" about people owning others as their property have been made pertinent to the issue at hand by the relevant political principles that they become moral facts. For the intuitionist these are moral facts from the start and before any theoretical vetting takes place. The moral fact that slavery is wrong does not need to await the selection from behind the veil of ignorance to become one of history's most gruesome wrongs. The great evils of history speak for themselves. They need no confirmation from behind the veil to make their impact on sound political theorizing. The relationship goes the other way: sound political theorizing must heed the moral fact of people owning other people as property is wrong. As long as we stick to the basics of morality, the constructivist procedure does not add any "additional light." When it comes to drawing up principles and writing constitutions diplomats and theorists need to take these basic moral facts into account and be guided by them. At the end of the war there was no "framework of reasoning" that helped "identify the facts that are relevant from the appropriate point of view and to determine their weight as reasons" (*PL*, 122). The horrors of the Holocaust spoke for themselves, and once they were exposed, both ordinary people and diplomats were outraged. This shared revulsion about the existing facts led them to cooperate in the construction of a system of rules based on the moral norms that had been violated.

While Rawls believes that there is no conflict between a "constructivist political conception" of justice and "our common sense ideas of truth and matters of [moral] fact" (*PL*, 122), I do hold there to be a conflict between these two when it comes to the question of how human rights entered the international legal arena. Rawls asks the crucial question:

Why look for something to ground the fact that slavery is unjust? What is wrong with the trivial answer: slavery is unjust because slavery is unjust? . . . Political constructivism does not look for something for the reasonableness of the statement that slavery is unjust to consist in, as if the reasonableness of it needed some kind of grounding. We may accept provisionally, though with confidence, certain considered judgments as fixed points, as what we take as basic [moral] facts, such as slavery is unjust. But we have a fully philosophical conception only when such facts are coherently connected together by concepts and principles acceptable to us on due reflection. These basic [moral] facts do not lie around here and there like so many isolated bits. For there is: tyranny is unjust, exploitation is unjust, religious persecution is unjust, and on and on. We try to organize these indefinitely many [moral] facts into a conception of justice by the principles that issue from a reasonable procedure of construction. (*PL*, 124)

This is an example of Rawls's well-known "reflective equilibrium" approach to these kinds of questions. The approach asks us to move back and forth between "provisional" facts and the further reflections that solidify these facts into a "fully philosophical conception." We accept the laudable (but not necessary) aim of stringing even these basic moral facts together into a theory, such as Rawls's political liberalism or our own theory of inherent human rights, but we do not follow him when he swallows up the separate and independent discovery of these moral facts into the process of constructing a philosophical conception.

We do not go along with Rawls's claim that there are "indefinitely many" of these basic moral norms scattered around, so that we would not know what to do with them until political theorists came along to tell us how to handle them and construct them into a political conception of justice. After all, the international bill of human rights got on its way without significant input from political theorists. With the exception of the third generation of human rights that stresses group-based rather than birth-based rights, very few additions or omissions to the birth-based category have been made. The procedures Rawls and his disciples stress so much have far more to do with the implementation of human rights than with their initial discovery and enunciation, as in the Universal Declaration, for instance. We see these rights around us on the floor of history (past and present) in more or less isolated bits and pieces. They shock us, and we react in horror at the gross violations of human dignity they call to our attention. That—in nauseating bits and pieces—is in fact how we experience the evil of the world and why the Declaration can be read as a response to (as yet theoretically) unrelated gross violations of human dignity. These rights found their way into the Universal Declaration not because of any theorizing the drafters did or that should be done by others to legitimate them as bona fide human rights. They are already legitimate by virtue of their birth out of the Holocaust and their subsequent entry into the Universal Declaration. The Declaration's drafters found them lying around on the workshop floor of political theory before Rawls and others picked them up to use in their construction projects.

Another constructivist is Jack Donnelly, who in crisply and clearly written theoretical books has been defending the "Universal Declaration Model" of human rights.[23] Instead of sharing the inherence view of human rights, Donnelly looks on human rights as a "social construction." This construction of human rights out of a social vision of man's moral nature—which is only "loosely linked" to man's "scientifically ascertainable needs"—took place during the Enlightenment period in Western history. At that time, markets and sovereign nation states came to dominate international affairs and the societies affected by that onslaught reacted by constructing a "moral vision of human nature" that "set the limits and requirements of social (especially) state action" (14). In this way human rights can be seen as a collective "work of self-creation"; they tell us less "about the way people are than about what they might become" (15).

Ignoring the conscience of humanity as one possible epistemic route into the domain of inherent human rights, Donnelly briefly considers the route of reason. He finds that route wanting as well. He knows that an appeal like that of the Universal Declaration to "the inherent dignity . . .

of all members of the human family" has "often been accepted as persuasive," but for him we can never "through logic alone force the agreement of the skeptic" (18). This admission echoes Rorty's claim that we can never get a convinced Nazi to yield to arguments based on "logic alone." We agree with this assessment of the role of reason when left to operate by itself, which is why we rejected Gewirth's rationalization of the Golden Rule in section A above. Donnelly is therefore left, like Rawls, with a conception of human rights as a purely Western construct, and both theorists show no embarrassment in recommending that this construction be exported to non-Western societies. The constructivism of both theorists is infected by the kind of latent ethnocentrism that I believe stems from their initial rejection of human rights as inherent in the human person and therefore as not really being (metaphysically) universal. Neither theorist believes that we can find a defense of our belief in human rights that is not bound to a particular tradition, be it a Western or other postmodern one. Neither believes that people from very different traditions can nevertheless have similar moral reactions when faced with gross abuses of human dignity, reactions that lead them to believe that certain inherent rights of the victims are being violated. Donnelly's ethnocentrism reveals itself in what we might call the language test for the presence of human rights.

Donnelly holds that "non-Western cultural and political traditions, like the pre-modern West, lacked not only the practice of human rights but also the very concept" (74). He offers us "proofs" that Confucian China (80), traditional Africa (79), traditional Islam (76), and Hindu caste societies (83) had no conception of human rights. To make his case he administers a language test to these societies. For instance, he "cannot imagine how the Chinese managed to claim human rights without the language to make such claims" (81). "Other societies may have (similar or different) attitudes toward issues that we consider in terms of human rights, but unless they possess a concept of human rights they are unlikely to have *any* attitude toward human rights" (81). To read the language of human rights back into these premodern societies would be, he says, to misunderstand the "functioning of a society as a result of anachronistically imposing an alien analytical framework" (81). "'Human nature'—if we can even use that term without anachronism—differs in traditional India from person to person, or rather, from group to group" (83). We disagree, because unlike Donnelly we draw a line between the way the world with human nature in it is and the conceptions or constructions cultures use to interpret that world. Some of these constructions approach reality more closely than others. We agree with him that "Caste and human rights are clearly radically incompatible" because such a system "denies the equal worth of human beings" (83). When pressed for further elaboration Donnelly's answer becomes less and less clear.

He does not make clear to his readers precisely which of the following four claims he does or does not defend: (1) that people have inherent human *rights*, (2) that a society has or had the *idea or conception* of such rights, (3) that a society has or had the *language* to express that idea or conception, and (4) that a society has or had the social and legal *mechanisms* to implement these ideas or conceptions in practices it develops. We agree that claims (2) and (3) flow together and that it probably makes little sense to say that a society has a certain idea or conception of something without having the language (broadly conceived, which includes archaeological data, and so on) with which to express that idea. If it did not have the language, how else would we know that it had the idea? Donnelly's language test gets him from level 3 to level 2, but it leaves untouched and undiscussed the inherent human rights claim of level 1. Scholars of different cultures can disagree about whether Donnelly (or anyone else) has properly administered the language test to a certain society, but whichever side in a dispute like that turns out to be right, my level 1 claim of metaphysical inherence is still on the table. Donnelly admits that people have "competing intuitions" on this issue. We see, he says, the importance of traditional values; "at the same time, though, we feel a need to reject an 'anything goes' attitude" (84). The "conditions of modernization render the individual too vulnerable in the absence of human rights" (85). When he is charged with "too homogeneous a conception of cultures" Donnelly sticks to the point that "it is simply not true that all people at all times have had human rights ideas [level 2] and practices [level 4], if by 'human rights' we mean equal and inalienable paramount moral rights held by all members of the species [level 1]" (86). We see here how Donnelly injects claims about the ideas of level 2 between the metaphysics of level 1 and the social and legal practices of level 4. His argument goes from the absence of the language of human rights to the absence of a conception of human rights and from there to the (unjustified) denial of the metaphysics of inherence.

If Donnelly is right about this elusion of levels it would seem to follow that before Aristotle invented the terminology (or conception) of potentialities in things, sugar was not sol*uble*, a rubber band was not stretch*able* and people were not excit*able*? Aristotle invented this language of capabilities in order to be able to explain the empirical phenomena as he saw them. So even if his pre-Socratic colleagues did not have the concept of potentialities and practiced science without it, that fact by itself does not mean that things or people did not have the properties Aristotle gave us the language to describe. I want to say the same thing about the language and ideas of human rights. Persons have always had these rights as moral birthrights, but for centuries societies worked with conceptions of dignity and attendant social structures without using the terminology of human rights. Just as scientists today still use Aristotle's way of talking because it fits reality so neatly and has been repeatedly confirmed by further experience, so the eighteenth-century language of inherent rights has caught on all over the world because it fits human experience so well. While the legal structures and social practices of modernity are indeed socially and politically constructed, and while the *language* of human rights may well be a Western invention, as Donnelly and others contend, the rights they express and describe are not.

A close reading of Donnelly's text leaves us wondering whether at the end he finds "slavery, trial by ordeal, extrajudicial executions, female infanticide and untouchability" (93) "morally obtuse" because these practices violate a "natural given" (91) about the kinds of creatures human beings are or because they are uniformly rejected by contemporary international human rights regimes. He seems to lean toward the latter. When he comes to explain the "convergence on the particulars of the Universal Declaration model," he makes no use of the core of human nature and what is a natural given. He only brings up factors connected with "the political rise and practices of the West" (57) and so passes up the enormous epistemic and moral power yielded by belief in inherent human rights. He rejects the Hindu view of the variability of human nature by caste because "such views . . . are almost universally rejected in the contemporary world. For example chattel slavery and caste-based legal and political systems, which implicitly deny the existence of a significant common humanity are almost universally condemned even in the most rigid class societies" (91). But why is this so? Is it not because such systems violate the "common humanity" that the drafters unpacked in their articles?

At this point Donnelly injects a new layer into his analytical framework. Instead of going straight for the inherence of moral rights that might explain why no modern society really accepts chattel slavery or caste-based social organizations, he admits to the existence of "a few cross-culturally valid *values*, [which] . . . still leaves open the possibility of a radical cultural relativist denial of human *rights*" (91). He has come to accept the existence of these cross-cultural values not because he subscribes to inherent human rights, but because he believes that the widespread "rhetorical 'fashion'" with which the contemporary world has come to accept the language of human rights "must have some substantive basis" (91). This is the point where the metaphysics of inherence should make itself felt. Not so for Donnelly, for he falls back on the historical point that the "substantive basis" of these values "lies in the hazards posed by modern markets and states" (91). We are still caught in the constructivist circle of positions, practices, and more refined positions that lead to still more practices, without a way of jumping into the circle or having any idea how this construction cycle started. If we can trace gross human rights violations only back to the birth of the modern state and to the human rights projects of post-traditional modern societies, we have no way of condemning them in earlier periods of history. To be able to do that we must distinguish between the way the world is and how we come to know it is that way. The constructivist approach denies us that option.

Conclusion. Constructivists may respond to this charge (of having no way of condemning human rights violations before the modern era) with the claim that constructivism does let us talk about rights in those earlier periods, just not about *inherent* rights. They can plausibly argue that before the modern era of radical egalitarianism, the rights individuals had were based on their particular locations in the social and political hierarchies of the societies in which they lived. And those hierarchies were anchored in various metaphysical systems of right and good, such as Plato's theory of Forms, Aristotelian Nature as a source of value, neo-Platonic emanations, Stoic and other forms of Eudaimonism in late antiquity, or the theory of Natural Law that flourished in the later Middle Ages. Constructivists admit that these bygone metaphysical schemes clash with the doctrine of inherence, but that does not bother them, for, as they see it, each age is free to construct its own theory of justice to match the moral intuitions of its own time and place. Some of these old constructions are better than others, but none have a claim to priority, for there are no moral intuitions or arguments that cut across ages and cultures. We disagree on two counts.

First, in these first three chapters we have rejected the antimetaphysical claims of many contemporary human rights theorists as not in keeping with their founding document. We have given a description of the domain of inherent moral rights and shown how ordinary people can gain access to that domain. Second, the modern constructivist escape from metaphysics shares a fatal flaw with these premodern metaphysical systems. That is the flaw of anchoring duties before rights and committing what I call the fallacy of implementation. Just as in contemporary constructivist systems (where there is no ontological flow) the moral flow goes from duties (of mostly states) to individual or subjective rights, so in the older metaphysical systems the ontological and therefore also the moral flow went from duties to rights. There are in those older systems no inherent rights in the human person per se. Until we know someone's place in the social and political hierarchy of his or her day, we have no way of telling what the individual's rights were, for these rights flowed from the person's station and duties. Throughout antiquity and far into the Middle Ages people could only claim rights based on their place. As long as one was aware of one's duties and performed them, one could claim certain goods. There were goods one deserved, but one never deserved them simply on the basis of being a human being, for no rights at all came from being just that. There were rights, but they were not based on one's humanity.

The doctrine of inherence spells out a totally different conception of justice in human relations. It postulates inherent moral rights that all human beings possess regardless of the place they occupy in any social or political hierarchy in which they find themselves. As it says in UDHR Article 2, these rights belong to everyone regardless of any distinctions based on "race, colour, sex, language, religion, political or other opinion, national or social origin, property, birth or other status," and regardless of "the political, jurisdictional or international status of the country or territory to which a person belongs." That is the *via negativa* of human rights. Article 1 gives us the *via positiva* when it declares that "All human beings are born free and equal in dignity and [inalienable] rights." Human rights theorists disagree about when the radical egalitarianism of human rights first gained a metaphysical hearing from theorists. Most, like Rawls and Donnelly, who believe that their constructivism absolves them of the need to make an ontological commitment themselves, think the (to them unnecessary) metaphysics came in roughly at the time of the Enlightenment and with the rise of the modern state, which is why so many of them define a human right as a right that is held over against the state. For these theorists the political and metaphysical narratives of human rights started at roughly the same time. We will see an extreme case of this in Chapter 6 when we discuss Jürgen Habermas's view on the relationship between human rights and popular sovereignty. Starting these (metaphysical and political) stories at the same time makes some sense, for the political and juridical implementation of human rights did contingently coincide with the creation of national bills of rights that were added to the first constitutions in the eighteenth century. But that is not the only possible narrative that can be told about the metaphysics of human rights. In the next chapter we adopt Martha Nussbaum's capabilities approach to human rights, and she traces her cosmopolitanism (if not her approach to human rights) all the way back to the ancient Stoics.[24] And Nicholas Wolterstorff has argued that belief in people having inherent moral rights goes back to the Hebrew Bible and the Christian Scriptures.[25] If these earlier tracings stand up, they will split the metaphysical story about human rights off from the political story, for the juridical and political implementation of inherent moral rights does not go back to antiquity.

We do not take sides in this looming controversy as to whether the origin of human rights can be traced back to the (early or late) Enlightenment or the beginning of the Judaeo-Christian era. But we have taken sides in the dispute as to whether there is a need for making a metaphysical commitment in the first place, never mind how far back in the history of political theory we trace it. We answered this question in the affirmative by defending the doctrine of inherence (in Chapters 1 and 2) and by rejecting constructivism in this chapter. In the next chapter we go back to the metaphysics of inherence. I draw out its cosmopolitan implications and ground those in the fact that there exist species-wide capabilities that all human beings have (unless blocked) that form the metaphysical pillars of the rights in the Declaration.

Chapter 4
Human Rights Cosmopolitanism

The phenomenon of globalization that we see all around us has economic, technological, and cultural aspects or strands, each of which can
be made into the defining feature of a new cosmopolitanism. The cosmopolitanism of human rights differs from these others in that it looks at
our world as one unified ethical community. While cosmopolitan theories generally stress either individual or institutional factors, the human
rights kind includes both. It has in it the moral reach of an individualist
vision that sees all the members of the human family as living in one
"global ethical community."[1] But it also includes the practical reach of
worldwide institutional regimes and organs of justice that seek to make
this vision a reality. And while other accounts of what a human right is
often stress these institutional regimes of implementation, ours focuses
on the inherence of human rights in individual human beings, which—
since it includes all of them everywhere—leads to the moral cosmopolitanism that is the subject of this chapter. The cosmopolitanism of the
Universal Declaration steps across the boundaries of nation-states and
emphasizes the inherent moral rights individuals have as members of the
human family. It looks at the rights that come with citizenship in Westphalian type nation-states as derivative of, or as implementation vehicles
for persons' enjoyment of these other more basic (because inherent)
human rights. While in the next chapter we do also discuss some of the
implementation regimes, we do so because we need to answer the charge
that this chapter's cosmopolitanism leads to expectations that cannot be
met.

A. The Moral World Picture of the Declaration

Even a casual reading of the Universal Declaration tells us that the document has very little concern with the nation-states that for the most part
control our political lives. The drafters were not looking to establish
inter-national justice, if by that we mean a kind of justice that aims to

fairly distribute the resources of the planet among the nations and peoples that occupy it. To achieve that kind of international justice, states and their governments sign any number of treaties, covenants, and trade agreements among themselves. The drafters of the Declaration were not internationalists in that sense. I made the point against Rawls (in Chapter 3, section B) that, while the drafters spoke on behalf of their governments, they were not negotiating on the basis of reciprocity, which is what nations-states do in most of their dealings with one another. The drafters' focus was not on their own nation's interests, but on forestalling a repeat of Holocaust type abominations through the articulation of an "international" bill of rights. They changed that title to a "universal" bill of rights when they realized that what had driven them together was a vision of *cosmopolitan* justice, which views all human beings as members of one and the same family of mankind, each one of them born with inherent human rights. The drafters were therefore globalists or cosmopolitans and not internationalists. As cosmopolitans who had their minds set on individual human beings, they looked at the nation-states that dot our planet as no more (and no less) than the most important vehicles for the delivery of the enjoyment of people's—to use a redundancy—inherent birthrights.

A sure sign of this moral and individual cosmopolitanism is the fact that the Declaration is resoundingly silent on the role of the modern nation-state, a fact that speaks against the prevailing internationalist interpretation of the document. The Preamble makes certain references to nation-states because they are the units that make up the UN, and that is the international organization that sponsored the writing of the Declaration. Though the drafters tell us in the Sixth Recital that human rights are "essential" for "the development of friendly relations between nations," the body of their document makes only two very incidental references to the nation-state, one in Article 16(3) and one in Article 30. It cannot be that the visionaries who wrote this text already knew in 1948 that the marriage between political absolutism and the modern state had run its course. For as they were laying to rest (so they thought) the totalitarianism of the fascist state, they were awakened just then by an equally menacing totalitarianism of communist states. It was very much their experience with these absolutist versions of the modern state that made them keep all states, even genuinely democratic ones, at arm's length.

On the day they adopted the Declaration the drafters first passed an Egyptian motion stating that the obligations of states were to be spelled out at a later date, and in 1967 the UN adopted two international covenants that have since been ratified by some 150 of the world's nations. The Declaration's drafters themselves looked at the whole of our planet as one global, almost-everywhere-inhabited, cosmopolitan world. They paid very little attention to the nation-state, and what they wrote conflicts with the "state-centric conception" of a theorist like Jack Donnelly.[2] A theorist who takes his or her clue from the Universal Declaration would not say, as does Donnelly, that "Everyone has a [human] right to X" *means* that "Each state has the authority and responsibility to implement and protect the right to X within its territory" (34, emphasis added). From the drafters' cosmopolitan perspective the question of what it means to have a human right should not *in the first instance* be understood through reference to the responsibility of modern states, but with an exposition of the doctrine of inherence.[3] While Bhikhu Parekh is right in his claim that human rights are "addressed to all human beings and impose on them a duty to respect them and do all they can to facilitate their realization," he is wrong to say that the Declaration "takes a statist view of human rights and emasculates their universalist and critical thrust" and that the "rights [in it] are addressed to the state which alone is deemed to have the obligation to respect and realize them."[4]

Moral cosmopolitanism is the obvious heartbeat of the words "everyone," "all," or "no one" with which almost every article of the document starts: "all people and all nations" (Preamble), "All human beings" (Article 1), "Everyone" (2), "Everyone" (3), "No one" (4), "No one" (5), "Everyone" (6), "All" (7), "Everyone" (8), "No one" (9), "Everyone" (10), "Everyone" and "No one" (11), "No one" (12), "Everyone" (13), "Everyone" (14), "Everyone" (15), "All men and women" (16), "Everyone" (17), "No one" (18), "Everyone" (19), "Everyone" and "No one" (20), "Everyone" (21), "Everyone" (22), "Everyone" (23), "Everyone" (24), "Everyone" (25), "Everyone" (26), "Everyone" (27), "Everyone" (28), "Everyone" (29), and "In no case" and "Nothing" (30). This litany of universal terms reflects the drafters' conviction that there are no exceptions to the possession of human rights. All members of the human family possess them simply by virtue of that membership. Starting from the perspective of moral cosmopolitanism, every article of the Declaration carves out, to repeat Camus, "a part of man which must always be defended."[5] Besides being manifest in the litany of article openings, this cosmopolitan vision breaks through to the surface of the text in references to "the inalienable rights of all members of the human family" in the First Recital, in the admonition that we should "act toward one another in a spirit of brotherhood" in Article 1, and in Article 28's claim that "everyone is entitled to a social and international order in which the rights and freedoms set forth in this Declaration can be fully realized," which is reiterated in Article 29's assertion that "these rights and freedoms may in no case be exercised contrary to the purposes and principles of the United Nations."

While the Declaration is today increasingly seen as a legal document, that was not the case when it was first adopted. Because they could not in the time allotted to them come up with a draft covenant that would have had legal teeth, most of the drafters came to see their document at first as primarily an educational tool for teaching universal moral rights that are inherent in the human person. As a worldwide educational tool the Declaration has definite cosmopolitan aspirations, for the litany of the words "everyone" and "all" and the references to the "spirit of brotherhood" and "the human family" are clearly aimed beyond domestic contexts. They are imbued with the spirit of cosmopolitanism that we also find in this operative paragraph, where the drafters express the hope that "every individual and every organ of society, keeping this Declaration constantly in mind, shall strive by teaching and education to promote respect for these rights and freedoms and by progressive measures, national and international, to secure their universal respect and effective recognition and observance, both among the peoples of the Member States and among the peoples of territories under their jurisdiction." The individual human beings—who are the primary addressees and the subjects about whom the Declaration is being made—are not isolated, mutually disinterested, and possessive human beings. They are members of the family of humankind. The Declaration clearly supposes that the members of the human family share and experience the kind of solidarity that Camus says is awakened in us when any of the rights of any member is violated. As Martin Luther King put it in his Letter from Birmingham Jail, "An injustice anywhere is an injustice everywhere."[6]

While they spoke on behalf of the nations they represented, the drafters were also thinking of the teaming multitudes of individual human beings throughout the ages and in the greatest possible varieties of settings. That deeper interest shone through when, after two years of hard work and hundreds of meetings, the drafters looked back at what they had written. Early in the proceedings, General Carlos Romulo of the Philippines urged his colleagues to draft a bill that "would take the different cultural systems of the world into account" (SR 9/2). Vladimir Koretsky of the USSR "stressed his belief that the approach of the Bill should be such as would make its acceptance possible under any and all social systems" (SR 6/3). When the draft of the eighteen-member Human Rights Commission was delivered to the fifty-eight-member Third Committee, Enrique Corominas, the Argentinean delegate, urged that certain changes be made so as "to give mankind the satisfaction it expected" (GAOR Third, 88). Speaking for Ecuador, Jorge Carrera Andrade said that the Declaration "was a major expression of the human conscience" (36). As usual, Chilean representative Hernán Santa Cruz was more expressive. "It had been necessary," he said, "to reconcile the different ideologies of the Soviet Union and other Eastern European countries and of other Members of the UN, the difference between the economic and social rights recognized by Christian Western civilization and those recognized by the Oriental civilization; the varying legal systems of Latin and Anglo Saxon countries" (49).

Alluding to the Berlin Airlift that was then in place, Haitian delegate Émile Saint-Lot noted that "After the war, at a time unpropitious for the success of such a venture, with rival ideologies confronting each other, the United Nations representatives had sought out among old established or recent political, economic, social and cultural rights formulas which might be acceptable to men from the four corners of the earth." He therefore felt that "the text of the draft declaration represented a kind of common denominator for those various ideas" (GAOR Third, 853). Charles Malik, Lebanese delegate and president of the Third Committee, held the view that "the present declaration had been drafted on a firm international basis, for the Secretariat's draft was a compilation not only of hundreds of proposals made by governments and private persons but also of the laws and legal findings of all the Members States of the United Nations" (858). General Romulo thought the "document was in reality the first in history which, from a truly universal standpoint defined the basic rights and fundamental freedoms to which all men were entitled . . . [and] that the philosophy on which the declaration was based was valid for all peoples and all nations and was universally accepted " (867).

Repeating verbatim the operative paragraph of the document, Dutch delegate J. H. Van Roijen said the "moral force" of the Declaration would be strong enough to make it "serve as a common standard for all peoples and all nations throughout the world" (GAOR Third, 873). Minerva Bernardino of the Dominican Republic said her delegation "was convinced that the declaration for which men and women were anxiously waiting, would be approved by the General Assembly and would receive the unqualified support of all peoples" (903). Carrera Andrade explained that "throughout many centuries of political struggle to bring about human unity, the climax had now been reached with the preparation of the document in which 58 nations had expressed their common ideal and their identity of thoughts regarding fundamental human rights" (918). Continuing such reflections on the meaning of history, Syrian delegate Abduhl Rahman Kayaly said he realized "those earlier declarations had not been perfect and had not all been applied: civilization had progressed slowly through centuries of persecution and tyranny, until finally, the present declaration had been drawn up. It was not the work of a few representatives in the Assembly or the Social and Economic Council; it was the achievement of generations of human beings who had worked towards that end. Now at least the peoples of the world would hear it proclaimed that their aim had been reached by the United Nations" (922).

This cosmopolitan vision of the inherent dignity of men, women, and children the world over was a dominant motif in the comments delegations made in the final General Assembly debates on the evening of December 10, 1948. Brazilian delegate Belarmino Austregesilo de Athayde noted that the Declaration "did not reflect the particular point of view of any one people or any one group of peoples. Neither was it the expression of any one political doctrine or philosophical system. It was the result of the intellectual and moral cooperation of a large number of nations; that explained its value and interest and also conferred upon it great authority" (GAOR 878). To those who compared the Declaration to its Enlightenment predecessors, Ernest Davies, UK representative, pointed out that this time "More than fifty nations with different systems of governance and different social structures, religions and philosophies had adopted by an overwhelming majority the articles of the draft declaration under discussion" (882). Throughout the deliberations the Indian delegation had been particularly sensitive to the issues of multiculturalism. Looking back at the crucial Third Committee debates, Lakshimi Menon recalled "how insistently the Indian delegation had stressed the importance of avoiding mention of any political doctrine either in the declaration or in the preamble." She thanked that Committee "for having understood" India's point of view (894).

The vote was taken a few minutes before midnight: 48 votes for, 8 abstentions, and no negative votes were cast. The president of that Third General Assembly was H. V. Evatt, an Australian. He noted that the adoption of the Declaration "without any real opposition" was a great achievement. "It was the first occasion on which the organized community of nations had made a declaration of human rights and fundamental freedoms. That document was backed by the authority of the body of opinion of the United Nations as a whole and millions of people, men, women and children all over the world would turn to it for help, guidance and inspiration" (934). We know from the subsequent success of the Declaration that it has indeed lived up to these predictions. As I said in the Introduction, the language of human rights has become the moral lingua franca of our age, and the Declaration that contains its code has been translated into more languages than has the Bible. It has given hope and courage to millions of violated and oppressed people on all continents and in all countries. And it has spawned an entirely new section of international law that is dedicated to translating and transposing these inherent moral rights into domestic and global contexts.

This translating and transposing of inherent rights needs to be done—as was the case for the Declaration itself—in conjunction with a commitment to a strong (meaning broad) principle of nondiscrimination. We can see the cosmopolitanism of the Declaration not just in the long list of birth rights it says belong to all members of the human family, but also in the types of discrimination Article 2 prohibits. While I have repeatedly said that the drafters of the Declaration were content to publish a list of inherent rights without attaching measures of implementation, I also said that they used two ways of approaching these rights, the positive way of Article 1 ("being born free and equal in dignity and rights") and the negative, nondiscrimination way of Article 2, that "Everyone is entitled to all the rights and freedoms set forth in this Declaration, without distinction of any kind, such as race, colour, sex, language, religion, political or other opinion, national or social origin, property, birth or other status."

I end this section on the cosmopolitan outlook of the Declaration with an exposition of the way Article 2's negative route of nondiscrimination was used by the drafters to help bring their vision of one unified human family down to earth and into the text of their document. When we say that people have moral rights that belong to them regardless of their sex, caste, place of birth, or whatever else we put on that nondiscrimination list—and add (from 2(2)) that they have these rights regardless of the political or international jurisdiction under which they are born or happen to live—we arrive at a set of moral rights that belong to everyone simply because they are human beings. If we really respect the moral rights people still have after we strip them of their race, their sex, their opinions on various subjects, all information about their background, birth, and present economic or political status or jurisdiction, what we have left is a naked human being without frills. This stripping of nonessential features or characteristics is another way of saying that people have these rights by virtue of their unadorned humanity. After I explain the importance of this "negative" inherence pillar, I point out that nation-states are increasingly using this principle of nondiscrimination to enunciate their own versions of cosmopolitanism.

We can see how serious the drafters were about this principle of nondiscrimination by noting that they started each of their Articles with the words "everyone," "all," and "no one." E. J. R. Heyward, the Australian delegate to the Second Session, made this connection succinctly: "Logically, discrimination was prohibited by the use in each article of the phrase "every person" or "everyone" (E/CN.4/AC.1/SR.27/4). The same focus on discrimination is revealed by the fact that the drafters devoted two Articles (2 and 7) and not just one to this principle. While all the delegations were in favor of this nondiscrimination theme, the fact that it is so indelibly imprinted upon the document is the Marxist legacy of the communist delegations. They put the rights of the colonial peoples on the agenda of the Commission and into the text as the second paragraph of Article 2. They were responsible for the repetition of the discrimination prohibition in Article 16 (on marriage) and in Article 23 (on equal pay for equal work). The women's lobby received more help from them than from any other block of votes, with the result that from the feminist perspective the Declaration is a remarkably clean document. The communist delegations also saw more clearly than their drafting partners the crucial role that this principle could and should play in protecting the rights of members of minority groups. In short, Marxist egalitarianism very much helped shape the Declaration's cosmopolitan outlook on the world.

Professor Vladimir Koretsky, the USSR delegate at the start of the drafting process, noted that "the ideas regarding discrimination as expressed by the various drafts had not been developed sufficiently," at which point he mentioned the treatment of Indians in South Africa and the unequal treatment of women in all areas of life as examples (E/CN.4/AC.1/ SR.6/.3). In a later exchange the Soviet delegation wanted the Declaration to say that acts of discrimination "constitute a crime and shall be punishable under the law of the State" (E/CN.4/SR.34/10). When Chilean delegate Santa Cruz asked Alexei Pavlov why he was willing to put so much "power in the hands of the State, [since] . . . the State constituted the chief threat to the rights of the individual," Pavlov responded that "if no provision were adopted to prevent acts of discrimination, it would mean that such practices as lynching Negroes would continue" (E/CN.4/SR.34/10–11). He made this reference about the time President Harry Truman's Committee on Civil Rights publicly told him that "lynching remains one of the most serious threats to the civil rights of Americans."[7] These examples exhibit the historical connection that has always existed between the "prevention of discrimination and protection of minorities." This was in fact the name of the Sub-Commission that was asked by the Drafting Committee to vet what at that point was a nondiscrimination list of five items: race, sex, language, religion, or political belief (E/CN.4/AC.1/W.2/Rev.1/2).

That the Universal Declaration should bar discrimination on the basis of race and color was a foregone conclusion. Not only is race the first item on the short Charter list of nondiscrimination items, the Declaration itself was also drafted in response to the horrible excesses of Hitler's racist policies and political philosophy. The first thing the Allied Powers did after the war was to dismantle Hitler's racist legal structures, which is why the fourth political principle announced at the 1945 Potsdam Conference stated that "All Nazi laws which provided the basis of the Hitler regime or established discrimination grounded on race, creed or political opinion shall be abolished." The peace treaties with other Axis powers also included provisions for the repeal of all racist legislation and discriminatory practices (E/CN.4/Sub.2/3/9). It is therefore inconceivable for the

Universal Declaration not to have prohibited discrimination on the basis of "race" and "colour," the first two items on the list in Article 2.

The Sub-Commission that had received the nondiscrimination list from the First Drafting Session of the Commission did not itself add color to the list. Instead, its report contained a note saying that "The Sub-Commission, in adopting the text, thought there was no need for a special mention of 'color,' as that was embodied in the word 'race'"(E/CN.4/52/.4). M. R. Masani, the Indian expert on the Sub-Commission, formally proposed that the word "color" be added to the list of items on the basis of which discrimination was to be prohibited. His reasoning was "that race and color were two conceptions that did not necessarily cover one another" (E/CN.4/Sub.2/4/3). He pointed out that the American Federation of Labor "had seen fit . . . to refer explicitly to color as well as race in connection with discrimination" (E/CN.4/Sub.2/SR.4). Experts from Haiti, the United States, and Belgium objected because they did not want to go beyond the Charter and because recent international conferences had not mentioned both terms either. After an extended discussion about whether there was such a thing as a scientific definition of race, the above-mentioned note ("It being understood that the term 'race' includes the idea of 'color'") was added to the text of the Declaration" (5). In the Second Session of the Commission it was again the delegation from India that sought to have the item color moved from this note to the formal list in Article 2 on the ground that in the Draft Covenant that was also under consideration the word "color" did follow the word "race" (E/CN.4/SR.34/.10). Supported by arguments from the Lebanese and Philippine delegations, the Indian amendment to add the word "color" was adopted "by ten votes to none, with six abstentions" (5).

I give these details to make the point that it was experts and delegations from countries that had significant experience with ethnocultural diversity who sought to have the word "color" included on the Declaration's list of nondiscrimination items. Race involves the classification of people on the basis of inherited physiological characteristics (like eye color and form, shape of the nose, stature, cephalic index, and blood groups) of which skin color is only the most obvious and frequently used; all are used to draw insidious distinctions that are arbitrary from both the scientific and the moral point of view. Making this addition to the list of Article 2 was therefore crucial for the protection of members of minority groups whose skin color differs from that of the bulk of the population around them. If we combine the prohibition of discrimination on the basis of race and color with the other Articles of the Declaration we immediately come to see the reach of the cosmopolitan vision at stake.

Behind the item "national origin" on the list in Article 2 lies the same kind of story. According to a note it added to the text, "the Sub-Commission wished to make it clear that the words 'national origin' should be interpreted by taking this conception, not in the sense of citizen of a State, but in the sense of national characteristics," which gloss the Commission of Human Rights accepted. The gloss resulted from a long discussion in the Sub-Commission about how the USSR expert Vladimir Borisov, who proposed the addition of this item, meant it to be understood (E/CN.4/Sub.2/SR.6). One of his colleagues thought that "national origin" might be "synonymous with nationality," while another "suggested omitting the words 'national or social' leaving the word 'origin' to cover everything" (E/CN.4/Sub.2/SR.4/.15). Borisov responded that he did not think the word "origin" by itself would suffice because the Soviet Union had "various nationalities of the same origin." While he was willing to entertain substitutes for the word "social" (such as class or caste), he was quite adamant on retaining the term "national." He felt that it was "in the interests of countries where people of different national origins lived together under the same government that the words "national origin" should be specifically mentioned (9). C. H. Wu, the expert from China, seconded the USSR position on the grounds that "In some countries there existed national groups that needed to be protected against discrimination. If the words 'national origin' referred to such groups he thought that they should be retained" (10). Borisov agreed with Wu that the phrase "national origin" pertained not to the question of citizenship rights but to the one of national minorities living under the security umbrella of one and the same state. The note that the item "national origin" should be interpreted as a reference to "national characteristics" and not to the matter of "citizenship" reflects these Sub-Commission discussions (E/CN.4/SR.4–6). As before, these drafting details show that delegations that had experience with the phenomenon of national minorities were especially interested in expanding the short UN Charter list to what we have in Article 2 of the Declaration, which has come to serve as a model for a host of domestic nondiscrimination clauses.

Since the Declaration does not contain a specific article on the protection of the rights of members of minority groups the list of Article 2 is a crucial place for us to look for that kind of protection. Article 2 opens with the assertion that "Everyone is entitled to all the rights and freedoms set forth in this Declaration" without discrimination based on the list of characteristic that follow. If we multiply the eleven items on the nondiscrimination list by the number of rights in the Declaration, counting one right per relevant Article (excluding Articles 1, 2, 29 and 30), we get 11 x 26 = some 286 areas of interest that are protected by this combination. Members of ethnocultural, national, religious, gender, social, or marginalized minority groups have just as much a human right to freedom of movement (Article 13) or to a fair trial (Article 10) as do members of the majority grouping. And so on for all the rights in the Declaration, including Article 27, which says that "Everyone has the right freely to participate in the cultural life of the community, to enjoy the arts, and to share in scientific advancement and its benefits." While the most natural way to read the double use of the definite article "the" is to assume that drafters were thinking of participation in the national culture of nation-states (which no doubt they were), their expansion of the nondiscrimination list from four items in the UN Charter to the long list in Article 2 clearly shows that they were very interested in extending all the rights in the Declaration to members of ethnocultural and national minority groups. The combination of the Article 2 list with the rights of Article 27 means that in their enjoyment of the right to cultural liberty no one is to be discriminated against on grounds "such as race, colour, sex, language, religion, political or other opinion, national or social origin, birth or other status." In section C of this chapter I explore the link between this right to participation in culture and the right to use one's minority language in parent operated schools.

Some kind of discrimination against some minority group or other is frequently how violations of human rights start and then grow to disastrous proportions. The Nazis began by tinkering with the marriage laws and ended up with the ovens of Auschwitz.[8] The communists began by denying the right to freedom of political opinion to some opponents (even if socialist) and ended up with the Gulag in Russia and the Cultural Revolution in China. Theocratically inclined Islamic governments in the Middle East and North Africa began by curtailing freedom of public expression of opinion and end up with unfair and secret trials, sometimes even with assassination attempts on apostate authors. Numerous capitalist-inclined governments began by denying the right to unionize and ended up allowing near-starvation conditions for thousands of their working-class citizens. The health care discrimination in the United States is thought by a great number of citizens to be a minor glitch in an otherwise fine system, while in reality it spells premature death for thousands. The violation of the human right to property and land has turned millions of indigenous people into second-class citizens on the very soil they were the first to inhabit and cultivate. We must admit that, whatever is wrong with Marxism as an ideology and whatever went wrong with the communist regimes that collapsed in the practice of it, its emphasis on nondiscrimination is one of its main contributions to political philosophy.

There is, I believe, a human rights lesson to be drawn from the drafters' purposeful expansion of the UN Charter's nondiscrimination list. When we seek to grade a country's human rights record, we should not just look at what rights of the Declaration are enshrined in that country's constitution or embraced by its legislative system, we must also take note of the kinds of discrimination a country allows or does not allow with respect to whatever rights it has constitutionally or legislatively embraced. An official nondiscrimination list (let alone the practice of it) can be very telling in its length or brevity, as the case may be. In the way Article 2 of the Declaration gives us a glimpse into the cosmopolitan mindset of the drafters, so a country's standard nondiscrimination list gives us a glimpse into the public philosophy of a nation at the time it adopted the list. Such lists reflect the history and spirit of a nation, and they often get changed after revolutions and other momentous events. The First Amendment to the U.S. Constitution ("Congress shall make no law respecting the establishment of religion, or prohibiting the free exercise thereof") has been the envy of a great many nations because it has protected religious liberties for Americans since their country's founding days. The Thirteenth Amendment abolishes slavery, the Fourteenth stipulates equality before the law, and the Fifteenth prohibits discrimination in voting "on account of race, color, or previous condition of servitude." These are clear references to the history of slavery in that country. The Nineteenth Amendment does the same for women's right to vote. These amendments were followed by Acts of Congress (and related Supreme Court decisions) that banned discrimination based on race, color, sex, religion, and national origin (1964), on age (1967), on disabilities (1990), on sexual preference (passed the House in 2007, but awaiting Senate approval), and on genetic information (2008).[9] These federal and numerous state and local legislative measures (and related court decisions) strengthen the cosmopolitan melting-pot aspect of life in the United States.

The official nondiscrimination lists of other countries are similarly revealing and often rewritten to help members of minority groups.[10] Many of them model themselves after the UDHR list, sometimes with telling variations. The 1991 Colombian constitution adds "family" to its list and ends it with "philosophy" (Article 13). The 2002 East Timor constitution ends its list with "physical or mental condition" (Article 2). Ghana's 1992 nondiscrimination list includes the item "occupation" (Article 3). Article 4 of the 1995 Constitution of Bosnia and Herzegovina pretty much follows the Declaration list, but inserts "association with a national minority" (Article 3). And so on for most of the countries of the world. Under specified circumstances, any item on any of these lists can be used by someone with an unusual (and therefore minority) skin color, religion, language, sexual preference, or occupation to gain enjoyment of the right in question, whether that be the right to vote, get an education, or stay in publicly offered accommodations, assuming that a country has translated that particular human right into a civil or constitutional right.

The communist delegations put up an enormous fight to have the item "political opinion" removed from UDHR Article 2. They were honest about not wanting multiparty elections and the like, even if it meant sharing power with other socialists. Because Cuba (in 2008) is still a communist country, Article 42 of its 1976 Constitution bans discrimination "based on race, color of the skin, sex, national origin, religious creeds, or any other type offending human dignity," among which it does not count "political opinion." That item is also missing from the lists in Article 40 of the 1971 Egyptian Constitution and Article 19 of the 1993 Russian one. It is not surprising that the 2003 Constitution of Rwanda, where thousands were killed in the horrible 1994 genocide, makes discrimination based on "tribe" punishable by law (Article 11). Because the people of Bangladesh knew what the Hindu caste system can do to a society, they included "caste" on their 1972 nondiscrimination list: "No citizen shall on grounds only of religion, race, caste, sex or place of birth be subjected to any disability, liability or condition with regard to access to any place of public entertainment or resort, or admission to any educational institution" (Article 27(3)). The constitutions of Sri Lanka (1978, Article 12(2), Burkina Faso (1991, Article 1), and Nepal (1990, Article 11(3)) contain the same stipulation. We speculate that the Netherlands will amend Article 1 of its 1983 Constitution (which prohibits discrimination on grounds of "religion, belief, political opinion, race, or sex or on any other grounds whatsoever.') to say that these "other grounds" include nationality, birth, place of origin, culture, and ethnicity. Because Iran is (in 2008) an Islamic Republic, Article 19 of its Constitution states that "Whatever the ethnic tribe or group to which they belong, all people of Iran enjoy equal rights, and factors such as colour, race, and language do not bestow any privilege." The phrase "such as" does not make up for the absence of standard items like "religion," sex," and "political opinion." Compare this list to the one of South Africa after apartheid. Article 9(3) of that country's 1996 Constitution concretizes everyone's equality before the law with a prohibition of discrimination "directly or indirectly against anyone on one or more grounds, including race, gender, sex, pregnancy, marital status, ethnic or social origin, colour, sexual orientation, age, disability, religion, conscience, belief, culture, language and birth."

A country's political philosophy can be seen not just in how many rights of the Declaration it has embraced in its legal system, but also in how long and specific its nondiscrimination list is. Serious cosmopolitanism requires two solid columns: a long positive column that translates the human rights of the Declaration into domestic bills of civil or constitutional rights and a long negative column of the grounds on which discrimination in areas of the first column is forbidden and punishable.

While the U.S. Bill of Rights is not a very impressive one (lacking most second-generation rights), its numerous nondiscrimination measurers tell a more positive story. Socialist Iran, on the other hand, does quite well in the first column, but falls far short in the second because of discrimination against women and members of certain religious minority groups. The presence of "sexual orientation" and "disability" on the 1996 South Africa list tells us as much about the inclusivity of that society as does the absence of "political opinion" about the closed character of absolutist societies or the absence of "religion" and "sex" in the theocratic ones. I return to issues of nondiscrimination toward the end of section C ("Fitting in Patriotism and Multiculturalism") of this chapter.

B. The Capabilities Approach to Human Rights

In the present section I want to forge a link between the drafters' cosmopolitan sentiments and the claim that all the human rights in the document were thought of by the drafters as (more or less) inherent in the human person. There are two parts to this link. I explored one in Chapter 1, when we argued that for every possessor of a human right there is a duty-bearer somewhere who has the duty to deliver the goods to which the right-holder is said to have a human right. And since a human right is held over against the whole world, it is held over against the entire human family. We explained that there is an asymmetry between the easily identifiable holders of inherent rights (because they are all human beings) and whoever (parent, village, government institution, police officer, or international aid organization) stands closest in the line of duty-bearers to give the help needed. In spite of this asymmetry, the correlation creates a moral bond between all the members of the human family, for they all have the same human rights and they all have their places in the multiple lines of duty-bearers that might be called on to help protect human dignity.

The task of this section is to forge the other part of this link between inherence and cosmopolitanism: to show how we can and should look on each right in the Declaration as inherent in the human person or as linked to human nature in a nonessentialist way. I noted in the Introduction that anyone who is interested in how a pack of lions operates would do well to study the kinds of animals lions are. Just so, anyone interested in what (besides the genetic code) binds together the human family would do well to study the kinds of animals human beings are. That is our interest in the capabilities approach. This approach, pioneered by economist Amartya Sen and philosopher Martha Nussbaum,[11] helps us place all the different kinds of rights in the Declaration on an equal philosophical footing, and to see them all as (more or less) equally inherent in the human person. Adopting this view will also help me rebut utopian criticisms (discussed in the next chapter) that stress the legitimacy of civil and political rights at the expense of social, economic, and cultural ones, for I argue that these species-wide capabilities underlie all the rights in the Universal Declaration. The approach grounds human rights in Aristotle's distinction between potentiality and actuality. It thinks of human beings as having a distinct set of potentialities or capabilities, or, in Thomas Aquinas's terms, natural inclinations. The point of a human life is to have these human capacities actualized and brought to fruitful functioning, which at the end of a long and fulfilled life can be said to have produced happiness. After considering Sen's and especially Nussbaum's modern application of Aristotelian capabilities, I join Nussbaum in using the idea of the conscience of humanity to argue that any denial of the flourishing of these human capabilities is a violation of human dignity and should not be tolerated. If we keep the cases clear enough, it turns out that the same metaphysics and the same epistemology can be used for most of the articles in the Universal Declaration. In each case the right is inherent and our moral sense tells us when it has been grossly violated.

Sen's Contribution. Amartya Sen was the first major theoretician who sought to bend the economic track of macro-national development toward a simultaneous interest in human rights, except that he used his own cumbersome terminology of "spaces," "capabilities," and "functionings" instead of the language of human rights. The title of his popular book *Development as Freedom* is purposely ambiguous between the following two kinds of development: the microdevelopment of the human personality, the right to which we find spread throughout the Declaration, and the macroeconomic development of whole nations and regions that has been the assignment of developmental economists.[12] Though the microdevelopment of the human personality is the problem at which he aims most of the statistics he cites, Sen sees freedom as the key to both micro- and macrodevelopment. The influence of Sen's approach can be seen not just in the fact that his books have been widely read and reviewed, but also in his collaboration with the World Bank and the United Nations Development Programme, organizations whose publications bear the stamp of his advice and influence.

As Sen sees the field, developmental economists have been too exclusively concerned with the income of developing nations, as measured in their GNPs, and the per capita income of their inhabitants. Since money and income can be measured like height and temperature, economists and bankers employed on the economics track have produced an enormous number of tables of statistics on various economic aspects of developing and developed countries. They use these statistics to evaluate their client countries' economic growth, as well as their own aid plans. Sen's increasingly vocal complaint has been that the development and growth statistics collected by his colleagues are not the right ones to help in assessment of public policies of developing nations, not if what we seek is the (micro) development of individual human persons.

The aggregate data collected by economists are too rough. They hide inequalities of distribution within national expenditures and within the groups covered. Income perspectives focus on GDP or national income. When we divide national income by the number of people in the population we get the per capita income of the population of a certain country for a certain year. That allows us to compare income levels for different populations, like the 2001 average income in Algeria at $1,650 with that for someone in the United States at $34,280 or in India at $480 or in Bangladesh at $360. Because one dollar can buy a lot more in a poor developing nation than in an industrialized one, we must figure in the PPP, the purchasing power parity factor, for each nation. That leaves the 2001 per capita income for an average American at the same $34,280, but increases it for someone in Algeria to $5,910, in India to 2,820, and in Bangladesh to $1,600. What such low figures mean is driven home when we learn that in 2000, 34.7 percent of the Indian and 36 percent of the Bangladeshi population lived on less than a dollar a day. Similar tabulations have been made for most countries of the world, from the advanced industrialized to the least developed, all yielding a wealth of statistics. The dramatic statistics for the least-developed countries tell a tale of poverty and starvation.[13]

Sen's objection is that this emphasis on income as money misses what he calls "the conversion factor" that needs to be included in our calculations if we are to evaluate the (micro) development of individual persons and not just look at aggregate (macro) figures for whole regions and nations. He points out that the same amount of money (that is, income) will do much more for a healthy, young, able-bodied male to help him reach his goals than that same sum will do for a female (in almost any country), a chronically ill person, an elderly person, a pregnant woman, or someone living in a high-crime area or epidemiological atmosphere.[14] The young healthy male can convert the fixed amount of money in ways he prefers to function much more easily than can a member of the other groups mentioned. To measure individual human development by dividing a nation's GDP by the number of people in its territory and come up with per capita income is, argues Sen, grossly inadequate. It fuzzes over enormous inequities among groups and even individuals within groups. What someone can do with a certain income depends a great deal on the "class, community, caste and gender" of the individual, and on personal handicaps such as "a high metabolic rate, or a large body size or a parasitic disease that wastes nutrients" (*Inequality*, 55, 111). To judge and evaluate development programs, we must factor in, if we can, the personal and group variations and then see what people are actually capable of doing. Since a person who is fasting is functioning at a low level of nutrient intake rather than involuntarily starving himself to death, we must not be simplistic and merely look at functioning as such, but rather look at what capabilities a person has, and what that person can do with earnings.

The freedom in *Development as Freedom* is the freedom to develop one's capabilities into types of actual functionings. Income or earnings or monetary grants is only one of the "spaces" in which we can compare inequalities between individuals and groups. The other spaces are those of Rawlsian primary goods, libertarian kinds of liberties, Ronald Dworkin's resources, utilitarian interpersonal preferences, and, of course, the income baskets of economists. Against all these, Sen argues that they are too crude because they ignore the conversion factor (as is the case with primary goods and resources), or they are too narrow (the weakness of libertarianism), or they cannot be measured (which he feels is true of personal preferences). In practice the preferences or utility functions that utilitarian social scientists would but cannot measure boil down to a crude comparison of shopping baskets consumers use to express these preferences. And that, Sen says, brings us right back to a comparison of income levels and its shortfalls in terms of the conversion factor. He therefore presents his own capabilities and functionings approach as a more refined way of evaluating government policies and welfare proposals.

Sen even proposes that we evaluate theories of justice by the kind of information they advocate collecting. If they stop short at income or resource levels, at shopping baskets, or at a short list of civil and political liberties, they have the "wrong" informational base from which to proceed. Since he himself has had a hand in what data are being collected, the statistical tables of the World Bank and the UN Development Programme are coming closer and closer to the information required by Sen's capabilities approach. For some years now theoreticians of all persuasions have been able to look up for most of the world's countries statistics for adult literacy, primary and secondary school enrollments, availability of clean water, the presence of telephones, child mortality rates of before five and after five, and a host of other factors related to microdevelopment in macrocontexts.

Unfortunately, Sen does not use the articles in the Universal Declaration as possible spaces for comparison. When he asks "Inequality of What?" in his book *Inequality Reexamined*, he could have broken up the concept of inequality into the different areas protected by the rights in the Declaration. That would have given him the moral perspective with which to judge and criticize the data and policies developed by economists. He instead gives us his own five "instrumental freedoms that contribute, directly or indirectly, to the overall freedom people have to live the way they would like to live" (38). The five types of freedoms are (1) "*political freedoms*" that "refer to the opportunities that people have to determine who should govern and on what principles"; (2) "*economic facilities*" that cover the capacities to "utilize economic resources for the purpose of consumption, or production, or exchange"; (3) "*social opportunities*" that include "arrangements societies make for education, health care, and so on"; (4) "*transparency guarantees*" that require "transparency and lucidity" in people's dealing with each other and that help fight "corruption, financial irresponsibility and underhanded dealings"; and finally (5) "*protective security*" that is meant to "provide a social safety net for preventing the affected population from being reduced to abject misery and in some cases even starvation and death" (38–39).

These five instrumental freedoms cover the entire range of the Declaration, but (disappointingly) Sen does not say that people have a *human right* to any of these freedoms, nor does he say that people have a *right* to "live the way they would like to live." The closest he comes to a normative point of view is to say that people have "reason to attach great importance" to these five instrumental freedoms, "including escaping avoidable mortality, being well nourished, and healthy, being able to read, write and count, and so on" (*Freedom*, 66). These are "things that would be strongly valued and desired by nearly all of us" (*Freedom*, 14). No reason, other than that most of us seem to like all these things (which might also be true of chocolate chip cookies), is given for attaching great importance to these capabilities. Of course, we can easily surmise that Sen must think (though he does not say it) that people have a right to the flourishing life that results when these instrumental freedoms are in place.

Sen's language here is too weak. He repeatedly passes up an opportunity to undergird his alarming statistical messages about inequalities in these five functionings with an overt appeal to internationally accepted human rights norms. He presupposes that all of the world's people have an equal basic right to their development as the persons they are, but he does not connect that supposition to the explicit claim in UDHR Articles 22, 26, and 29 that everyone has a right to the full and free development of his or her personality. His liberal cosmopolitan readers are "taken in" because they share Sen's assumption that (to use Dworkin's term), equality is the "sovereign virtue."[15] Sen admits that every ethical theory nowadays must make claims to equality in some space or other, whether that be in primary goods (for Rawls), in resources (for Dworkin), in liberties (for libertarians like Robert Nozick and Maurice Cranston), or in preference calculations (for utilitarian-minded economists). They all operate with some claim to basic equal treatment for the subjects of the domains their theories stake out. Sen's own theory is no different, for his numerous examples of unequal statistics are meant to arouse us to action based on the implied belief of a right to equal treatment both domestically and, if there are not enough resources at that level, globally. But Sen nowhere defends this presumption of equal treatment, except to say that anyone who favors unequal treatment must offer an argument that can convince all those affected by such treatment.[16] I will argue against this burden when (in Chapter 6) I reject any kind of intrinsic or conceptual connection between democracy and popular sovereignty. Sen should come right out and say (as Locke did about people in the state of nature) that people are roughly equal in their capabilities or in their desires for the five instrumental freedoms and that they have an inherent moral right to their development. He shifts the burden of proof too quickly to anyone who countenances an unequal distribution. Having broken open the path between the moral and economic tracks, he has left it for others to pave. Martha Nussbaum's more refined capabilities approach helps us do that.

Nussbaum's Capabilities Approach. Nussbaum has given us two very similar versions of a more overtly philosophical capabilities approach to questions of justice, one in *Women and Human Development* (here referred to as *WHD*) and a later, more elaborate one in *Frontiers of Justice.*[17] She offers us the later book "to provide the philosophical underpinning for an account of core human entitlements that should be respected and implemented by the governments of all nations, as a bare minimum of what respect for human dignity requires" (*Frontiers*, 70). These "entitlements" are the human rights of my theory, and I shall use her (and Sen's) capabilities to develop a metaphysics of human rights and to flesh out the concept of inherence introduced in Chapter 1. To do this I will have to highlight her metaphysics, which she allows much of the time to remain dormant, stressing its political utility instead. I have phrased my report and critique in terms of her first account, qualifying that when necessary by her later emendations. The biggest change, as I see it, is that in her later account she has sought to draw the line between the metaphysical and the political more clearly. My criticism is that she still does not appreciate enough the power of the concept and language of human rights, and fails to openly place those norms between her metaphysics of capabilities and the political use she wants to make of those universal human capabilities.

Like Sen, Nussbaum criticizes the resource-based approach as not "going deep enough to diagnose obstacles that can be present even when resources seem to be adequately spread around, causing individuals to neglect to avail themselves of opportunities they in some sense have (such as free public education, or the vote, or the right to work)" (*WHD*, 68–69). She says that "if we operate only with an index we will frequently reinforce inequalities that are highly relevant to well-being." She wants an approach to development that "is respectful of each person's struggle for flourishing that treats each person as an end and as a source of agency and worth in her own right" (68–69). Her "core idea is that of the human being as a dignified free being who shapes his or her own life in cooperation and reciprocity with others rather than being passively shaped or pushed around by the world in the manner of a 'flock' or a 'herd' animal. A life that is really human is shaped by these human powers of practical reason and sociability" (72). In other words, we ourselves, as the persons we are, must take an active part in the development of our own capabilities. For doing so is one of our most basic human rights. Our reason and sociability inject into that development a large area of choice as to the precise manner in which we would like to see our capabilities developed.

We must be careful when we use the passive language of international human rights documents, which use the noun "development" and, like the Declaration, speak of "everyone" in the third person as having the right to the "free (and full) development of his personality" (Articles 22 and 29) or having his or her education "directed at the full development of the human personality" (Article 26). The use of the noun "development" leaves unsettled who has the primary responsibility for this development of one's personality. It could be society and state, which are mentioned in 26(3) and alluded to in 25(2). Or it could be parents, who are given a "prior" say in these matters in 26(3). These references pertain primarily to the development of our personalities and capabilities when we are still in our childhood. The implication is that when we are no longer in life's earlier stage, the end of which is defined differently in different societies, then it is we ourselves who are the primary duty-bearers that correlate with our right to develop our personalities. It is only when things happen to us that are, to use the crucial words of 25(1), "beyond our control" that the state and society must step in and help us function with dignity. This includes the "normal" rights to social security mentioned in Articles 22 and 25, as well as the times when we speak up for people outside the mainstream, who for reasons beyond their control have fallen to the margins of our societies.

So a large part of the development of our capabilities is very much a matter of the personal choices we ourselves make in the course of living our lives. Central to this development is the concept of human dignity that is the ground floor of all international human rights documents, the Declaration included. Nussbaum believes that her way of understanding human dignity does and should have "cross-cultural resonance and intuitive power" (*WHD*, 72). Her example is that of a tragic art work in which the tragic character "is assailed by fortune in a way very different from the way we react to a storm blowing grains of sand in the wind." When these typically human powers are blocked in their development, we invariably experience an assault on our idea of human dignity and at times are filled with horror. And when the "forces of chance" have "not completely eclipsed the humanity of the person" we often stand in awe and wonder (72–73). We are even more profoundly repelled and horrified when this involves not the forces of chance but the voluntary behavior of other human agents gone berserk, as in the Holocaust and other massacres and genocides before and after. "One way of seeing this," she says, "is to think about the ways in which tragic plots cross cultural boundaries; certain deprivations are understood to be terrible, despite differences in metaphysical understandings of the world" (74). Human beings from a wide range of cultures and traditions share (unless their consciences are somehow blocked) these intuitive fixed starting points, for "there is a tragic aspect to any choice in which citizens are pushed below the threshold in one of the central [capacity] areas" (81). Nussbaum rejects, as I did in Chapter 3, any account of justice that is purely procedural. Her approach "involves an intuitive idea of human dignity and arguments to the effect that a certain entitlement is implicit in the idea of human dignity (*Frontiers*, 37)," but she stops far short of embracing the theory of moral intuitionism I placed as a framework around these intuitions.

In both her accounts Nussbaum gives us the same list of ten "central human functional capabilities" (*WHD*, 78; *Frontiers*, 77). They are (1) Life; (2) Bodily Health; (3) Bodily Integrity; (4) Sense, Imagination, and Thought; (5) Emotions; (6) Practical Reason; (7) Affiliation. Being able to live with and show concern for others. Having the social bases of self-respect; (8) Other Species. Being able to live with concern for and in relation to animals, plants, and the world of nature"; (9) Play; (10) Control over one's environment. Political and Material. Her capabilities approach derives from Aristotle's distinction between potentiality (capability) and actuality (functioning). Human beings the world over are the sorts of creatures that have these roughly (because the list can be amended) ten capabilities, which means that—unless they are in some way handicapped by internal or external causes—it is natural for them to develop these capabilities. Any development that stops short of the full and free development of these capabilities is a violation of human nature and dignity.

Nussbaum wisely refrains from claiming that these ten human capabilities constitute the essence of what it means to be human, but her desire not to be infected by the essentialist virus also makes her unnecessarily shy about saying, as we just did, that it is natural for humans everywhere to develop these capabilities. She claims that "the capabilities approach is fully universal" in the sense that "the capabilities in question are held to be important for each and every *citizen*, in each and every nation, and each *person* is to be treated as an end" (*Frontiers*, 78, emphasis added). The shift here between "citizen" and "person" shows that her primary interest is still in the political use she wants to make of her list of capabilities (which we applaud) and not in supplying a metaphysics for the concept of human rights, the use to which I propose we put her list. She moves rather quickly when she admits that her capabilities approach is "in this [universal] way similar to the international human rights approach," without telling us what the deeper reason for that similarity might be (78). That said, we can and should read the Declaration as saying that all human beings have equal rights to develop the (for now) ten "central human functional capabilities" mentioned by Nussbaum.

The Declaration's first two articles can be read as stating Sen's and Nussbaum's basic presupposition that "all human beings are born free and equal" with rights to the development of these capabilities. Since almost all our human capabilities can be brought to blossoming only in a communal context, it goes without saying that we can only catch the centrality or basic character of these capabilities if we state them in a very abstract way. By stripping away all local factors we reach this abstract level and isolate the fundamental right to a basic functional equality of all the members of the human family. Article 2 does this when it says that "without distinction of any kind, such as race, color, sex, language, religion, political or other opinion, national or social origin, property, birth or other status," all human beings "are entitled to all the rights and freedoms set forth in this Declaration." By saying that these local and birth factors are irrelevant, the drafters did not mean to suggest that they do not enter the picture at all, which would be absurd and unfortunately has led to many misunderstandings about the concept of what a human right is. Our question is not whether local factors enter in, but concerns what role they do and ought to play in the development of our personality.

Nussbaum holds that the dignity she defends as at the base of these capabilities is an equal dignity.[18] Article 2 of the Declaration forbids the destructive application of any of these nondiscrimination factors when it forbids using them to deny the fact that some human being has one of Nussbaum's ten capabilities. These capabilities are constitutive of our human nature and ordinarily come with our birth, which is why the rights (my word) or entitlements (Nussbaum's preference) to their development are said to be inherent in us and inalienable. While she uses the same normative link between capabilities and the call for government programs aimed at their development, Nussbaum never does say that these "entitlements" are inherent in the persons that have the capabilities or that they are inalienable. This omission may be due to the fact that for a good many of these human capabilities a great deal of nurture by family, community, and state is called for if they are to blossom. This outside involvement brings the local factors rejected in the abstract formulation of these rights back into the development picture in a positive, nondiscriminatory manner. In this way nature (stripping away the local factors to see what capabilities are central to our humanity) and nurture (having family, community, and nation provide essential support for capability development) complement each other.

These background assumptions allow us to read into each article of the Declaration one or several of Nussbaum's ten capabilities (the numbers for which I give in parentheses): Article 3's rights to life, liberty, and personal security protect our capacity for having a life and being at liberty to come and go as we please in the knowledge that we are secure in our persons (1–3); Article 4's right to freedom from all forms of slavery and servitude protects our capacity to live that life rationally, to form our own conception of "the good and to engage in critical reflection about planning one's life," which we cannot do if we are not free (1, 6); Article 5's prohibition of torture and degrading treatment or punishment protects not just our "Bodily Integrity," but also "the social bases of self-respect and non-humiliation" (3–5, 7B); Articles 6 through 11 explore what it means to be "a person before the law" and so secures our "being treated as a dignified being whose worth is equal to that of others" (5B, 10A); the privacy rights of Article 12 protect our capacity for developing emotional "attachments to things and people outside ourselves; to love those who love and care for us." It protects us against having our "emotional development blighted by overwhelming fear and anxiety, or by traumatic events of abuse or neglect" (4, 5, 7A, 10B); Article 13's right to freedom of movement protects our "Bodily Integrity" by enabling us "to move freely from place" and to secure ourselves "against assault, including sexual assault, child sexual abuse, and domestic violence" (3); Article 14's right to ask for asylum in other countries seeks to protect that same "Bodily Integrity" and often prevents people from "dying prematurely, or before one's life is so reduced [by persecution] as to be not worth living" (1, 3); the right to a nationality in Article 15 must be seen as protection of our "Bodily Integrity" when our government comes to our aid, and of our capability to control our political environment through participation, free speech, and association.

The marriage rights of Article 16 protect our capacity "for sexual satisfaction and for choice in matters of reproduction" as well as our capability for "Affiliation," which allows us "to live with and toward others" (3, 7); the property rights of Article 17 protect our capability to control our "Material Environment" in terms of holding "property (both land and movable goods), not just formally but in terms of real opportunity [and] . . . on an equal basis with others" (10B); Article 18's rights to freedom of thought, conscience, and religion protect the capabilities of our "Senses, Imagination and Thought." These are used by us in numerous contexts, a crucial one being one's "search for the ultimate meaning of life in one's own way" and to do this critically and rationally (4, 6); Article 19's right to freedom of opinion and expression continues this capability and duplicates Nussbaum's "guarantees of freedom of expression with respect both to political and artistic speech, and freedom of religious exercise" (4); Article 20 protects our capability for "Affiliation" in all its varied forms. It protects our ability "to recognize and show concern for other human beings, to engage in various forms of social interaction; to be able to imagine the situation of another and to have compassion for that situation; to have the capability for both justice and friendship" (7); Article 21's dual rights of citizenship in terms of having input by voting and standing for office protect the basic human capability to control our "Political Environment" and one's capacity "to participate effectively in political choices that govern one's life" (10A);[19] the work related rights in Article 23 protect our capability "to work as a human being exercising practical reason and entering into meaningful relationships of mutual recognition with other workers" (7B); Article 24's right to leisure and holidays with pay protects our fundamental capability "to laugh, to play, to enjoy recreational activities," which we need to exercise in part as a respite from work; Article 25's list of social security rights protect both the items Nussbaum mentions under "Bodily Health" (2) as well some of those that come with our capacity for caring and being cared for that fall under various types of "Affiliation" (7); Article 26's right to an education protects our capacity to "imagine, think and reason—and to do these things in a "truly human" way, a way informed and cultivated by an adequate education, including, but by no means limited to, literacy and basic mathematical and scientific training" (4); Article 27's right to participation in culture takes this one step further in that it recognizes and protects our own capacity to produce or to enjoy "the self-expressive works and events . . . religious, literary, musical and so forth" of others (4).

In a note Nussbaum tells her readers that capability no. 8—the capacity "to be able to live with concern for and in relation to animals, plants and the world of nature"—"has been the most controversial item on the list"

(*WHD*, 80, n.85). She feels that a government can do "quite a lot about this capability, through its choice of policy about endangered species, the health and life of animals, and the ecology. Norway, for instance, places tremendous emphasis on this capability" (80). In chapter 6 of *Frontiers of Justice* she has greatly expanded on this theme of "justice for nonhuman animals," and shown us how we can and should both foster the development of the capabilities of nonhuman animals as well as acknowledge our own capabilities for compassion for and for companionship with them. We may also give the National Park and preservation systems in the United States, Canada, and numerous other countries as further examples of the protection of and companionship with nature and other animal species that find refuge in them from the ever-encroaching human world. Article 28's human right "to a social and international order in which the rights and freedoms set forth in this Declaration can be fully realized" has been interpreted as protective of this desire and capability to live in harmony with the rest of the biosphere. In fact, Thomas Pogge reads Article 28 "as holding that the moral quality, or justice, of any institutional order depends primarily on its success in affording all its participants secure access to the objects of their human rights."[20] In Chapter 1, section A, we criticized Pogge's metaphysical openness as too focused on institutional structures, but that does not mean that we do not agree with him when he claims here that "There can be, at any given time, only one global order" and that a "*single universal* standard" is given to us in the Universal Declaration (177, emphasis original). The capability involved gives ontological grounding to the stated moral right. Together they have in recent years led to advances in international environmental law. Nussbaum repeatedly calls her capabilities account "a species of" the human rights approach (*Frontiers*, 284–86) and not the exact same thing, because nonhuman animals (who make up an important part of her theory) also have capabilities and entitlements to develop them, but they cannot be said to have human rights and are therefore not a part of our own theory, other than in this indirect way: through our own capacity to live with and have concern for nonhuman animals.

The advantage of adding capabilities to an analysis of the Declaration is that it gives us a clear way of saying something about the adjective "human" in the clause "human rights." Most books about human rights tell us a great deal about what a *right* is (a justified claim that can activate the duties of others), but they frequently fail to tell us about the import of the adjective *human* in the crucial juxtaposition of these two words. Also, the capabilities approach can answer the charge of utopianism. Having one and the same intellectual umbrella for all the rights in the Declaration will amplify the answers to the Cranstonite challenge which I discuss in Chapter 5. With the capabilities approach under our belt, we can answer anyone who wants a much shorter list of human rights than the Declaration gives us with the retort that we can intellectually afford the wide scope of the rights in the Declaration because they all are organically linked to an ontological network of capabilities, a network that fleshes out the widely used concept of human dignity. One can also legitimately argue that throughout the entire Declaration runs the theme of a person's fundamental right to the full and free development of his or her personality; this breaks through to the surface of the text in Articles 22, 26, and 29. This right summarizes what in my previous study I referred to as "The Socialist Shape of Work-Related Rights."[21] I argued there not that the Declaration was a socialist document, but that the socialist nations of Latin America fortunately had a strong hand in its writing. No one can say that the document imposes a possessive individualist or libertarian view on the rest of the world, for the text and *travaux* belie such a claim. I made the point that the majority of the drafters wanted to steer a middle ground between capitalist and socialist ways of organizing a nation's economy, which we can tell from Article 17's assertion that "everyone has the right to property alone *as well as* in association with others" (emphasis added). Nussbaum's earlier statement of the capabilities approach captures the levels of community and state involvement needed for the development of various of our capabilities. That is what we might expect and as it should be.

In her earlier account Nussbaum reserves the connection between human rights and capabilities for a subgroup she calls "combined capabilities." She defines these "as internal capabilities *combined with* suitable external conditions for the exercise of the function" (*WHD*, 85, emphasis original). A nonmutilated widowed Indian woman has "the internal capability for sexual expression" and citizens living under repressive nondemocratic regimes have "the internal capacities but not the combined capacities to exercise thought and speech in accordance with their consciences" (85). In each case the social and legal environment blocks "the exercise of practical reason and the other major functions" of these central human capabilities. Nussbaum unnecessarily complicates things when she puts the connection between human rights and more basic capabilities in this parenthetical comment: "Once again, we must distinguish the claim that 'A has a right to shelter'—which frequently refers to A's moral claim by virtue of being human, possessing what I call *basic capabilities*—from the statement that 'Country C gives its citizens the right to shelter.' It is the second sentence whose analysis I am discussing here" (98, emphasis original). In both her accounts Nussbaum comes at the connection between human rights and capabilities from the point of view of the second statement in these parentheses. This reveals her interest in the political use of the capabilities approach. Because my interest is metaphysical and not political, my account of this connection focuses instead on the first sentence in these parentheses. I want all the capabilities—and not just the combined ones—equally identified as good grounds for human rights claims. I look on the social and political forces that are needed to turn a basic capability into a combined one as measures of implementation that it is for duty-bearers to deliver. Nussbaum's idea is that some capabilities are "basic" and embedded in our biological nature. These (like the exercise of the five senses) require only little communal input. Others, such as an "internal" one (like speech) or a "combined" one (like religious practice) require a great deal of family, community, or national input to be brought to full and free blossoming. I note these differences, but see them more as nuances that the duty-bearers need to be attentive to than as relevant to a deep connection that exists between human rights and only some (but not all) of the species-wide capabilities.

In her second account Nussbaum has dropped these distinctions between basic, internal, and combined capabilities and offers all of them as key components of human dignity and thus as all equally worthy of being developed. Since I am interested in the metaphysics of these capabilities and not just in their political use, I much prefer her first and fuller account. The distinctions between "basic," "internal," and "combined" capabilities are helpful in that they bring out the communitarian character of the human rights that ride piggyback on these capabilities. Even though all the capabilities are inherent in the human person because we are born with them, it is obvious that different community and state involvement is called for in the case of different capabilities. Just like a flower is really that flower when it stands in full bloom, so the human person spoken of in the Universal Declaration is only and really such when he or she expresses all these different capabilities fully and freely. These human and therefore universal (unless blocked) capabilities are constitutive of the human personality, which it is the point of my continued references to the full and free development of the human personality that we find in Articles 22, 26, and 29.

I am not claiming that the drafters always had these capabilities in mind when they discussed their articles. They probably did not. Nor do I claim that Nussbaum set up her list with the Declaration in mind. She probably did not. But I also do not believe that it is sheer coincidence that the list of rights in the Declaration and the list of central human functional capabilities fit so well together. This fit is the result of the deep connection between human rights and human nature that, as I have shown in Chapter 1, the drafters did not want to give up, even though they voted to delete a reference to "natural rights" from their text. While they rejected the strong natural rights language that travels with Cartesian essentialism, we can now see the kind of connection they wanted to preserve between the rights they proclaimed and the person-hood they sought to protect. It is one with multiple capabilities that need to be brought out and developed with a great deal of family, community, national, and international support.

Since Nussbaum's list is of universal human capabilities, she faces the same questions that any theorist of human rights does: what makes this theorist think that people have these capabilities universally and why should governments honor them? Her expanded account in *Frontiers of Justice* stresses that the capabilities are universal and thus possessed by every human being, but she is still too reticent to make overt connec-tions between her universal entitlements and there being such a thing as human nature. She confesses that she is sympathetic to John Rawls's shift to the neutrality of political justice. That makes her avoid all the deeper philosophical questions of metaphysics, ontology, and theology. These are to be settled by people when they construct their own personal world views, but they are not part of the liberal political agenda espoused by Rawls and Nussbaum. "In general, the account of political justification that I favor," she writes, "lies close to the Rawlsian account of argument proceeding toward reflective equilibrium: we lay out the arguments for a given theoretical position, holding it up against the 'fixed points' in our moral intuitions; . . . For example, among the provisional fixed points might be the judgment that rape and domestic violence are damaging to human dignity. We look to see how the various conceptions we exam-ine correspond to that intuition" (*WHD*, 101). These intuitions are the justificatory basis of Nussbaum's list of universal human capabilities. A capability is placed on the list as a "fixed point" when a gross lack of de-velopment of that particular capability strikes us as an affront to human dignity. The life stories of the women in India whose capabilities Nuss-baum found stifled by discriminatory social and cultural practices show us that "certain human abilities exert a moral claim that they should be developed" (83).

She adds that "this must be understood as *a freestanding moral idea*, not one that relies on a particular metaphysical or teleological view. Not all actual human abilities exert a moral claim, only the ones that have been evaluated as valuable from an ethical viewpoint. (The capacity for cruelty, for example, does not figure on the list.) Thus the argument begins from ethical premises and derives ethical conclusions from these alone, not from any further metaphysical premises" (*WHD*, 83). That is her earlier disavowal of metaphysics. Here is her later version: "I consider the list to be a freestanding 'partial moral conception' to use Rawls' phrase: that is, it is explicitly introduced for political purposes only, and without any grounding in metaphysical ideas *of the sort that divide people along the lines of culture and religion*" (*Frontiers*, 78, emphasis added). I have italicized the differentiating clause that she has tagged on at the end. It works in favor of a sort of metaphysics, for the metaphysics she rejects, as she puts it some pages later, "are ideas of the sort that divide people along lines of culture and religion, or the idea of god or gods" (*Frontiers*, 297). So there is one sort of metaphysics (theological) that is not acceptable, and another sort (Aristotelian) that is.

Having just been told by Nussbaum about the existence of at least ten "central human functional capabilities," we must take her disavowal of metaphysics with a grain of salt. Nussbaum feels that

we can get a consensus of the requisite sort, for political purposes, about the core of our moral argument concerning the moral claim of certain human powers. Human beings are creatures such that, provided with the right educational and material support, they can become fully capable of all [ten] of these human functions. . . . When a human being is given a life that blights powers of human action and expression that does give us a sense of waste and tragedy—the tragedy expressed, for example, in Mrinal's statement to her husband, in Tagore's story, when she says, "I am not one to die easily." (83)

In this short statement Nussbaum has repeated both the metaphysics and the epistemology of inherent human rights. Human beings are "creatures such that . . ." is the metaphysics of the theory, and her use of violations of human dignity to justify placing some capability or other on the list of demands for development provides the matching epistemology. The Declaration's drafters, too, were ready to adopt a clause or an article if it was shown that Hitler had violated it in some gross manner. In both cases the presumption is that human beings worldwide recognize and condemn gross violations of human dignity. It is from this shared recognition that a political consensus can be developed, whether it is on a list of human rights or on Nussbaum's list of human capabilities.

The capacity for cruelty is not on the list, for although human beings are capable of acts of torture, that capability does not flesh out the intuitive idea of human dignity that is Nussbaum's justificatory point of departure. Going where she probably does not want to go, we may be able to sort out these capabilities the way Aquinas sorted out what he called our "natural inclinations." He said that those that were common were good and proper to man, and those that were not common were not good and proper, and that in any case "all the natural inclinations belonging to the other powers must needs be directed according to reason."[22] Cruelty is not common and therefore not good. To critics who suggest that this makes the capability for sexual intimacy between persons of the same sex not good because it is clearly is not as common as the heterosexual inclination is, I respond with Aquinas that these powers or capabilities must in each case "be directed according to reason." The test of being "directed according to reason" will ban cruelty but not gay and lesbian sexual inclinations. Nussbaum makes the same point as Aquinas did when she lifts up practical reason and affiliation as two capabilities that are of "special importance" in that they run through the use of all the others. What she says about the use of senses can be equally said of all the other capabilities, including sexuality: "To use one's senses in a way not infused by the characteristically human use of thought and planning is to use them in an incompletely human manner" (82). Work also "must involve being able to behave as a thinking human being, not just as a cog in a machine; and it must be capable of being done with and toward others in a way that involves mutual recognition of humanity" (82). A test like this must have helped Nussbaum construct her list of capabilities. For not literally all people have these ten capabilities on a functioning level. Tumors, bad governments, or bad parents can stand in the way. These capabilities are all more or less natural in that they are either basic ones that are woven into our biological system or internal ones that are woven in but come out progressively (instead of instantly). In her earlier account she calls these latter ones "combined capacities" because they need a great deal of environmental input to flourish. Wanting to stay clear of metaphysics, Nussbaum no longer recommends this way of selecting the capabilities for her list. Her preferred epistemic route is the appeal to our shared intuitions and moral revulsions whenever we see a gross lack of their development.

We must now discuss Nussbaum's main complaints against the language of human rights. She contends that the idea of it is "by no means a crystal-clear idea" and that "difficult theoretical questions are frequently obscured by the use of [human] rights language" (*WHD*, 97; *Frontiers*, 284). By inserting the term "human" here I mean to draw attention to the fact that both of Nussbaum's accounts suffer from a lack of clarity on the difference between inherent human rights and ordinary legal rights. My insertion fits her first account best, for there the citation comes from a section entitled "Capabilities and Human Rights" (*WHD*, 96). In her later account the same citation is drawn from a section entitled "Capabilities and Rights" (*Frontiers*, 284). The title change suggests that in *Frontiers of Justice* she makes fewer claims about what a human right is than she did in her earlier discussion, but it does not help to clear things up. The same ambiguities plague both accounts. Because she operates with an incomplete set of human rights theories, Nussbaum still fails to see the tremendous complementarity that exists between her capabilities approach and human rights. What follows draws on both accounts.

The first problem arises because "people differ about what the *basis* of a rights claim is: rationality, sentience, and mere life have all had their defenders" (*WHD*, 97, emphasis original; *Frontiers*, 285). Here my answer is that it is none of these singly, but all of them together form the basis of a human right. One of the things that makes Nussbaum's list of capabilities appealing as a metaphysical grounding theme for the articles of the Declaration is that each capability carves out its own area of functioning. All three of the foundational candidates (reason, sentience, and life) are involved in every one of these functionings. Even so, we are not bound by this list. New capabilities that have lain dormant in human nature can be discovered, as for instance has happened with the need for and the consequent human right to privacy. It is this open-ended and empirical character of the list of capabilities that keeps our account from being essentialist. I do not deduce the rights in the Declaration from any one of these basic characteristics or capabilities, but make them piggyback along on the list as it expands. So we need not be afraid of a return to the Cartesian essentialism the drafters rejected in favor of plain human rights discourse. We have a right to life, liberty, and security of person not simply because, as a disciple of Descartes might say, we are "thinking things," but because the (for now) ten capabilities that Nussbaum mentions are universal ones that may not be thwarted. Nussbaum often says that the two lists complement each other, but I wish to hold her to her statement that the capabilities approach provides "the philosophical underpinning for core human entitlements" (*WHD*, 66). Her set of capabilities does more than complement the list of rights in the UN Declaration; it grounds them in human nature, understood in a nonessentialist fashion. Instead of being "free floating," the list of capabilities describes the kinds of creatures humans are.

Nussbaum's second account stresses that the basis of a person's claim to the development of one of her capabilities is "the very birth of a person into the human community" (*Frontiers*, 285) and that the capabilities do not derive from that person's birth as the unique person he or she is; instead, the capacities involved are "characteristic of the human species" (285). We entirely agree and have based the metaphysical universality of human rights and of the doctrine of inherence on this line of thinking. Speaking of the entitlements of someone who suffers from congenital cerebral palsy and severe mental retardation (96), Nussbaum says that "they would not exist were capabilities based only on individual endowment, rather than on the species norm" (285). She is also right when she adds that "most human rights approaches fail to give definite answers to such questions." True, but we wish to claim an exception for the theory proposed in this book. While other human rights theorists may well dispute among themselves about the basis of human rights, we take all Nussbaum's capabilities and use them as metaphysical stepping stones to attendant moral rights.

The second controversy has to do with whether human rights are "prepolitical or artifacts of laws and institutions" (*WHD*, 97; *Frontiers*, 285). We saw in Chapters 1 section C and 3 section B that there is indeed a strong trend in the human rights literature to define a human right as an artifact constructed by lawmakers and judges or even by the customs of the ages, and I accused theorists of committing the fallacy of implementation. It is probably with these accounts in mind that Nussbaum observes that there is "one significant tradition" that holds even human rights to be "political artifacts" (*Frontiers*, 285). Our theory does not belong to that tradition. Since we have openly linked human rights to Nussbaum's own list of capabilities that are clearly prepolitical, I have also strengthened the case for the prepolitical or prejuridical character of human rights. While the prepolitical character of some of the civil rights (for example, the right not to be tortured) is rather obvious and readily agreed on as being a universal value, the rights to political participation, to hold a job, to get married, and to participate in culture can now also be seen as inherent to the human person because they are linked to universal human capabilities. If for even a moment Nussbaum thought of her list of capabilities as *not* prepolitical, her entire project of using the list to call the world's governments to task for not fostering these capabilities for women and disabled persons under their jurisdiction would come to naught. Unless they are very severely physically or mentally handicapped, all people are more or less (because the combined ones require a great deal of environmental input) born with these capabilities. Therefore, if the capabilities that lie behind the rights in the Declaration are prepolitical, the rights that piggyback along must also be so. Governments cannot legitimately decide to foster some capabilities in their peoples and let others go by the wayside. That would amount to a violation of the human right to the free and full development of one's personality, which I have been mentioning as the one right (in Articles 22, 26, and 29), that seems to summarize or collect within itself all the other rights in the document.

In her earlier account Nussbaum correctly claims that rights theorists differ about the relationships between rights and duties: "if A has a right to S, does this mean that there is always someone who has a duty to provide S, and how shall we decide who that someone is?" In her later account she tackles this question not in the section on capabilities and rights, but before that when she rejects O'Neill's insistence on the priority of duties over rights (*Frontiers*, 277). Since I have already dealt with this query in my discussion of the asymmetry between human rights and their correlative duties (Chapter 1, section C), I can be brief here. We noted in that discussion that the assignment of correlative duties, as opposed to inherent rights, depends on local, domestic, and often international factors. If the primary caregivers and duty-holders shirk their duties and do not (for instance) feed their children, and if the village and state are in such political turmoil that they fail to act, and if the Red Cross trucks happen to have been disabled or robbed by bandits, then in the final analysis it might be up to the citizens of other countries to act through the UN or through any of the thousands of national and international NGOs that on a daily basis solicit our money or other kinds of support.

The capabilities approach also helps resolve a dispute or ambiguity about whether (human) rights are to be seen negatively or positively, which in our response to Cranston (in the next chapter) we will settle in favor of the latter option. For Nussbaum this ambiguity is "about what rights are to be understood as rights *to.* Are human rights primarily rights to be treated in certain ways? Rights to a certain level of achieved well being? Rights to resources with which one may pursue one's life plan? Rights to certain opportunities and capacities with which one may make choices about one's life plan?" (*WHD*, 97). Or what? The last suggested option of "rights to certain opportunities and capacities" is recast in the later account as "the affirmative task" of governments to help secure the rights of all citizens to the development of all the ten capabilities on the list (*Frontiers*, 287). As such it is opposed to the Enlightenment tradition of negative liberty, which leaves "things notoriously indeterminate as to whether impediments supplied by the market or by private actors are to be considered violations of fundamental [human] rights of citizens" (286). The examples Nussbaum picks are the rights to political participation, free exercise of religion, and free speech, which, she says, we should think of as "secured to people only when the relevant capabilities to function are present" (287). If such a right only "exists on paper" it cannot be said to be secured to the citizens.

It is at a point like this that Nussbaum's failure to differentiate clearly between human rights and legal rights is most evident. It leads her to flirt with the implementation fallacy that pulls the measures of implementation into the very definition of what a human right is.[23] Says she: "But by defining the securing of rights in terms of capabilities, we make it clear that a people in country C don't really have an effective right to political participation . . . ; they really have been given the right only if there are effective measures to make people truly capable of political exercise" (*Frontiers*, 287). The "capabilities" here must be understood in terms of Sen's "functionings," for they are the "effective measures" of implementation and place citizens in positions of really being capable of doing X, Y, or Z. This need for measures of implementation is part of what it means (broadly speaking) to have a legal right. Such rights are not the rights they are said to be if the procedures in which they are embedded have broken down or are shot through with loopholes and corruption. On paper the citizens have the right to participate politically, but, as is so often the case with single-party systems, in reality they do not. Because legal rights are created and defined procedurally, they cannot be said to exist where those procedures, including enforcement ones, have totally broken down. But the case is different with inherent human rights or entitlements and their attendant ten capabilities. These all accrue to us at birth, and our possession of them *as rights or entitlements* does not depend on any measures of implementation. Since our enjoyment of them *does* so depend, we want to have them secured in our legal systems as legal rights, not just on paper but in reality.

We must therefore read Nussbaum's observation that certain "rights" are "best thought of as secured to people only when the relevant capabilities to function are present" on two levels. First, we must secure, tie down, or implement the already existing inherent human right to, for instance, freedom of expression. We do that through constitutional and statutory legal enactments. Second, we must secure or implement the legal right we have just been "given" (Nussbaum's word) through "effective measures," so that they do not remain "nominal" rights that exist only on paper. Nussbaum's entitlements float back and forth between the first and the second level. They are comparable to our human rights when we see them as rights to the development of our species capabilities. But she just as often leads us to read them simply as legal rights that must be followed up by effective implementation measures to be the entitlements they are said to be. I believe that the above passage about "country C" is a case in point.

She moves even farther from the human rights approach with the claim that her capabilities approach is better suited to dealing with the inequalities women have for centuries suffered "inside the family" in terms of "inequalities in resources and opportunities, educational deprivations, the failure of work to be recognized as work, [and] insults to bodily integrity" (*Frontiers*, 290). The reason she gives is that "Traditional rights talk has neglected these issues" because "rights language is strongly linked with the traditional distinction between the public sphere, which the state regulates and a private sphere which it must leave alone" (290). This may well be true of "traditional rights talk," but it does not hold for the tradition of human rights, for they were from the start aimed at breaking down the distinction between public and private realms. We can see this in the (relative) absence of sexist language in the Universal Declaration,[24] and in international human rights norms generally, as well as in the attention that has been given to the rights of children.[25] From the human rights point of view women and children are every bit as entitled to the development of their species capabilities as are men and adults. The right to the development of our personalities was chosen as a theme precisely because it would also catch those who have been marginalized by domestic legal systems. As will be clear from our response to the Cranstonites in the next chapter, I do not dispute Nussbaum's lesson that "securing a right to someone requires more than the absence of negative state action" (288). Nor do we dispute her claim that the distinction between the first and the second generation of human rights is a "misleading" one that serves no great purpose (289).

Alhough, as I just argued, Nussbaum should have retained her earlier distinctions between "basic," "internal," and "combined" capabilities, her second and more expansive account of the capabilities approach still supports the metaphysics of inherent human rights. To give an example of this support in the realm of justification, Nussbaum sees her list of capabilities not as deductively "derived from" the intuitive idea of human dignity, but as a "fleshing out" of the ideas of dignity and respect (*Frontiers*, 174). I likewise have rejected deductive accounts based on the Golden Rule (in Chapter 3) and have given support to the idea of the conscience of humanity with a discussion of the doctrine of manifest illegality (Chapter 2, section B). In her earlier account Nussbaum differentiated between basic capabilities (like seeing, tasting, hearing, and touching) and internal ones (like thought and speech) that come with growing into mature adults, and the further implementation of the internal ones with the creation of legal and other institutional environments that turn them into combined capabilities. Making these distinctions was not futile. She rightly felt that there was a distinction to be made between an internal and a combined capability because "even a highly trained capability can be thwarted," as when "a person accustomed to exercising religious freedom and freedom of speech" is legally and environmentally blocked from exercising these internal capabilities. "Here we feel that the internal capability is fully present, but the combined capability is not." Also, "Many women who, driven by material need, are eager to work outside the home, and who have skills that they could use to do some work, are prevented from working by familial or religious pressures" (*WHD*, 85–86). She took from these examples the lesson of the "twofold importance of material and social circumstances, both in training internal capabilities and in letting them express themselves once trained" (86).

These examples help us realize that the human rights to the development of our species capabilities require a nuanced and greatly varied system of implementation. After the necessary support from family, community, and state, it is hoped that all the capabilities "at a certain point . . . are there, and [that] the person can use them" (*WHD*, 84). For example, a "woman who has not suffered genital mutilation has the *internal capa-*

bility for sexual pleasure; most adult human beings everywhere have the *internal capability* for religious freedom and the freedom of speech," but that does not mean they can freely function in those areas (84). Like Sen, Nussbaum is sensitive to the conversion factor and warns us, for instance, not to simply "think of the right to shelter as a right to a certain amount of resources" because "giving resources to people does not always bring differently situated people up to the same level of capability to function" (99). By contrast, "Analyzing economic and material rights in terms of capabilities . . . enables us to set forth clearly a rationale we have for spending unequal amounts of money on the disadvantaged, or creating special programs to assist their transition to full capability" (99). In this way the capabilities approach helps us see the importance of the nondiscrimination list in Article 2 of the Declaration and especially of the need to add to that list the item "disability."[26]

The upshot is that while the capabilities approach helps us develop a metaphysics for human rights, Nussbaum at the same time underestimates the power that has accrued to the language of human rights in our world. As she puts it in *Frontiers of Justice*, "the language of [human] rights still plays an important role in public discourse, despite its unsatisfactory features" (*Frontiers*, 290). Earlier she had said that "The language of capabilities has [this] . . . advantage over the language of [human] rights: it is not strongly linked to one particular cultural and historical tradition, as the language of rights is believed to be" (*WHD*, 99). She there catches herself by adding: "This belief is not very accurate: although the term 'rights' is associated with the European Enlightenment, its component ideas have deep roots in many traditions," including those in India.[27] "So 'rights' are not exclusively Western, in the sense that matters most; they can be endorsed from a variety of perspectives. Nonetheless, the language of capabilities enables us to bypass this troublesome debate. When we speak simply of what people are able to do and to be, we do not even give the appearance of privileging a Western idea. Ideas of activity and ability are everywhere, and there is no culture in which people do not ask themselves what they are able to do, what opportunities they have for functioning" (100).

True, the metaphysics of capabilities is universally available, and that is why we are using it here to strengthen our doctrine of inherence and with that our answer to the challenge of Western ethnocentrism. Additionally, the human rights movement has advanced far enough that there is no longer a need to "sidestep" the debate about the universality of human rights. In the next chapter I show that the implementation of human rights has become a genuinely international activity, participated in by more than 150 nations around the world and by hundreds of intergovernmental agencies. Given that her agenda is an overtly political one,

Nussbaum needs to make human rights discourse a much bigger item on her agenda. All the more so because she admits that "there is no doubt that one might recognize the basic capabilities of people and yet still deny that this entails that they have rights in the sense of justified claims to certain types of treatment" (*WHD*, 100). The existence of universal capabilities has been known for ages, and Nussbaum's list is no surprise to anyone. It therefore requires the up-front moral punch that a theory of human rights can give it. In her earlier account she realizes this, which is why she gives us four reasons for keeping "the language of [human] rights . . . despite its [supposedly] unsatisfactory features" (100).

To begin with, Nussbaum admits that this language reminds us that "people have justified and urgent claims to certain types of treatment, no matter what the world around them has done about that" (*WHD*, 100). This "no matter what" clause moves her approach in the direction of our doctrine of human rights as inherent in their possessors. She points out that what she herself calls "natural rights" (without putting the phrase in quotes) "usually proceed by pointing to some capability-like feature of persons (rationality, language) that they actually have on at least a rudimentary level." She adds: "And I actually think that without such a justification, the appeal to rights is quite mysterious." True enough, which is why we have incorporated the capabilities approach into our theory of inherent human rights. But there still is for Nussbaum a gap to fill between explaining and observing universal capabilities and making moral claims about their development. This is-ought gap is difficult to fill and I do not see that she has filled it any better in her second account than in her first. She is aware that "appealing to rights communicates more than does the bare appeal to basic capabilities, without any further argument of the sort I have supplied" (*WHD*, 100) and that "the idea of capability all on its own does not yet express the idea of an urgent entitlement based on justice" (*Frontiers*, 290). The only "ethical" argument she gives her readers to fill the gap between the "is" of capabilities and the "ought" of rights or entitlements is the appeal to the shared revulsions in tragic situations when people's development of one or more of their capabilities has been blocked. We began our discussion of her approach with those appeals and see them as very much in harmony with our intuitionist moral epistemology of human rights.

Nussbaum's second reason for keeping the language of human rights is that it "places great emphasis on the importance and the basic role of these spheres of ability" (*WHD*, 100). To press human rights in the face of oppressive parents or regimes is more "rhetorically direct," she feels, because it tells people that these functionings, which we claim are suppressed or blocked, are in fact "backed up by . . . a justified claim that all humans have to such things by virtue of being human" (100). It is not just rhetorically more direct, it is also philosophically more correct, since the claim is thought of as "justified" precisely because it is based on our very humanity.

Nussbaum's third reason for hanging on to "rights language" is that it "has value because of the emphasis it places on people's choice and autonomy" (101). Mixing choice with capabilities sets her theory of capabilities apart from "the more passive approaches to capabilities in Marxist Aristotelianism and some forms of Thomist Catholicism" (101). The element of choice in the implementation process for these moral rights is a welcome refinement of those more traditional approaches, and we accepted that feature when we admitted that we ourselves often are the first-duty bearers to bring about the enjoyment of our own inherent rights. So, we must not understand the Declaration's right to full and free development of our personality in the passive voice only.

Nussbaum's fourth and last reason for wanting to keep the language of human rights in addition to capabilities is that it preserves "a sense of the terrain of agreement . . . when the claims of utility, resources, and capability are still being worked out" (101). She believes that the discourse of human rights will preserve this terrain even when "there is no proper analysis of rights talk" on which theoreticians agree. Naturally, we hope that our theory of inherent human rights will lead to that kind of agreement.

Nussbaum is right about the great popularity of the language of human rights. This is why she cannot turn the clock back and make the capabilities approach precede or supersede the human rights approach. Our discussion has shown that capabilities are indeed metaphysically prior to human rights, for the latter are birth rights that ride on those capabilities and come along with them. Oddly enough, we would argue that from Nussbaum's own political policy perspective, human rights should come first, for the modern media have spread this ideology far and wide, to the most remote corners of our planet.

C. Fitting in Patriotism and Multiculturalism

Contemporary education systems and the states that control them are each pinched by two conflicting movements. They are pinched from above by cosmopolitan forces (in part caused by the increased recognition of international human rights) that seek to bring about a greater unity of vision, and from below (or internally) by multicultural forces that draw them in the opposite direction of greater fragmentation and disunity. Each of the two subsections that follow will be devoted to one of these movements in the field of education. In the first subsection I defend the thesis that patriotism in school curricula is best taught within the larger cosmopolitan framework developed in the first two sections of this chapter. Fitting patriotism within this larger cosmopolitan human rights framework gives it a civic shape that should keep it from degenerating into a kind of nationalism that can, and, as we saw in Chapter 2, does sometimes lead to the grossest human rights violations. In the second subsection, I use this civic (or constitutional) nationalism to place boundaries around the multicultural interests of the numerous groups that demand educational recognition in contemporary nation-states.

Morally and educationally speaking, we have three concentric circles to contend with in an ideal curriculum: (1) a very large one that comprises the human family, (2) many medium-size ones that make up the school curricula set by nation-states, and (3) millions of parent organizations with their own multicultural interests. The purpose of this section is to make a case for the way these three circles fit inside each other. I use Thomas Aquinas's distinction between the order of being and the order of knowing to explain how we might do that. I believe that in the order of being the flow goes from the largest to the smallest circle, that is, from cosmopolitanism to patriotism to multiculturalism. In the order of pedagogy and of knowing, the flow most often (though not always) goes from the smallest to the largest circle, from multiculturalism to patriotism to cosmopolitanism. Keeping the difference between these two orders or flows in mind will help us make sense of theoretical discussions of these matters.

The Universal Declaration was proclaimed to the world as an educational or pedagogical tool for human rights education. In what is called the operative paragraph, the drafters tell us that the peoples of the UN adopted this list of rights "to the end that every individual and every organ of society, keeping this Declaration constantly in mind, shall strive by teaching and education to promote respect for these rights and freedoms and by progressive measures, national and international, to secure their universal and effective recognition and observance, both among the peoples of Member States themselves and among the peoples of territories under their jurisdiction." There are three tiers of addressees here. The first includes human beings everywhere whose rights are being proclaimed, the second is that of educators around the globe, and the third includes the nation-states where these people and their educators live. The second and third tiers are asked to spread word of the Declaration to the people of the first tier, who are the real addressees of the document. Educators and states are asked to spread respect for human rights through national and international cooperative measures in the hope of achieving "effective recognition and observance" of these rights among all member states of the UN and among the territories under their jurisdiction.

This ambitious pedagogical goal is complicated by the fact that member states guard their own sovereignty just as much in the field of education as they do in security. States create systems of education and curricula that are openly geared toward patriotism and nationalism and that seek to mold citizens who have loyalty, love, and respect for their own country, usually at the expense of the larger cosmopolitan connections I have drawn out in the other sections of this chapter. The drafters were fully aware of this patriotic dominance over cosmopolitan sentiments and wrote the nuts and bolts of Article 26(1) with the practical needs of nation-states in mind. It states that: "Everyone has a right to education. Education shall be free, at least in the elementary and fundamental stages. Elementary education shall be compulsory. Technical education shall be made generally available and higher education shall be equally accessible to all on the basis of merit." I reported elsewhere on the adoption of these nuts and bolts and shall not repeat the obviously justifiable state-centered issues they raise.[28] Our interest here is in the intellectual challenges that arise from the other two additional paragraphs that are also part of this education article in the Declaration. Paragraph 26(2) brings us the challenge of cosmopolitanism, while 26(3) brings us the challenge of multiculturalism. I take them in this order.

Patriotism Within Cosmopolitanism. In the fall of 1994 the *Boston Review* published a special issue entitled "Patriotism or Cosmopolitanism?" The issue was billed as a "debate" between Martha Nussbaum and twntynine scholars who responded to her defense of "the very old ideal of the cosmopolitan person whose *primary* allegiance is to the community of human beings in the entire world" and not to his or her own nation-state.[29] The suggestion of not owing first allegiance to one's own country gave this debate bite. Nussbaum expressed the view that in education (as elsewhere) nationalism "subverts, ultimately, even the values that hold a nation together because it substitutes a colorful idol for the substantive universal values of [cosmopolitan] justice and right" (3). The debate was a heated one because most of Nussbaum's commentators did not agree on the insertion of the word "primary" in the above citation, and in any case felt that against the background of the American founding documents with their proclamation of inalienable rights, her charge of jingoism and ethnocentrism did not ring true. Nussbaum traced her cosmopolitanism to that of the ancient Stoics and to the Enlightenment philosophies of Kant in the West and Tagore in the East.

She pleaded that the U.S. student can love her country, ethnicity, and religion, "But she must also and centrally learn to recognize humanity, undeterred by traits that are strange to her, and be eager to understand humanity in its 'strange' guises" (4). Nussbaum followed the Stoics by placing each human person at the heart of a series of concentric circles that move further and further outward or (depending on how one reads their evolution) more and more inward. They go from the self and one's immediate family, to one's neighbors and local groups, to one's fellow "city-dwellers," and from there to one's compatriots—at which point Nussbaum interjects the observation that "we can easily add to this list groupings based on ethnic, linguistic, historical, professional, social, gender and sexual identities"—finally to the largest circle of all, "humanity as a whole" (4). She reiterates the reasons Stoics gave for their view that education should first of all aim to make people citizens of the world: (i) studying humanity helps us "see ourselves more clearly," (ii) it helps us solve our problems more quickly, and (iii) this study is "intrinsically valuable" because "it recognizes in persons what is specifically fundamental about them, and most worthy of respect and acknowledgment: their aspiration to goodness and their capacities for reasoning in this connection" (4). If that is where our first allegiance goes, it follows, says Nussbaum, that it should go to "no mere form of government, no temporal power, but to the moral community made up by the humanity of all human beings" (4). But we should ask whether the words "first" and "primary" are to be understood in the order of being or in the order of knowing and pedagogy. The Declaration can be read either way, depending on which paragraph of Article 26 we pick as our point of departure.

When the drafters had written the first, nuts-and-bolts paragraph of Article 26(1) and had said nothing (yet) about the larger cosmopolitan vision that drove them together in the first place, A. L. Easterman, a nonvoting representative of the World Jewish Congress, spoke up. He noted that "the article on education provided a technical framework of education but contained nothing about the spirit governing education which was an essential element. Neglect of this principle in Germany had been the main cause of two catastrophic wars," He proposed that the following article be added: "This education shall be directed to the full development of the human personality, to strengthen respect for human rights and fundamental freedoms and shall combat the spirit of intolerance and hatred against other nations or racial or religious groups everywhere" (E/CN.4/SR.8/4).

Strong support for this article, which with slight differences became Article 26(2), came from the UNESCO representative. He pointed out that under the Hitler regime "education had been admirably organized but had, nevertheless, produced disastrous results. It was absolutely necessary to make clear that education to which everyone was entitled should strengthen respect of the rights set forth in the Declaration and combat the spirit of intolerance" (SR.8/12). The reference to "the activities of the United Nations and the maintenance of peace" that we have in our final version was added on the suggestion of the Mexican delegation to the Third Committee and received a great deal of support. Its delegate, Pablo Campos Ortiz, argued that "support of an educated public opinion was essential for the success of the United Nations." Lack of public support had been the downfall of the League of Nations, and the need to create that support had been the reason the Third General Assembly had adopted Resolution 137(III), which was a recommendation that "the purpose and principles of the United Nations should be taught in the schools of the Member States" (GAOR Third, 583). We may therefore interpret the drafters' adoption of 26(2) as demonstrating their desire to forge a link between their document's moral cosmopolitanism and the education machinery of member states.

The question Nussbaum leaves us with is not whether cosmopolitanism is a proper educational goal, but whether more specific patriotic goals should, as I put it in the title of this subsection, be conceived of *within* this cosmopolitanism, or the reverse.

Many commentators wanted Nussbaum to reverse the order of the circles, making the patriotism circle larger than the cosmopolitan one, which would fit within it and be subordinated to it. Sissela Bok asked Nussbaum about the direction taken in the concentric circles metaphor: "Is it [pedagogically] better to begin at the outer edges and to move inward? To move back and forth between the two? Or to begin with the inner circles and to move outward?" (32). Bok clearly had pedagogy in mind, for she wanted to know: "Must the educator she has in mind—inviting children to view themselves primarily as citizens of the world—instruct them to regard all claims to national or other identity as morally irrelevant?" The word "irrelevant" is far too strong no matter what order (of being or knowing) one has in mind. More to the point is Bok's observation that "without learning to understand the uniqueness of cultures, beginning with one's own it may well be impossible fully to honor both human distinctiveness and the shared humanity central to cosmopolitanism" (32). Michael Walzer also focused on the circles metaphor from a developmental point of view. I quote him at some length: "Nussbaum's image of concentric circles is more helpful than her idea of world citizenship—precisely because it suggests how odd it is to claim that my *primary* allegiance is or ought to be to the outermost circle. My allegiances, like my relationships, start at the center. Hence we need to describe the mediation through which one reaches the outer circles, acknowledging the value of, but also passing through, the others. That is not so easy to do; it requires a concrete, sympathetic, engaged but not absolutely engaged account of the inner circles—and then an effort not so much to draw the outermost circle in as to open the inner ones out" (29, emphasis original). Walzer believes we "should extend our sense of moral fellowship and neighborliness to new groups of people, and ultimately to all people.[30]

We might bring the cosmopolitan and communitarian sides in this debate closer together if we adopt what Barry and others have called "civic patriotism."[31] Several of Nussbaum's respondents took this approach. Benjamin Barber granted Nussbaum's point that in "an overly tribalized world cosmopolitanism might be a useful counterpoint," but it cannot be a commitment to a mere abstraction (14). Instead, according to Barber, "we require . . . healthy democratic forms of local community and civic patriotism rather than abstract universalism and the thin gruel of contract relations. This civic patriotism works in two directions at once: it fosters "an affection for the general" and also wards off other "pathological versions of blood kinship that are around today." Echoing Thomas Paine, Barber argued that the sources from which Americans derive their sense of national identity are the Declaration of Independence, the Constitution, and the Bill of Rights, with the result that their "civic nationalism . . . is a celebration of internationalism, a devotion to values with a cosmopolitan reach" (14). We can see how this is done in U.S. civics textbooks, which invariably link patriotism to acceptance of the American Constitution with its Bill of Rights. Paine puts it this way: "The independence of America, considered merely as a separation from England, would have been a matter but of little importance, had it not been accompanied by a revolution in the principles of governments. She made a stand, not for herself only, but for the world, and looked beyond the advantages she herself could receive."[32]

My report on this debate had a twofold purpose. First, I do believe that the kind of civic patriotism described by Walzer and others is an excellent home base for a human rights curriculum that can give a global reach to our patriotic impulses. My second reason was to show up the general neglect of human rights in U.S. public thinking about education policies. Only two of the twenty-nine commentators caught Nussbaum's almost casual question "But is this sufficient?" in response to the suggestion that "a commitment to basic human rights should be part of any educational system and that this commitment will in a sense serve to hold many nations together" (4). Both Charles Beitz and Amy Gutmann followed up on this offhand comment. Beitz made the observation that "As a matter of educational practice I suspect that the international doctrine of human rights can serve as a valuable organizing principle for a form of moral education that is both civic and cosmopolitan" (24). This doctrine, he noted, is "the closest the international community has come to a cosmopolitan moral language; there is simply no alternative remotely as legitimate." Gutmann answered that "teaching human rights . . . cannot be fairly characterized as a *thin* conception of anything" (16). She urged educators not to make pupils choose between "being above all citizens of our own society or above all citizens of the world" (17). She suggested that "public education ought to cultivate in all students the skills and virtues of democratic citizenship," and unpacked that statement in terms of the "capacity to deliberate about the demands of justice for all individuals, not only for present-day citizens of the United States" (17). Unfortunately, that belief has not led her to be a strong advocate of human rights education, which receives scant attention in her book on this subject.[33] I conclude that at least in the United States, because of its unique founding conditions, the political context comes before the cosmopolitan one. But that is in the order of knowing. In the order of being the inherent human rights that make up the central core of democratic education come first. They are the ones that bind the human family together and should place boundaries around the kind of patriotism being taught in a nation's schools.

To say that the order of being should influence the order of knowing and pedagogy, as Nussbaum and Beitz[34] would have us do, may not calm patriotic anxieties over which loyalties come first. I therefore add these further explanatory assurances. As part of a defense of the same position that I have taken here, Kok-Chor Tan has helped evaluate the various ways cosmopolitans have sought to defend their priority status.[35] Some of them do not work because, as Tan notes, they "need not deny the irreducible nature of the ties of nationality (that some nationalists want to claim); they need only insist that the expression and exercise of these national ties be *constrained by* cosmopolitan principles" (150–51, emphasis added). I accept this distinction between patriotic ties—which have their own justification from which special obligations flow—and the fact that these patriotic obligations are limited by cosmopolitan duties that come with our commitment to human rights. By placing our civic patriotism within this larger cosmopolitan circle we have no intention of demeaning or belittling special patriotic obligations that have their own philosophical and historical roots. We do not mean to suggest that our obligations to our neighbors and fellow citizens are not different from those to strangers in other countries; they are quite different and testify to the fact that living a moral life involves far more than adhering to a code of human rights. All we mean to do is restrict these special personal and patriotic obligations by placing them within a larger human rights framework.

Tan uses the analogy of friendship and family ties that also have their own special associative obligations, but which can be restricted and overruled by more general moral duties. "Cosmopolitanism," we agree, "plays a limiting role with respect to patriotism, not a justificatory role as such" (160). Our more local duties are part of commonsense morality, but that does not mean that we need to "endorse patriotism as it is conventionally practiced" (147). That is why we have chosen a civic and not an extreme kind of nationalistic patriotism as our home base for human rights education. We have left open the ways one might want to justify our special patriotic obligations to our fellow citizens, which many nationalists say are based on special associative relations, much like those of friendships and family ties. Those special ties are not derived from or justified by more general principles, but they can be limited by these external principles. We each have our personal mix of duties at home and duties abroad. And while we ourselves often feel that we do not do enough on either front, our governments should do more. With some eighteen million people starving to death annually due to no fault of their own, citizens of rich countries should lobby their governments to work much harder at alleviating world poverty and other gross human rights violations, even at the expense of doing less for their own compatriots. This would lead these citizens to scrutinize their countries' economic policies as practiced in their World Bank, IMF, and WTO memberships.

This leads me to one other reason, omitted by Tan, for putting our patriotic obligations on a cosmopolitan lease. U.S. exceptionalism is the belief that in international affairs and law the U.S. experience is—because of its birth and life story—unique and therefore cannot be judged against external standards. Some of Nussbaum's critics can be read as leaning in this direction. Translated into the field of human rights, it means that the United States does not need adhere to international human rights norms the way other nations do and should. Americans, so goes this line of thinking, can help write international covenants, but then hold back on ratifying them and, if they do ratify them, they can make some very important reservations. Since U.S. programs to protect children are (supposedly) so good, the United States does not need to worry about ratifying the Convention on the Rights of the Child that every other member of the UN (except Somalia) has ratified. Finally, all the treaties that Americans have ratified—and they have ratified some[36]—are said to be non-self-executing, which means that even upon ratification by Congress, laws need to be adopted that incorporate these treaties into our legal system so that the rights in them can be used as grounds for litigation. Without that extra legislative step, even ratified treaties such as the International Covenant of Civil and Political Rights are stillborn. Since the United States did ratify the Convention on the Elimination of Torture and Cruel and Unusual Punishment, and since Congress did in this case want to make the rights in the treaty part of the U.S. legal system, it also adopted a federal Anti-Torture statute. As we saw in the discussion of manifest illegality (Chapter 2, section B), it was that very statute that worried the U.S. attorney general and led him to advise President Bush as to how he might avoid having CIA and army interrogators be accused of violating our own narrower laws against torture. I put the circle of patriotism *within* the bigger one of cosmopolitanism to guard us against this type of exceptionalism. Other civilized nations also need to place their own patriotic educational goals—which no doubt differ from ours in their historical and cultural details—within the same human rights cosmopolitanism. Nations can do this by making reference to international human rights norms in their constitutions, and many newly written constitutions contain such references. That sets the tone for the nation's conduct of international relations and for the structure of its governmental branches. Such a constitution should have in it an enumeration of at least the most important rights in the Universal Declaration. American exceptionalism or American Exemptionalism (as Michael Ignatieff has dubbed it)[37] undercuts the excellent reputation the United States began with when the Universal Declaration was drafted under the leadership of Eleanor Roosevelt, who received thunderous applause the evening it was adopted.

Multiculturalism Within Civic Patriotism. The relationship between the Declaration and the cultural dimension of life is ambiguous. The text itself takes us in two conflicting directions. Article 27(1) suggests that there is such a thing as a national culture for each nation-state because it provides that "Everyone has the right freely to participate in *the* cultural life of *the* community, to enjoy the arts and to share in scientific advancement and its benefits" (emphasis added). This provision places the Declaration at the heart of contemporary debates between liberal theorists (like Rawls, Barry, Gutmann, and Miller)[38] who believe that the liberal democratic state can and should be more or less neutral toward the phenomenon of culture, and multiculturalists (like Taylor, Kymlicka, Parekh, and Benhabib)[39] who believe that such neutrality is an impossibility and that language like that of 27(1) discriminates against members of ethnocultural minority groups. Seemingly going in the opposite, multiculturalist direction, the drafters assert in Article 26(3) that "Parents have a prior right to choose the kind of education that shall be given to their children," which I show below includes minority language rights. Seeing this potential conflict, we might say that the drafters were confused because in 27(1) they ascribed to the assimilationism that was in the late 1940s very much part of North Atlantic and Latin American nations, while in 26(3) they adopted a key ingredient of the contemporary multiculturalist agenda specifically designed to combat that same assimilationism. There is no escaping the fact that in the late 1940s many delegations were operating in the assimilationist mode, but I argue here that the text before us allows for a realistic interpretation that removes the conflict between an assimilationist nationalism, on the one hand, and a strident multiculturalism that undercuts civic patriotism, on the other. While the Declaration as such places patriotism itself inside the larger circle of cosmopolitanism, we now interpret Articles 27(1) and 26(3) as placing the numerous more immediate familial and ethnocultural attachments inside the circle of civic patriotism. As I put these two segments of text in line with this thesis, I also defend its soundness.

The double use of "the" (participation in "*the* cultural life of *the* community") highlights the fact that Article 27(1) does not speak of everyone's right to participation in the cultural life of his or her own particular ethnocultural community. That other kind of language would have given the state the duty of protecting these minority cultural liberties. As it reads, the text seems to suppress the possibility (and the likelihood) that for many people being a citizen of a certain state and participating in the cultural life of one's own community do not point to one and the same experience. The article seems to assume that all of a nation's citizens want to identify with that nation's national culture. There seems to be here no hint of any room for multiculturalist or pluralist endeavors. I say "seems" because much depends on what kind of nationalism or patriotism we discern in Article 27. While it is true that many delegations from around the North Atlantic and Latin America clearly brought an assimilationist mindset to the drafting table, many other delegations did not. Yet these nonassimilationist delegations also voted for the present text, which suggests that there might be a middle way between what can be read as the conservative nationalism of Article 27 and what can be read as a radical multiculturalism in Article 26(3). Conservative nationalism postulates a link between citizens' personal identities and a specific majority-driven nationalist and assimilationist cultural agenda that is frequently insensitive to minority cultural attachments. Article 27(1) can—but need not—be read this way. Radical multiculturalism goes to the other extreme by denying any need to link statecraft to a national cultural agenda, leaving each cultural group to feed the personal identities of its own members in its own way. It is hoped that respect and dialogue between cultural groups will avoid a clash between them. Article 26(3) can also—but need not—be read in this extreme way.

The supposed dilemma is that either there is one thick national culture that feeds into the personal identities of all citizens, or there is no national cultural agenda at all, and each citizen's identity is fed by his or her own cultural embeddedness. Our theory chooses the middle way of civic patriotism, which we see as a liberal rather than narrowly tribal kind of nationalism. This thinner kind of nationalism brackets issues of personal identity as not needing to be linked to political programs and structures, but it does follow Article 27(1) in holding that all citizens have a right to participate in that national culture, thin as it might be. As they so participate, people can feed their personal identities at whatever troughs they find for themselves, be they religion, culture, ethnicity, or sports. This third option fits the Declaration far better than either of the extremes I mentioned because it realistically accounts for both segments of text, Articles 27(1) and 26(3). So, let me explain this middle way.

David Miller defines a nation as "a community (1) constituted by shared belief and mutual commitment, (2) extended in history, (3) active in character, (4) connected to a particular territory, and (5) marked off from other communities by its distinct public culture."[40] Article 27(1)'s language of "the culture of the community" gives us Miller's fifth component of a "distinct public culture" for each nation. When we search Miller for the content of this public culture we run into the obvious fact that nations differ enormously in how they go about constructing and safeguarding this national culture. We also find that his description is mostly negative. It is not determined by "biological descent," which most certainly the drafters also rejected since they wrote their international bill in response to Hitler's racism. This opens the door to having a large mixture of ethnic groupings participate in the same national culture. That culture also cannot be determined by who is and who is not born "there," on the chunk of land that a people claim and protect. Concludes Miller: "So immigration does not pose a problem, provided only that immigrants come to share in a common national identity, to which they may contribute their own distinctive ingredients" (26). Surveys do indeed show that immigrant loyalty to a nation-state is no less and often more intense than the loyalty of citizens by birth. Miller's stipulation that a nation is a community stretched out in history helps explain why we did not derive our civic patriotism (in the preceding subsection) from cosmopolitan premises as a means to their end. A nation's extension in history explains why our compatriots matter a great deal to us; it gives its present members special, specific obligations to past and future generations (for example, honoring battlefields of the past and saving national parks for the future) that differ from the more general human rights obligations we have to all members of the human family.

A public culture is a vague conglomeration of various beliefs and practices, some social, some religious, and some political, none of which Miller wants to list as an absolute requirement for his definition of what counts as a "national culture." These beliefs and practices feed into "a set of understandings about how a group of people is to conduct its life together," a set that will also include "political principles" of some sort. Miller adopts here what I call "civic patriotism," for he says that these political principles express a people's political aspirations that set them as a nation apart from other ethnocultural groups. While most nations at one time arose from one or several dominant ethnic groups, it is not a requirement that a group's earlier domination will persist. The shifting demographics of many contemporary nation-states testify to this fact. Usually the language of that originally dominant group survives the longest in the melting pots created by modern demographic movements. The phenomenon of "hyphenated American" fits well into this picture. The sharing of "political principles" that help define the public cultures of nations sets civic patriotism apart from more conservative and emotive types of nationalism.[41] It fits the text of the Declaration because it recognizes that underneath the political machinery of the modern state lies "a people" who use this machinery to construct a government that represents them both at home and in world affairs.

UDHR Article 21 acknowledges this deeper layer when it tells us that "*the* will of *the* people shall be the basis of the authority of government" (emphasis added). In Chapter 3, section B, I criticized Rawls's treatment of human rights in his *Law of Peoples* as ethnocentric. With that important caveat in place, we do here support Rawls's unusual position that peoples and not states are the primary units of international law. Taken together, Article 27 (on culture), Article 21 (on participation in government), and Article 15 ("Everyone has the right to a nationality") validate the modern phenomenon of the nation-state, where the state and its government act on behalf of its "people," the term being understood as the civic (rather than national or tribal) body politic. Article 15 puts pressure on the international community not to have anyone fall between the cracks of the nation-state system, as, we know, millions of people still do. Nation-states themselves cannot be the basic moral building blocks of our theory of human rights, for they do not create—yet they must protect—inherent human rights. Because in our modern world they still are the main protectors of human rights, states do come in a close second to the individuals who are the carriers of those rights. Parents, extended families, and a host of other more voluntary civic groups mediate between the level of the individual possessor of human rights and that of the nation-state where most of the power to protect resides. Together with various national symbols and customs the political principles that make up the civic part of a national culture help bind compatriots together so as to prevent a nation's nationalism from drifting into racist or tribal directions.

One drafting episode that might seem to conflict with a liberal nationalist reading of UDHR Article 27 does in fact support it. In the Third Session of the commission, Charles Malik proposed that the following provision be added to the article: "Cultural groups shall not be denied the right to free self-development" (E/CN.4/140). The proposal was neither discussed, nor voted on, nor reintroduced in the larger Third Committee, where it might have had a chance. One way to read this neglect is to ascribe to the drafters a willful intent to discriminate against cultural minorities. But that is not the only possible interpretation. In an article elsewhere on cultural genocide and minority rights I discussed the 1948 overlap between the proposal to add a cultural genocide article to the Convention on Genocide and the proposal to add a minority rights arti cle to the Declaration. Malik may have dropped his amendment because he wanted to wait until the question of cultural genocide had been decided on. Or we can speculate that this particular addition to Article 27 was merged with or eclipsed by the various proposals (one by Malik's own delegation) that sought to add a separate minority rights article to the Declaration. If this is what happened, it presents us with one more example of how the unfulfilled expectation of later addition of a minority rights article ended up impoverishing the document.[42] As I pointed out at the start of this chapter, Article 2's list of nondiscrimination items ("such as race, colour, sex, language, religion, political or other opinion, national or social origin, property, birth, or other status") gives a great deal of protection to members of minority groups. I explained the drafters' note that we should interpret "national origin" in this list "not in the sense of citizen of a State, but in the sense of national characteristics" (E/CN.4/Sub.2/SR.17/6). This gloss supports a liberal nationalist reading of Article 27(1).

If the political principles that lie at the heart of a nation form the main component of a national culture as most liberal nationalists see it, then citizens can participate in that national cultural life to a greater or lesser extent. Not only do they have leeway in interpreting these political principles all the way to acts of nonviolent civil disobedience as practiced by Mohandas Gandhi and Martin Luther King, Jr.; they can also share in the rest of the national cultural trappings to a greater or lesser degree. Multiculturalists are right when they insist that even a modern and liberal state cannot be totally neutral toward cultural meanings. Simple things like holiday schedules and laws about food, medicines, and public behavior quickly show their leanings in one direction or another. Since national cultures differ enormously in their patriotic holidays and language policies, for some citizens this national cultural life is that of their own dominant cultural group and hence is probably the culture that informs the policies of the government, even if only thinly so. Others, while loyal citizens of the state, do not find their personal identities fed by the dominant culture that informs these state structures. From a human rights perspective it is not politically relevant where citizens ground and feed their identities as long as the government does not bar them from those grounds. Language and religion are the most prominent of these grounds, which is why I have singled them out for further discussion, language here and religion in a forthcoming volume. I begin with some observations that I have taken from the 2004 UNDP report, *Cultural Liberty in Today's Diverse World*.[43]

In its discussion of what it calls the "right" to cultural liberty, the report takes the position that states can and should be neutral on ethnicity and religion, but that such neutrality "is impractical for language [because] [t]he citizenry needs a common language to promote mutual understanding and effective communication" (60). The report supports the thesis that the unity of a nation requires one or several national languages and subscribes to UNESCO's recommendation that governments support a three-level model of languages: one global language of commerce and diplomacy, one (or two) national languages to facilitate communication between different linguistic groups, and one mother tongue for each minority linguistic group. The report correctly places minority language rights within the framework of larger patriotic and civic interests, but it does not belittle the importance of local mother tongues. A plural language policy should say: "Let us each retain our own language in certain spheres, such as schools and universities, but let us also have a common language for joint activities, especially in civic life" (60). "Countries need to recognize all three as official languages or at least recognize their use in different circumstances such as in courts and schools." On a national level, nations must cultivate one or several national languages that cut across ethnocultural groups, but a program of nation building must also leave enough room for the cultivation of mother tongues at the local level, for that is where the connection between culture and language is the strongest.

Different versions of this three-language model exist. Since 1956, Indian state boundaries "have been drawn along linguistic lines," with the result that each state has "one dominant state language, each with its own script, rich vocabulary and literature going back hundreds, if not thousands of years" (62). Most countries in sub-Saharan Africa have local language education in the first three grades, but after that almost all switch to French or English or Portuguese, a national language they inherited from their respective colonial pasts. The report notes that "Since knowledge of Western language is often a means of upward mobility, the goal is not to remove Western languages, which would narrow choices and access to international knowledge" (63). In the forty-five languages of that region we find fifteen core languages that serve as links across borders and as national languages supplementing the inherited colonial ones. A nation needs to be careful when deciding on its national language(s), for a narrow choice can lead to violence by a suppressed minority. In Mali the "exclusive use of English" in parliamentary discussions and government publications "creates a barrier between the political elite and the masses and reduces the pool of possible legislators," whereas in Tanzania political participation is enhanced by the official use of Kishwahili as one of the national languages (63). In 1956,

Sinhali, which is spoken by the majority of citizens of Sri Lanka, was made the official language. Much of the violent civil war that has torn that country apart can be traced to the disaffection of the Tamil minority "who wanted both Sinhali and Tamil to be recognized" (60), much the way Canada, Belgium, and Switzerland have more than one national language. The report's conclusions that "Assimilation without choice is no longer a viable—or a necessary—model of integration" and that countries "do not have to choose between national unity and cultural diversity" (3) invite us to explore what human right, if any, parents have to set up their own school systems alongside government-controlled systems, and to decide on the language of instruction in those schools.[44]

While there is no explicitly stated human right in the Declaration to the use of one's mother tongue, that right is clearly implied by other stated rights. One of these is the right to freedom of expression in Article 18, which includes "freedom to hold opinions without interference" and to get and pass on information "through any media and regardless of frontiers." Another very important link is the one in Article 11, according to which "Everyone charged with a penal offence has the right to be presumed innocent until proven guilty according to law in a public trial at which he has had all the guarantees necessary for his defence." The *travaux préparatoires* make it clear that these guarantees include a defendant's right to competent counsel and to address the court in "a language that he can understand."[45]

Other international human rights instruments have drawn out the implications of these texts, especially Article 26(3), which I discuss below. Article 27 of the ICCPR, which is a document that more than 150 states have ratified, is the locus classicus for minority language (and other) rights in international human rights law. This key text says that "In those States in which ethnic, religious or linguistic minorities exist, persons belonging to such minorities shall not be denied the right, in community with other members of their group, to enjoy their own culture, to profess and practice their own religion, or to use their own language."[46] Together Articles 13(3) and 13(4) of the ICCPR make the same point as does UDHR 26(3). According to the education Article 13(3) "The States Parties to the present Covenant undertake to have respect for the liberty of parents and, when applicable legal guardians, to choose for their children schools other than those established by the public authorities, which conform to such minimal educational standards as may be laid down or approved by the State and to ensure the religious and moral education of their children in conformity with their own convictions." Article 13(4) adds the stipulation that "No part of this article shall be construed so as to interfere with the liberty of individuals and bodies to establish and direct educational institutions," subject to state supervision that is defined in terms of minimal standards, which includes the promotion of tolerance and friendship among all nations, racial, ethnic, or religious groups, and the furtherance of the activities of the UN for the maintenance of peace. These and other goals, spelled out in Article 13(1) of this covenant, place the multicultural and religious liberties granted in paragraphs 3 and 4 within our larger patriotic and cosmopolitan circles.

Article 30 of the Convention on the Rights of the Child (CRC) applies Article 27 of the ICCPR directly to children: "In those States in which ethnic, religious or linguistic minorities or persons of indigenous origins exist, *a child* belonging to such a community or who is indigenous shall not be denied the right, in community with other members of his or her group, to enjoy his or her culture, to profess and practice his or her own religion or to use *his or her own language*" (emphasis added). Article 29(1) of the CRC starts with the same educational goals as those in UDHR 26. It places "respect for the child's parents" in the context of our three concentric circles of respect for a child's "cultural identity, language and values" (our multiculturalism), of respect for "the national values of the country in which the child is living" (our civic nationalism), "the country from which he or she may originate" (back to the mother tongue), and of respect for "civilizations different from his or her own" (our cosmopolitanism). This Convention also forbids interference with "the liberty" of parents and guardians "to establish and direct educational institutions," subject to the usual limitations found in UDHR 29.

Article 17 of the CRC "Encourage[s] the mass media to have particular regard to the linguistic needs of the child who belongs to a minority group or who is indigenous." Forbidding the use of a minority language, as did Turkey in 1994 when it forbade the use of Kurdish in public places, violates these international norms.[47] The government of Guatemala also violates the language rights of its indigenous peoples by "not recogni[zing] their language in schools, law courts and other official arenas" (7). The 2004 UNDP Report shows that in the year 2000 in sub-Saharan Africa only 13 percent of the population had access to education in their mother tongue; in East Asia and the Pacific, 62 percent; in South Asia, 66 percent. In Central and Eastern Europe and the CIS, the percentage rose to 74 percent; while for the high-income Organisation for Economic Co-operation and Development (OECD) countries it was 87 percent, and in Latin America and the Caribbean, 91 percent (34, Fig. 2.4). I am not arguing that not having any education in one's mother tongue leads automatically to cultural dislocation and discomfort. However, if there is a human right that links facility in one's mother tongue to an appreciation of one's cultural roots, as I believe there is, then these data show that many parents have not availed themselves of that right, probably for reasons outside their control.

Since UDHR Article 26(3)—"Parents have a prior right to choose the kind of education that shall be given to their children"—is the bedrock of these later, more detailed and explicit norms and findings, I will briefly explore the original 1940s rationale for this crucial right. I must state up front that I do not mean to imply that governments must organize and pay for the implementation of this "prior right" of parents or guardians. The UDHR drafters left that question open. All I mean to argue is that parents or guardians have the right to organize schools outside the public system, where they can give their children "the kind of education" they think their children should have.

When Article 26 came to the Third Committee it did not contain this prior right of parents, but three delegations submitted proposals that it be put in. Since the Lebanese amendment ("Parents have a priority right to choose the kind of education that shall be given to their children" A/C.3/260) was the shortest of the three, it was the one adopted. The other two came from the Dutch and Danish delegations. Having just witnessed Hitler's attempt to brainwash an entire generation of German youth with a sick racist and anti-Semitic ideology, the delegates saw the point of curtailing the power of the modern nation-state in matters of education. I will quote the Dutch rationale and then give the vote that led to the adoption of the shorter Lebanese version. The Dutch delegate spoke for a country that in the nineteenth and early twentieth centuries had gone through a school struggle that ended with three parallel state-funded education systems, one for Catholic children, one for Protestant children, and a secular alternative. This Dutch "three pillar" system, as it was called, does not figure into the delegation's rationale, but it does explain the passion that informed the Dutch plea for passage. Dutch representative L. J. C. Beaufort argued that

Parents would be unable to bear the primary responsibility unless they were able to choose the kind of education their children should have. Nazi Germany, where Hitler Youth deprived parents of control of their children and provided an experience which should never be permitted to recur. It might be objected that such a provision restricted the child's right to education in that it deprived it of protection against negligent or unwise parents. Such cases would be exceptions, and, in any case, the influence of teachers and educational organizations would most probably prevent any real damage. . . . He had no wish to interfere with the State's responsibility for the system of teaching, but parents must retain the right to select the atmosphere they considered best for their child. He had no objection to compulsory education since that system had been in force in his country for more than fifty years. (GAOR Third, 582)

The Dutch delegate successfully shifted the burden of proof onto those who would deny parents primary say over their children's education.

This speech set the tone for the rest of the discussion, and led to narrow passage of the Lebanese amendment by 17 votes to 13, with 7 abstentions. The roll was called, and it shows the following delegations voting for the "prior right" of parents to determine the character of their children's education: Argentina, Australia, Belgium, Chile, Denmark, India, Lebanon, Luxembourg, the Netherlands, Pakistan, New Zealand, Paraguay, Philippines, and Sweden. Voting against: Afghanistan, BSSR, Ecuador, France, Mexico, Poland, USSR, UK, U.S., Uruguay, Venezuela, and Yugoslavia. The following were present, but abstained from voting: Canada, China, Czechoslovakia, Dominican Republic, Honduras, Peru, and Turkey. A few moments later the whole education article was adopted by 34 votes to 0, with 2 abstentions.

Most of those voting in favor of the amendment had been impressed by the argument that parents had a right to protect themselves against acts like the recent Nazi abuses of state power. Shaista Ikramullah, from Pakistan, thought it "was essential to guarantee freedom to choose education, a principle flagrantly violated by the Nazis. The argument that parents might refuse to give their children an education was not pertinent because the article gave them only the right to choose the kind of education they wished, but not the right to totally withhold education from their children" (GAOR Third, 584–85). Belgian delegate Carton de Wiart argued that

In effect the family had prior rights over the State, which it would be useful to recognize in one way or another in a statement of principle such as article 23 [26]. The Netherlands representative had expressed the horror which the Nazi-occupied countries still felt at the thought that the State could compel children to be deformed morally and intellectually by the doctrine of the party in power. . . . It would in fact be an error not to retain the rights of the family in an article of such importance, especially as it could not be assumed that the rights and duties of the State in the field of education had been disregarded by so doing. (GAOR Third, 594–95)

Philippine representative Melchor Aquino said he "would vote for the Lebanese amendment, which without giving excessive authority to the parents gave them the right to decide the type of education which they wished their children to receive. That provision would provide protection against the risk of undue intervention by the State in the sphere of education" (593). The negative vote of the United States was a big surprise, for all along that delegation had insisted that private institutions be explicitly mentioned.[48] Yet now Eleanor Roosevelt opposed the Lebanese and Dutch amendments because they "might be interpreted as giving [parents] the right to supervise school curricula, which clearly might have undesirable consequences" (590). To most of those who voted for 26(3) that was not so clear at all.

The distrust of state power that made the majority vote for the "prior right" in Article 26(3) also led some of them to oppose the use of the word "compulsory" in Article 26(1). Just before the vote, Lebanese delegate Karim Azkoul sought to win over some of the doubters by making the point that his third paragraph would serve as a balance to the power given to the state in the first paragraph. "It was important to proclaim the rights of parents. By stating [in 26(1)] that education was compulsory, the state would be authorized to force parents to send their children to school. Were the parents not entitled, on the other hand, to select the school to which they would send their children and the type of education they intended to give them? The Lebanese amendment," he said, "was intended to simply assert that right" (GAOR Third, 598). That is precisely what the communist delegations objected to. They did not share the Dutch and Lebanese mistrust of the power of the state, and certainly did not support the Dutch suggestion that parents might want to organize schools from a religious perspective. Alexei Pavlov of the USSR "could see no reason to omit the word 'compulsory.' A child had an absolute right to education, independently of the wishes of its parents," he said. "Education should be compulsory because a child could not claim the right as it had no strength to defend it" (589). Kaminsky from the BSSR also interpreted the proposed priority right of parents as a restriction to which he was opposed because "The culture and intellectual development of all peoples were in fact based on education" (591).[49]

For us it is important to know that the majority of delegates probably viewed the specific language provisions of the Danish text ("All persons belonging to a racial, national, religious or linguistic minority have the right to establish their own schools and receive teaching in the language of their choice" A/C.3/250) as included within the wider scope of the adopted Lebanese text. The 1940s constitutions of member states went both ways on this issue. While some explicitly gave minorities the right to use their own language in their own schools (Belgium, BSSR, Canada, Czechoslovakia, Syria, USSR, and Yugoslavia),[50] a constitution like the Brazilian one went in the opposite direction. It stated that "Primary schooling . . . may be given only in the national language."[51] That stipulation put Brazil in collision with the nondiscrimination prohibition of Article 2, which says that "everyone is entitled to all the rights and freedoms set forth in this Declaration, without distinction of any kind," including "language." "All the rights" includes the "prior right" of parents in Article 26(3). Because 26(3) also gives parents the right to set up schools that teach from a religious perspective, the communist delegations voted against the amendment, even though they were strong supporters of multicultural language rights. It had been the great virtue of the Danish amendment that it made these connections explicit. Belgian delegate de Wiart said that he thought all three amendments "made the same essential point" (GAOR Third, 594). Shaista Ikramullah of Pakistan said she would have supported the Danish text had it not been withdrawn. She shifted her support to the Dutch amendment on the supposition that it be read "in conjunction with the substance of the Danish" text (584). As the provision in the Brazilian constitution shows, the delegations from the Americas still clung to their assimilationist views.[52] This was the 1940s, and I have cited the UNDP surveys that gainsay these fears. Whatever is left of them must be weiged against the arguments we have advanced for the adoption of minority language rights.

Chapter 5
The Charge of Unrealistic Utopianism

The cosmopolitanism of the preceding chapter is not without its critics. The very idea of looking at the entire human race as one big transhistorical and cross-cultural family—the members of which have inherent rights and correlative duties to take care of each other—is open to serious criticisms, if not outright ridicule. While it is true that since the end of World War II the human rights movement has made enormous progress and has been able to enlist in its various causes pretty much all nations of the world and millions of their inhabitants, there also is an enormous and scary underbelly to this cosmopolitan vision of one unified ethical world. We saw in Chapter 2 that nations regularly and grossly violate the human rights of their own citizens. The Westphalian system of international law and affairs that has been in place since 1648 is not protecting the people within the borders of these autonomous states all that well. That is why the international community felt it necessary to create the permanent International Criminal Court that we discussed in Chapter 2, section B. Additionally, roughly 50 million people are not really covered by this Westphalian system. Among them I count 11 million stateless people (who have no state to protect them), 10 million refugees or asylum seekers who have fled their own states because of fear of persecution, and some 25 million who are displaced within their own failed or failing countries, mostly because of civil wars.[1] These millions of people are not enjoying the goods to which they have inherent moral birthrights. They live in poorly functioning Westphalian states or they have fallen between the cracks of that system. It can therefore be argued that the moral cosmopolitanism that we have drawn out of the Declaration is far too utopian to be a realistic moral vision.

Our response is that none of this should affect either of the two universality theses that we defended in the first two chapters of this book. The existence of this horrible underbelly does not show that those millions of victims do not have the moral birthrights the Declaration says they have. They have these rights, but the delivery systems for the enjoyment of these rights have broken down. In a specific incident of torture our theory does not say that the torturer takes away the victim's *right* not to be tortured. The victim has that right no matter what; it is the victim's *enjoyment of that right* that the torturer is taking away. We see no metaphysical difference between this single case and the millions of victims that make up the huge underbelly of our cosmopolitan world. To question the idea of metaphysical inherence as a result of these uncomfortable truths would be to commit the fallacy of implementation, which is the pulling of the measures of implementation into the very definition of what a human right is. It says that human rights do not exist whenever they are not implemented in any way. We have rejected that line of thinking in Chapters 1 and 2, and we now hold on to inherence even in the case of these magnified violations. We cannot silence the voice of humanity that affirms our belief in the birthrights of these victims and tells us that they have been or are being grossly wronged.

Our reaction should be, as it fortunately often is, to rush to fix the system whenever delivery gaps are occurring. When the truck breaks down, it has to be fixed, or another one has to be called in to deliver the goods. That is in fact the story of the incredible growth of the human rights movement. It explains why some 150 of the world's 192 nations signed and ratified the two international covenants that came out of the Declaration in the mid 1960s, and why new human rights treaties have been written that focus on the birthrights of neglected groups such as children, immigrants, and the disabled. It is also the story of the increase of human rights items on the agenda of the UN and its affiliated agencies. It explains why the World Bank, the IMF, and even the WTO are finally waking up to their human rights mandates. It is the reason why the number of domestic (like battered women's shelters) and international (such as Human Rights Watch) NGOs with human rights agendas has grown exponentially in recent decades from mere hundreds to the hundreds of thousands. Because many groups and corporations have started to supplement and even replace traditional government services (like the delivery of healthcare or prison management), the international community is now in the process of applying human rights norms to these new non-state actors as well. It is not a pretty sight to see so many brokendown or only partly effective vehicles scattered about, but the system does work and it is growing.

Unfortunately, even if we use the notion of inherent human rights as part of our response to the failures of the Westphalian delivery system, that still is not a good enough answer to the charge of unrealistic utopianism. There is another far more specific utopianism charge that is often leveled at the Declaration itself that we must answer before we can go back and address any malfunctioning of the overall Westphalian system.

While section B of this chapter does look briefly at that general system, the more specific charge that we discuss in sections A and C has to do with the scope and the range of the rights listed in the Declaration and not just with the general vision that animates the document.

In 1972 Maurice Cranston wrote an essay attacking the Declaration's cosmopolitan vision for a new international order as a philosophically muddled utopian pipedream. Our problem is not that Cranston used a definition of what a human right is that differs greatly from the one I am using in this book. He, too, thinks that a "human right is something of which no one may be deprived without a grave affront to justice. There are certain deeds that should never be done, certain freedoms which should never be invaded, some things which are supremely sacred."[2] He gives the example of a black student from South Africa whose government refused to give him a passport so he could accept a scholarship at the University of Oxford. This was an "invasion" of the human right to freedom of movement across borders. The annihilation of the Jews by the Nazis was "an atrocious abuse" of the right to life. Also, those who are held in prison without a trial have had their human rights to liberty and a fair trial violated. These are Cranston's examples of "real" instead of "supposed" moral rights that belong to "all people at all times and in all situations" (Cranston, 126). They are genuine human rights in that they "pertain to a human being merely because he is a human being."

As Cranstonites see it, the difficulty with documents like the Universal Declaration is that some of "What are now being put forward as universal human rights are social and economic rights such as the right to unemployment insurance, old-age pensions, medical services and holidays with pay" (Cranston, 121). Whatever one might say about most of the rights in the first half of the Declaration, these other kinds of rights, they maintain, cannot be considered inherent in the human person. The Declaration contains a good many examples of what Cranstonites see as "interlopers" in the human rights domain: the Right to Own Property (Article 17), the Right to Social Security (Article 22), the Right to Desirable Work and to Join Trade Unions (Article 23), the Right to Rest and Leisure (Article 24), the Right to Adequate Standard of Living (Article 25), the Right to Education (Article 26), and the Right to Participate in the Cultural Life of the Community (Article 27). To the Cranstonites, these social and economic interlopers "do not make sense" and are "of a different logical category." They are not inherent. The genuine human rights to freedom of movement, to life, and to a fair trial "belong to a totally different moral dimension from questions of social security and holidays with pay" (127). Cranston gave shape to frequently heard complaints that the social, economic, and cultural rights in the second half of the document should be called "ideals" or "manifesto rights," because the material wealth of a country frequently does not allow for immediate realization of goals like unemployment insurance or holidays with pay. An ideal is in this way different from a right. While "an ideal is something one can aim at" (127), "a right *must* be respected here and now" (128). The rights to work, to join a trade union, to health care, to an education, and to leisure time, all fit into the realm of social policy, but it is difficult to view them as moral rights that "belong to all people at all times and in all situations." "What ought to be done, what is obligatory, what is right, what is duty, what is just," writes Cranston, "is not what would be nice to see done one day" (128), which is just how social and economic rights strike a great many people. Cranston speaks here for all those U.S. citizens who think it would be nice if all their fellow citizens had health insurance some day soon, but who do not think of this as a matter of 45 million human rights violations in their own country. To refer to these policy matters as issues of basic inherent human rights is, so goes the challenge, sheer utopianism.

I respond to this Declaration-focused charge of utopianism in three ways. In section A, I give an exegesis of Articles 22 and 28 of the Declaration. These two articles play a crucial role in my defense of the view that the drafters gave all of the rights they proclaimed the same ontological status of inherence. While Cranstonites seek to break up the document and split it into two conflicting halves, I defend the unity of all human rights as together grounded in the inherent dignity of the human person. The difference lies in the fact that the drafters came to realize that *if* we look at social, economic, and cultural rights as also inherent in the human person, *then* we must not look at the human person as only embedded in Westphalian-type states. That is how Cranstonites look at individuals, but it is not the cosmopolitan framework the UDHR drafters used. They called in Articles 22 and 28 for a new post-Westphalian international order that enables us to think of these newer rights as also genuinely inherent in the human person. We follow the definition from Chapter 1 and think of these rights as being held or possessed *against the whole world,* for that idea is built into the very notion of what it is to have a moral right that is based on our (shared) humanity. This means that the duty-bearers who correlate with these inherent human rights might be found outside the borders of the states in which the victims live, in other countries, for instance, that have citizens who can share their wealth with their foreign brothers and sisters in need. The charge of unrealistic utopianism rests on too narrow a conception of who the duty-bearers are that correlate with inherent right-holders. They are not just located in our own families, neighborhoods, or countries, but may be found outside our borders in the wider world of the UN and its affiliated agencies, and especially among the wealthier citizens of other countries.

The Internet has shown us that the bonds of humanity know no boundaries. Cranston has set up three quite legitimate tests for sorting out the supposed from the real human rights. The thesis of my first section here is that the cosmopolitan outlook developed in the preceding chapter shows how the social, economic, and cultural rights of the Declaration can pass these Cranston tests just as well as can the older civil and political rights. Either all flunk or all pass.

To further answer this challenge, I add in the second section the idea of human rights thresholds to my definition of what a human right is. We need that concept in order to avoid the charge of utopianism, for not all inequalities in the world should be thought of as human rights violations. While we defend the thesis that social, economic and cultural rights have the same status as civil and political ones, we do not subscribe to a worldwide egalitarianism that is implicit in any Cranston-type charges. In the third section, I refer to the International Covenant of Economic, Social and Cultural Rights in discussing international activity that exemplifies human rights threshold construction. We give examples of the process by which the abstractions of the Declaration are lowered into their domestic and local contexts. By showing how this concretizing of the UDHR abstractions works in practice, I hope to take some of the sting out of the utopianism charges. But first the Cranston tests.

A. New Rights Call for a New World Order

When the drafters looked back at what they had done in two years of drafting, they were especially proud of having included social, economic, and cultural rights in their text, and they did call them "rights." Guy Peres Cisneros of Cuba said he liked the fact that "social rights, which were a feature of the twentieth Century, occupied a prominent place in the draft declaration." As he saw it, "the draft declaration expressed in particular clear and precise terms the most noble aspirations of twentieth Century man." Referring to U.S. President Roosevelt's 1941 Four Freedoms speech, he predicted that the "declaration would mark the advent of a world in which man, freed from fear and poverty, could enjoy freedom of speech, religion and opinion."[3] (These four freedoms did find their way into the Declaration's Second Recital.) General Carlos Romulo observed that "the new declaration recognized rights which were perhaps not even contemplated in the Magna Carta, the 1789 Declaration of the Rights of Man, or the American Declaration of Independence. That recognition was based on the fact that a traditional declaration of political rights would be insufficient unless buttressed by a declaration of economic and social rights." Lakshmi Menon called attention to "the rights to equal pay for equal work; the rights of mothers and children to social protection, whether the children were born in or out of wedlock; the right to an education; equality of rights for men and women." She saw these rights as "the expression of a new social order, of true democracy based on social justice" (GAOR Third, 893). Jorge Carrera Andrade called to mind "the right of man to work, and his right to benefit from his leisure, the right to a decent standard of living and the right to social security," all of which rights, he said, "constituted the real triumph of the twentieth Century and were the foundation of the modern democratic system which believed that social peace depended on the well being of the individual" (918). Baghat Badaoui Bye also thought that in addition to the classical "public freedoms," the social and economic rights "must certainly be included" in the Declaration (59). Surprisingly, the communist delegations gave the social, economic, and cultural rights only backhanded praise.[4]

All this praise in Paris stands in stark contrast to the postwar history of human rights implementation. In the 1950s and 1960s the same commission that drew up the inclusive list of the thirty articles in the Declaration was forced to break up the Declaration list into two (instead of the planned one) legal international covenants. Because of the influence of the Cold War, the UN adopted one covenant for the civil and political rights and another, different covenant for the social, economic, and cultural rights. Also, the 1950 European Convention of Human Rights contains only civil and political rights. It took eleven more years to add to that convention the European Social Charter of 1961 that deals with social, economic, and cultural rights. This Social Charter was updated and revised in 1988, 1995, and 1996. While the 1948 Bogotá Declaration of the Association of American States does have in it some social, economic, and cultural rights, the Human Rights Convention sponsored by the same organization does not, and it leaves the implementation of these rights to the 1988 Protocol of San Salvador. This dual implementation process has created the temptation to think that there are in the Universal Declaration two very different kinds of human rights, some of which are genuinely inherent in the human person, some not.[5] Cranston's 1972 essay "Human Rights, Real and Supposed" fit well into this Cold War battle and gave intellectual credence to this split understanding of the Declaration and of the domain of human rights generally. Since the Universal Declaration is the mother of all human rights norms, any potential crack in this foundation stone needs to be thoroughly investigated.

There is a certain urgency to this investigation because a working group of the UN Commission on Human Rights is presently debating the feasibility of adding an optional protocol to the International Covenant on Economic, Social and Cultural Rights (ICESCR) that would allow individuals and groups to lodge complaints against states for violating this covenant. This kind of quasi-juridical complaints process was attached to the Civil and Political Covenant when it was adopted in 1966. Attaching a similar mechanism to the other covenant can be seen as the coming of age of the social, economic, and cultural human rights. Article 22 of the Declaration plays a role in this debate because those who oppose this additional protocol use the presence of Article 22 in the Declaration as evidence that the drafters of the Declaration did not look on all the human rights as having the same status, so that they do not require the same implementation treatment.[6] Article 22 raises the question why the drafters felt the need to introduce the social, economic, and cultural rights of their document with a special introductory article. It reads as follows: "Everyone, as a member of society, has the right to social security and is entitled to realization, through national effort and international cooperation and in accordance with the organization and resources of each State, of the economic, social and cultural rights indispensable for his dignity and the free development of his personality." The presence of this article just before the list of social, economic and cultural rights in Articles 23 through 27 can be interpreted in at least three ways. It can mean that the drafters viewed these newer rights as *less* important and therefore wanted to set them apart from the civil and political rights that preceded them in the document. The article can also indicate that the drafters viewed these newer rights as *more* important than the older more established rights. The third reading, which I will defend, is the benign or neutral one that sees the article as included to draw attention to these newer rights, not because of any ontological weakness, but because the drafters realized that implementation of these "newer" rights would require a great deal of international cooperation.

The first two readings reflect the Cold War rhetoric of capitalist versus communist ideologies, where the former stressed the first half of the document and the latter the second half, each claiming superiority for its own list. The first interpretation feeds into Cranston's famous attack on the Declaration. Cranstonites view social, economic, and cultural rights as phony philosophical interlopers. The second interpretation is a mostly Marxist one, according to which the social, economic, and cultural rights are the intellectual starting base for the whole set of human rights, the older ones existing to serve the newer ones. On both of these readings the domain of human rights is split in half, the difference being which half is given ontological priority. As I already noted, this fight did eventuate in the 1967 adoption of two (instead of just one) international covenants. Our theory sees no philosophical or ontological significance in the presence of Article 22, but holds that it was included for strategic and practical reasons.

The main purpose of Article 22 was to underline everyone's entitlement to the realization (or implementation) of the social, economic, and cultural rights of the Declaration.[7] In the context of a discussion on the right to work, a subcommittee was appointed "to work out a special article concerning the measures to be taken in order to ensure enjoyment of economic and social rights" (EC.4/SR.65/11). This subcommittee consisted of representatives from France, Lebanon, the UK, the USSR, and the United States. It reported out the following article: "Everyone has the right to a good social and international order in which the rights and freedoms set out in this Declaration can be fully realized" (SR.67/2). With the deletion of the word "good," the Third Committee made this is our Article 28. The Sub-Committee adopted this umbrella article unanimously and we note that it does not make explicit reference to the duties of states and that it does not single out the social, economic, and cultural rights for special attention. For that very reason the French delegation moved for the adoption of a text that was more in keeping with the Committee's mandate: "Everyone, as a member of society, has the economic, social and cultural rights enumerated below, whose fulfillment should be made possible in every State separately or by international collaboration" (E/CN.4/120). René Cassin moved for the adoption of the article with the observation that this text "was more specific and applied to the economic, social and cultural rights which the commission was examining at present." Some later additions turned this French text into Article 22.[8] The drafters' discussion of the relative merits of Articles 22 and 28 could not avoid the Cranstonite question of whether there are two kinds of human rights in the Declaration, or whether they are all cut of the same inherent moral cloth.

Charles Malik argued that Article 22 was made "redundant" by the presence of Article 28. "To make special reference to the economic, social and cultural rights would be to favor them in comparison with other rights and freedoms which was inadmissible," he said (SR.67/5). "He failed to find anywhere in the beginning of the Declaration an article parallel to that proposed by the French representative. While [Article 3] was a declaratory statement of the rights and freedoms of human beings, there was no statement to the effect that society must be so organized as to guarantee those rights and freedoms to the individual." He therefore felt that the "adoption of the French proposal would mean that economic and social rights . . . would be given preferential treatment over other rights of equal importance . . . [and] would create a bias in favor of economic and social rights" (SR.72/5)

Picking up on Malik's own use of the phrase "as a member of society," Cassin made some malignant-sounding comments that I interpret as benign. He initially argued "the previously adopted articles for the most part dealt with the natural rights of individual human beings," whereas Articles 22 and 28 "viewed human beings as members of organized society." He felt that this "difference should be noted in the Declaration" (SR.72/2). Hinting at the notion of progressive implementation that was later used to separate the two international covenants, he argued that "Most States would agree that the liberty of conscience or the right to live should be safeguarded as soon as possible, but few would be in agreement on detailed undertakings regarding social security, social insurance, full employment, and other subjects" (AC.1/SR.5/3). Cassin was an internationalist and a strong union supporter who saw labor rights as genuine human rights. When he was asked by his colleagues to streamline the list of rights submitted by John Humphrey, director in the Secretariat's Division of Human Rights, he had a chance to reduce Humphrey's list of no fewer than ten social, economic, and cultural human rights. He left all but one of them in place. His initial opposition to inclusion of the newer rights was based on his belief that there was not enough time to nail down the "detailed undertakings" required for states to make legal commitments about them. We must read this hesitancy in the context of Western European economies having been devastated by the war.

When it became obvious that a Declaration would be adopted and when Article 28 had already been put on the table, Cassin felt no compunction about lobbying vigorously for the adoption of Article 22 as a necessary way of achieving the progressive implementation of social, economic, and cultural rights. He told his Third Committee colleagues that the presence of Article 22 was an indication that social rights "were different in character from any rights outlined in earlier declarations of man. They all had in common the fact that national effort and international cooperation were needed for their realization" (GAOR Third, 499). In a 1958 lecture he said that the new social, economic, and cultural rights had been included in the Declaration because they were "en un certain sens indivisibles" (in a certain sense indivisible) from the older civil and political rights.[9]

Instead of reading Cassin's defense of Article 22 in an ontologically malignant way, as Michael Dennis and David Stewart do,[10] I suggest that we see it as a (benign) pronouncement of a new vision for a new world order that went far beyond the eighteenth-century precedents that consisted largely of civil and political rights. For Cassin the differences between the "old" and the "new" lay in how much administrative effort and financial support were involved in their implementation, which is why the drafters called for a new post-Westphalian world order.

Similar, stronger support for Article 22 as a second umbrella article came from the Cuban and the Chilean delegations (GAOR Third, 509, 500). Australian delegate Alan S. Watt argued that Article 22 "placed the problem in its true light by emphasizing the need for international co-operation as well as for national action in accordance with Article 56 of the U.N. Charter" (508). Going in the other direction, communist delegations were worried that the presence of Article 22 would suggest that these newer rights had been selected for attention because they were weaker or less important. Alexei Pavlov rephrased and proposed for adoption an earlier Yugoslav text that fixed these shortcomings.[11] This Soviet text was rejected by both the Third Session and the Third Committee for reasons that support our interpretation of Cassin's intent.

The only objection to Article 22 that might be read as somewhat malignant came from the U.S. delegation. The drafters had all along worked with a policy of not making references to the obligations of states. By calling for "international co-operation," Article 22 also ran the risk of coming into conflict with this policy. Governments could, however, take cover by stressing the voluntary character of the call for cooperation by pointing to various "escape" clauses also included, which is precisely what the U.S. Department of State asked its representative to do. Dennis and Stewart have a case when they cite the United States as opposed to Article 22 because of skepticism about the genuine character of the rights involved, but the case is not a direct one in that it is based on the escape clauses.[12] They point to Eleanor Roosevelt's explanation that Article 22 was a "compromise between views of certain governments which were anxious that the State should give special recognition to the economic, social and cultural rights of the individual and the view of Governments, such as the US Government, which considered that the obligation of the State should not be specified" (GAOR Third, 501). The Declaration "should enunciate the rights of man and not the obligations of States. Furthermore, economic, social and cultural rights, though important, were not more important than political rights" (501). Roosevelt stressed that to her delegation the phrases "through national effort and international co-operation" and "in accordance with the organization and resources of each State" were the key ones of the article. When the competing USSR text was rejected by 27 votes to 8, with 8 abstentions, Article 22 was left standing as a unifying bridge between the first and the second halves of the Declaration (512).

After Article 22 had been adopted, the question was whether the eclipsed Article 28 was still needed as well. In the Third Session it read as follows: "Everyone has the right to a good social and international order in which the rights and freedoms set forth in this Declaration can be fully realized" (78–79). Charles Malik, who had been the original sponsor of Article 28, admitted that the ideas of the article were "to some extent expressed in the Preamble [Article 22] that had just been adopted. He nevertheless felt that the Declaration should clearly set forth the right of mankind to have in the United Nations a world organization, as well as a social order, in which the rights and freedoms could be realized" (78–79). In spite of the article's telling us that everyone is "entitled"[13] to this new world order, Robinson thinks that "it is obvious that Article 28 is not a 'right' in the accepted sense of the word because there is no one to implement it."[14] We disagree. The new international world order envisioned in Articles 22 and 28 is full of all kinds of duties that attach themselves to individuals, groups, states, and the UN with its affiliated organizations: UNDP, UNESCO, World Bank, and IMF, all of which have human rights duties, which in the case of these worldwide organizations are legally anchored in the seven human rights references in the UN Charter. The debates about UDHR Articles 22 and 28 forecast the enormous growth in human rights and humanitarian law that have taken place in recent decades, all of it aimed to protect individual human beings.

I mention of the successful Soviet proposal (641) to have the adjective "good" deleted from the just cited text of Article 28 because it shows us how keen the drafters were about *not* slanting the new world order demanded by their document in the direction of any one political or economic ideology, just so long as all the rights in the Declaration are being honored and realized. The Third Committee accepted the deletion of the adjective "good" (34 votes to 2, with 2 abstentions), but it did not accept Pavlov's reasoning. The communists felt that "as long as there was [any] private ownership of the means of production, the social order could not possibly be a good one" (638), which narrow view the drafters rejected with the inherent right to property that can be held "alone as well as in association with others" (Article 17). Malik supported the deletion of the word "good" from Article 28 because the expression "good social and international order" did not "apply to any particular system, whether capitalist or socialist" (639). The Norwegian, Syrian, UK, and Peruvian delegations all also felt (in the words of Canadian Ralph Maybank) that "should the rights set forth in the Declaration be achieved the social and international order would be good, whether it came within the framework of capitalism, communism, feudalism, or any other system" (640–41). Since the Declaration includes a great many human rights, no system or ideology can easily claim to have dominated the drafters' vision. Article 28 was adopted by 25 votes to 3, with 8 abstentions (642). The general and inclusive character of Article 28 has since been used to strengthen the international character of the rights in the Declaration and to expand the reach of human rights law into international environmental and trade law.[15]

I will now use this call for a new post-Westphalian world order to comment on the three tests that Cranston uses to sort out "real" from merely "supposed" human rights. To help with this leveling process I will also invoke the capabilities approach to human rights that we introduced in the Chapter 4 as a crucial unifying factor for human rights.

1. The Test of Universality. This test states that "everyone" must have the right; otherwise it will not be a universal right and therefore not a genuine human right. While the right to life clearly fits everyone from the moment of birth (if not before), the idea of holidays with pay does not fit, for it presupposes that one is an employee of some kind. This might be a moral right that some people have, but they will have it because they belong to a certain class of people or live in a certain society, and not simply by virtue of their humanity. So argue the Cranstonites. Our response is that people everywhere do have the capability for relaxation and the associated moral right to the development and practice of that capability. Also, whatever the merits of this view are, it cannot be used to divide the rights in the Declaration into real and utopian ones. Even in the second half of the document we meet with capabilities and rights that seem to fit us just as human beings, like the right to an education (Article 26), to participation in culture, and to the benefits of scientific research (Article 27). Going the other way, it is very easy to find rights in the first half, both civil and political, that obviously only fit us as members of certain groups. Most legal rights can only be claimed if one is an adult, and only then if one is a citizen of a certain country (Article 21), if one has been arrested or detained by security forces (Article 19), or if one has been put on trial (Article 10) or charged with a penal offense (Article 10). All normal and healthy people always possess the capabilities that undergird these rights, as well as the rights themselves, but—and this is crucial—they will not find a need to *claim* any of these rights unless they find themselves in one of the situations described in one of these articles. It is only when one has been arrested that one's right to a fair trial and an impartial judge or jury kicks in and becomes claimable. At the start of the proceedings one can, for instance, claim one's human right against arbitrary arrest. Similarly, no one who is not, in the words of Article 16, "of full age" has the human right to marry and start a family.

To see why, in spite of the specificity of when we can claim these rights, we nevertheless should see all of them as genuinely inherent and therefore metaphysically universal, we need to recall the distinction made in Chapter 1 between the inherent possession of a human right and the need to claim it, or to have it claimed for us by others. According to UDHR Article 1, we all possess these human rights by birth, but it is clear that the lucky ones among us only rarely, if ever, need to claim them as a *human* right. We (the lucky ones) almost never need to call on the authorities or our friends to stop a violation from being perpetrated against us. But millions of people, even in the developed world, are not that lucky. When they are arrested, they do have their moral birth rights to a fair trial or humane treatment violated. Some couples who do not share the sexual preference of the majority find "the free and full consent" clause of their right to marriage violated even though they clearly are of "full age." Since some of the capabilities that undergird our inherent human rights can only be exhibited as functioning capacities when they are exercised in group contexts (as the right to association always is), Cranston's point will not be totally lost. But he cannot draw any kind of line between real and supposed human rights, since all the capabilities discussed in Chapter 4 are universal foundation stones for human rights.

2. *The Test of Paramount Importance.* Cranston thinks that it "is a paramount duty to relieve great distress, as it is not a paramount duty to give pleasure" (127). Then he gives the earlier-mentioned examples of the South African student who was denied a travel visa to accept a scholarship at Oxford University, of the victims of the Nazi genocide, and of someone imprisoned without a fair trial. To Cranston the rights involved in these three cases are of "paramount importance" because with them "we are confronted by matters which belong to a totally different moral dimension from questions of social security and holidays with pay" (127). Social, economic, and cultural rights are not "supremely sacred" and their violation is not a "grave affront to justice." This affront to justice (or paramount importance) test can be used against Cranston and other libertarian and conservative thinkers. All of us tend to pick affronts to justice that suit our own ideological predilections. Conservatives point to abuses of religious human rights, while liberals point to prison labor or sweatshops. Conservatives point to the violation of political human rights in Saudi Arabia and liberals to the lack of land distribution in Brazil. And so on. An honest and objective reader of news and television reports can without much trouble find or recall "great affronts to justice" that involve the entire scope of the Universal Declaration. Our theory of human rights explains all these affronts in terms of the same theory of moral intuitionism introduced at the end of Chapter 2. Cécile Fabre has made the point that "the adverse consequences of neediness on people's prospects for a decent life can be as bad as the consequences of infringement of freedom of speech, of being tortured, of not being able to associate."[16] This affront to justice is her main argument for the inclusion of welfare rights to food, clothing, housing, and healthcare in the constitutions of nations.

When Franklin Roosevelt was the U.S president during the years of the Great Depression, he did not think that these kinds of rights needed to be added to the U.S Constitution. But he did use the same affront-to-justice test to defend a legislative and executive approach to codifying these new rights. Cass Sunstein gives a fitting title to the chapter in which he details the horrors of the Great Depression that led Roosevelt to propose a second, economic bill of rights for the U.S people: "Rights from Wrongs: Roosevelt's Constitutional Order." Sunstein describes how the numerous agencies that were part of Roosevelt's New Deal "were concrete expressions of the emerging conception of rights."[17] It was the government's task, Roosevelt felt, to deliver these newly enunciated rights to the U.S people. Roosevelt's second bill fleshed out the third and fourth of his famous four freedoms of expression and religion, and from want and fear.[18] The rights in this second bill were seen as a correct response to "a particular set of social wrongs" pushed into national consciousness by the Great Depression. The obvious affronts to human dignity suffered by millions of people due to no negligence on their own part led Roosevelt to reconsider the original U.S. bill of rights as far too narrow for the advancing industrial age.

Jeremy Waldron also defends these liberal rights as genuine, not just because they sometimes are means to the implementation of civil and political rights (voters need to be able to read, for instance), but also because "death, disease, malnutrition, and economic despair are as much matters of [moral] concern as any denials of political or civil liberty."[19] Like Cranston, Waldron picks the human right to "periodic holidays with pay" (Article 24) as his main example. He imagines the life of a man who since the age of twelve did back-breaking work without ever having had "reasonable limitation of working hours," who collapsed at forty with a body riddled with disease but had no insurance to pay the bills. He could never take a day off to rest up because that would have meant he could not feed his family. Comments Waldron:

to demand in addition "periodic holidays with pay" is to try and claw back as well some larger blocks of leisure time, time measured in whole days rather than hours, so the rest of life can be led. There *is* a universal human interest—recognized (though not necessarily respected) in all cultures—in having longish periods (days rather than hours) of sustained respite from the business of securing subsistence, whatever that involves: fiestas (as opposed to siestas), holy days, vacations, communal celebrations, and so forth. "Periodic holidays with pay" expresses a particular culture-bound conception of that interest, but the wider interest is there and its importance in the constitution of a bearable human life is undeniable. (11)

Life can be made unbearable in numerous ways—some more obvious than others—which is why the need and the right for holidays with pay has escaped many a reader of the Declaration. Admits Waldron: "The urgency of the other socioeconomic demands is more evident: health care, social security, a minimum standard of living" (11).

3. *The Test of Practicability.* This third test especially has fed into the

widespread charge of utopianism in a directly Declaration-specific way. "If it is impossible for a thing to be done," argues Cranston, echoing Emmanuel Kant, "it is absurd to claim it as a right" ("Human Rights," 126). If ought implies can, then individuals or even whole nations can only be blamed for things they did or could have done, and not for things they did not do or could not have done. If it is impossible for a nation to implement certain human rights, then we cannot blame its government for violating its people's dignity in that particular way. Cranston believes that this test of practicability disqualifies most social and economic rights of the Declaration because "it would be totally impossible to translate them in the same way into positive rights by analogous political and legal action" (124). Cranston starts his practicality test with a mention of the problem of justiciability, but then soon shifts to questions of resources and money. I will do the same.

Those who object to judicial mechanisms (in a global or domestic setting) for the settlement of violations of social, economic, and cultural rights argue that these rights cannot be easily legislated and decided by judges and juries because the language (and therefore the standards) involved is by its very nature vaguer and less precise than the language we supposedly find in statutes about civil rights and political entitlements. For some theoreticians this difference in language stems from a deep division in the realm of rights itself between negative ones and positive ones. Since negative rights are phrased negatively as involving freedom *from* certain interferences with one's life (like torture and blockage of movement), it is the government's job to legislate those freedoms. It can easily do this by punishing those (including its own officials) who interfere in an unacceptable way in the lives of its citizens. This is done when murder, assault, theft and the breaking of contracts are made punishable by law. We see on a daily basis how prosecutors, courts, judges, and juries deal with the violators of these so-called negative rights. They are obviously justiciable.

Positive rights, on the other hand, are seen as rights *to* something, like housing, education, or welfare. Here one thinks of claims *to* and of freedoms *for* obtaining certain goods, rather than freedoms *from* interferences with one's activities. Charles Fried seeks to draw a rather precise line between negative rights "that something not be done to one" and positive rights that are "inevitably claims to scarce goods" such as material supplies or the attention of a lawyer or doctor.[20] Here the government has to do more than just keep our paths clear; it has to allocate scarce resources and supply services that sometimes cost a great deal of money. The rights Cranston criticizes as interlopers make up much of the content of the ICESCR, whose wording one scholar has called "misleading" and "regrettable" because it introduced "a notion of 'right' . . .

that is utterly different from the concept of 'right of an individual' as it is traditionally understood in international law and employed in practice"[21] The arguments of this chapter take issue with this thesis.

It is not at all clear to me that the language of positive rights is by its very nature less nuanced and less precise than that of so-called negative rights. There does not seem to be much, if any, difference in precision and therefore in justiciability between everyone having, on the one hand, the Declaration's negative rights "to life, liberty and security of person" (Article 3) and, on the other, having its positive "right to education" (Article 26). Both types seem to be perfectly comprehensible and therefore equally susceptible to legal disputes. In the next section I will give examples of countries that do treat social, economic, and cultural rights as justiciable and without apparent chaos in their courts. It turns out that the issue of justiciability is more one of political ideology than of what the law and the courts can or cannot handle. The committee that monitors the Covenant of Social, Economic and Cultural Rights, which is based on the second half of the Declaration and has been ratified by more than 150 countries, recognizes that different states have different legal cultures and ideologies, but even so it has stated that "there is no Covenant right which could not, in the great majority of systems, be considered to possess at least some significant justiciable dimensions."[22] Our investigation leads to the opposite conclusion from that of Dennis and Stewart, who conclude their analysis of these debates with the observation that "The rights and obligations contained in the ICESCR were never intended to be susceptible to judicial or quasi-judicial determination" (515). As to the skills judges need to adjudicate these rights, Cécile Fabre sees no reason "why specialized judges could not be trained to acquire those skills, or could not seek advice from independent experts, as they actually already do."[23] In the next section on threshold construction I will have occasion to mention the administrative law judges in the United States who help adjudicate complaints filed with the National Labor Relations Board alleging unfair labor practices.

The real force of the practicality test lies not in what courts are able to do, but in what nations are able to pay. This alleged difference in cost has been used to accentuate the difference between negative and positive rights, where the cheaper negative ones turn out to be mostly civil and political rights, and the more expensive positive ones turn out to be mostly social, economic, and cultural rights. This terminology is meant to indicate that some rights involve little or no expenditure of resources (negative ones) or that they do require such (positive ones). However, ever since Henry Shue made his contribution to this discussion, the consensus is that no right is really totally negative in the sense that it involves little or no cost to implement it.[24] All human rights call on the resources of the community for their implementation. And while there obviously is a difference between rights in terms of implementation costs, that difference does not draw a useful line between civil and political rights on the one hand and social, economic, and cultural ones on the other. Take, for instance, the human rights to "freedom to leave any country including his own" (Article 13), to "seek and enjoy in other countries asylum from persecution" (Article 14), and "to a nationality" (Article 15). These rights correlate with duties to set up a system of international law that protects persons against violations of these particular rights. Since they involve the jurisdiction of several countries, these rights cannot just refer to negative duties on the part of our government to let us be, which is what a strict negative-rights approach would suggest. These international rights call on governments to get involved on an international level, which costs a great deal of money. It means countries have to heed UDHR Articles 22 and 28 and take their UN membership seriously. They have a duty—based on the inherent rights of the victims—to cooperate with one another in the creation of international regimes that help refugees relocate, and to combat the problem of the millions of stateless people that we meet with in the "underbelly" described at the start of this chapter.

Even domestically, one can readily see that every right listed in the Declaration involves public expenditures that turn such rights into positive claims on community resources. The call of Article 16 for "protection [of the family] by society and the State" could easily involve some form of welfare assistance, which is just what Article 23 indicates when it says that a worker has a right to have wages "supplemented, if necessary, by other means of social protection." At a minimum the rights involving our physical security (Article 3) involve good police academies and ample police personnel, especially in more dangerous neighborhoods. The rights "to security of person" of Article 3 meant a great deal more to the drafters than that a person be left physically secure or alone. The Latin American sponsors of this clause meant it to be a reference to all the social, economic, and cultural rights that are listed later in the Declaration.[25] Sometimes governments need to go to great extremes to ensure everyone's right to "take part in the government of his country" (Article 16), as they do when they invite international monitors or are told by courts to guard voting stations and buy new voting machines.

Though it serves as a special bridging article in the document, Article 22 cannot be used to draw a sharp line between two very different kinds of human rights, with those that cost next to nothing placed in the first half of the document and those that cost a great deal in the second half. We have seen that the drafters inserted this bridgelike article not to cast aspersions on the rights that follow but to draw attention to them so that they would not be monetarily starved into oblivion as the younger siblings in the family of rights. Since 9/11 we have learned that an expensive human right can just as well be a security-related civil or political one as a social or cultural one. It all depends on the circumstances.

I have not yet mentioned what I see as the greatest weakness of the Cranstonite position: it views the international arena as broken up into discrete national entities that do not interact with each other. Cranstonites work with an outmoded Westphalian view of the world as one made up of completely sovereign states that engage one another through voluntary treaties, and that are never responsible for feeding, clothing, or otherwise caring for one another's citizens. Taking India as his example, Cranston asserted in 1967 that its government "simply cannot command the resources that would guarantee each one of the 480 million inhabitants" what Article 23 demands, namely, 'a standard of living adequate for the health and well-being of himself and his family,' let alone 'holidays with pay'"(Cranston, 126). The word "resources" here covers both material and human resources, all of which differ enormously from country to country.

This claim is still true today, when it has been suggested that India presents a challenge to Amartya Sen's thesis that democracies never let famines happen within their own borders.[26] We can easily fortify Cranston's point by noting that the 2002 UN Development Report, which ranks the nations of the world according to their standard of living, ranked 49 nations below India, which was no. 124 out of a possible low of 173 (Sierra Leone) spots.[27] India was placed in the medium human development range together with Mexico (no. 54), Bulgaria (no. 62), Ukraine (no. 80), Ecuador (no. 93), Algeria (no. 106), Namibia (no. 122), Kenya (no. 134), and 76 others. The 35 "low human development" countries were, of course, even worse off. In that range we find Sudan (no. 143), Bangladesh (no. 146), Nigeria (no. 151), Tanzania (no. 156), Rwanda (no. 164), and Ethiopia (no. 171). So, if India does not have the resources to bring the full range of social, economic, and cultural rights to its people, neither do a great many other countries. In 2002, Cranston's practicability objection could be made to apply to some hundred and twenty nations in the world. The 2008 numbers are not all that different. If his argument is valid, it will indeed make the Declaration a very utopian and unrealistic kind of document.

The only way for the newer rights not to flunk this practicality test is for us to heed the demand the drafters make in Articles 22 and 28 for a new, non-Westphalian international order that is structured so as to let people everywhere enjoy the goods referred to in their inherent social, economic, and cultural rights. This means that we must merge the moral track of human rights (based on the Universal Declaration, which fleshes out the seven references in the UN Charter) with the economic development track that came out of the 1944 Bretton Woods Conference (held in the Connecticut town of that name), where the World Bank, IMF, and (what is now) the WTO were born. Until the beginning of the twenty-first century, human rights theorists and activists on the moral track worried only about the microdevelopment of the individual human person all around the world, and economists on the development track worried only about the macroeconomic development of whole regions and client nations on all continents. These two systems did not really cross over into each other's territories. They therefore also did not publicly quarrel a great deal. It might even have seemed to theoreticians that their two tracks, though they never planned it, would by some invisible hand end up working toward the same goal of the development of both human beings and the countries in which they live. Each set of institutions did what it was designed to do, and no intentionality was brought to bear to make sure there was no conflict between human rights and economic development, or to make sure the theoreticians on each track stayed in touch.

This lack of communication lasted until the turn of the twentieth-first century, when experts on both tracks came to see that they needed to start working more closely together. It would have been a great source of satisfaction to the drafters of UDHR Articles 22 and 28 to see that human rights experts have now started to look at what the Bretton Woods experts are doing and saying, and to see that economists have discovered that they cannot achieve economic development without paying attention to the moral guidelines in human rights norms. The Reports of the UN Development Programme are a good example of this new awareness. The subtitle of its *Human Development Report 2000* is very telling in this regard: *Human Rights and Human Development.* The term "development" was left intentionally ambiguous between the microdevelopment of the human person and the macroeconomic development of whole regions and nations. About the approach of the preceding decades the report had this to say: "Until the last decade human development and human rights followed parallel paths in both concept and action—the one largely dominated by economists, social scientists and policy makers, the other by political activists, lawyers and philosophers. They promoted divergent strategies of analysis and action—economics and social progress on the one hand, political pressure, legal reform and ethical questioning, on the other" (2). Both the title and much of the content of the report give the impression that the merger is finally taking place. We see evidence of it all around us, as when huge international corporations impose codes of ethics on their partners in the developing world. We can also see it in the fact that thousands of domestic and hundreds of international NGOs lobby governments with a mix of moral and economic agenda items.

The exegetical, philosophical, and political arguments of this chapter mean to make a contribution to the ongoing conversation between these two different international communities of experts. The remarkable scope of the Universal Declaration—containing as it does both civil and political and social, economic, and cultural rights—makes it a natural bridge between these two tracks. By offering a unified theory of inherent human rights that is drawn from this crucial text we hope to further the dialogue and cooperation that is starting to take hold between theoreticians and practitioners on these different tracks. The merger has not yet taken place, for, as Philip Alston has shown, even within the world of the UN itself, huge segments of its operations that should be merging are still like "ships passing in the night."[28] His example is the lack of contact between experts charged with implementing the UN millennial goals (adopted in the fall of 2000) and human rights experts. These 147 government heads pledged themselves to: " (1) eradicate extreme poverty; (2) to achieve universal primary education; (3) promote gender equality and empower women; (4) reduce child mortality; (5) improve maternal health; (6) combat HIV/AIDS, malaria, and other diseases; (7) ensure environmental sustainability; and (8) develop a global partnership for development" ("Ships Passing" 756). Clearly, there is an overlap between these well-known development goals and the moral aspirations of the human rights movement. Yet, in spite of a strenuous effort in 2003 to get the two tracks to accept a "Common Understanding on the Human Rights Based Approach to Development Cooperation,"[29] the sixty reports from countries on how much progress they have made toward these eight goals make scant or no reference at all to the human rights of the people they are trying to save. And, just as negligent, the various committees that oversee the human rights track have in their work totally ignored the Millennial Development Goals.

This is a sordid state of affairs that cries out for more synchronization across the globe. Concludes Alston, "It is paradoxical that the HR community, which has been so quick to criticize the reluctance of development agencies to take human rights considerations on board, has itself shown a significant degree of obstinacy when it comes to making the necessary outreach to ensure that its own agenda is effectively promoted within the context of the international community's development agenda" ("Ships Passing," 827). We rightly detect some optimism in the title of a 2005 volume of essays, *Human Rights and Development: Towards Mutual Reinforcement.*[30] With contributions of more than twenty-five experts (mostly in the development field), Mary Robinson rightly points to a "sea change" in "the relationship between development and human rights." But she does not believe that the experts on the two tracks have really started to speak "the same language. If mutual curiosity has increased, confidence is far from being safely established" (31). The essays in the volume bear out this judgment. Perhaps we should speak of a conversation about mutual interests rather than of a merger of two fields or even of two visions. Whatever the nature of this rapprochement is, we can rest assured that it is *not* being directed by any sort of invisible hand that synchronizes the efforts of the two tracks.

Citizens of affluent democratic societies can help speed up the merger of these two tracks by lobbying their own government's representatives at the World Bank and IMF when loans to weaker and less developed nations come up for a vote; by closely monitoring the bilateral trade pacts their governments sign with other countries; by insisting that the next WTO treaty include clauses that protect all (those in advanced postindustrial economies, those only now in the process of industrializing, as well as those still almost totally dependent on agricultural exports) of the world's workers and their dependents; and by insisting that their own country actively participate in the Millennial Development Goal of cutting the number to those living in poverty in half by the year 2015.

B. The Construction of Human Rights Thresholds

The Need for Built-In Thresholds. Since 1990 the above-mentioned the UN Development Program has published a biannual Human Development Index. This index is a compilation of data in one large international index that ranks all the countries in the world from highest to lowest in terms of human development. A country's ranking is based on three sets of data: life expectancy at birth, gross school enrollment, and Gross Domestic Product per capita (PPP, in U.S. dollars). The first tells us about the average life and health of the people; the second, about their average level of education and literacy; and the third, about their income, which may indicate a measurable level of poverty. In the 2002 index, Canada (which had ranked first for many years) was overtaken by Norway, which in that year had a life expectancy at birth of 78.5 years, an adult (age 15 and above) literacy rate of 100 percent, a gross (primary, secondary, and tertiary) school enrollment figure of 97 percent, and a per capita income of $29,918 that was arrived at against the equivalent of U.S. dollars in 2000. As I indicated earlier, Sierra Leone, as no. 173, ranked last. There life expectancy was a mere 38.9 years, the adult literacy rate was only 36 percent, and the per capita income was 490 U.S. dollars per year, which (given that the rich had a much higher income) means that most of the population had to get by on less than a dollar a day and were starving to death. The middle position between these extremes was held by Turkmenistan, which was no. 87, with an average life expectancy of 70.9, an adult literacy rate of 82.8, a school enrollment rate of 70 percent, and a per capita income of 4,598 U.S. dollars. The connection between poverty, disease, and public policy can be seen in the fact that between 2000 and 2010, 23 percent of the teachers in Zimbabwe will die of AIDS, as will 18 percent of teachers in Zambia, 15 percent in Kenya, and 5 percent in Uganda (26). In 2000 close to 600 of every 100,000 women in South Asia died while giving birth, and close to 1,000 did so in sub-Saharan Africa (22). That same statistic for the rest of the world was below 200. The Food Security and Nutrition Index gives us the daily per capita supply of calories, protein, and fat, and the percentage of household consumption that went to food for nearly all the nations in the world. We could therefore ask whether the United States (with 8 percent) should help pull Morocco (with 45 percent) down to its own low level, and whether it should be concerned about the 28 percent of Greece.

Global data like these on a great variety of issues or problems are being gathered and published on a regular basis. The World Bank, a veritable geyser of statistics, publishes its own *World Development Report*, which for 2004 was based on more than 800 indicators, complemented by "a separately published database that gives access to over 1000 data tables and 800 time-series indicators for 225 economies and regions."[31] The result is an overwhelming jungle of statistics on which the human mind naturally wants to impose some order, human rights theorists being no exception. These theorists approach this jungle from either of the two directions I mentioned at the start of my cosmopolitanism chapter. Those that are interested in *inter-national* justice start with a domestic conception of justice and seek to extend that conception to the global context, while those I called cosmopolitans start with a *cosmopolitan* mandate and work their way back to nation-states as the best vehicles to fulfill that global mandate. Since the first group looks at states, societies, and peoples as the primary actors in international affairs, it does not share the ethical or normative individualism of the Declaration, and so is not really exposed to the utopianism charges that are the subject of this chapter. We put John Rawls and the Cranstonites of section A into this internationalist camp.[32]

As Chapter 4 made clear, my interest lies with the cosmopolitan group. Unlike internationalists, cosmopolitans (as I define them) are less likely to think of human rights as created by international lawyers and diplomats. They look on the whole world as one unified ethical community, where all the members of the human family have both their own inherent rights and the correlative duties to respect the same rights of their brothers and sisters around the globe. On this moral individualist view, nation-states are still the most important delivery vehicles for the enjoyment of inherent human rights. But states are not the only ones, and they are not the ethically basic ones. Moral cosmopolitans see adult human beings as the first duty-bearers who created and now sustain the international institutions that dot our globe. Groups (whether governmental or nongovernmental), organizations, communities, and, yes, even states that human beings are born into, create, and maintain are very necessary tools for the implementation of inherent moral rights. It is the perspective of these different kinds of duty-bearers that brings us to the important role that the idea of human rights thresholds plays in this chapter's answer to the charge of unrealistic utopianism.

The idea of a human rights threshold is needed because it gives a developmental floor to every person's right to the development of his or her personality, while it leaves further development goals up to local geography and domestic or international politics. We take it from the preceding chapter that every human being has the right to the development of his or her capabilities. We now add that that is a right only *up to a certain threshold level*. Our definition of a human right will then say that "when A has an inherent human right to X over against B, then B is obligated to deliver *threshold satisfaction* of X to A on pain of dereliction of duty." Beyond that threshold point our theory leaves the right to the development of one's personality up to domestic and international theories of justice. A theory of human rights needs to be able to mark out a unique human rights domain within the wealth of statistical information available and so deflect the charge of utopianism. Human rights activists are not trying to level the global playing field. They do not regard all the inequalities revealed by the statistics as showing that human rights have been or are being violated. Just those statistics that point to individuals or groups that have fallen below the official level of a particular threshold indicate a human rights violation. The work on which I report in this and the next section has to do with the construction of these thresholds.

The very concept of what it is to have a human right to substance X demands that a limitation be placed on the quantity or amount of X, where X is the substance of the right in question, be it security, health care, or education. A threshold of any particular human right (and thresholds obviously differ for different rights) stipulates the minimum below which no human being should be allowed to fall in the enjoyment of the right in question. One important reason for stressing this threshold concept is that if human rights correlate with duties, as I hold they do, then duty-bearers have a right to know what they are responsible for and when they can be charged with a dereliction of duty. This holds for individual human agents as well as for the groups, governments, and international organizations that individuals have created, including the states that sign and ratify human rights treaties. A second reason for the incorporation of these thresholds into the theory of human rights is to help cosmopolitans avoid the pitfalls of utopianism when they face reams of statistical data. It is one thing to say that all persons must be treated with equal threshold respect and concern and another to claim that the world's resources must be equally shared by all. The difference lies in what it is that human dignity requires, a question that the threshold idea answers far short of a worldwide egalitarian scheme of distribution. Too often theorists and the media conflate these questions and thereby dilute the support a more narrowly defined conception of human rights might have received. Here I will mention some cosmopolitan theorists who might want to use the idea of thresholds to rebut charges that they are courting utopianism.

Cosmopolitan theorists start with the idea of the moral unity of the human race and then work their way back to nation-states as necessary vehicles for the delivery of whatever goods have to be shared. Leif Wenar, for instance, defends "a cosmopolitan economic original position that is supposed to yield an argument that relates individuals [the world over] fairly to each other regarding the effects they have on each other through international economic activity."[33] The distributive justice Wenar seeks is initially one not between nations or states, but between individual human beings that inhabit these states. Wenar overlooks the fact that the very idea of human rights that he wants introduced into a global Rawlsian original position comes with built-in thresholds, the result of which is that rich Westerners owe individuals living in much worse-off places only the safety nets that would prevent them from falling below internationally constructed thresholds for their state or region. There is a difference between our duty to bring others up to human rights thresholds and our duty, if there be such, to pull them up toward where we are ourselves. The first is our duty to deliver global justice and involves our commitment to universal human rights, while the second gets us involved in detailed questions of inter-national justice that have to do with legal relations between states that are primarily based on the treaties they have or have not signed with each other.

When Charles Beitz picks Frankfurt's standard of each person "hav[ing] enough" or "meet[ing] a standard of well being" over the much lower standard of "merely having enough to get along" or "mak[ing] life marginally tolerable" he raises the bar far too high and so courts the charge of utopianism.[34] Human rights thresholds are not aimed at giving people "a reasonably successful life" but at giving them "a minimally decent life." And even that is a stupendous challenge to meet. Rainer Forst also ignores the idea of human rights thresholds in his argument (derived from the principle of reciprocity) that "none of the parties concerned may claim certain rights and privileges it denies to others."[35] For him, even in a global context all persons have "a qualified veto-right against any norms and practices which cannot be justified reciprocally and generally or, to use a modified version of Thomas Scanlon's phrase, against norms that can reciprocally and generally be rejected" (Forst, 178). In Chapters 3 (on the Golden Rule) and 6 (on democratic participation) I defend the view that reciprocity and inherence do not fit well together, to which criticism I now add the point that even if it succeeded in the abstract (which I believe it does not), this approach elicits unrealistic utopian aspirations. If given a choice between meeting only minimal human rights thresholds and being offered a reasonably successful life people in the third and fourth world will naturally pick the latter. We ourselves pack no more into the conception of global justice than that all people be brought up to their human rights thresholds. The rest belongs to international justice broadly conceived. We want to know what kinds of human rights questions we should raise about the above-cited statistics, especially about the figures at the lower end of the tables that scream out at us about obvious human rights violations. From this perspective the UN *Human Development Report 2000* is a disappointment. The *Report* has the promising subtitle of *Human Rights and Human Development,* but it fails to explicitly acknowledge that all human rights have built-in thresholds that block any arguments toward an unrealistic global egalitarianism. It does not even tell us what the UN has done to help define these thresholds.

I should mention that both Sen and Nussbaum have used, but not stressed enough, the notion of a human rights threshold. Donnelly also fails to tell the readers of his "Universal Declaration Model" how we might reach what he calls an "overlapping consensus" or what "the large common core" for each of these rights includes (98). In what follows I discuss the construction of these common cores or thresholds, and in the process I hope to shed some light on how that construction feeds into the international consensus that is the heart of Donnelly's model. Sen has observed that when it comes to "severe deprivations," there is likely to be quite a bit of agreement in the midst of social and cultural differences. He adds that this agreement is more likely when we focus more on people's "capability to avoid hunger or severe undernourishment than on the significance of having an adequate supply of particular food items (e.g. some specific types of meats or fish or grains or pulses) to serve those functionings."[36] In other words, the capability/functioning approach is itself seen as a minimum threshold that can cut across cultural and social differences better than can baskets of commodities and income levels. Even within these capabilities there are levels of development (from, for instance, basic literacy to advanced graduate work). Sen recognizes this when he recommends that we see "poverty as the failure of basic capabilities to reach certain minimally acceptable levels" (109–10). These "minimally acceptable" or threshold levels of personal development "vary from elementary physical ones such as being well nourished, being adequately clothed and sheltered, avoiding preventable morbidity, etc. to more complex social achievements such as taking part in the life of the community, being able to appear in public without shame, and so on." (110). We need a further description of what is to count as "minimal," "elementary," "well," "adequate," and "preventable." All these adjectives point to the existence of a universal or international threshold below which no one should be allowed to fall in his or her capability development.

Nussbaum also has made it clear that that the capabilities approach "uses the idea of a threshold: for each important entitlement, there is some appropriate level beneath which it seems right to say that the relevant entitlement has not been secured" (*Frontiers*, 291–92).[37] The relevant goods or services needed to develop a person's capabilities "must be available at a sufficiently high level" to help make that person flourish. In the case of some capabilities, adequacy of resources or services need not necessarily lead to equality in the possession of instrumental goods, housing being an example. Here, "what seems appropriate is *enough*" (293; emphasis original). Regarding other capabilities, such as primary and secondary education, political liberty, or religious freedom, adequacy of development would seem to entail the need for roughly equal development. It all depends on how close a capability is to the heart of human dignity. To live in a modest house is not an affront to human dignity, but to be denied a basic education or be forbidden to worship as one would want is.[38] Nussbaum rightly cites Adam Smith's point that societies differ enormously in how they flesh out the idea of human dignity when it comes to how people do or do not dress.

Her claim that with the capabilities approach "we can arrive at an enumeration of central elements of truly human functioning that can command a broad cross-cultural consensus" rings true, but it also points up her own neglect of the role of the international community in the construction of these thresholds (*WHD*, 74). She realizes that this "threshold level of each of the central capabilities will need more precise determination, as citizens work toward a consensus for political purposes" (77). But she only goes so far as to envision that this further determination will take place "within each constitutional tradition, as it evolves through interpretation and deliberation." She often uses the constitutional tradition of India as an example. My point is that the international community has for some time now placed these domestic activities within an international monitoring system that is aimed at producing the consensus of which Nussbaum and other theorists speak. The construction of international human rights thresholds or minimums has been an international project ever since the Declaration was adopted in 1948. In their attempts to domesticate the rights they find in the Universal Declaration, states and their governments find themselves enmeshed in an already-existing network of oversight and monitoring. It is in this activity of monitoring and matching international norms with local domestic customs and legal systems that human rights thresholds can be seen being constructed.

The Role of the International Community. The first big step in this international construction effort came with the writing and adoption of the two international covenants in 1966, one on civil and political rights and one on social, economic, and cultural rights.[39] Between them, these two covenants spell out in much greater detail all the major rights listed in the Universal Declaration, with the exception of the right to property of Article 17. These legal texts tell signatory states what they should do to bring their domestic legal systems and public policies in line with the obligations they have incurred by ratifying these conventions. In section C below I give specific examples from the Covenant on Economic, Social and Cultural Rights of how this system works. In addition to these two covenants as portals of delivery, many individual articles of the Declaration (or clusters of them) have inspired more narrowly aimed, separate international conventions. The right to an education was (with the help of UNESCO) further refined in the 1989 Covenant on the Rights of the Child. Marriage rights were further spelled out in the 1962 Convention on Consent to Marriage, Minimum Age for Marriage and Registration of Marriages and in the better-known 1981 Convention on the Elimination of All Forms of Discrimination against Women. The meaning of the right to protection against torture is further explained in the 1984 International Convention against Torture and Other Cruel, Inhuman or Degrading Treatment or Punishment. The Declaration's call for the special protection of "all children, whether born in or out of wedlock" is further worked out in the 1989 Convention on the Rights of the Child. The UN has also sponsored and is awaiting the coming into force of the International Convention on the Protection of the Rights of All Migrant Workers and Members of their Families. The General Assembly has made any number of more or less hortatory declarations (on care of the elderly and minority rights, for instance) that are slated to be translated into conventions with legal teeth. Many of the provisions of these less familiar instruments are also covered by the two major international covenants that came into force in 1976.

Enforcement of these international treaties and covenants comes primarily by way of shaming into compliance those countries that fall behind in their required reporting, which happens because their enforcement has been grossly defective or because the tremendous overlap in international monitoring systems has placed undue burdens on their administrative capacities. This shaming is an inadvertent side effect of having experts publicly ask a country to explain or defend its lack of progress in domesticating the rights of these covenants or conventions. After a country submits its periodic reports to the committee that monitors a certain covenant or convention, that committee will then often invite a representative of the country to speak with committee members. These members are experts on the matters covered by the text of the convention they monitor. The committee then publishes what are called Concluding Observations (on specific country reports) and numbered General Comments on how the committee believes one or several articles of "their" text should be interpreted. Countries are supposed to heed these Observations and Comments (in addition to questionnaires they receive) in their next reports to the various committees.

It is in this process of reporting and communication between countries' representatives and international experts that we can see human rights thresholds being constructed and put into place locally. Since the Observations and Comments grow out of national attempts to implement the demands of the covenants, the emerging human rights thresholds will fit most domestic contexts. They are, so to speak, being tailor-made for those domestic contexts. The monitoring committees monitor the country reports that are sent in and engage selected ones in periodic dialogues aimed at improvement of a country's human rights record. This monitoring has both an enforcement aspect (when the meaning of the norm is not in dispute) and an interpretive aspect, when the local meaning of the norm needs to be clarified. Either way, a matching takes place between what the international human rights texts say and the local customs and laws of the reporting states. Frequently, NGOs and specialized agencies both inside and outside the UN supply information that helps with this dialogue. Since there are at least six of these conventions, there are also six monitoring committees.

The fact that the monitoring committees are always strapped for time and money is one reason why the construction of human rights thresholds is going so slowly. Still, it is obvious that the abstract language of the Universal Declaration is, by way of the enforcing mechanisms attached to these conventions, slowly being lowered into place around the globe. The committees of these conventions function in effect as global courts of meaning. Their pace may be glacial, but as a threshold comes closer to being clarified, it becomes easier for the international community to call for protection of individuals against standard threats that involve questions solely of enforcement rather than interpretation. Anyone interested in the construction of a particular human rights threshold can follow its progress on the UN Web pages that record the work of these committees.[40] The monitoring committees for the International Covenant on Civil and Political Rights (ICCPR) and the ICESCR are good places for a generalist to take a first look at an ongoing construction. Countries' reactions when faced with this international system of norms differ greatly. A few refuse to sign and ratify these conventions for fear of having their domestic policies found wanting. Others gladly comply and do a good job in their reports, and many find ways to drag their domestic feet and fall behind in their reporting obligations.

Nussbaum's leap from capabilities straight to the constitutional tradition of India and other countries requires a bridge. She is right to suggest that there is a need for a local body or organ to interpret abstract statements about the rights (entitlements) people have to develop their capabilities. The human rights listed in the Declaration are in that sense no different from the bills of rights that are part of many national constitutions such as the Indian, South African, and U.S. documents. Provisions in these domestic constitutions are often just as abstractly stated as those of the Universal Declaration, which, I hasten to add, was not intended to be and has not become a constitution for the world. It does not call for a world government by any stretch of the imagination. The Declaration started out as a set of moral prescriptions for all people and all nations against which they can measure their own and other peoples' moral progress, much in the way the 1789 French bill was drafted to make it possible for "the acts of the legislative and executive powers of government . . . [to be at] every moment compared with the end of political institutions" (Melden, *Human Rights*, 140). Because these constitutional bills of rights are couched in general terms and lack specificity, countries that have such bills also have courts that interpret these bills to make them fit particular circumstances. It may take decades and even centuries for the meaning of a certain constitutional article or clause to become reasonably precise.

It may thus take a long time for the norms in the Declaration to receive the precise meanings they will have in all the different countries around the world. While in most national contexts the much-needed community of interpreters is constituted by a nation's own high court, no such single community of interpreters exists for human rights (or for the rest of international law). This lack of a hierarchy has led to the creation of several overlapping communities of interpretation in the human rights field, described in this section. Additionally, Europe, the Americas, and Africa have their own regional human rights courts that interpret regional conventions. The 1950 European Convention for the Protection of Human Rights and Fundamental Freedoms was the first major regional construction effort and has been very successful. It has served as a model for the later adoption of regional courts for the Americas and (much more recently) Africa. The European Court has developed an enormous body of decisions that circumscribe what the European nations that are subject to its jurisdiction must and cannot do in their application of this convention that provides the authoritative text for this regional court. Since these three regional texts and courts focus primarily on civil and political rights and do not have the breadth of the Declaration—and for reasons of space—I forgo discussing these important regional contributions in my description of international threshold construction activities.[41] These courts and their affiliated commissions function as communities of interpretation for the texts involved. But such communities of interpretation need not be courts, just so long as they have the requisite authority to interpret the norms stipulated in the various human rights texts. The committees that monitor the various international human rights conventions are not courts, but they do function as arbiters of meaning. All of these hermeneutical communities serve as mediators of meaning between these international or regional norms and the local, domestic bodies, organs, or courts that do the actual domestic work of implementation.

In addition to these regional human rights monitoring committees and regional courts, domestic high courts are increasingly taking note of each other's human right decisions. They talk to each other in workshops that have opened them up to what Sandra Day O'Connor of the U.S. Supreme Court has called "persuasive authority."[42] This kind of authority is different from the old-fashioned hierarchical and coercive kind, where we might have envisioned the International Court of Justice in the Hague (the legal arm of the UN) laying down the law to member states that have accepted its authority. Anne-Marie Slaughter describes an emerging community of national courts that dialogue with each other over what international norms (like the above-named human rights conventions) mean domestically. She cites Justice Claire L'Heureux-Dubé of the Supreme Court of Canada as saying that "More and more [national] courts . . . are looking to the judgments of other jurisdictions, particularly when making decisions on human rights issues" (*New World Order*, 70). Slaughter points out that the new constitution of South Africa goes out of its domestic way to "permit" the Constitutional Court of that country "to consult foreign law in its human rights decisions" (70–71). That is indeed what that court has been doing.[43] The South African Constitution has intentionally modeled itself on the norms of the Social, Economic and Cultural Covenant, several of which it states explicitly.[44] After the Indian Constitution lists basic rights in Part III, Part IV is devoted to "Directive Principles of State Policy." That Part expressly states that these principles "shall not be enforceable by any court, but the principles therein laid down are nevertheless fundamental in the governance of the country and it shall be duty of the State to apply these principles in making laws."[45] For a long time these Directive Principles did not have much effect on the interpretation of the political and civil rights of Part III. But under the leadership of Justice Bhagwati in the 1980s, the court has allowed for social activist litigation and ruled, for instance, that the right to life (Article 21) and personal liberty (of Part III) had to be interpreted as including "the right to live with dignity and all that goes along with it, namely, the bare necessities of life such as adequate nutrition, clothing, and shelter" and we can safely assume access to health care facilities (P. Hunt, *Reclaiming Social Rights*, 159).[46]

While the South African and Indian Supreme Courts have been particularly helpful in showing that social and economic rights are justiciable, other courts have also entered the global dialogue on human rights threshold construction. Chief Justice Smith of the Norwegian Supreme Court has gone on record stating that "his" court "should especially contribute to the ongoing debate on the court's position on international human rights" (70). As a signatory of the European Convention of Human Rights, Norway is bound by the decisions of the European Court of Human Rights, which has developed a large body of case law that is consulted by many courts in non-European nations when they are asked to interpret human rights texts that resemble or overlap the 1950 European Convention. Even the group LawAsia, which Slaughter describes as "a form of regional bar association composed of different kinds of legal associations across the region," has adopted "the promotion of human rights and administration of justice throughout the region" as one of its goals (73). Considering that the ivy of formal human rights is thinnest on Asian soil, this is an encouraging development. Since the United States is known as an infrequent signer and ratifier of international human rights conventions, it is also encouraging to read that several of the justices of the U.S. Supreme Court are "remarkably self-conscious" about not closing the door to the "persuasive authority" of the courts of other nations, even when it comes to human rights issues. According to Ruth Bader Ginsberg, one of the U.S. justices, "In the area of human rights, the experience in one nation or region may inspire or inform other nations or regions" (76). Slaughter concludes her survey with this observation: "To the extent that pockets of global jurisprudence are emerging, they are most likely to involve issues of basic human rights" (79). That may count as a prediction that in the future the construction of human rights thresholds will increasingly be a collective juridical effort.

C. Social and Economic Covenant Examples

A discussion of human rights thresholds is important for any general answer to the charge of utopianism. But it is especially necessary for a defense of the inherence of social, economic, and cultural rights in the human person.[47] By calling, in Articles 22 and 28, for a new post-Westphalian order, the Universal Declaration drafters started that process. Because these rights gained recognition later than civil and political ones, the process of determining what counts as the minimum for these older rights is much more advanced than that for social, economic, and cultural rights, which is why these newer rights are eliciting the call for new international structures of cooperation. For that reason I use the remainder of this chapter to give some specific examples of threshold construction from the covenant that deals with economic, social, and cultural rights.[48]

Articles 6, 7, and 8 of this covenant give additional details on the work-related rights in UDHR 23. Article 9 picks up the umbrella right to social security of UDHR 22 and the details of UDHR 25. Article 10 elaborates on the protection of the family and of mothers and children, which are stated in UDHR 16(3) and 25(2). Article 11 enunciates the right to an adequate standard of living as seen in the rights to food, clothing, and housing, also taken from UDHR 25, and goes out of its way to "recognize everyone's fundamental right to be free from hunger." Article 12 expands on the right to health also mentioned in UDHR 25. Article 13 elaborates on the right to an education, as found in UDHR 26. Article 14 makes special mention of the right to "compulsory primary education, free of charge." Finally, Article 15 is a restatement of the right to participate in the cultural life of the community and to benefit from scientific research.[49]

The writing of these covenant articles provided the first step toward international construction of thresholds for the social, economic, and cultural rights of the Universal Declaration. Right after and closely connected to it came the second step, the interpretation by the monitoring committee of what this still-abstract (but less so than the Declaration) text of the covenant means in local or domestic situations. I have chosen three examples of this two-step process: (1) work-related human rights, (2) the right to housing as part of social security packages, and (3) the right to health care. Even though the United States has not ratified the ICESCR, I pull that country's human rights record into this discussion in the hope that someday it will sign, ratify, and come to respect these inherent human rights.

1. Thresholds for Work-Related Rights. In ICESCR Article 6 "The States Parties recognize the right to work, which includes the right of everyone to the *opportunity* to gain his living by work which he freely chooses or accepts" (emphasis added). The use of the term "opportunity" suggests that we must read the agency that informs the ideology of human rights in the active voice. As UDHR 23 ("Everyone has the right to work [and] to free choice of employment") reads, one might think that the government owes everyone a job, which is not feasible under any economic system. The Covenant drafters corrected this impression when they rephrased the article in terms of the *opportunity* to be gainfully employed without coercion. Article 6 goes on to mention steps governments must take to create the optimum conditions for the realization of this capability to work. Matthew Craven reports that these steps include the institution of "technical and vocational guidance and training programs, policies and techniques to achieve steady economic, social and cultural development and full and productive employment under conditions safeguarding fundamental political and economic freedoms to the individual."[50] The drafters of the Covenant wanted to go beyond the UDHR, which they did by borrowing these steps from various ILO instruments.[51] The monitoring committee has accepted the following elements for the construction of the right to work threshold from ILO instruments: (1) access to (meaningful) employment, (2) equality of that access, (3) free choice of employment, and (4) guarantee against arbitrary dismissal. The third element comes straight from the "freely chooses or accepts" clause in 6(1); it gives someone the right not to work and also forbids slavery and policies of "forced labor" like those still practiced in many parts of the world.[52]

The list of rights in Covenant Article 7 adds quite a few details to the work related rights of UDHR Articles 23 and 24.[53] It also adds the idea that what is stated in the article is to count "as a minimum" and should therefore be considered as a threshold below which workers should not be allowed to fall. Some nations felt that this might act as a ceiling and prevent even better remuneration schemes. But it was "finally accepted . . . on the basis that it would have considerable utility in the context of less developed countries" (Craven, 228). The covenant drafters also agreed that "workers" here must not be taken to refer just to industrial workers, but should be "seen as all categories of workers" (228). They repeat their prohibition of discrimination from Covenant Article 2(2) and their demand for gender equality from Covenant Article 3. The "just and fair remuneration" of the UDHR 23 are here replaced by "fair wages and equal remuneration for work of equal value," while the UDHR phrase "an existence worthy of human dignity" is here replaced by the phrase "decent living" for "themselves and their families." The "decent living" clause has the advantage of "emphasizing that the term 'remuneration' also covered matters that fell outside mere financial remuneration, such as social security benefits and cheap housing" (230). This, too, points to a threshold built up in terms of elements that go beyond the paycheck, a point made obvious by the addition of "safe and healthy working conditions," which was first proposed by Yugoslavia, picked up by the ILO, and "found its way with little discussion into the final text" as paragraph b (230). Spain proposed the addition of remuneration for public holidays in the repetition of UDHR 24 paragraph d. Others went along on the supposition that these free days were not covered by the phrase "periodic holidays," by which was meant "that workers should be given consecutive holidays of not less than two weeks' duration at least once a year" (232).

At Sen's suggestion economists have constructed what is called the Gini index. This index "measures the inequality over the entire distribution of income or consumption [with] a value of 0 represent[ing] perfect equality and a value of 100 perfect inequality" (*UNDP 2000*, 197). Obviously no country has ever had perfect equality of income and consumption, for even in socialist economies, large differences show up between the bureaucratic administrative class and the bulk of ordinary workers. And similarly, no country can sustain perfect inequality for long, for then one person or dictator (and a very few cronies) would need to own and consume everything, and the rest of the population nothing. So the question really is the size of the spread between the haves and the have-nots, with those closer to the 100 figure being riper for turmoil or revolution than those farther away from the 100 mark. As we might expect, the stable European democracies and some former communist countries have the lowest figures on the economic inequality index.

Let us call "good equality" countries those that in 2000 had a score of 30 or less, like the following: Belarus (21.7), Belgium (28.7), Bulgaria (26.4), Czech Republic (25.4), and Egypt (28.9), Hungary (24.4), New Zealand (27.3), Norway (25.8), Slovakia (19.4), Slovenia (28.4), Sweden (25.0), and Ukraine (29.0). All a good score means is that the pie of national wealth (however large or small) is *relatively* evenly divided. This occurs far less evenly in the countries that scored over 50 on the index, and which for that reason can be said to be courting the danger of upheaval or revolution: Brazil (60.7), Chili (56.6), Colombia (57.1), Guatemala (55.8), Honduras (56.3), Mexico (53.1), Nicaragua (60.3), Paraguay (57.7), South Africa (59.3), Swaziland (60.9), Zimbabwe (50.1), and many others that are known to be in trouble or barely functioning. We can further speculate that countries with a score in the 40s should not be too smug about their stability, since they are more like the ones with bad equality scores than like the ones with good scores. This group includes Kenya (44.9), Peru (46.2), Panama (48.5), and Venezuela (49.5). Recent exposés help us see why it also includes the United States (40.8). In March 2007 the *New York Times* reported on the findings by Emmanuel Saez and Thomas Pikkety, who analyzed data from the U.S. Internal Revenue Service. Their study shows that "income inequality grew significantly in the year 2005," with the result that the United States now has its "greatest" income inequality since the Great Depression of the 1920s.

"The new data show that the top 300,000 Americans collectively enjoyed almost as much income as the bottom 150 million Americans."[54] Since the pie the United States divides is the largest in the world, the shame that attaches to this high and still increasing inequality score is also very large. We cannot escape the Marxist insight that the elites at the top are exploiting a growing "underclass."

The United States did not ratify this covenant, but if it had, the monitoring committee might well say about it what it has said about Kenya, namely, that the level of minimum wages appears "to be far too low to even allow a very modest standard of living" (Craven 235). We might respond that there must be an enormous difference between poverty in Kenya and in the United States. That is true, and it is the reason two poverty indexes are published, one for the richest nations and one for all the others. It takes far fewer dollars to make it in Kenya than in the United States, but when the PPP (parity purchasing power) is factored into the comparison, it turns out that someone with $34,000 in the United States is just as bad off as someone with $7,000 in Botswana or with $1,000 in Kenya. On the separate index for the seventeen richest nations in the world, the United States ranks last, with the most poverty for the year 2002.[55] Barbara Ehrenreich's and Beth Shulman's accounts show why that is so.[56] Ehrenreich was trying to live on the minimum wage in U.S. cities like Miami, Portland, and Minneapolis-Saint Paul, and could not do it. Shulman's statistics back up this failure. She tells us that the value of the minimum wage in the United States fell by 21 percent between 1979 and 1999 (*Betrayal of Work*, 157). This drop has created a veritable "underclass" of thirty million working Americans whose work has none of the dignity international standards call for. This class is made up "security guards, nurse's aides and home health-care aides, child-care workers and educational assistants, maids and porters, 1-800 call-center workers, bank tellers, data-entry keyers, cooks, food preparation workers, waiters and waitresses, cashiers and pharmacy assistants, hairdressers and manicurists, parking-lot attendants, hotel receptionists and clerks, ambulance drivers, poultry, fish, and meat processors, sewing-machine operators, laundry and dry-cleaning operators, and agricultural workers" (45–46). They all have several part-time jobs, do not have health insurance, cannot afford child care, and are not given maternity leave or vacations.

The threshold element of paragraph 7(b)—that working conditions be safe and healthy—was constructed with the 1981 ILO Occupational Safety and Health Convention in mind. Clearly, millions of workers in third-world sweat shops and in Mexican factories south of the U.S. border, as well as those working in the hundreds of poultry-processing plants north of that same border or on construction sites in New York City, have this threshold element of the right to work constantly violated. In its guidelines the committee asks numerous ILO-inspired questions that seek to prod countries into establishing national policies regarding matters of labor safety and health conditions. It criticized New Zealand for putting too much of the burden for collecting compensation claims on the victims, and Italy for failing to provide information about inspection systems (Craven, 242 and n. 125). Updates for the United States concerning similar infractions of labor safety rules can be found by browsing the Human Rights Watch Web site.[57]

Covenant Article 8 expands everyone's right in UDHR 23(4) "to form and to join trade unions for the protection of his interest" into a separate article with four paragraphs. In the first one the States Parties "ensure" everyone's right "to form trade unions and join the trade union of his choice, subject only to the rules of the organization concerned, for the promotion and protection of his economic and social interests." The rest of this paragraph and of the article has to do with the kinds of restrictions that governments can place both on this right to join and on the rights unions themselves have once they are formed. The clear intent was to cut down on government control over the union movement to just what "is necessary in a democratic society in the interests of national security or public order or for the protection of the rights and freedoms of others." Paragraph 1(b) gives unions the right to federate, while (d) gives unions the right to strike, "provided that it is exercised in conformity with the laws of the particular country." The main rationales for including these trade union rights were that these rights are "a necessary instrument for implementing economic, social and cultural rights" generally and that they are mentioned in the Declaration, which it was the express purpose of the covenant to amplify and codify.[58]

These union-related rights provide us with a good example of how the monitoring committee interprets the often cited stipulation in Article 2(1) of the ICESCR that each State Party "undertakes to take steps" to achieve "progressively the full realization of the rights recognized in the present Covenant by all appropriate means, including particularly the adoption of legislative measures." Cranstonites tend to exploit this allowance for "progressive realization" with the argument that these kinds of rights are better viewed as goals and not as enforceable rights. Responding to this challenge, the monitoring committee has on several occasions urged governments to seek a balance between progressive implementation and legislative steps that can and therefore need to be taken immediately after a country has ratified the covenant. The right to unionize is included in the Committee's list of immediate action items included in its Third General Comment: Article 3 (§4) (forbidding gender discrimination), 7(a)(i) (forbidding gender discrimination), 8 (union rights), 10(3) (protection of children), 13(2)(a) (free and compulsory primary education), 13(4) (the right to start schools) and 15(3) (the freedom of scientific research).[59] All these rights "would seem to be capable of immediate application by judicial and other organs in many national legal systems" (Craven, 374). Since General Comments are authoritative interpretations of the text of the Covenant and, by extension, of the Declaration, we cannot say that the Covenant allows nations to pick and choose, dragging their feet on the "progressive" implementation of human rights in their territories. The Comments press states to take the "appropriate means" called for in Article 2(1) and the committee "recognizes that in many instances legislation is highly desirable and in some cases may even be indispensable" (Craven, 373). Also, the Committee has made it clear that "the ultimate determination as to whether all appropriate measures have been taken remains for the Committee to make" (374). It has criticized Jamaica for reading Article 8(1)(d) as giving the freedom but not the right to strike (280), and has ruled that an individual who participates in a strike should not be dismissed just for that reason (278). Members of the Committee have expressed concern about various restrictions on this right in, for instance, the legal systems of Morocco, Senegal, the Dominican Republic, and Panama.

The United States is in a curious position regarding Covenant Article 8. It did not ratify this Covenant, but it did ratify the ICCPR, according to which "Everyone has the right to form and join trade unions for the protection of his interests." These linkages create a genuine obligation for the United States to protect and help secure the right to unionize and to bargain collectively. We cannot help but wonder what the monitoring committee for the covenant would say when asked about U.S. efforts in this regard. A 2000 publication by Human Rights Watch, *Unfair Advantage: Workers' Freedom of Association in the United States Under International Human Rights Standards*, answers this query.[60] This NGO did a series of case studies involving this particular right (and the ancillary rights to bargain collectively and to strike) across the full range of the U.S. economy. All the evidence supports the contention that a country's legal system is very much a reflection of its political (lack of) will, and that at this time in its history the United Sates lacks the will to stop systematic violations of this particular human right. This study clearly shows that the much-lauded flexibility of the U.S. economy is bought at the expense of the legal dignity of millions of workers. By "legal dignity" I mean that the loopholes in the law and the delays in the handling of cases are an affront to justice. It turns out that the real obstacles to the United States fulfilling its labor law obligations under either of the two international covenants are not practical or monetary ones, as is so often thought, but are mostly due to a lack of political will to make the details of the law and the speed of the decisions conform to our sense of justice.

Another important weakness in U.S. labor law is the fact that, strictly speaking (as one should speak in matters of law), a huge chunk of the labor force in the United States falls outside the scope of the laws that govern labor relations. Certain clauses in the 1947 National Labor Relations Act cut out from coverage some 1,000,000 domestic workers, 700,000 independent contractors, 4,000,000 people defined as supervisors, 10,000,000 listed as managers, 300,000 college professors, 100,000 Indian casino employee, 500,000 employees of religious communities (Human Rights Watch, *Unfair Advantage*, 189).[61] Naturally, some of these millions seek admission to whatever protection labor laws do give. Their attempts have led to numerous protracted labor disputes, involving 40,000 mostly legal Mexican immigrant pickers in the Washington state apple industry, 6,000 high-tech computer programmers at Microsoft corporation also in Washington, 15,000 drivers at 300 Airborne subcontractors around the country, 120 snack food workers in a Detroit suburb, and groups of New York sweatshop workers seeking to bargain through UNITE, the main apparel industry union. The dilemma is that "Either they are not employees as defined in labor laws, or the proprietor of the place where they work is not their "employer" under the law" (Human Rights Watch, *Unfair Advantage*, 162). Since the law says that a worker has a right to bargain collectively with his or her employer, these temps (who are sent out to different places of work each day) often do not know who their coworkers are or how to get in touch with them. And once they do, their agency has folded, opened up shop in a new location, and started to hire new temps who will be sent to the same place of work. The main employer, be it Microsoft, Airborne, K-Mart, Ann Taylor, some other brand-name company, or your very own university, has "nothing" to do with what the subcontractor pays its workers and whether that contractor flaunts overtime and vacation rules.[62] The larger companies are shielded by the hierarchical structure (company-contractor-subcontractor-worker) that is replacing the horizontal (employer-employee) model in many industries, and a climate of fear has been created in the lower and even middle layers of the workforce, which explains why "unionization rates plummeted during the eighties, falling from 25 percent of the workforce in 1979 to 16 percent in 1990," and from there to 11 percent in 2003 (Shulman, 131). It is no accident that in the 2008 U.S. presidential election so much attention was paid to the spread of poverty among laid-off industrial workers and the need to strengthen the union movement. It has become very clear that the much-lauded flexibility of the U.S. economy had been bought at the price of gross legal and other indignities endured by millions of its workers.

2. *Thresholds for Social Security and Housing.* Covenant Article 9 expands the scope of these labor rights by repeating UDHR 22's right to "social

security," adding that it includes the right to "social insurance," which is a phrase the Universal Declaration drafters rejected but the details for which they did put in UDHR 25, where they say everyone has the "right to security in the event of unemployment, sickness, disability, widowhood, old age or other lack of livelihood in circumstances beyond his control." These UDHR rights are given a more detailed shape in Articles 6, 7, 8, 9, and 12 of the ICESCR. In Covenant Article 11(1) the States Parties "recognize the right of everyone to an adequate standard of living for himself and his family, including adequate food, clothing, and housing, and to the continuous improvement of living conditions." Craven suggests that Article 11 "is the area in which the Committee's practice is most developed" (288), yet it wisely has not sought to monitor the "continuous improvement" clause (294–95) and, just as smartly, it has not given an independent meaning to the phrase "adequate standard of living" (302). Instead, the committee has focused on individual components within this larger social security concept, particularly on the rights to adequate food and adequate housing. We take the latter as our example.

Jeremy Waldron's thesis in "Homelessness and the Issue of Freedom" is that property rights, laws, and regulations are very much tied in with the range of liberty that persons in a society enjoy. In advanced industrial societies most of the property is privately owned, which means that the owner can call the police to have an uninvited intruder removed. We also have rules against doing certain things (like making love or urinating) in public areas. We do things like that in our own homes or in office buildings and other places of work where we have connections. Waldron's point is that homeless people do not own or have legal access to their own domicile; and being unemployed, they also have none of the other connections. Since cities pass specific laws that forbid people to sleep, urinate, or make love in subway cars, tunnels, parks, or under bridges, the upshot is that the homeless are stuck without a place or a room of their own. They are stuck because laws forbid them to do in public what other people do in private. Since every human being requires a place to exercise these most basic of human capacities and needs (such as the need to defecate), the freedom of the homeless, and with it their human dignity, is frequently reduced to zero. Using less dramatic examples, Sunstein makes the same argument in terms of the legal realist foundations supplied by Robert Hale and Morris Cohen to help justify Franklin Roosevelt's New Deal legislation, including the National Resources Planning Board, which drew up an economic bill of rights that included the right to adequate food, clothing, shelter, and medical care.[63]

"One of the tasks of a theory of human rights," according to Waldron, "is to pick out a set of actions it is thought particularly important from a moral point of view that people should have the freedom to perform, choices it is thought particularly important that they should have the freedom to make, whatever other restrictions there are on their conduct" ("Homelessness," 332).[64] That is why we have bills of rights that give people the freedom to worship, get married, educate their children, and do a host of other things. While Henry Shue picked security, subsistence, and liberty as "basic rights" that are prerequisites for the exercise of any other rights, Waldron adds a place to urinate and sleep as just as basic: "Though we say there is nothing particularly dignified about sleeping or urinating, there is certainly something deeply *un*dignified about being prevented from doing so. Every torturer knows this: to break the human spirit, focus the mind of the victim through petty restrictions pitilessly imposed on the banal necessities of human life" (334). To this point we need to add "that any restriction on the performance of these basic acts has the feature of being not only uncomfortable and degrading, but more or less literally *unbearable* for the people concerned" (334; emphasis original).

What happens, of course, is that many of the better-off citizens of the advanced societies here under discussion often, but not always correctly, believe that the homeless are not legally barred from renting a place of their own. However, what frequently prevents them from exercising the option to rent is their "position" in society, and that fact brings us right back to the Covenant Committee's insistence that the threshold of "adequate housing" should include far more than simply a "roof over one's head." Property and shelter is partly about enabling people to perform a range of very basic human functions in private, and partly about restrictions. Homeless people bear *all* the restrictions, and because of that they have been deprived of some of the most basic enabling capabilities. Waldron's point is that our industrialized system of property rights begs the very question of freedom. We cannot go and stand on a free spot outside the property system and say of the homeless that they simply do not have the will to freely step inside that system and rent a place, for liberty and property are intertwined in our societies as well as in the personal histories of all of us. If we go back into the lives of most of the homeless, we will probably find a lack of basic education and social services, a lack of electricity or of good water, an absence of transportation, a lack of access to trained medical personnel, or "access to land as an entitlement" ("Homelessness," 380). Depending on which homeless persons in which country one chooses to make the focus, any one of a number of different threshold components is likely to have been a contributing cause to the undignified status of these members of our human family. This brings us to the expansive way the Committee has chosen to interpret the right to "adequate housing" in Covenant Article 11.

At its seventh session in 1951, the UN Human Rights Commission that was drafting the Covenant considered two versions of the right to housing, one from the Soviet Union and one from the United States. Probably because it wanted to avoid all implications of property rights, the USSR version spoke of "a right to living accommodations," while the U.S. version spoke of "a right to housing" (Craven, 290). As it had done when the Universal Declaration was drafted, the Chinese delegation proposed and got accepted the insertion of "food, clothing, and . . ." before the word "housing." The U.S. text, with this Chinese insertion, was adopted. Craven also tells us that the term "adequate" was inserted before these three items because that term was used in the Declaration and because of the underlying supposition that these "components of the standard of living should be maintained at a certain level" (291, 293). Against the rejection of a Chinese proposal to add the right to "means of transport," consider these facts from the *World Bank Atlas 2003*: "in Morocco girls' attendance in primary school more than tripled after a road was paved"; "in Africa, 11 percent of people surveyed say that the high cost of transport—or its absence—is the major barrier to health care"; and "in central Peru, a rural road project reduced travel time by half for more than 2.5 million people providing access to health clinics, schools, and jobs."[65] Roads do matter. Many delegates considered the rights to "adequate food, clothing, and housing" so crucial that they voted to add a second sentence, in which the States Parties commit themselves to take "appropriate steps to ensure the realization of this right, recognizing to this effect the essential importance of international co-operation based on free consent." This unusual sentence was adopted on account of the essential character of the rights involved, and with the understanding that the addition "based on free consent" took the legal sting out of the moral commitment (Craven, 297). This reminds us of the new international order called for by UDHR Articles 22 and 28 that we discussed in section A.

Because the United States was the main sponsor of the international human right to adequate housing, we are faced with the paradox that this right's main sponsor is also known to be one of this right's main violators among advanced industrialized nations. In 1991 the Committee published its General Comment No. 4 on this particular right, pointing out that "a disturbingly large gap" exists between this right and its implementation around the world: "While the problems are often particularly acute in some developing countries which confront major resource and other constraints, the Committee observes that significant problems of homelessness and inadequate housing also exist in some of the most economically developed societies" (General Comment No. 4; Craven, 377–78). The committee bemoaned the lack of good data,[66] but Americans know this truth first hand. They have shelters for the homeless in all their major cities, which manifestly fall far short of what the monitoring committee has given as a definition of adequate shelter: "adequate privacy, adequate space, adequate security, adequate lighting and ventilation, adequate basic infrastructure and adequate location with regard to work and basic facilities—all at a reasonable cost."[67] The Committee goes on to explain what various components of the housing threshold mean: "protection against forced eviction, safe drinking water and energy for cooking, washing and food storage, site drainage and emergency services, affordable modes of financing, and the *Health Principles of Housing* published by the WHO." It has pressed governments to make sure that "such disadvantaged groups as the elderly, children, the physically disabled, the terminally ill, HIV-positive individuals, persons with persistent medical problems, the mentally ill, victims of natural disasters, people living in disaster prone areas and other groups should be ensured some degree of priority consideration in the housing sphere" (379). After pointing out that location should allow for access to "employment options, health-care services, schools, child-care centers, and other social facilities," and that housing units should allow for the expression of "cultural identity," the Committee quoted the Declaration right "not to be subjected to arbitrary or unlawful interference with one's privacy, family, home, or correspondence" as part of the right to adequate housing. It called for a "mix of public and private sector measures . . . because experience has shown the inability of Governments to fully satisfy housing deficits with publicly built housing" (381). As for the problem of justiciability, it pointed out that many legal housing measures can be taken immediately, foremost among them (a) providing legal appeals in advance of planned evictions, (b) providing compensation for illegal evictions, (c) instituting complaint procedures in relation to rent levels and maintenance, (d) protection against discriminatory practices and (e) instituting complaint procedures against landlords concerning unhealthy or inadequate housing conditions (382).

Since the United States has not signed this Covenant it does not have to write reports to the Committee on its housing policies or its homelessness problems. But a little reflection will show that few to none of these requirements are what U.S federal, state, and local statutes and policies provide or even aim at. The Committee's view of what counts as adequate housing goes far beyond what most large U.S cities provide in the shelter programs that give the homeless, in the Committee's words, "a roof over one's head" and that view "shelter exclusively as a commodity." The ultimate goal would, of course, be to have the United States sign and ratify the much broader provisions of this Covenant and be coached into constructing the various components laid out by the Committee. As a first step, Americans have to be brought to an acceptance of this "roof over one's head" minimum as a moral duty that is activated by the inherent right to housing that homeless people have.

3. Thresholds for Health Related Rights. For the construction of the right to health, the drafters of the ICESCR had to choose between a narrow definition of health as mostly access to medical services and a broader one that also put into the threshold certain "preconditions" for good health. They stayed with the broader context that this right has in UDHR 25, where it is seen as part of an adequate standard of living. In Covenant Article 12(1) the "States Parties to the present Covenant recognize the right of everyone to the enjoyment of the highest standard of physical and mental health." This may not look like strict clinical threshold language, but we must read this text against the expansive Constitution of the World Health Organization, according to which "Health is a state of complete physical, mental and social well-being and not merely the absence of disease or infirmity." The Covenant drafters took over the "highest standard of physical and mental health" part of that definition, but dropped the equation of health with "social well-being" as "inappropriate" because, as the Dutch representative argued, "it was quite easy to conceive of a perfectly healthy person whose morality might be questionable"[68] Luckily, in more recent years the WHO has focused on immunizations for diseases like diphtheria, tetanus, whooping-cough, measles, poliomyelitis, and tuberculosis.

While the Covenant drafters did not want to define the right to health as broadly as the WHO has done, they did want States Members to take certain "steps" "to achieve the full realization of this right." Brigit Toebes begins her fine study *The Right to Health as a Human Right in International Law* with a brief survey of the history of public health.[69] She reminds us of "the construction of water supply and draining systems" in ancient Egypt, India, Crete, Troy, and the Inca society. She also tells us how the "medical police" in nineteenth-century German-speaking countries kept an eye on public health and sought to improve the sanitation and hygiene in the big cities of Western Europe (8–9). Some U.S cities apparently also had this kind of police. Her point is that public health measures or "steps" are historically linked to the health of the republic whose public it is. We are reminded of this connection between the health of a republic and that of its own public with the spread of the HIV/AIDS pandemic that affects huge percentages of the population of some nations and, it has been calculated, will decimate the workforce in several African countries by the year 2020: Botswana (30 percent), Cameroon (13 percent), Guinea-Bissau (10 percent), Mozambique (25 percent), South Africa (25 percent), and Zimbabwe (30 percent).[70]

As is the case with nutrition standards and the right to food, the precise health threshold cannot be constructed other than in the presence of and (usually) in consultation with the person having the right. That was one of the points we sought to make with our adoption of the capabilities approach. In even the most advanced industrial states there exist no precisely defined health thresholds if by that we mean the exact level of clinical care that is everyone's birthright. That minimum threshold is always the outcome of a complicated interplay of government budgets, shared with provincial or regional organizations that themselves set guidelines and levels of care in consultation with hospitals, ethics boards, and doctors' organizations, and (in the United States) with private companies that provide health insurance. The final stage of this lengthy process is the doctor-patient relationship where the final threshold delivery takes place. However, good thresholds require a solid grounding in well-thought-out public policies that include these individually tailored final threshold pieces. From this public policy perspective some of the Western debates about patients' autonomy and bills of rights are too narrowly focused. Since the actual medical care that a patient or victim needs obviously varies with each case and is to be determined by the attending physician or nurse, it will come as no surprise that the Committee that monitors the international human right to health has placed most of its emphasis on the public health policies (or lack of them) of the reporting nations.

The first required step stated in Covenant Article 12(2)(a) reaches back to Chapter 4's discussion of the right to life itself and the right to the full and free development of our personalities. It asks governments to provide "for the reduction of the stillbirth-rate and of infant mortality and for the healthy development of the child." Worldwide statistics confirm the assumption (built into this demand for a reduction) that the number of stillbirths is still very high: 98 per 1,000 life births in the least developed countries compared to 6 in high-income OECD countries in 2000.[71] In spite of the fact that "mortality of children has been declining at an average of 1 percent a year," the World Bank reports that in 2001 in most of Africa, 10 percent of the children born died before the age of five (*World Bank Atlas*, 21). So as not to be paralyzed by statistics like these, monitors have borrowed the concept of a *benchmark* from the world of sports and exercise. When a nation's already high percentage of infant deaths per 1,000 life births drops only a little in the thirty years from 1970 to 2000—as for Angola (180/172), Nigeria (120/110), Chad (149/118), Ethiopia (160/117), Niger (197/159), and Sierra Leone (206/180—then it is safe to say that the right to life finds no protection there. And when the number of child deaths has gone up instead of down, as they have between 1990 and 2001 in Côte d'Ivoire (155/175), Kazakhstan (52/99), Tanzania (163/165), and Zambia (192/202), then we know something has gone drastically wrong (21). The demand of Article 12 for a *reduction* in stillbirths and under-five deaths does not mean that the rights to life and health are not inherent in the human person. The use of benchmarks recognizes the fact that it is better to work with incremental improvements than to throw up one's hands in despair. This approach helped Bolivia in the 1990s bring down its infant death rate from 122 to 77. India, where in 1970 more than 200 children died before they were five years old, brought that rate from 123 in 1990 to 93 in 2001.

The setting and meeting (often with international help) of realistic benchmarks lies at the heart of the Committee's dialogues with reporting nations. Since between 1970 and 2000 the aggregate figures of infant mortality for the least-developed countries have dropped from 118 to 98 and for under-five deaths from 240 to 155, it is tempting to think that the fight for the right to live is being won around the world. Sooner or later—so we hope—all the world's nations will arrive at the figures that the rich OECD countries reported for the year 2000. There, out of each 1,000 life births, 6 infants died in childbirth and no more than 6 children died before they reached age five, at which point they are hopefully on the way to the full and free development of their personality.

The fourth step called for by Covenant Article 12(2)(d) is "The creation of conditions which would assure to all medical service and medical attention in the event of sickness." This demand also fits well with a narrowly defined threshold. It is probably the step most of my readers think of when it comes to the human right to health care. Many industrialized nations have no problem meeting this demand because they have some version or other of universal health coverage, which assures the rights mentioned in Article 12(2)(d). We can use any number of indicators to measure access to medical services and medications, ranging from the number of physicians per 100,000 people to the percentage of public monies spend on health care as compared to defense. Advanced industrialized nations frequently have more than 200 or even 300 physicians per 100,000 people, middle-group nations range from 530 in Cuba to 25 in its neighbor Surinam, while least-developed nations often have no more than 10 physicians for each 100,000 people. The Cuban figure shows that political ideology does make a difference.

The great embarrassment in these comparisons is the case of the United States, where access to medical services is very uneven. While in the 1990s the United States averaged 279 doctors per 100,000 people, it is a widely known fact that at the turn of the twenty-first century roughly 45,000,000 Americans have no access to medical services because health insurance is unavailable or too expensive. The working poor whose plight I described above generally do not receive health insurance through their part-time jobs or are asked to pay far too large a chunk of their own paychecks to get coverage. They will pay for a roof over their heads before spending money on visits to a clinic. We are again faced with the anomaly that in the richest country on earth, one of the most basic of human rights (health care defined as access to medical services and medications) is being violated on a very large scale. What keeps this abomination from being a crime against humanity is the fact that hospitals in the United States must by law treat emergency cases brought in. The ideology that creates this state of affairs is one that does not look on health care as a genuine human right, which is one reason the U.S. Senate refused its consent when, in 1977, President Carter sent the Covenant to the Senate for ratification and implementation.

Sunstein calls these kinds of rights "constitutive commitments" because they have worked themselves into U.S culture as basic public commitments, even though they are not mentioned in the original Bill of Rights (Sunstein, *Second Bill*, 175ff.). They remain in this limbo state as the different compositions of the Supreme Court bow in their direction or shun them. They have achieved their status as a result of legislative enactments and not because they were placed up front in the constitution, as is the case in Finland, India, Ireland, Nigeria, Norway, Papua New Guinea, Peru, South Africa, Spain, Switzerland, Syria, and most of the former Soviet block countries.[72] Their socialist perspective made many of these countries in the 1940s vote to include the second generation of human rights in the Declaration.[73] It made them in the 1970s and 1980s draft, sign, and ratify ICESCR, and in more recent years it has made them willing to dialogue with the monitoring committee of that Covenant about the best way to implement the right to health care. As I have already mentioned, the closest the United States has come to embracing these "new" rights was under the presidency of Franklin Roosevelt. The U.S. government does not recognize as inherent the social, economic, and cultural rights that it should enact and reify for its citizens. Instead, on the whim of the legislature or a change in the composition of the Supreme Court, these entitlements can be and have been drastically changed.

While step (a) (the reduction in stillbirths and under-five deaths) and step (d) (access to medical facilities) are the threshold components on which medical personnel are usually focused, steps (b) and (c) fit better with what public health officials set their sights on. Article 12(2)(b) demands "The improvement of all aspects of environmental and industrial hygiene," and 12(2)(c) demands "The prevention, treatment and control of epidemic, endemic, occupational and other diseases." Toebes refers to these items as the "underlying preconditions for health" and points out that they find their echo in many international human rights texts.[74] As such we can either include them in the threshold or view them as the soil on which a good threshold can be built. She has studied the health reports that were sent in by some thirty nations from 1986 up to December 1997 and analyzed the reactions of the monitoring committee to these reports. It is clear from the dialogues between the signatories and the Committee that many nations have come to see these preconditions as important features of the health threshold. These dialogues, which are ongoing as more periodic reports are submitted to the Committee, give us a glimpse of the wide range of issues involved when a right like the one to health care is lowered into the enormous variety of domestic contexts found around the globe.

South Korea reported in 1990 that "most communicable diseases have disappeared as a result of improvement of living conditions (safe water supply, improvement of food, hygiene, etcetera)" (Toebes, 122). The "Romanian representative reported that in Romania there was a high incidence of cardiovascular diseases due to an incorrect diet" (122). The representative of Syria indicated that access to drinking water in 1990 was 73 percent, versus 45 percent in 1980 (124). Zaire wrote that it was planning to set up 250 rural hydrology teams to supply drinking water by the end of 1991 to 50 percent of the rural population (124). Tunisia took measures for water treatment "to restrict the spread of water-borne and feces-borne diseases" (125). The Committee pointed to "the insufficient number of labor inspectors" in Mauritius (126). The Federal Republic of Germany reported on a new law that requires firms with more than fifty employees to "appoint doctors specializing in industrial medicine for the medical supervision of the employees." Cameroon reported that it was "about to ratify the convention prohibiting the use of asbestos" (127).

The Netherlands reported that the most important tool in fighting the AIDS pandemic was health education. Since in Mali some 75 percent of girls and women had been circumcised, and in Gambia more than half, "the Committee expressed its concern about the prevalence of female circumcision" in those countries (129). It "noted that in Mali, legislation in effect for 30 years prohibiting such practices had never been enforced." The representative of the Philippines reported on his country's "difficulties in containing population growth because of the fact that 'Catholics and Muslims together constitute 90% of the Filipinos'" (130). One Committee member engaged with the Philippine representative in a discussion on the extent to which the Philippine government was realistic about the incidence of people suffering from AIDS. In this same context the Colombian representative worried that in his country "the disease was spreading very rapidly" (134). The eightfold increase in HIV infection in what then was still the Russian Republic led the Committee to ask Russia to "adopt laws to prevent discrimination against HIV-positive persons." "Algeria's State representative reported that young people in Algeria were hardly ever committed to prison and were usually subjected to fines for drug consumption, something that was in line with the Government's policy for treating drug users as patients rather than criminals." On that topic South Korea reported that "a special decree prevented the infringements of the human rights of drug addicts in medical facilities" (137). Cameroon, Ecuador, and Cyprus all reported that abortion was illegal there, and the representative of Ecuador "admitted that the 'inadequate facilities for such operations, including a lack of blood supplies, had led to an increase in the mortality rate" (131).

The Committee has openly worried about the numerous restrictions in the Iranian constitution that grant a certain right, but then qualify it with phrases like "provided it is not against Islam" and "with due regard to Islamic standards." These led it to conclude that "the authorities in Iran were using religion as a pretext to abuse these rights" (103). Given that in 1986 Morocco had only one doctor per 4,188 inhabitants, the country rightly aimed its "health policy" at the promotion of "primary health care and access of all citizens to health care, in particular those living in remote areas" (104). The policy paid off, for Morocco brought down its under-five mortality from 184 in 1970 to 46 in 2000 (UNDP). The groups most frequently mentioned as being most disadvantaged in this respect are "people living in remote, rural areas, minorities and indigenous populations, women, children, the elderly, the mentally ill, disabled persons, persons with HIV/AIDS, and drug and alcohol addicts" (Toebes, 116–17). For instance, not that long ago UNICEF asked nations to pay far more attention to the health rights of indigenous children.[75]

These fragments of the international dialogue about health thresholds show how diverse the issues are when we lower abstract international norms into their local contexts and final resting places. The reader can find updates of these early dialogues and numerous other more recent segments on the Web site for the Office of the UN High Commissioner for Human Rights.[76]

Chapter 6
Human Rights and Democratic Participation

The Universal Declaration contains several types of human rights. There are the civil and political rights that dominate (but are not limited to) the first half of the document. And there are the social, economic and cultural ones that dominate (but are not limited to) the second half. In Chapter 5 we discussed the lack of usefulness of dividing the rights in the document into just these two large groupings. Between them these two main categories harbor at least five types of human rights: civil (like the right to marry), political (like the right to vote), social (like the right to privacy), economic (like the right to work), and cultural (like the right to an education). Since these are all inherent moral rights that are supposed to be implemented in domestic legal systems around the world, legal rights are imbedded in (or implied by) all five of these categories. These categories are fluid and overlap, in that many articles and rights can be housed in more than one of these five categories, depending on how one unpacks the right in question. The broad subject of this chapter is the group called "political human rights," which includes Article 19 (freedom of expression), Article 20 (freedom of assembly), and Article 21, with its three paragraphs devoted to democratic rights.

Grouping these rights together under the rubric of "democratic participation" links them up to the utopianism challenge of the preceding chapter. For it can be argued that the claim in Article 21 that "everyone has a [human] right to take part in the government of his country" raises very unrealistic expectations. Most of the world's people never have lived and still do not live in a democratic country and so cannot be said to be enjoying the substance of this right. If we add to this the thought (accepted by many scholars) that the democratic idea was not really born until the seventeenth century, it would seem that it makes no sense to speak of the right to democratic participation in earlier times and in premodern societies. This then raises not just the utopian challenge of people living without the goods to which they have a human right, but also the charge of Western ethnocentrism, the argument being that the right to democratic participation is a typically Western and modern invention or development that more than any of the other "interlopers" weakens the moral force of the Declaration. To fight off the more general charge of utopianism we insisted in Chapter 5 that everyone only has a human right to the minimal level of the substance (be it health care, food or an education) that is mentioned in any given right. People have a human right to no more than is needed to live a life with dignity. If we allow for appropriate changes in the goods involved, this could be said to apply to all periods of history. Health care in the Middle Ages is not the same thing as health care in the twentieth century, but at least people have a right to the threshold amount of the good involved in that right. The adoption of the capabilities approach in Chapter 4 helped us link the full range of the articles and rights in the Declaration to these species wide capabilities and in that way to human nature. Such linkage to human nature sets the rights (demands or claims) of the Declaration apart from other kinds of claims that are not so widely based. My examples from the Social, Economic and Cultural Covenant showed that the whole set of these capabilities and rights form an organic unity, with some being the means to the development of others. I admitted that not all of these rights need to be claimed all of the time and in all circumstances, just as we do not use all of our body parts all of the time, though we need them to be part of us all of the time.

The point of the present chapter is to place the right to democratic participation in that tapestry of human rights. This right deserves its own chapter because it brings with it more than do most other rights in the Declaration the charge and the fear of Western ethnocentrism. If democracy is a modern Western invention and if it is not as clearly linked to human nature as most other human rights seem to be, then why did the drafters include it in their Declaration? Were they being Western chauvinists, or what? And why raise false expectations if benevolent dictatorships can deliver the goods just as well? Other rights, like the one to unionization, also can raise this same question, but the right to democratic participation catches these others in its net, which is why I have singled it out for special treatment. I begin with a discussion and critique of Jürgen Habermas's theory of human rights because he thinks that there is an essential and epistemic (and not just a historical or sociological) connection between human rights and popular sovereignty or, as I shall call it, democratic participation. For Habermas, the justification of our belief in human rights completely overlaps with whatever justification we give for the political procedures of democratic participation. This overlap has, of course, a very Western ring to it, which is why I begin with a critique of Habermas's thesis. I end by opposing his purely procedural definition of democracy to a more substantive kind of democracy that I find in the Declaration and propose we include as part of a more effective theory.

A. Habermas on Popular Sovereignty and Human Rights

Which comes first, the chicken or the egg? Does democracy give birth to human rights, as Habermas maintains, or do human rights precede democratic procedures, as the Declaration and our theory would have it? If democracy gives birth to human rights, then people did not have human rights before there were democratic governments, which (depending on one's definition) was not really until fifth-century Athens or the Enlightenment. In this case the presence of Article 21—with its right to participation in a government that is based on the "will of the people"—in the Declaration is not puzzling in the least. As the birthplace of human rights, the article becomes the lynchpin of the entire document, as indeed it is for Habermas and his followers. Habermas meets the charge of Western ethnocentrism head-on and in the affirmative: yes, human rights were born in the West whenever it was that democratic types of government were first instituted, and, yes, human rights can exist only in societies that have these types of governments. Because human rights are constructed in the actual democratic procedures of government, we have no independent epistemic access to these rights outside whatever justification we have for those same democratic procedures. To justify or defend democracy and to justify or defend belief in human rights amount to one and the same thing. While Jack Donnelly makes this point on an external historical and sociological level (which we criticized at the end of Chapter 3), Habermas draws the connection between popular sovereignty and human rights even more tightly by making this connection an internal and conceptual one. Both thinkers agree that human rights should be exported and they make no apologies for the "invention" of human rights in the West, just as they would not make them for exporting penicillin.

On the other hand, if human rights are inherent in the human person and precede the development of democratic procedures of government in the seventeenth and eighteenth centuries, the presence of Article 21 in the list of internationally accepted human rights poses the challenge of Western ethnocentrism. Since the inherence view holds that people have their human rights by virtue of their humanity—which, of course, they possessed long before the development of democratic nation-states—the relationship between human rights and Article 21 presents a challenge to interpreters of the Declaration. Rawls answers this query by limiting the list of human rights "proper" to the ones found in Articles

3–18 of the document and leaving the political rights of Articles 19, 20, and Article 21 especially in limbo. We saw him do this when he invited "decent" hierarchical societies into the society of well-ordered peoples, all present members of which had sworn to "honor human rights," but who were inviting new peoples that did not (really) honor Article 21 and often not fully Articles 18 and 19 either. Habermas's approach is in a crucial way the opposite of Rawls's in that for Habermas human rights are *essentially* juridical, and not, as they are for Rawls, contingently so. This has to do with the fact that Habermas does not work with two different justificatory contexts, a liberal domestic one where individual human rights are the focus, and a global one where whole peoples are the focus. For Habermas popular sovereignty in democratic regimes and universal (or global) human rights are internally and conceptually linked in a most intriguing way.

Habermas shares with the later Rawls the deep concern that political theory be responsive to our multicultural world. He believes that we live in a posttraditional and postmetaphysical world where shared moral codes have been cut off from their old, mostly religious moorings and where they also can no longer be based on other metaphysical ideas, such as the doctrine of inherence defended in this book. Even if there were such a domain of inherent rights, Habermas does not think that we have the epistemic equipment to gain access to it. This makes him reject all versions of the Golden Rule, whether that be Kant's categorical imperative or Gewirth's rationalized version of it, and it makes him reject as well any appeal to the conscience of humanity that I claimed (in Chapter 2) is built into international legal developments and for which I offered the theoretical framework of classical moral intuitionism.

Of all the Enlightenment thinkers, Rousseau is the one Habermas follows most closely, because "Rousseau starts with the constitution of civic autonomy and produces a fortiori an internal relation between popular sovereignty and human rights."[1] Unlike Locke, who thought that inalienable rights existed in the state of nature before any government was formed, Rousseau believed that these rights only resulted when the sovereign body of the people (gathered as a whole in a Geneva-like setting) decided to make their General Will effective through making laws for the territory under their control. Since laws (to be real laws) are not supposed to make reference to the private interests of any one particular citizen, all the members of the body politic, thought Rousseau, had their rights as human beings guaranteed. To violate the dignity of any one of them the legal system would have to discriminate between citizens on a level Rousseau's social contract would not allow. Habermas thinks this is naïve and that Rousseau places far too much faith in the form or format of the law, as such. I quote him: "Apparently, the normative content of the original human right [to equal treatment] cannot be fully captured by the grammar of general laws alone, as Rousseau assumed. The substantive legal equality that Rousseau took as central to the legitimacy claim of modern law cannot be satisfactorily explained by the semantic properties of general laws. . . .The form of universal normative propositions says nothing about their validity" (*Facts and Norms*, 102). As I also argued at the end of my exposition of Gewirth's argument for human rights (in Chapter 3, section A), appeal to the Golden Rule supposes that its basic content is poured in from elsewhere.

We can see Habermas' objection to Rousseau in the latter's observation that someone who is outvoted in a session of the sovereign people should simply say this to himself: "When a law is proposed in the people's assembly, what is asked of them is not precisely whether they approve or reject, but whether or not it conforms to the general will that is theirs. Each man in giving his vote, states his opinion on this matter, and the declaration of the general will is drawn from the counting of the votes. When, therefore, an opinion contrary to mine prevails, this proves merely that I was in error, and that what I took to be the general will was not so."[2] He deepens the muddle with the assertion that our very freedom is constituted not just by our membership in the nation, but by our voting the way of the General Will, which is drawn from the counting of the votes: "If my private opinion had prevailed, I would have done something other than what I had wanted. In that case I would not have been free" (Rousseau, 82). This is a purely procedural definition of democracy because it mentions no side constraints on the will of the majority. In other places Rousseau mentions the common good as a side constraint, but the decision of what that good is lies with the General Will. Below I will defend a substantive kind of democracy over this procedural kind and give contemporary examples of both. Habermas is right to point out that Rousseau's type of democracy does not provide enough safeguards against a majority's perverse understanding of what the general will in a given case might be. Rousseau, he complains, "cannot explain how the normatively construed common will can, without repression, be mediated with the free choice of individuals" (*FN* 102). The question for us is whether Habermas's own view of the epistemic link between popular sovereignty and human rights avoids Rousseau's mistake of exposing his general will to being hijacked from within by a radically evil majority that does not, for instance, hesitate to violate the most sacred of human rights the way Hitler did.

The issue for Habermas is one of "rational political will formation," which is the process where our wills are both rationally and politically shaped so as to give at one and the same time expression to our individual autonomy (as the persons that we are) and to the public autonomy (of the citizens that we are). The "co-originality" of these two autono-mies—that of the private individual and that of the public citizen—is what makes him link the very concept of a *human* right to the concept of citizenship and to a government's equal respect for all of its citizens. For Habermas the title of the 1789 French Declaration of the Rights of Man and of the Citizen is wrongly conceived because he sees these two categories of rights as coextensive. Says he: "The co-originality of private and public autonomy first reveals itself when we decipher, in discourse theoretic terms, the motif of self-legislation according to which the ad-dressees of law are simultaneously the authors of their rights" (104). That description fits the civil rights of citizens, but not the rights that are inherent in the human person and of which that same person cannot also be the author. Yet, that is how Habermas wants us to understand the concept; we are supposed to pull ourselves up by our own bootstraps.

This private and public will formation can take place in any of three modes that I label as Habermas identifies them. According to the first mode (that is Kant): "If the rational will can take shape only in the indi-vidual subject, then the individual's moral autonomy must reach through the political autonomy of the united will of all in order to secure the private autonomy of each in advance via natural law" (103). This is also the option my own theory adopts, except that it replaces an emphasis on reason with one on our moral intuitions as the initial causal factor in the formation of our moral wills. Those wills are being formed as our intuitions gain us access to the domain of the inherent rights of people, which moral rights we then seek to impose, guided by the golden rule, on the political realm of our existence both domestically and internation-ally. Habermas denies this separation of law and morality because "it is only participation in the practice of *politically autonomous* lawmaking that makes it possible for addressees of law to have a correct understanding of the legal order as created by themselves" (121). That includes what-ever moral underpinnings that legal order may be thought to have and thus leads to a view of human rights as collectively man-made. Therefore, according to the second mode (that is Rousseau): "If the rational will can take shape only in the macro subject of a people or a nation, then po-litical autonomy must be understood as the self-conscious realization of the ethical substance of a concrete community; and private autonomy is protected from the overpowering force of political autonomy only by the nondiscriminatory force of general laws" (103). We also find this mode of political will formation in the extreme organic theories of the state in fascism and Nazism. As I said, it does not give individuals sufficient protection against violations of their private autonomy by a deranged or thoroughly corrupt majority. The political autonomy of the people as a whole is too powerful and the general formulations of its laws are too porous not to let great abuse and oppression by the party or the executive branch run rampant. This calls for a third mode, which is Habermas's own refinement and update of Rousseau.

That mode blends private (Kant) and public (Rousseau) will formation through participation in public discussion and argumentation. According to it the other two conceptions "miss the legitimating force of a discursive process of opinion and will formation, in which the illocutionary binding forces of a use of language oriented to mutual understanding serve to bring reason and will together, and lead to convincing positions to which all individuals can agree without coercion" (*FN* 103). This is the idea of deliberative democracy with the addition of the "illocutionary binding forces of a use of language" that is aimed at coming to a meeting of the minds of all those affected by the norms to be adopted. The results of these discursive processes are summarized in Habermas's all important Discourse Theoretic Principle: "Just those action norms are valid to which all possibly affected persons could agree as participants in rational discourses" (107). Since it makes reference to "action norms" in general, this principle can function both on a moral and a legal level. On the first level it is (not surprisingly) called the moral principle and on the legal level it is referred to as the principle of democracy. Habermas's theory of human rights involves the interplay of these three principles.[3] Since the moral principle and the democratic principle are two sides of the same Discourse Principle, they can only be institutionalized and concretized together, which is why human rights (think of the moral principle) and popular sovereignty (think of the democratic principle) are conceptually linked. Our problem is that while Habermas holds that in his theory "the moral principle and the democratic principle reciprocally explain each other" (94), to us he seems to be traveling in a circle here. He holds that as individuals we cannot come to know what our human rights are outside the context of our roles as citizens in a body politic, but then he explains that public role in terms of our observance of human rights, as if we already had had access to that realm. His admission that "I take as my starting point the [initial] *rights* citizens must accord one another if they want to legitimately regulate their common life by means of positive law" (82, emphasis added) is trivially true if it is meant legally, but open to questioning if it is meant morally. For instance, the moral rights to which the conscience of humanity gives us access have a positive shape the rough contours of which we know regardless the political situation in which we find ourselves. Their existential epistemic scope is far broader than the roles citizens have in democratic societies.

Habermas seeks to get around this point by making all of us members of an abstract communicative society. That society is governed by a morality that "first results when one specifies the general discourse principle for those norms that can be justified if and only if equal consideration is given to the interests of all those who are possibly involved" (108). When we ask what the domain is of "all those possibly involved" the answer we get is that with "*moral questions* humanity or a presupposed republic of world citizens constitutes the reference system for justifying regulations that lie in the equal interest of all. In principle the decisive reasons must be acceptable to each and everyone" in this republic of world citizens.[4] Habermas is not aiming at a world government, nor does he mean by "humanity" the actual human family of which we are all members. Much as Rawls wanted us all to be represented behind his abstract veil of ignorance, so Habermas views us all as members of an abstract and ideal community of discourse that seeks to adopt rules for any kind of discursive or argumentative process. Once these rules have been worked out, they can then be lowered into place in political communities and be rebaptized as the democratic principle. Habermas lists and defends these rules of his "Discourse Ethics" in his book *Moral Consciousness and Communicative Action,* and they look nothing like any of the rights listed in the Universal Declaration.[5] They cannot look like that because they are at least one whole step removed from the level of actually living together in a real historical community. They are instead the rules we need for the rational (instead of coercive or intuitive) formation of our wills to prepare those wills for further argumentation or discourse with others about what rights we do and do not need for living together in a real historical situation.

The abstractness or remoteness of this discourse theoretic community creates an epistemic gap between how we come to know the moral rules of discourse ethics and how (I have argued) we come to know the moral rights articulated in the Universal Declaration. In my critique I follow some of the objections Hilary Putnam has raised against the way Habermas derives the rules of his communicative ethics. Putnam's first objection reminds us of what critics of logical positivism have said about the principle of verifiability that positivists used to establish their claim that the propositions of ethics, theology, metaphysics, and aesthetics had no truth value. The critics rightly said that this powerful Verification Principle was itself not being subjected to the verifiability test. While the principle lorded it over all other propositions, it itself had not been vetted against the empirical data that supposedly knocked out huge areas of human inquiry as delivering pieces of knowledge. Putnam's criticism of Habermas's Discourse Principle (which is a summary of the discourse ethics rules) is that this principle itself was not adopted in the manner that it prescribes should be used for adopting rules of discursive engagement in real life. I quote Putnam: "Since all of the norms and maxims of discourse ethics are built into the description of the ideal discussion situation, they will, by the very definition of the situation, be accepted by all the participants. But then *their* justification—and they constitute essentially the whole of Habermasian ethics—*isn't* that they are the *outcome* of an indefinitely prolonged Peircean inquiry at all!"[6] The Discourse Principle itself is not the result of a collective discursive session that lasted until a consensus on the rules was reached. How then can Habermas set up that very principle as the master rule for the adoption of all other rules, including the moral ones that inform the procedures of democratic participation that lead to the adoption of human rights?

Habermas's pure procedural approach to questions of political justice is not democratic in its inception because it derives from the logical *dicta* of discourse ethics. This robs him of a chance to criticize our own theory of human rights for not being a purely procedural one either. This presumption that the initial agreement on the construction of norms must be made by consensus is borrowed from the social contract tradition, to which point I add the reminder that for Locke (whom we follow) that unanimous contract is made *after* the rights in the state of nature have already played a substantive role. Because Habermas follows Rousseau, the consensus requirement precedes the adoption of the rules for discursive engagement and—with the help of the principle of reciprocity—shapes the Discourse Ethics test, according to which only those rules are justified which have been accepted by or are in principle acceptable to all the relevant parties to which they are applied, which in Habermas's case ends up being an idealized and hugely abstract community of discourse that includes all of humanity.

Putnam's second criticism focuses on the fact that argumentative sessions do not always end in consensus and cannot last forever. They must often end at a time when the community as a whole has not yet come to a perfect meeting of the minds. For an example he goes to Wittgenstein's discussion of whether there is a rule for telling when someone is feigning an emotion. Wittgenstein says there is not, and Putnam agrees that such a discussion must end in favor of those who "have more *Menschenkenntnis* (understanding of people) than others, and *Menschenkenntnis* cannot be reduced to a system of rules" (Putnam, 126) Just so, Putnam argues, there also is not in "a dispute as to whether an act is cruel" or not (127). Take the case of a father who is teasing his child to tears and who may either be obtuse or have a streak of sadism in him. Putnam's point is that the community as a whole probably will not come to an agreement on this question, even if they perfectly follow all Habermas's discourse ethics rules. "What is wrong with the discussants in the above situation *isn't* that they aren't obeying the norms of discourse ethics. What is wrong is stateable *using the thick ethical vocabulary appropriate to the particular ethical problem*" (127–28).

In a discussion like this, there are no strict rules that tell us when terms like "obtuse" and "having a streak of sadism" are correctly used. Without claiming that Putnam supports our theory of classical moral intuitionism (which he does not), his point about "thick" ethical terms that fit their precise context does go in that direction. Our moral sense and intuitions cannot be reduced to a set of rules for settling disputes involving those "thick" terms, not even, for instance, when, to use Putnam's example, a large number of members in a community are obtuse or blinded by a trace of sadism. In the end, we may have to decide that the conscience of humanity speaks through us and not through the majority of a particular community whose consciences are somehow blocked or warped. This is what the Israeli Court did when it executed Eichmann in spite of the fact that he claimed to have lived his whole life according to Kant's categorical imperative as he saw it practiced in the Third Reich.

Putnam borrows his third criticism of Habermas from Lyotard and thinks that it is not quite on target, though I think it is well aimed. Lyotard's objection is that "discourse ethics marginalizes or excludes the 'inarticulate,'" to which we add the weak, the invisible poor, and all other exploited and oppressed persons (129). Putnam thinks that this is not a good objection because the members of Habermas's ideal speech community must not just obey the rules when they argue with one another, they must also regard inarticulate and marginalized persons as members of their group "(otherwise it does not include all affected persons), and every member must have a non-manipulative attitude towards every other" (130). This might well be what Habermasians would say, but to us the answer ignores an important difference between the ideology of human rights and ordinary democratic processes of representation. There is an important difference between, on the one hand, representing others by *speaking for* them or on their behalf, and on the other hand, *speaking-up-for* them. By merging the justification of human rights with the justification of normal democratic procedures (without remainder), Habermas ignores this difference. Altruistic motivations are a viable part of the ideology of human rights activism. Those motivations lead to a different kind of representation from what is involved in the ordinary democratic procedures that Habermas justifies with an appeal to the principle of reciprocity he has built into his ideal speech community.

Since elected representatives must know what their constituents are saying, needing or wanting, a modern political representative has to communicate regularly with those constituents. Members of different political parties (such as Democrats and Republicans in the United States, or Christian Democrats and the Green Party in Germany) differ in their goals and platforms, but they do not differ on the fundamentals of representative government. Their elected representatives inform themselves on a regular basis of what their constituents want and therefore are able to speak on their behalf and *for* them. Habermas's ideal speech community accommodates this point by asking us to pretend that all humanity or all world citizens (and everyone is that) are present. But that answer does not capture Lyotard's or Nussbaum's point about the weak and the exploited being left out of the imagined dialogue or, if not left out, at least not given the special attention they should be given if we take human rights seriously.

In the speaking-up-for others the Habermasian communication element between the speaker and her constituents need not necessarily be present. In some cases the train of thought of activists leads from a belief in (1) *inherent rights* to (2) a belief in the *universal possession* of these rights, to an observation that (3) these rights have been *grossly violated* (by some state, person or agency), to the claim that (4) the victims' *need the actual enjoyment* of the violated rights, and from there to (5) their *speaking-up-for* the victim(s) and demanding that action be taken. Since the inherence lies in the human personhood of the victims, Albert Camus' metaphysical solidarity extends to all the members of the human family, which is why so many NGOs dealing with human rights issues have sprouted up in recent decades. The victims want full enjoyment of all their inherent rights, and since these rights are equally inherent in both victims and "representatives," the latter know what it is the former want and need.

Our belief that the victims have what Nussbaum calls species-wide capabilities makes us reject the charge of paternalism that Habermasians might want to level against our doctrine of inherence. From our point of view, with the abstract rights already in place in a document like the Declaration, what remains to be done is for the world to be informed on the extent of the violations, to determine which duty-bearers are shirking their duties and which "representatives" are willing and able to ring the alarm bell. The entire Declaration is premised on the fact that the victims of the Holocaust no longer had a voice and could not speak for themselves. There are also numerous instances of this altruistic kind of representation. All the sessions of the Human Rights Commission and of its Drafting Committee were attended by representatives of some fifty NGOs. The growth of this advocacy network has been phenomenal. Steiner and Alston tell us that "well over half of the 3,240 persons who participated in the 1999 session of the UN Commission on Human Rights were NGO representatives," and that according to UN estimates "the number of international NGOs grew from around 1300 in 1960 to more than 36,000 in 1995, and the number has increased significantly since then."[7] To these thousands of international groups we must add the millions of grass-roots domestic groups that deal with human rights issues, all speaking-up-for different marginalized groups in their own or other countries. Depending on our own educational history and sensitivities, our altruistic feelings of solidarity with marginalized and violated persons are probably being channeled through one or several of these groups.

We find this motif of speaking-up-for others on all levels of international society. At the very top, the UN has been overseeing a global system of more than 200 human rights instruments with treaties and declarations that speak up for every kind of oppressed, neglected, or ignored victims imaginable: for children, for people suffering from HIV-AIDS, for the homeless, for indigenous peoples, for women, for those suffering from discrimination, especially the racial kind. And so on. This system has developed precisely because the diplomats and human rights activists who drew up these human rights instruments felt that the members of these groups did not have enough or any voice or vote in the ordinary political processes of whatever state or region they were inhabitants. These marginalized persons needed to be spoken-up-for because they had been left out of ordinary political processes. The monitoring committees that oversee the implementation of UN sponsored human rights norms stress to their reporting countries the obligation to deliver human rights to the marginalized groups in their midst. The same thing is true at the bottom of the international pyramid. About once a month the members of our campus chapter of Amnesty International set up a table in the University Center where they ask students who walk by to write a letter and to speak-up-for designated prisoners of conscience. Amnesty's researchers have determined that these prisoners have not engaged in any violent acts. Their human rights (to personal security, movement, or a fair trial) were violated when they were imprisoned, tortured or went missing, simply because they spoke their consciences, frequently to help yet others whose human rights were being violated by their own governments. The speaking-up-for these dispossessed, missing or tortured persons is a process that takes place entirely outside and even in lieu of ordinary democratic processes and for that very reason is not likely to be captured by justificatory arguments that bind themselves to those ordinary processes that Habermasians tend to emphasize.

From the point of view of our doctrine of inherence Habermas's co-originality thesis that tightly binds together the justification of belief in human rights and the justification of democratic procedures of government fails in two directions. It has the implication that before there were democratic regimes of any kind (and no justifications for them were even thought of) people did not have human rights, which clearly does not fit with the idea of human rights as birth-based rights. The thesis also suggests that people who do not now live under democratic regimes cannot strictly speaking be said to have human rights. That is not really what Habermas wants to say (which is why the discourse ethics community is constituted by the entire human family), but it has led some of his followers to postulate another basic right just above the more "mundane" human rights that we find in democratic constitutions, from which basic right those more mundane ones can be derived. In that case, the list would not need to be drawn exclusively out of the lower level democratic procedures.

A prominent U.S. example of driving a wedge between the two processes of justification (for human and constitutional rights) can be found in Seyla Benhabib's 2006 Presidential Address to the Eastern Division of the American Philosophical Association, entitled "Another Universalism: On the Unity and Diversity of Human Rights."[8] Benhabib speaks of the "tension generated by the context- and community-*transcending validity* dimension of human rights on the one hand, and the historically formed, culturally generated and socially shaped specificities of existing juridico-civil communities on the other" (23, emphasis added). For us, this is the tension between independently discovered inherent human rights and the implementation of these rights in communal networks and domestic legal systems. I see Benhabib struggling to make true the "transcending validity" factor that I italicized above. She views the justification of human rights as "a dialogical practice [that] is not mired in the metaphysics of natural rights, natural law or possessive individual selves" (19). "Rights [to her] are not about what there is but about the kind of world we reasonably ought to want to live in" (12).

This wholesale rejection of metaphysical universality includes that of our doctrine of simple inherence. Benhabib rejects that doctrine because to her all descriptions of human nature are tainted with the virus of essentialism, just as they were for her communitarian companions MacIntyre and Rorty, whose views we discussed at the end of Chapter 1, section B. Moral universalism, she says, "does not consist in an essence or human nature which we are all said to have or possess, but rather in the experience of establishing commonality across diversity, conflict, divide and struggle" (21). She refers to this "commonality" also as "the unity" and "the moral core" of human rights that needs to be given "legal form" (23). That could be a lead-in for some minimalist metaphysical independence. However, she in no way wants to equate this core with anything that is birth-based and not man-made. For her "natality itself cannot ground human rights claims which need intersubjective confirmation and validation among human beings" (42). This is Benhabib's affirmation of Habermas's postmodern, intersubjective method of justifying belief in human rights. She can now follow Habermas and link this intersubjective justification of human rights essentially and conceptually to the establishment of democratic procedures, or she can separate these two processes, in which case she owes her readers an explanation of our belief in human rights that views the right to democratic participation as just one human right among many, and not as the linchpin of the whole system, which it is for Habermas.

To break the overly tight conceptual linkage between human rights and democracy, Benhabib posits "the right to have rights" as the most fundamental of all human rights. She shares Hannah Arendt's belief that persons have at least one basic moral right, which is the right "to be recognized by others as a being who is *entitled* to the equal respect of his or her legal personality" (10, emphasis added). While Arendt views this entitlement as created by the modern state and therefore also as being taken away by the arrangements those states made in her lifetime, in the case of Benhabib the source of this entitlement is left unclear between being an independently established or discovered *moral* right and being a *legal* right that emerges out of modern democratic procedures.[9] We agree that this right to have rights embodies "the inviolability of the person," and that we should be able to "proceed from" this principle to "the norms of equal respect and concern" that we often meet with in democratic polities, where respect and concern get spelled out in various bills of civil rights (24). However, we question Benhabib's account of how we should go from the principle of the inviolability of the human person (which we accept) to those democratic procedures that reflect equal respect and concern and get translated into bills of rights. In our theory this gap is filled by the idea of inherent birth rights, while in Benhabib's case it is filled by the principle of reciprocity that we have criticized in Chapter 3.

We agree that the local contexts in which these legal derivations take place differ a great deal in their history, culture and topography, and that "there [therefore] is a legitimate range of variation and interpretation even in implementation of such a basic right as that of equality before the law" (25). Our concern is with the origin of this basic right to have rights, which for Benhabib is the heart beat of moral universalism, which type of universalism she defines as "the principle that all human beings, regardless of race, gender, sexual orientation, and ethnic, cultural, linguistic and religious background are entitled to equal moral respect" (7). This negative definition of moral universalism is no accident, for the drive toward greater inclusivity is the mark of Benhabib's much appreciated contribution to contemporary political theory.[10] Given a choice between the first two articles of the Declaration, she would pick the second, non-discrimination one over the first, birth-based one, because a list of non-discrimination items fits far better with the principle of reciprocity than does the metaphysics of natality in Article 1. For her all rights claims, including the most basic right to have rights, follow this schema: "I can justify to you with good reasons that you and I should respect each other's *reciprocal claim* to act in certain ways and not to act in others, and to enjoy certain resources and services" (emphasis added; 11). This is none other than the Golden Rule, which we have found wanting when it is meant to serve as the sole justification for our belief in human rights. Benhabib seeks to strengthen it with the principle self-government or democracy, which is how we finally arrive back at Habermas's co-originality thesis.

Speaking of the range of legitimate diversity in the interpretation of equality before the law, Benhabib observes that "the legitimacy of this range is crucially dependent upon the principle of self-government" and democratic procedures (25). Just how crucial "crucial" is comes out when she herself wonders how we can "assess whether [genuine] democratic iterations have taken place rather than demagogic processes of manipulations or authoritarian indoctrination?" Her answer to this query is that she "accept[s] Jürgen Habermas's insight that the democratic principle states that *only* those statutes may claim legitimacy that can meet the assent (Zustimmung) of all citizens in a discursive process of legislation which has been legally constituted" (28, emphasis added; cited from *Facts and Norms*, 110). We must keep in mind that the "statutes" involved here are the ones that are to establish what human rights people do or do not have in a given polity. That means people only have those human rights that they as fellow citizens give to each other in a genuine democratic give and take, involving public debates in which any citizen has a veto over proposals others make. "There is," says Benhabib, "an intrinsic, and not merely contingent, connection between human rights and democratic self-determination" (32). The word "intrinsic" makes UDHR Article 21 the linchpin of the entire system of human rights, a claim that we reject because it ignores our doctrine of inherence that we fleshed out with the species capabilities approach. Also, in our theory it is possible that an authoritative regime (that, let's say, suppresses free speech of opponents to the regime) honors the human right not to be tortured, even though the statute that implements that moral right was enacted in violation of internationally accepted standards of democratic participation. Our interpretation of the Declaration does not require that there be an *intrinsic* and therefore definitional connection between honoring the human right not to be tortured and the right to democratic self-determination. The former can be honored where the latter is not. I do, however, hold that both these rights are expressions of human dignity. The right to democratic participation should be seen as inherent because it expresses our species capacity to control our environment and because it is a means for the delivery other human rights, which last point I defend in section B below.

One cannot help but think that Benhabib is having her cake and eating it too. On the one hand, it turns out that "'The right to have rights' *means* the right to action and to opinion in a polity the laws of which govern one's existence" (28, emphasis added). This makes the having of human rights and the living in a democratic regime one and the same thing, which is belied by the scenario in the preceding paragraph. Probably in recognition of this fact, Benhabib assures us that the cake has not been eaten, for "the two are not identical." She then eats it when she says that "*only* through the self-determination of the citizens and residents of a polity can justifiable distinctions among them be generated and the range of legitimate variation be judged" (28, emphasis added). The world "only" conflicts with the claim that the two rights are not the same. Because it cuts out any chance of appealing to the inherent moral rights that we correlate with the capabilities humans typically have, it makes the connection between human rights and democracy too tight. It leaves the justification of our belief in human rights up to the strength of the Golden Rule or the principle of reciprocity, neither of which, we argued in Chapter 3, can by itself be trusted to carry that weight.

B. The Right to Participation in Substantive Democracies

Having rejected Habermas's attempt to connect human rights conceptually and without remainder to the right to democratic participation, I do owe the reader an account of how that (ordinary) democratic right fits into our theory of inherent human rights. After I mention the consensus among theorists of international law that there is indeed an emerging right to democratic participation, I report on the debate that took place when UDHR Article 21 was adopted. The three paragraphs of this article are "(1) Everyone has the right to take part in the government of his country, directly or through freely chosen representatives. (2) Everyone has the right to equal access to public service in his country. (3) The will of the people shall be the basis of the authority of government; this will shall be expressed in periodic and genuine elections which shall be by universal and equal suffrage and shall be held by secret vote or by equivalent free voting procedures." I then use the authority of this text and the *travaux* to take sides between those who opt for a procedural definition of democracy (as we have just seen Habermas does) and those who look for a more substantive definition of democracy, which is the side we support. I end with some observations about the means-ends relationship that exists between the right to democratic participation as a means to the enjoyment of other crucial human rights like health care and freedom of thought.

It is amazing how many of the issues raised in contemporary democracy discussions were also raised when the Declaration was drafted. More than twenty international law scholars wrote lengthy contributions to a 2000 volume entitled *Democratic Governance and International Law*.[11] These scholars agree that we are witnessing the birth of a new internationally recognized human right called democratic entitlement. They are not all equally sure as to what this right's content is and what the depth of its anchor in international law is, but none of them argue that no birth at all is taking place; they simply differ on how far the birthing process has gone. Space limitations allow me to mention only three of these essays.

Looking at the enormous election monitoring activities of the UN and the European and Latin American regional bodies, Thomas Franck concludes that "the opinions of mankind have begun in earnest to require that governments, as a prerequisite to membership in the community of nations derive their just powers from the consent of the governed."[12] His evidence is that "as of late 1997, approximately 130 national governments were legally committed to permit open, multiparty, secret ballot elections with universal franchise" (27). He points out that just in the year "1996–97 elections were observed in Algeria, Ghana, Madagascar, Mali, and Yemen; further [that] electoral assistance was also provided to Bangladesh, the Comoros, Gambia, Guyana, Haiti, Liberia, Mali and Mexico" (31). And he is of the opinion that a failure like the one in Angola is "balanced by successes in Namibia, Cambodia, Nicaragua and El Salvador" (41) In recent years the Organization of American States has sent monitors to Surinam, El Salvador, Paraguay, Panama, and Peru. A lot of election monitoring was done in Eastern Europe with the post 1989 transition from communism. To facilitate the emergence of this right to democratic participation, in 1992 the UN added an Electoral Assistance Division to its Secretariat.

Franck believes that as a result of all this election aid and monitoring activity "a global canon of legitimate rules and procedures" is developing and that with this canon we can judge "the democracy of nations" (42). He also thinks that this canon "has trumped the principle of noninterference" enunciated in Article 7(2) of the UN Charter. Gregory Fox investigated international legal texts and court decisions and came to the same conclusion as Franck, namely, "that the right to political participation has established a firm grounding in both treaty law and international practice."[13] "The particulars of a human right to political participation," observes Fox, "once a flashpoint for grand ideological battles, now appears rather pedestrian. That receipt of an electoral mandate bestows legitimacy upon governments, that genuine choice in an election requires multiple political parties, that incumbent regimes cannot monopolize the mass media during a campaign, and that the other elements of fair elections must be provided, all seem to flow inevitably from treaties announcing commitment to representative government" (Fox, 89). He wrote this after a thorough investigation of the text of Article 25 of the ICCPR and of decisions by the Human Rights Commission, by the Human Rights Committee (of the ICCPR), by the European Commission, by the European Court, of those found in the Latin American and African systems, and as stated in the Helsinki Accords of the OSCE.

Both Franck and Fox mention Article 21 of the Universal Declaration as the moral and legal anchor for these developments, but they do not nearly give it the attention it deserves.[14] The Declaration was written in a shared mood of rebellion (metaphysical and otherwise) against the Nazi abuses of state power. While we might be inclined to see the inclusion of Article 21's democratic entitlement to be a piece of Western ethnocentric thinking, the drafters themselves had no such compunctions. The only time they ever raised any kind of qualification is when they added the clause "or by equivalent free voting procedures" at the end of Article 21(3). This was done on the insistence of the Haitian delegation, which reminded the members of the Third Committee that they were drafting a declaration that was addressed not solely to the Western hemisphere, but to the entire world;, and according to figures supplied by UNESCO, illiteracy was still very common, 85 percent of the population of the world being illiterate.[15] The drafters of ICCPR Article 25, which was copied from UDHR 21, deleted the clause, but in 1998 about one quarter (24.8 percent) of the world's adults over fifteen years old were still illiterate.[16]

We know, of course, that military and other kinds of dictatorial regimes can manipulate elections so that they seem free but in reality are not. In the 1948 debates the Lebanese delegate also made this point when he observed that "the Nazi government could have subscribed to all of those ideas [in Article 21] and its elections would still not have been free" (GAOR Third, 456). The UN election monitoring teams are sent in precisely because, even if elections are held periodically and by secret ballot, that by itself does not assure that they will be free. What made Hitler's elections not free was the intimidation and incarceration of opposition party figures, which is why the communist delegations wanted to keep the item "political opinion" from the nondiscrimination list in UDHR 2. When Article 21 came up for discussion in the First Drafting Session, Hernán Santa Cruz of Chile suggested that "a provision concerning the right to form political parties be added" to Article 21. At that point in time UDHR Article 20 (on the right to association) included a list of legitimate reasons for which association should be allowed, which included political purposes. This fact resulted in a withdrawal of the Chilean suggestion as unnecessary. Unfortunately, that list of particular purposes was later deleted from the article on association. When the Belgian delegate, Fernand Dehousse, brought up the same point much later in the Third Committee, he ran into solid opposition from USSR delegate Alexei Pavlov, who gave his colleagues a free lecture on the benefits of one party systems in people's democracies. When Dehousse withdrew his suggestion, Eduardo Plaza, the Venezuelan delegate, openly regretted this conciliatory Belgian move. Still, the weight of the evidence is that the kind of democracy called for by the Universal Declaration is a multiparty one. This gives added sanction to recent pronouncements by the human rights judicial organs that Fox surveyed as to what a "genuine" election entails.

As I indicated earlier, the communist delegations fought to have the item "political opinion" removed from the nondiscrimination list in UDHR Article 2. They realized that together with Article 21 this item has the implication that democratic multiparty forms of government are the only legitimate ones for nations to have. Any other type of government, whether a single party system or a dictatorship, is a violation of the human rights of the people living under its jurisdiction. Related fights occurred when Articles 19 and 20 came up for adoption. The communist delegates wanted an exception built into these rights so that they could not be practiced by Nazi and fascist groups or persons. They lost all of these drafting battles. The result is that Article 21 of the Declaration stands unencumbered at the center of a well articulated right to democratic participation.

By locating the authority of government in the will of the people and then also spelling out how that will is to be determined, Article 21 conflicts with what until recent years was standard procedure in international law and practice. That practice was for member nations not to judge how applicant nations came to have control over their people and territory. As long as governments were seen to have firm de facto control and could be relied on for treaty purposes they were judged legitimate. UN membership is, for instance, (still) not formally based on the character of the government that asks to join the organization. UDHR Article 21 creates a different standard. If it is to serve as a "common standard for all nations," then the good standing of nations or peoples within the community of nations must at least in part be judged by whether they have an electoral democratic type of government, or they must at least be in transit to this goal. Either that, or Article 21 is the most Western ethnocentric article in the document. The broader rights stated in Articles 19 (to freedom of expression) and 20 (to freedom of association) also become heavily political when combined with Article 2, which forbids discrimination on the basis of "political opinion" and other factors. The combination of these articles stipulates electoral democracy as the mandated form of government.

In their joint essay Fox and Nolte spell out the basic difference between procedural and substantive democracies. I end this chapter with a defense of the substantive kind, both because it fits the Declaration best and because it helps us answer the challenge of Western ethnocentrism that the presence of Article 21 raises so directly. In procedural democracies there are no limitations on the rights to free speech and association that would prevent opposition figures and their parties from participating in elections, after which point they could throw away the very ladder by which they climbed into office. The authors give as examples the Nazi grab for power in 1933 and the 1991 Algerian military coup that prevented a similar grab from taking place there. The question is how far democracies are allowed to go to prevent themselves from being taken over by parties or dictators who once they have grabbed power with much popular support, afterwards do away with elections and the rest of UDHR Articles 19, 20, and 21. Can such democracies ban individual citizens and even whole parties from freely speaking out and standing for office? Fox and Nolte argue that they can and should ban them, thereby defending a substantive kind of democracy. Democracies can, they hold, legitimately put substantive requirements in their constitutions or elsewhere in their legal systems, and in that way safeguard their democracies from being overtaken from within. As examples of weak (which they call tolerant) substantive democracies they discuss France, Canada, and India (Fox and Nolte, 411), while they pick Germany, Israel, and Costa Rica as examples of strong (meaning militant) substantive democracies. Their examples of procedural democracies are the UK, Botswana, and Japan (weak); and the United States, which they see as a militantly procedural democracy. Without commenting on their choice of examples, I shall defend the view that, given their classification scheme, the Universal Declaration must be said to be calling for a substantive and not for a merely procedural type of democracy.

The story is a complicated one, since it appears initially as if the Universal Declaration puts no limitations, other than those of Article 29, on the rights to free speech and free association, even for political purposes. The Soviet delegation repeatedly sought to have limitations added to Articles 19 and 20 that barred the use of these rights to Nazi groups, but failed every time.[17] The idea was that, while the Nazis and other axis powers were not invited to help write the Universal Declaration, once a democracy has been set up on the basis of respect for human rights, then it should be quite tolerant of groups that are themselves known to be intolerant. Contemporary democracies differ on this issue; the Fox-Nolte procedural ones allow antidemocratic individuals and parties almost the same rights to free speech and association as other individuals and parties, while the substantive democracies have constitutional and other safeguards to protect themselves against such citizens and their political parties.

My reason for saying that the Declaration takes a substantive path is the much overlooked last clause of the second sentence of Article 7. In the Second Session of the Commission the communist delegations got an important assist from the Belgian delegation.[18] The result is that second sentence, the last clause of which I have italicized: "All are entitled to equal protection against any discrimination in violation of this Declaration *and against any incitement to such discrimination.*" The UDHR leaves open the question as to how democratic governments are to provide this protection to their citizens, except that they did not want individual citizens to be cut off at the start, which is what happens when Articles 19 (on expression) and 20 (on association) are circumscribed in the individual civil as well as in political group rights.

We also need to bring to mind Article 30 of the Declaration: "Nothing in this Declaration may be interpreted as implying for any State, group or person any right to engage in any activity or to perform any act aimed at the destruction of any of the rights and freedoms set forth herein." The adoption discussions for this article are quite relevant to our own ongoing discussions of how democracies should deal with hate crimes and fanatical political parties.[19] At the time this issue came to be seen as one of the spirit of the laws. A legal system can seem quite all right on the surface, but in its spirit and application flaunt human rights regularly, especially in cases where political opponents of the regime are involved. U.S. delegate Eleanor Roosevelt pointed out that "Nazi Germany had appeared to be legally fulfilling the duties and obligations of the state, but in practice had been destroying all human rights and liberties" (E/CN.4/AC.1/SR.74/8). It was her considered opinion that no text could protect the spirit of the laws. Charles Malik, the Lebanese representative, countered this view with the observation that that was precisely the reason an article like this should be included in the Declaration. Pierre Ordonneau of France also saw the "danger against which Article [30] was aimed [as] a serious one" (SR, 74, 8). He felt that it "was essential that the Declaration should at least recall the dangers of Nazism" and that "it was wrong to deny a possible recurrence of Nazism." When in the later Third Committee meetings the United States still objected to the article, Pavlov, the Soviet delegate, argued that this particular article "was the only one that could be used as a weapon against Nazism." "He appealed to the committee to consider its responsibilities before rejecting the article, which might in the future serve as a weapon against Nazism and fascism" (7).

The French delegation proposed that the word "group" be inserted into the text of Article 30 because "experience had shown that it was rarely states or individuals that engaged in activities aimed at the destruction of human rights; such activities in recent times had been pursued by groups sometimes acting on the instructions or with the connivance of states" (GAOR Third, 666). After Pavlov pointed out how Hitler's and Mussolini's paths to power had been paved "by constant infiltration and propaganda," he added the example of the Ku Klux Klan in the United States. He wanted to answer the argument of those who belittled the influence of these kinds of hate groups because "their membership was very small and their activity of little consequence." That rationale, he said, was exactly what had also been used in the early stages of Hitler's and Mussolini's political careers, "the disastrous consequences of such indifference were unfortunately all too well known" (671). Dehousse from Belgian also thought that the drafters should "prevent a repetition of the experiences of a number of countries in the years immediately preceding the war" (667). The word "group" was included in Article 30 unanimously by 42 votes, with just 1 abstention, as was the whole article with no abstentions (672–74).

I interpret these votes to mean that the drafters of the Universal Declaration, which is the mother norm of all human rights norms, intended not to let democracies be taken over from within, either by military coups, by individuals, or by subversive groups, among which we may count political parties that have no intention to honor and respect human rights once they gain power by "legitimate" means such as the ballot box. This is the paradox of democracy. Just as in defenses of personal liberty political theorists of almost all persuasions hold that a person has no right to sell herself into slavery and so loose the very condition of liberty that allows her to make the deal, so, too, a democracy must protect itself against subversion from within and adopt measures and tactics that help her do that. That is a strong, substantive kind of democracy that cannot be undermined by its own procedures. It is the kind called for by the UDHR and supported by recent developments in international law. Present-day discussions of what the democratic entitlement entails suggest that Pavlov's future is here, for the Fox and Nolte constitutional survey shows that the question newly born and therefore fragile democracies often face is just that, how tolerant to be of members of militant political groups that abuse the freedoms of Articles 19 and 20 to come to power and then refuse to implement Article 21. While in Chapter 3, section B, we I took exception to Rawls's excessive proceduralism, we here subscribe to his own earlier apt observation that "justice does not require that men must stand idly by while others destroy the basis of their existence."[20]

Now that we have decided that the right to democratic participation is a genuine human right and should therefore have a place in the Declaration, we still need to say something about its relationship to the rest of the document. This is a debt we owe to Habermas and other pure proceduralists who want to give Article 21 pride of place, which idea we rebuffed for epistemological reasons. While in international human rights law a distinction is made between human rights that are derogable (that is, suspendable) in times of national emergencies and those that are not derogable, the drafters did not use such distinctions. They viewed all the rights in their document as equally important and did not attach particu- lar importance to where in the line-up a certain right was placed, as long as it was placed in the cluster that it had naturally fallen into during the seven drafting stages. The line-up in the document grew organically, and the decision made at the end was to leave them as they had grown. *Pace* Rawls, Articles 18, 19, 20, and 21 were seen as a natural cluster, as were the legal rights in Articles 6 through 12. The status of the right to demo- cratic participation was the same as that of the other articles. This onto- logical equality does not mean that we ourselves cannot view some rights as a means to the delivery of other rights within or outside the same cluster. The drafters themselves did that when in Article 23 they listed "the right to form and join trade unions" after "the right to favorable and just remuneration" because the former is an indispensable means to the implementation of the latter. The idea is that if X is the only means to come to enjoy Y, and Y is a human right, then X should also be seen as human right. A weakening of that causal link would weaken X's claim to being a human right, unless X could claim that status independently of its connection with Y, which it usually can.

For instance, the right to democratic participation is increasingly being accepted as a separate human right by the international legal commu- nity for two reasons. First, theorists and practitioners have in numerous ways come to see that in order to flourish human beings need to be given choices, including in the political realm. When I matched Nussbaum's species capabilities list with the articles in the Declaration, I pointed out that under the ability of having "Control over One's Environment" she first lists our "Being able to participate effectively in political choices that govern one's life; having the right of political participation, protections of free speech and association" (*Frontiers*, 77). These are the capabilities that underlie Articles 19, 20, and 21 of the Declaration. They help make up what leads to human flourishing and the "full and free development of our personalities," as called for in Articles 22, 26, and 29. This connec- tion with human capacities and abilities to function also underlies the title of Sen's book *Development as Freedom*, which figured in our discussion of his views in Chapter 4, section B.

Already in 1981 Sen had made the connection explicit between world poverty and the right to democratic participation.[21] He showed that some of the greatest famines in modern history (like those in Bengal in 1943, Ethiopia in 1972–74, the arid African Sahel in 1973, and Bangladesh in 1974) could have been prevented by the politicians and statesmen in charge at the time. The cause of these famines was not that there was not enough food in the nation or region where the famine occurred, but that those starving to death had no legal access or entitlement to that food. While they were morally entitled to be saved from starvation that was not of their own making, these mostly peasant workers or migrants to cities could no longer grow their own food or purchase it from others. Their production and exchange opportunities were cut down to zero. So they starved to death. Sen argues that better planning on the part of authorities and politicians could have prevented the local shortages from taking place where they did. These millions of deaths were primarily caused by a failure of political leadership. We know this is also true of the great famines caused by Stalin's cruel resettlement policies and by Mao's Great Cultural Leap Forward. Thomas Pogge has given the same disturbing explanation for the roughly 18,000,000 starvation deaths that annually occur in our own times.[22]

His explanation is disturbing to Westerners because Pogge traces these millions of deaths to the political failures of rich Westerners to actively oversee their own countries' foreign policies and aid budgets, among which he counts the trade pacts these governments negotiate. While Sen stressed the right to democratic participation at the effect end of the causal chain, in the lands where the victims lived, Pogge puts his finger on the causal end of that same chain, that is, on the (mostly) rich Westerners that fail to stop their own democratically elected governments from "allowing" corrupt regimes to rob their peoples and countries of their natural resources. Sen's and Pogge's complementary theses are probably still true in 2009, even though we are witnessing a sharp increase in the world's food prices and therefore an increase in starvation deaths due to several nonpolitical causes, such as the world's running out of oil, overall climate change, and more local natural disasters. Sen, for instance, has modified but not withdrawn his previous analysis in light of these new developments.[23] I think it is safe to conclude that the UDHR drafters were decades ahead of their time when—as a reaction to Hitler's crude suspension of the political rights of all his opponents—they placed the right to democratic participation on their list of real human rights. To them that right was no interloper in the domain of genuine human rights.

The means-ends relationship between democratic participation and other human rights has also been confirmed by Joseph Siegel, Michael Weinstein, and Morton Halperin. These researchers took World Bank development indicators from 1960 to the present and designated as poor countries those that had a GDP per capita under $2000 in constant 1995 dollars.[24] They also used the Polity IV index of the University of Maryland, which scores countries from 0 (least democratic) to 10 (most democratic), and called those with a score between 8 and 10 democracies and those with a score between 0 and 2 autocracies. Overlapping these two sets, they ended up with a total of 38 poor autocracies and only 14 poor democracies. While they focused on growth rates for the economies of these countries (which except for eastern Asia were 50 percent higher for poor democracies), they also compared how the respective peoples fared in terms of the "broader measures of well-being." These other measures included such indicators "as life expectancy, access to clean drinking water, literacy rates, agricultural yields and the quality of public-health services." These indicators are of interest to us because they correlate well with people's enjoyment of their human rights. The authors found that when it comes to these measures of well-being low-income democracies "dramatically outdo their autocratic counterparts" (59). In other words, the right to democratic participation is a proven means to the enjoyment of the right to life, to health care and to the development of one's personality generally.

These world poverty data confirm the drafters' supposition that the right to political participation is a key component of the organic tapestry of human rights and should not simply be seen as a Western imposition on the rest of the world. The 1940s moral consensus that conceived the international bill with this right in it was remarkably prescient.

Notes

Introduction: The Need to Think Beyond the Political

1. The results of those archival diggings were published under the title *The Universal Declaration of Human Rights: Origins, Drafting, and Intent* (Philadelphia: University of Pennsylvania Press, 1999) (hereafter cited as Morsink, *Origins*).

2. Lynn Hunt, *Inventing Human Rights: A History* (New York: Norton, 2007), 150–51.

3. Says he: "Whoever becomes the master of a city accustomed to freedom, and does not destroy it, may expect to be destroyed himself; because, when there is a rebellion, such a city justifies itself by calling on the name of liberty and its ancient institutions, never forgotten despite the passing of time and the benefits received from the new ruler"; Niccolo Machiavelli, *The Prince*, trans. George Bull (New York: Penguin, 1981), 48.

4. See Hunt, *Inventing*, chap. 4, "'There Will Be No End of It': The Consequences of Declaring," note 2. See also Jon Elster, "Arguing and Bargaining in Two Constituent Assemblies," *University of Pennsylvania Journal of Constitutional Law* 2 (March 2000): 345. Both authors discuss both the French and the American debates.

5. See note 1.

6. Michael Ignatieff, *Human Rights as Politics and Idolatry*, ed. Amy Gutmann (Princeton, N.J.: Princeton University Press, 2001).

7. William F. Schulz, *In Our Own Best Interest: How Defending Human Rights Benefits Us All* (Boston: Beacon Press, 2001).

8. Isaiah Berlin, *The Proper Study of Mankind*, ed. Henry Hardy and Roger Hausheer (New York: Farrar, Straus and Giroux, 1997), 194.

9. For an elaboration of this claim, see Alan Gewirth, *The Community of Rights* (Chicago: University of Chicago Press, 1996).

10. See, for instance, the essay by David Lyons, "Human Rights and the General Welfare," in *Rights*, ed. David Lyons (Belmont, Calif.: Wadsworth, 1979). For other explorations of the relationship between utilitarianism and human rights, see the essays in R. G. Frey, ed., *Utility and Rights* (Minneapolis: University of Minnesota Press, 1984), and the essays by John Gray, Allan Gibbard, and James Fishkin in *Human Rights*, ed. Ellen Frankel Paul, Jeffrey Paul, and Fred Dycus Miller (Oxford: Blackwell, 1984).

11. Plato, *The Republic*, trans. G. M. A. Grube (Indianapolis: Hackett, 1974), 357b–d.

12. Emil Fackenheim, *To Mend the World: Foundations of Post-Holocaust Jewish Thought* (Bloomington: Indiana University Press, 1940), 250.

Chapter 1. The Metaphysics of Inherence

1. United Nations General Assembly, Official Records (GAOR), Third Session, Third Committee (1948), 37. Unless otherwise indicated, the UN documents cited in this book are from the years 1947 and 1948. The designation "GAOR" refers to just the December 1948 General Assembly debates, while "GAOR Third" refers to the debates in the Third (Humanitarian, Social and Cultural) Committee that were held earlier that fall. The "E/CN.4/SR" designations in the text refer to the numbered 1947 and 1948 Sessions of the Human Rights Commission or, when preceded by "AC.1," to the Sessions of the Drafting Sub-Committee. "AC.2" refers to one of the Working Groups set up by the Second Session. The very last number in these UN textual references is the page number of whatever document is being cited.

2. Cited in A. I. Melden, *Human Rights* (Belmont, Calif.: Wadsworth, 1970), 138–39.

3. Except for those citing Melden, the references in this section to early American documents are to the seven volumes by Francis Newton Thorpe, *The Federal and State Constitutions* (Washington, D.C.: Government Printing Office, 1909). This first citation is to volume 5, where we also read that "all men have a *natural and inalienable right* to worship Almighty God" (5:3082). For similar natural rights language, see the 1784 New Jersey Constitution (5:2599), the July 1977 Vermont Constitution (6:3737), the July 1780 Massachusetts Declaration (3:1889), and the 1784 New Hampshire Constitution (4:2451).

4. This (37) and all other references to texts surrounding the French Revolution and from the debates in the French General Assembly of 1789 are taken from Lynn Hunt, *The French Revolution and Human Rights: A Brief Documentary History* (Boston: St. Martin's, 1996); emphasis added throughout.

5. The existence of slavery and the slave trade became an obvious testing ground for these "rights of humanity." In 1770 Abbé Raynal anonymously published his *Philosophical and Political History of the Settlements and Trade of the Europeans in the East and West Indies.* He pleads with his readers to "hasten to the *light of reason and the sentiments of nature* [rather than] to the blind ferociousness of our ancestors" (Hunt, 55).

6. For this point, see Pauline Maier, *American Scripture: Making the Declaration of Independence* (New York: Knopf, 1997), 167.

7. Paul Gordon Lauren, *The Evolution of International Human Rights: Visions Seen,* 2nd ed. (Philadelphia: University of Pennsylvania Press, 2003), and Lynn Hunt, *Inventing Human Rights: A History* (New York: Norton, 2007). Even more recently, Nicholas Wolterstorff has defended the thesis that the origin of the idea of human or natural rights goes all the way back to the Hebrew Bible and the New Testament Gospels, from which it intruded on the reigning eudaimonistic theories of late antiquity to find its way to the Enlightenment, which is where most theorists wrongly (according to Wolterstorff's well-constructed case) begin their narrative. See Wolterstorff, *Justice Rights and Wrongs* (Princeton, N.J.: Princeton University Press, 2008).

8. In her interpretive study *Inventing Human Rights*, Hunt gives additional references that come close to our phraseology of "human rights," such as Richard

Price's reference to "the rights of humanity" (1776), those from seventeenth-century natural law theorists Hugo Grotius and Samuel Pufendorf, and especially the eighteenth-century adaptation of these views by Jaques Burlamaqui.

9. Thomas Pogge, *World Poverty and Human Rights* (Malden, Mass.: Blackwell, 2002), 56.

10. I discuss Rawls's views on human rights in Chapter 3, section B.

11. In his commentary on Article 1, Tore Lindholm admits that the "locution 'are born' (etc.) was interpreted by most speakers . . . to indicate the pre-positive and normative status of freedom and equal dignity." See Bjørn Eide et al., eds., *The Universal Declaration of Human Rights: A Commentary* (Oslo: Scandinavian University Press, 1992), "Article 1: A New Beginning," 48, referred to in the text as *Comm.*

12. Several Catholic South American countries objected to the phrase "are born" because it did not go back to the beginning of a person's life. See, for instance, the Venezuelan and Mexican observations made in the Third Committee (111, 122).

13. For a fuller discussion of these issues, see Morsink, *Origins*, section 8.1.

14. See Alasdair MacIntyre, *After Virtue: A Study in Moral Theory* (Notre Dame, Ind.: University of Notre Dame Press, 1981), 51–52.

15. Richard Rorty, "The Priority of Democracy to Philosophy" in *Prospects for a Common Morality*, ed. Gene Outka and John P. Reeder, Jr. (Princeton, N.J.: Princeton University Press, 1993), 255.

16. Allan Gewirth, *Human Rights: Essays on Justification and Applications* (Chicago: University of Chicago Press, 1982), 12. Richard Wasserstrom says that a human right "must be possessed by all human beings, as well as only by human beings," which amounts to the same thing. See Wasserstrom, "Rights, Human Rights, and Racial Discrimination," in *Rights*, ed. David Lyons (Belmont, Calif.: Wadsworth, 1979), 47.

17. Judith Jarvis Thomson, *The Realm of Rights* (Cambridge, Mass.: Harvard University Press, 1990), 88.

18. See Morsink, *Origins*, Chapter 7.

19. Onora O'Neill, "Agents of Justice," in *Global Justice*, ed. Thomas Pogge (Malden, Mass.: Blackwell, 2001), 190.

20. See the American Declaration of the Rights and Duties of Man, adopted in Bogotá, Colombia, 1948. This and many other documents are available on the Web and reprinted in Ian Brownlie and Guy S. Goodwin-Gill, eds., *Basic Documents on Human Rights* (Oxford: Oxford University Press, 2006), 927–32. In these notes I give readily accessible URLs for these instruments. See American Declaration of the Rights and Duties of Man, http://www1.umn.edu/humanrts/oasinstr/zoas2dec.htm (from the University of Minnesota) linked from the ASIL database. Also found from the UN database, http://daccessdds.un.org/doc/UNDOC/GEN/GL9/001/94/PDF/GL900194.pdfOpen Element

21. See African Charter on Human and Peoples' Rights, adopted June 17, 1981, http://www.hrcr.org/docs/Banjul/afrhr.htm.

22. For good discussions of the interface of human rights with these and other organizations see Philip Alston, ed., *Non-State Actors and Human Rights*; Alston, ed., *Labour Rights as Human Rights* (Oxford: Oxford University Press, 2005); and relevant essays in Philip Alston and Mary Robinson, eds., *Human Rights and Development* (Oxford: Oxford University Press, 2005).

23. Martha C. Nussbaum, *Frontiers of Justice* (Cambridge, Mass.: Belknap Press of Harvard University Press, 2006), 277.

24. This is Joel Feinberg's phrase in "The Nature and Value of Rights," in Lyons, ed., *Rights*, 89. Feinberg uses this very feature of generality and vagueness to question the universality of social, economic, and cultural rights, but I do not see why his own criterion of when a claim can be said to be valid should apply only to civil and political human rights, not social and economic ones as well.

25. Wasserstrom, "Rights, Human Rights and Racial Discrimination," 50.

26. Supplementary Convention on the Abolition of Slavery, the Slave Trade, and Institutions and Practices Similar to Slavery, 226 U.N.T.S. 3, *entered into force* April 30, 1957, http://www.unhchr.ch/html/menu3/b/30.htm.

27. Ibid.

28. Declaration on the Elimination of All Forms of Intolerance and of Discrimination Based on Religion or Belief, http://www.unhchr.ch/html/menu3/b/d_intole.htm.

29. International Covenant on Civil and Political Rights, Adopted and opened for signature, ratification and accession by General Assembly resolution 2200A (XXI) of 16 December 1966 - http://www.unhchr.ch/html/menu3/b/a_ccpr. htm, and International Covenant on Economic, Social and Cultural Rights, Adopted and opened for signature, ratification, and accession by General Assembly resolution 2200A (XXI) of 16 December 1966, http://www.unhchr.ch/html/menu3/b/a_cescr.htm.

30. International Convention on the Protection of the Rights of All Migrant Workers and Members of Their Families, http://www2.ohchr.org/english/law/cmw.htm.

31. Vienna Declaration and Programme of Action, http://www.unhchr.ch/huridocda/huridoca.nsf/(Symbol)/A.CONF.157.23.En

32. See http://www.un.org/documents/ga/res/43/a43r173.htm.

33. See http://www.un.org/documents/ga/res/45/a45r111.htm.

34. Convention Against Torture and Other Cruel, Inhuman or Degrading Treatment or Punishment, http://www.unhchr.ch/html/menu3/b/h_cat39. htm. The hard copy for this reference can be found in *Human Rights: A Compilation of International Instruments*, vol. 1 (First Part), *Universal Instruments* (New York: United Nations, 2002), 460.

35. See http://unesdoc.unesco.org/images/0010/001096/109687eb.pdf.

36. See http://www.unhchr.ch/html/menu3/b/o_nonnat.htm.

37. See Wesley Newcomb Hohfeld, *Fundamental Legal Conceptions* (New Haven, Conn.: Yale University Press, 1919). Carl Wellman's definition of what a human right is contains an especially clear echo of some of the concepts Hohfeld analyzed. According to Wellman, a human right is a "cluster of ethical liberties, claims, powers and immunities that together constitute a system of ethical autonomy possessed by an individual human being vis-à-vis the state." See his "A New Conception of Human Rights," in *The Philosophy of Human Rights*, ed. Morton E. Winston (Belmont, Calif.: Wadsworth, 1989), 93. See also L. W. Sumner, *The Moral Foundation of Rights* (Oxford: Clarendon Press, 1987); Diana Meyers, *Inalienable Rights: A Defense* (New York: Columbia University Press, 1985). For a recent, very incisive discussion of Hohfeld's theory, see Nicholas Wolterstorff, *Justice Rights and Wrongs* (Princeton, N.J.: Princeton University Press, 2008), 249–63.

38. Wellman, "New Conception of Human Rights," 93. See also Sumner: "It is thus quite inconceivable that we have any rights simply because we are human. If this is what is implied by the rhetoric of human rights, then that rhetoric has been used to serve a discriminatory, because speciesist, programme" (*Moral Foundation of Rights*, 206). And Carlos Santiago Nino, *The Ethics of Human Rights* (Oxford:

Clarendon Press, 1991), 36: "We must accept that . . . moral citizenship is not a question of biological theory (or, for that matter, of any other factual theory) but of political theory, that is, of moral theory in a broad sense. That means we need a radical change in philosophical strategy in the characterization of moral personality. We must begin with the moral principles from which basic rights derive, and then go on to define the class of moral persons as the class of all those individuals (or entities) who possess the properties which are in fact necessary to enjoy or exercise those rights." Both Sumner and Nino defend various systems of moral principles from which they then construct or deduce moral rights human beings possess. As these citations show, neither of them believes that we have such things as inherent human rights by virtue of membership in our species.

39. Rex Martin, "Human Rights and Civil Rights," in Winston, ed., *Philosophy of Human Rights*, 79, n. 30.

40. Martin explains and defends the thesis that "Rights, for Rawls, are not free floating claims, of the sort often called moral. They are, rather, details of an institutional arrangement in which the claims and the means for delivering on it are linked closely together." See Rex Martin, *Rawls and Rights* (Lawrence: University Press of Kansas, 1985), 28. For a similar assessment of Rawls's position on human rights, see Stanley Hoffmann's review of Stephen Shute and Susan Hurley, eds., *On Human Rights: The Oxford Amnesty Lectures* (New York: Basic Books, 1993), *New York Review of Books*, November 2, 1995, 52ff.

41. Rex Martin, *A System of Rights* (Oxford: Clarendon Press, 1993), 90–91.

42. Raymond Geuss, *History and Illusion in Politics* (Cambridge: Cambridge University Press, 2001), 139.

Chapter 2. Obeying the Conscience of Humanity

1. See the comments by Minerva Bernadino of the Dominican Republic, at GAOR Third, 93; Abdul Rahman Kayala of Syria at UNGA 922; Geoffrey Wilson of the UK at ECN.4/SR.50/8; Ulla Lindstrom of Sweden, at Third, Article 16, 403); Michael Klekovkin of the Ukrainian Socialist Republic at Third, Article 3, 175; and Peng Chung Chang of China at ECN.4/SR.50/17.

2. René Cassin, "Historique de la Déclaration," in Cassin, *La pensée et l'action* (Paris: Lalou, 1972), 118.

3. Alan Dershowitz, *Rights from Wrongs: A Secular Theory of the Origins of Rights* (New York: Basic Books, 2004).

4. See Dershowitz, *Rights from Wrongs*, chap. 2, "World War Two as Catalyst."

5. Cass Sunstein, *The Second Bill of Rights: FDR's Unfinished Revolution and Why We Need It More Than Ever* (New York: Basic Books, 2004), chap. 3, "Rights from Wrongs: Roosevelt's Constitutional Order."

6. Because Gewirth does hold that human rights really are inherent in the human person, his dialogical approach is not merely justificatory in the way Rawls's and Habermas's approaches are. That is why we are far more sympathetic to Gewirth's use of reason (though in the end it falls short) than to the arguments of Rawls, Habermas, and their followers.

7. Lynn Hunt, *Inventing Human Rights: A History* (New York: Norton, 2007).

8. UN DOC No. 96 (1) (1946) and E/CN.4/46/ 7 (1948).

9. Philippe de la Chapelle, *La Déclaration universelle des droits de l'homme et le catholicisme* (Paris: Pichon et Durand-Auzias, Librairie Générale de Droit et de Jurisprudence, 1967), 44.

10. American Anthropological Association, "Statement on Human Rights," in *The Philosophy of Human Rights*, ed. Morton E. Winston (Belmont, Calif.: Wadsworth, 1989), 116.

11. Abdullahi Ahmed An-Na'im, "Conclusion," in *Human Rights in Cross-Cultural Perspectives: A Quest for Consensus*, ed. Abdullahi Ahmed An-Na'im (Philadelphia: University of Pennsylvania Press, 1992), 427–28. He defends this view in his own contribution to this collection ("Toward a Cross-Cultural Approach to Defining International Standards of Human Rights The Meaning of Cruel, Inhuman, or Degrading Treatment or Punishment," 20–43) and especially in "Problems of Universal Cultural Legitimacy for Human Rights," in *Human Rights in Africa: Cross-Cultural Perspectives*, ed. Abdullahi Ahmed An-Na'im and Francis Deng (Washington, D.C.: Brookings Institution, 1990), 331–68.

12. Adamantia Pollis and Peter Schwab, "Human Rights: A Western Construct with Limited Applicability," in *Human Rights: Cultural and Ideological Perspectives*, ed. Adamantia Pollis and Peter Schwab (New York: Praeger, 1980), 1.

13. Alison Dundes Renteln, *International Human Rights: Universalism Versus Relativism*, Frontiers of Anthropology 6 (Newbury Park, Calif.: Sage, 1990), 53.

14. As quoted by James Silk, "Traditional Culture and the Prospect for Human Rights in Africa," in An-Na'im, ed., *Human Rights in Cross-Cultural Perspectives*, 309.

15. Antonio Cassese, "The General Assembly: Historical Perspective, 1945–1989," in *The United Nations and Human Rights: A Critical Appraisal*, ed. Philip Alston (Oxford: Clarendon Press, 1992), 31.

16. See the last sections of Susan Sontag, *Regarding the Pain of Others* (New York: Farrar, Straus Giroux, 2003), where she discusses the importance of the settings in which atrocity photographs are displayed.

17. Pollis and Schwab, *Human Rights*, 4.

18. Amy Eckert, "Universality by Consensus: The Evolution of Universality in the Drafting of the UDHR," *Human Rights & Human Welfare* 1, 2 (April 2001): 21–24.

19. See Morsink, *Origins*, chaps. 5, 6.

20. See ibid., section 2.5.

21. See ibid., section 1.3.

22. See ibid., section 8.1.

23. See ibid., section 3.5.

24. Eleanor Roosevelt, chairperson of the proceedings (of both the Commission and its drafting subsidiary) had far too much integrity to let this happen, and it was not even attempted. For her role, see ibid., section 1.5.

25. John P. Humphrey, *Human Rights & the United Nations: A Great Adventure* (Dobbs Ferry, N.Y.: Transnational Publishers, 1984).

26. For details on both clauses see Dershowitz, *Rights from Wrongs*, chap. 3, section 2.

27. For details of these debates see A/C.3/400; A/C.3/AC.4/3; 400/Rev.1/856–863. I summarize them in *Origins*, section 3.2.

28. See ibid., section 1.4.

29. See ibid., section 3.1.

30. See ibid., section 2.4.

31. Martha C. Nussbaum, *Upheavals of Thought: The Intelligence of Emotions* (Cambridge: Cambridge University Press, 2001), especially chap. 8, "Compassion and Public Life."

32. Jonathan Glover, *Humanity: A Moral History of the Twentieth Century* (New Haven, Conn.: Yale University Press, 2000), 345.

33. See Susan Walz, "Universal Human Rights: The Contribution of Muslim States," *Human Rights Quarterly* 26 (2004): 799–844.

34. Christopher L. Blakesley et al., eds., *The International Legal System Cases and Materials*, 5th ed. (New York: Foundation Press, 2001), "The Nuremberg Principles Report of the International Law Commission," 1265 (hereafter Blakesley).

35. "Nuremberg War Crimes Trials" (1947), 1, *Trial of Major War Criminals* 171, Blakesley, 1268.

36. See Morsink, *Origins*, section 2.3.

37. Cited in Henry J. Steiner and Philip Alston, eds., *International Human Rights in Context: Law, Politics, Morals*, 2nd ed. (Oxford: Oxford University Press, 2000), 124.

38. As reported by Jonathan Glover, *Humanity: A Moral History of the Twentieth Century* (New Haven, Conn.: Yale University Press, 1999), 63.

39. *United States v. Calley*, U.S. Court of Military Appeals, 1973, 48 C.M.R. 19; Blakesley, 1299–1300.

40. *United States v. Staff Sergeant (E-6) Walter Griffin*, RA 17542182, U.S. Army, Company D, 1st Battalion (Airborne), 8th Cavalry, 1st Cavalry Division (Airmobile), APO San Francisco 96490 CM 416805; Blakesley, 1306.

41. Mark J. Osiel, *Obeying Orders: Atrocity, Military Discipline, and the Law of War* (New Brunswick, N.J: Transaction Publishers, 1999), 25.

42. *In Re Eck and Others (The Peleus)*, Hamburg, British Military Court, October 20, 1945, 13 Am. Dig; Blakesley, 1282.

43. *Public Prosecutor v. Leopold*, Austria Supreme Court 1967; Blakesley, 1294.

44. *The Finta Case*, Supreme Court of Canada, 1994 28 C.R. (4th) 265; Blakesley, 1309.

45. Yoram Dinstein, *The Defence of "Obedience to Superior Orders" in International Law* (Leyden: Nijhoff, 1965), 9.

46. Cited in English by Carlos Santiago Nino, "The Duty to Punish Past Abuses of Human Rights Put into Context: The Case of Argentina," *Yale Law Journal* 100 (1991): 2625, n. 28.

47. The first redraft of the code was disappointing in its view that "anyone acting under orders during the dirty war should be presumed innocent." See Ian Guest, *Behind the Disappearances: Argentina's Dirty War Against Human Rights and the United Nations* (Philadelphia: University of Pennsylvania Press, 1990), 552–53, n. 2.

48. See Nino, "The Duty to Punish," 2633.

49. Argentine National Commission on the Disappeared, *Nunca Más* (New York: Farrar Strauss & Giroux, 1986).

50. *New York Times*, July 15, 2005, A3.

51. UNGA/RES/57228B/Article 1, May 2003.

52. Steven R. Ratner and Jason S. Abrams, *Accountability for Human Rights Atrocities in International Law: Beyond the Nuremberg Legacy*, 2nd ed. (Oxford: Oxford University Press, 2001), 270–76.

53. For both citations see Cambodian Royal Decree NS/RKM/1004/006 (Reach Kram) of October 4, 2006 (accessed June 3, 2008), Articles 3 and 29, pp. 2, 8 respectively, http://www.cambodia.gov.kh/krt/pdfs/Kram percent20and percent20KR percent20Law percent20amendments percent2027 percent20Oct percent202004 percent20—percent20Eng.pdf

54. Carlos Santiago Nino, *Radical Evil on Trial* (New Haven, Conn.: Yale University Press, 1996), 180.

55. See "AR 15–16 Investigation of the Abu Ghraib Prison and 205th Military

Intelligence Brigade LTG Anthony Jones pages 6–33 and AR 15–16 Investigation of the Abu Ghraib Detention Facility and 205th Military Intelligence Brigade MG George R. Fay," 34–176, reprinted under the heading "The Jones/Fay Report" (401–579) in *Torture and Truth: America, Abu Ghraib and the War on Terror*, ed. Mark Danner (New York: New York Review of Books, 2004), 423. A good start for an outside (nongovernmental) report on this Abu Ghraib scandal can be found in Philip Gourevitch and Errol Morris, *Standard Operating Procedure* (New York: Penguin, 2008)

56. "New Army Rules Snarl Talks with McCain on Detainee Issue," *New York Times*, December 14, 2005, A1, A15: "The new manual, the first revision in 13 years, will specifically prohibit practices like stripping prisoners, keeping them in stressful positions for a long time, imposing dietary restrictions, employing police dogs to intimidate prisoners and using sleep deprivation as a tool to get them to talk, Army officials said. In that regard, it imposes new restrictions on what interrogators are allowed to do. Those practices were not included in the manual in use when most of the abuses occurred at Abu Ghraib in Iraq in the fall of 2003, but neither were they specifically banned." The next day (October 15) the House followed the Senate and voted to adopt the McCain amendment banning torture with 308 votes for and 122 against; as it turned out, however, some crucial compromises allowed the president far more room than the public had been made to believe.

57. The *New York Times*, March 2, 2008, Wk10 gave this list of practices the Manual presently bans: "forcing a prisoner to be naked, perform sexual acts or pose in a sexual manner. Placing hoods or sacks over the head of a prisoner, and using duct tape over the eyes. Applying beatings, electric shocks, burns or other forms of physical pain. Waterboarding. Using military working dogs. Inducing hypothermia or heat injury. Conducting mock executions. Depriving a prisoner of necessary food, water or medical care."

58. *New York Times*, June 30, 2006, A21.

59. "Whether the Soldier or contractor knew, at the time of the acts, that the conduct violated any law or standard, is not an element of the definition. In other words, the conduct that met the definition would be 'abuse' independent of the actor's knowledge that the conduct violated any law or standard" (Jones-Fay 423). Soldiers involved in these more serious cases "knew they were violating the approved techniques and procedures" (424).

60. Army Field Manual, "Remedies for Violations of International Law; War Crimes, Section IV Defenses Not Available," chap. 8, para. 509, http://www.globalsecurity.org/military/library/policy/army/fm/27–10/Ch8.htm (accessed June 3, 2008).

61. Army Field Manual, para. 154: "The United States normally punishes war crimes as such only if they are committed by enemy nationals or by persons serving in the interests of the enemy state. Violations of the law of war committed by persons subject to military law of the United States usually constitute violations of the Uniform Code of Military Justice and are prosecuted under the UCMJ. Commanders must insure that war crimes committed by members of their forces against enemy personnel are promptly and adequately punished."

62. For these texts, see International Covenant on Civil and Political Rights, http://www.unhchr.ch/html/menu3/b/a_ccpr.htm and Convention Against Torture and Other Cruel, Inhuman or Degrading Treatment or Punishment, http://www.unhchr.ch/html/menu3/b/h_cat39.htm. I am here relying on the legal analysis by the Association of the Bar of the City of New York, Committee

on International Human Rights [and] Committee on Military Affairs and Justice, "Human Rights Standards Applicable to the United States' Interrogation of Detainees," report, April 2004, in *The Torture Papers: The Road to Abu Ghraib*, ed. Karen J. Greenberg and Joshua L. Dratel (Cambridge: Cambridge University Press, 2005), 557–611.

63. Article 1 defines torture as "any act by which severe pain or suffering, whether physical or mental, is intentionally inflicted on a person for such purposes as obtaining from him or a third person information or a confession, punishing him for an act he or a third person has committed, or intimating or coercing him or a third person, or for any reason based on discrimination of any kind, when such pain or suffering is inflicted by or at the instigation of or with the consent or acquiescence of a public official or other person acting in an official capacity. It does not include pain or suffering arising only from, inherent in or incidental to lawful sanctions."

64. The domestic legal texts also include the Foreign Affairs Reform and Restructuring Act of 1998, together with the Immigration and Naturalization Service regulations that effectuate the FARR Act. Included as well is Section 2340 of the U.S. Criminal Code; both are meant to implement the Torture Convention and both also domesticate the meaning of the key terms involved. For support of this claim see the New York City Bar Association report, "Human Rights Standards."

65. All references in the text to the articles of the Yugoslav Tribunal Charter are taken from the official UN version, adopted May 25, 1993, as amended May 13, 1998, http://www.un.org/icty/legaldoc-e/basic/statut/statute-feb06–e.pdf (accessed June 3, 2008). The first category of crimes comprises "serious violations of international humanitarian law" (Article 1) and of "grave breaches of the Geneva Conventions of 1949" (Article 2), many of which have to do with the treatment of prisoners of war, such as "willful killing"; "torture or inhuman treatment, including biological experiments"; and "taking civilians as hostages." The second category, involving "violations of the laws and customs of war" (Article 3), prohibits "poisonous weapons"; "wanton destruction of cities"; and "willful damage to religious, educational and cultural institutions." The third category prohibits the crime of genocide and forbids, for instance, "killing members of the group," "causing serious bodily or mental harm to members of the group," and "imposing measures intended to prevent births within the group" or "forcibly transferring children of the group to another group." The fourth and last power is the one to prosecute "Crimes against humanity" (Article 5). In this ICTFY statute these crimes are still linked to situations of "armed conflict," a connection dropped in Rwanda ICC statutes cited below. It holds any person responsible for crimes "directed against any civilian population: (a) murder; (b) extermination; (c) enslavement; (d) deportation; (e) imprisonment; (f) torture; (g) rape; (h) persecutions on political, racial and religious grounds; (i) other inhumane acts."

66. The main defendants before the Yugoslav Tribunal are, of course, deceased President Slobodan Milosevic and "his" generals, such as Radovan Karadzic, apprehended 2008, and Ratko Mladic, still at large. For a discussion of various types of responsibility and the differences between them, see Norman Cigar and Paul Williams, *Indictment at the Hague: The Milosevic Regime and Crimes of the Balkan Wars* (New York: New York University Press, 2002), 39.

67. "After Srebrenica fell to besieging Serbian forces in July 1995, a truly terrible massacre of the Muslim population appears to have taken place. The evi-

dence tendered by the Prosecutor describes scenes of unimaginable savagery; thousands of men executed and buried in mass graves, hundreds of men buried alive, men and women mutilated and slaughtered, children killed before their mothers' eyes, a grandfather forced to eat the liver of his own grandson. These are truly scenes from hell, written on the darkest pages of human history." ICFY Press Release, Tribunal Doc. CC/PIO/020-E (November 10, 1995), cited in Cigar and Williams, *Indictment at the Hague*, 46.

68. A *New York Times* editorial, April 20, 2008, Wk9, reported that Bush administration officials at the highest level of government had "squeezed in dozenz of meetings in the White House Situation Room to organize and give legal cover to prisoner abuse, including brutal methods that civilized nations consider to be torture" and that "Mr. Bush told ABC News this month that he knew of these meetings and approved of the result."

69. For an articulation of these and related questions, see, for instance, "The Torture Complex," *The Nation*, special issue, December 26, 2005.

70. Drazen Erdemovic was a Croat locksmith, whose defense counsel portrayed him as "an easygoing young man" of "honest disposition" who "showed no signs of bigotry or intolerance." This seems to be confirmed by the fact that he "married a wife of a different ethnic origin" and witness testimony that the accused used to be part of a group of "multi-ethnic friends." Also, his "lack of commitment to any ethnic group in the conflict is demonstrated by the fact that he was by turns a reluctant participant" in the Army of the Republic of Bosnia-Herzegovina, the Croatian Defense Council, and the Bosnian Serb Army. He said he chose the 10th Sabotage Detachment of the Bosnian Serb Army "because it did not involve the loss of human lives," because "there were other non-Serb soldiers" in it, and because "it did not have a reputation for brutality at the material time" (16iii). The couple have one child, and he told the Court that he joined these various armies to support his family. This information can be found in Sentencing Judgment of the Trial Chamber, handed down March 5, 1998, para. 16, "Mitigating Factors," 8–9, http://www.un.org/icty/erdemovic/trialc/judge ment/erd-tsj980305e.htm (accessed June 3, 2008).

71. For this citation, see Sentencing Judgment in the Trial Chamber, which contains extensive citations from what the defendant said before Trial Chamber I, May 31, 1996, http://www.un.org/icty/erdemovic/trialc/judgement/erd-tsj980305e.htm (accessed June 3, 2008).

72. See *Prosecutor v. Drazen Erdemovic*, Separate and Dissenting Opinion of Judge Cassese, Appeals Chamber, October 7, 1997, para. 16 (9), http://www.un.org/icty/erdemovic/appeal/judgement/erd-adojcas971007e.htm (accessed June 3, 2008) (hereafter "Cassese").

73. See *Prosecutor v. Drazen Erdemovic*, Sentencing Judgment, March 5, 1998, http://www.un.org/icty/erdemovic/trialc/judgement/erd-tsj980305e.htm, para. 7(b) (2) (accessed June 3, 2008).

74. See *Prosecutor v. Drazen Erdemovic*, Appeals Chamber, IV Disposition (4) (10), http://www.un.org/icty/erdemovic/appeal/judgement/erd-aj971007e.htm (accessed June 3, 2008).

75. All references to Articles of the Rwanda Statute are from the official UN Web site (accessed June 10, 2008), starting p. 43, http://69.94.11.53/ENGLISH/basicdocs/statute/2007.pdf. Whereas the Yugoslav Charter introduced this list (Murder, Extermination, Enslavement, Deportation, Imprisonment, Torture, Rape, Political, Racial and Religious Persecutions and Other Inhumane Acts) as criminal "when committed as part of a widespread attack against any civilian

population," the Rwanda Charter adds the clause "on national, political, ethnic, racial or religious grounds."

76. References to the trial of the two defendants discussed here are taken from the official UN Rwanda Tribunal Web site, http://www.ictrcaselaw.org/docs/doc9039.pdf. Numbers in parentheses are to paragraph numbers of this site.

77. Kayeshima was born into a Hutu family to a father who was first a teacher and then a janitor. His mother and seven siblings were "uneducated farmers" (§1.3). After being appointed registrar, he went on to study medicine and practiced at the National University of Rwanda and in a Ugandan refugee camp, where he was sent by the government. From 1986 to 1991 he was medical director of the hospital of Nyanza. In July 1993 he was appointed prefect of the Kibuye Prefecture, in charge of civil and police matters for that community. After the death of the Rwandan president he was reappointed to this post, putting him in a command position at the time the massacres took place. He is married to "a Rwandan woman by the name of Mukandoli," who has an advanced degree in psychology. Ruzindana was born into a wealthy, well-known, respected Hutu family. His father was Bourgmestre (mayor) of the Mugonero Commune. He set up a successful import-export company and married a woman he had known since childhood. His wife's father was a Tutsi, and she testified before the Court that it was possible to pay to have one's identity card changed to read "Hutu," which she did. The couple has two children.

78. (1) The Catholic Church and the Home St. Jean complex in Kibu town, "where thousands of men, women and children were killed and numerous people injured around April 17, 1994"; (2) the Stadium in Kibuye town, "where thousands of men, women and children were killed and numerous persons injured on about 18 and 19 April 1994"; (3) the Church in Mubuga, "where thousands of men, women and children were killed and numerous persons injured between about 14 and 17 April 1994"; and (4) the massacres in the Bisesero area, "where thousands of men, women and children were killed and numerous people injured between about 10 April and 30 June 1994" (§1.1).

79. The Tribunal records contain a similar account of hundreds of gruesome killings ordered and executed by Georges Anderson Nderumbumwe Rutaganda, a well-educated Seventh Day Adventist, agricultural engineer, and prominent member of Interhamwe zap MRND (a Hutu militia movement), where he served as second vice president of the organization's youth branch; http://www.ictrcaselaw.org/docs/doc5088.pdf.

80. All references to this case are from the official UN Web site for the Rwanda Tribunal with numbers in parentheses from the paragraphs of the indicated judgment. This first reference is to section 1.5 §51; http://www.ictrcaselaw.org/docs/doc15154.pdf.

81. Jonathan Glover, *Humanity: A Moral History of the Twentieth Century* (New Haven, Conn.: Yale University Press, 2000).

82. For the standard eighteenth-century exposition of these four tenets, see Francis Hutcheson, *A System of Moral Philosophy* (New York: Augustus Kelley, 1968). I will be using contemporary writers.

83. Michael Ignatieff, *Human Rights as Politics and Idolatry* (Princeton, N.J.: Princeton University Press, 2001), 88.

84. W. D. Ross, *The Right and the Good* (Indianapolis: Hackett, 1988), 33.

85. Cited by James H. Hutson in *The Founders on Religion: A Book of Quotations* (Princeton, N.J.: Princeton University Press, 2005), 148.

86. Judith Jarvis Thompson, *The Realm of Rights* (Cambridge, Mass.: Har-

vard University Press, 1990). Rex Martin, *A System of Rights* (Oxford: Clarendon Press, 1993); see Chapter 1 for a discussion of Martin and the fallacy of implementation.

87. Calley told journalist John Sach: "As for me, killing these men in My Lai didn't haunt me—I didn't—I couldn't kill for the pleasure of it. We weren't in My Lai to kill human beings. We were there to kill Ideology that is carried by—I don't know. Pawns. Blobs. Pieces of flesh, and I wasn't in My Lai to destroy intelligent men. I was there to destroy an intangible idea. . . . Personally, I didn't kill any Vietnamese that day. I mean personally. I represented the United States of America. My country" (Blakesley, 1294).

88. Among contextual intuitionists I count William H, Davis, "The Morally Obvious," *Journal of Value Inquiry* 19 (1985): 263–77; Mark T. Nelson, "Intuitionism and Conservatism," *Metaphilosophy* 17, 2 (April 1980): 127–34; John Kekes, "Moral Intuitionism," *American Philosophical Quarterly* 23, 1 (January 1986): 83–93; and Richard Rorty, "Human Rights, Rationality, and Sentimentality," in *Human Rights: The Oxford Amnesty Lectures 1993*, ed. Stephen Shute and Susan Hurley (Oxford: Oxford University Press, 1993), 111–35.

89. Margaret MacDonald, "Natural Rights," in *Human Rights*, ed. A. I. Melden (Belmont, Calif.: Wadsworth, 1970), 54.

90. For an in-depth development of this point, see Martha Nussbaum, *Upheavals of Thought: The Intelligence of Emotions* (Cambridge: Cambridge University Press, 2001). Her thesis is that human emotions, especially compassion, are in themselves, when rightly nourished, a vehicle of thought and knowledge and therefore worthy of epistemic attention.

91. "And indeed even when the decision of the moral faculty relates primarily to some particular action, there is commonly at least a latent belief that similar conduct would be right for all similarly constituted persons in similar circumstances." See Henry Sidgwick, *Methods of Ethics* (London: Macmillan, 1877), 88.

92. Albert Camus, *The Rebel* (New York: Knopf, 1956), 13.

93. Susan Sontag, *Regarding the Pain of Others* (New York: Farrar, Straus and Giroux, 2003), 40.

94. This speech was reprinted in *The Nation*, May 5, 2003, 11–14.

95. Sontag formulated the principle in this case as follows: "It's wrong to oppress and humiliate a whole people. To deprive them systematically of lodging and proper nutrition, to destroy their habitations, means of livelihood, access to education and medical care, and ability to consort with one another" (12).

96. UNESCO, *Human Rights: Comments and Interpretations* (Westport, Conn.: Greenwood, 1973), 263.

97. On Wednesday, December 3, 1947, Professor Fernand Dehousse, Belgian representative to the Commission, complained that he had been "very sorry" to find that UNESCO, a specialized agency, had just published a report on "The Bases of an International Bill of Human Rights," a report the UNESCO Committee had sent to the Human Rights Commission of the United Nations (E/CN.4/SR.26/11). The Commission decided "not to reproduce the [unauthorized] UNESCO report for distribution to all the members of the United Nations" (E/CN.4/SR.26/16). A few days later, on December 26, Jacques Havet, UNESCO representative to the Commission, wrote Eleanor Roosevelt, the Chairperson of the Commission, a letter explaining what the Commission had done and why. There is no indication that this explanation changed the Commission's lack of interest in rational arguments or intellectual constructions about human rights.

98. Stuart Hampshire, *Innocence and Experience* (Cambridge, Mass.: Harvard University Press, 1989), 90.

99. See Glover, *Humanity*, 78.

100. H. R. Pritchard, "Does Moral Philosophy Rest on a Mistake?" *Mind* n.s. 21, 81 (January 1912): 16.

101. William Gass, "The Case of the Obliging Stranger" *Philosophical Review* 66, no 2 (April 1957): 196–97.

102. David Little, "The Nature and Basis of Human Rights" in *Prospects for a Common Morality*, ed. Gene Outka and John P. Reeder, Jr. (Princeton, N.J.: Princeton University Press, 1993), 81–82.

103. For the first citation, see Little, "Nature and Basis," 80, 83; for the second see Ross, *The Right and the Good*, 26.

104. Sidgwick, *Methods of Ethics*, 85.

105. See Samuel P. Oliner and Pearl M. Oliner, *The Altruistic Personality: Rescuers of Jews in Nazi Europe* (New York: Free Press, 1988); Gay Block and Malka Drucker, *Rescuers: Portraits of Moral Courage in the Holocaust* (New York: Holmes & Meier, 1992); Eva Fogelman, *Conscience and Courage: Rescuers of Jews During the Holocaust* (New York: Anchor Books, 1994); Kristin Renwick Monroe, *The Heart of Altruism: Perceptions of a Common Morality* (Princeton, N.J.: Princeton University Press, 1996).

Chapter 3. The Shortcomings of the Golden Rule

1. Abdullahi Ahmed An-Na'im, "Problems of Universal Cultural Legitimacy," in *Human Rights in Africa: Cross-Cultural Perspectives*, ed. Abdullahi Ahmed An-Na'im and Francis M. Deng, (Washington, D.C.: Brookings Institution, 1990), 366. See also An-Na'im, "Toward a Cross-Cultural Approach to Defining International Standards of Human Rights: The Meaning of Cruel, Inhuman, or Degrading Treatment or Punishment," in *Human Rights in Cross-Cultural Perspectives: A Quest for Consensus*, ed. Abdullahi Ahmed An-Na'im (Philadelphia: University of Pennsylvania Press 1991), 19–44.

2. Tore Lindholm, "Prospects for Research on the Cultural Legitimacy of Human Rights: The Cases for Liberalism and Marxism," in An-Na'im, ed., *Human Rights in Cross-Cultural Perspectives*, 397. He writes: "Article 1 of the UDHR establishes that the proximate normative moral premise in justifying universal human rights is the moral principle that every human being is entitled to freedom and equal dignity, where 'entitled' indicates what human beings are due as a question of reciprocal moral recognition. . . . The universal reciprocal moral recognition among human beings in terms of inherent freedom and equal dignity is . . . the minimal common normative grounds for universal human rights" (395–96).

3. Tore Lindholm, "Article 1," in *The Universal Declaration of Human Rights: A Commentary*, ed. Asbjørn Eide et al. (Oslo: Scandinavian University Press, 1992), 42.

4. Alan Gewirth, "The Golden Rule Rationalized," in *Human Rights: Essays on Justification and Applications* (Chicago: University of Chicago Press 1982), 130; emphasis original.

5. Richard Rorty, "Truth and Freedom: A Reply to Thomas McCarthy," in *Prospects for a Common Morality*, ed. Gene Outka and John P. Reeder, Jr. (Princeton, N.J.: Princeton University Press 1993), 282.

6. Gewirth, *Human Rights: Essays*, 30.

7. For a detailed elaboration of this second set, see Alan Gewirth, *The Community of Rights* (Chicago: University of Chicago Press, 1996).

8. Bernard Williams, *Ethics and the Limits of Philosophy* (Cambridge, Mass.: Harvard University Press 1985), 69.

9. Robert Nozick, *Philosophical Explanations* (Cambridge, Mass.: Harvard University Press, 1981), the "Ethical Push" and "Ethical Pull" sections in Part 5, "Foundations of Ethics."

10. John Rawls, *The Law of Peoples* (Cambridge, Mass.: Harvard University Press, 1999) (hereafter *LP*).

11. John Rawls, *Political Liberalism* (New York: Columbia University Press, 2005) (hereafter *PL*).

12. John Rawls, *A Theory of Justice* (Cambridge, Mass.: Harvard University Press, 1971), 60.

13. This is the point David Reidy makes in "Political Authority and Human Rights," in *Rawls' Law of Peoples: A Realistic Utopia?* ed. Rex Martin and David A. Reidy (Oxford: Blackwell, 2006). Reidy reconstructs Rawls's cryptic remarks along the lines of the common good conception of justice as expounded by Philip Soper in *A Theory of Law* (Cambridge, Mass.: Harvard University Press, 1984), which Rawls cites in his construction of Kazanistan (*LP*, 66, 67n, 72n).

14. See especially Alistair Macleod, "Rawls's Narrow Doctrine of Human Rights," in Martin and Reidy, eds., *Rawls' Law*. Macleod does think that Rawls provides "neither a clear explanation nor an adequate defense" for his "sparse" (138) and "ad hoc" (141) list.

15. Allen Buchanan, in "Taking the Human out of Human Rights" (in Martin and Reidy, eds., *Rawls's Law*), also criticizes Rawls for "develop[ing] a theory of human rights in which the idea that these rights are grounded in our humanity is conspicuously absent" (140; cf. 150, 163, 167) and sees the list as "truncated" (150) without good reason and therefore as "a radical departure" from mainline philosophical views such as the capabilities approach that we defend in Chapter 4.

16. See *LP*, 80, n. 23.

17. For this same point, see also Buchanan, "Taking the Human out of Human Rights," where he defends inherence and "accuses" Rawls of using an unacceptable "stipulative redefinition" of what a human right is (65–67).

18. Here I agree with Reidy's argument (in "Political Authority") that Rawls's "human rights minimalism . . . is not a function of concessions to or accommodations of nonliberal, nondemocratic decent peoples," but must be traced back to within the earlier foreign policy caucus of the liberal club itself (178).

19. It is at this point, before the doors of the club have been opened to the other four types of peoples mentioned, that Rawls makes the observation that he "is not calling for a world government" (*LP*, 36).

20. René Provost, *International Human Rights and Humanitarian Law* (Cambridge: Cambridge University Press, 2002), 133.

21. Ibid., 135.

22. Rawls, *PL*.

23. Jack Donnelly, *Universal Human Rights in Theory and Practice* (Ithaca, N.Y.: Cornell University Press, 2003), chap. 2.

24. We will see that Nussbaum mostly sides with Rawls and is hesitant about anchoring human *rights* metaphysically, though in the third section we will also see that she see takes her cosmopolitanism back to the ancient Stoics. In any case, it would seem that the Stoic entry into the domain of inherent rights (if

there is such) was by way of reason instead of conscience. For a critique of Nussbaum's interpretation of Augustine and of the Stoics, see Nicholas Wolterstorff, *Justice Rights and Wrongs* (Princeton, N.J.: Princeton University Press, 2008), 202–4, 213–18.

25. Wolstersorff, *Justice Rights and Wrongs.*

Chapter 4. Human Rights Cosmopolitanism

1. Peter Singer, *One World: The Ethics of Globalization* (New Haven, Conn.: Yale University Press, 2004), 149.

2. Jack Donnelly, *Universal Human Rights in Theory and Practice* (Ithaca, N.Y.: Cornell University Press 2003), 34. I agree with Donnelly that "the need for an active state has always been especially clear for economic and social rights" (36), but we object to his drawing out of the Universal Declaration a "state-centric conception" of human rights.

3. Donnelly must therefore be added to the list of theorists who commit the fallacy of implementation, which we defined as the pulling of the measures of implementation into the very definition of what a human right is (Chapter 1, section C). He thinks that the Declaration was set up as "'as a common standard of achievement for all peoples and all nations'—and [*indirectly*] the states that represent them" (34). The word "indirectly" must be inserted here to make this claim fit with what the drafters were thinking, for they mostly ignored the fact that our world is broken up into nation-state units.

4. Bhikhu Parekh, *Rethinking Multiculturalism Cultural Diversity and Political Theory* (Cambridge, Mass.: Harvard University Press, 2000), 134.

5. Albert Camus, *The Rebel* (New York: Knopf, 1956), 19.

6. Martin Luther King, Jr., "Letter from Birmingham Jail," *Christian Century*, April 16, 1963, 1 §4, http://www.stanford.edu/group/King/frequentdocs/birmingham.pdf (accessed June 10, 2008).

7. *To Secure These Rights: The Report of the President's Committee on Civil Rights* (Washington, D.C.: Government Printing Office, 1947), at viii.

8. For details, see Karl A. Schleunes, ed., *Legislating the Holocaust: The Bernard Loesener Memoirs and Supporting Documents*, trans. Carol Scherer (Boulder, Colo.: Westview Press, 2001).

9. For perusal of discrimination law in the United States I recommend http://finduslaw.com/federal_employment_laws/employment_discrimination/age.

10. The references to and citations from the world's constitutions can be checked in www.cofinder.richmond.edu (accessed October 7, 2008).

11. For another recent and worthwhile version of this capabilities approach, not discussed in the text, see A. Belden Fields, *Rethinking Human Rights for the New Millennium* (New York: Palgrave Macmillan, 2003), chap. 3, "A Holistic Approach to Human Rights."

12. Amartya Sen, *Freedom as Development* (New York: Random House, 1999).

13. For these statistics, see International Bank for Reconstruction and Development/World Bank, *World Bank Atlas 2003* (Washington, D.C.: World Bank, 2003), 80–81, 56.

14. Amartya Sen, *Inequality Reexamined* (Cambridge, Mass.: Harvard University Press, 1992), 113.

15. See Ronald Dworkin, *Sovereign Virtue: The Theory and Practice of Equality* (Cambridge, Mass.: Harvard University Press, 2000). Human rights do not occur

in the index of Dworkin's challenging book. There are in Dworkin's scheme no prepolitical or prejuridical rights other than the single abstract right to equal treatment and concern. For instance, he cannot accept the Lockean idea that a person "owns" his mind and body and is therefore entitled to the fruits of both "because it uses the idea of prepolitical entitlement based on something other than equality, and that is inconsistent with the premise of the scheme of equality of resources we have developed" (90).

16. See Sen, *Inequality*, section 1.2, "Impartiality and Equality," 16.

17. Martha C. Nussbaum, *Women and Human Development: The Capabilities Approach* (Cambridge: Cambridge University Press, 2000); Nussbaum, *Frontiers of Justice: Disability, Nationality, Species Membership* (Cambridge, Mass.: Belknap Press of Harvard University Press, 2006). A still earlier account of her views can be found in her article "Capabilities and Human Rights," *Fordham Law Review* 66, 273 (1997): 273–300.

18. Nussbaum, *Frontiers*, chap. 5, section iv.

19. I skip Article 22 because in the preceding section we saw that it was meant as an introduction to some of the articles that follow it.

20. See Thomas Pogge, "Human Rights and Human Responsibilities," in *Global Justice, Transnational Politics*, ed. Pablo de Greiff and Ciaran Cronin (Cambridge, Mass.: MIT Press, 2002), section 4, "An Institutional Understanding of Human Rights Based in §28," 165.

21. See Morsink, *Origins*, chap. 5.

22. St. Thomas Aquinas, *Summa Theologica I-II*, in *Basic Writings*, vol. 2 (New York: Random House, 1945), Q94/Art.4/Reply Obj. 3, p. 778.

23. For a discussion of this fallacy see Chapter 1, section C.

24. For a discussion of this issue see Morsink, *Origins*, section 3.5.

25. For a discussion of the rights of children in the Declaration see *Origins*, sections 6.3, 7.2.

26. Nussbaum, *Frontiers*, chap. 3, "Capabilities and Disabilities," has a very helpful discussion.

27. For Enlightenment roots in India, see Amartya Sen's essay "Tagore and His India," *New York Review of Books* 44, 11 (June 1997).

28. See Morsink, *Origins*, section 6.3.

29. "Patriotism or Cosmopolitanism?" *Boston Review* 19, 5 (October/November 1994): 3.

30. Hilary Putnam doubts that there even is such a thing as "a world way of life" ("Patriotism," 13), while Nathan Glazer questions that there could be a "cosmopolitan political loyalty" (26).

31. See Brian Barry, *Culture and Equality* (Cambridge, Mass.: Harvard University Press, 2001).

32. Thomas Paine, *Rights of Man* (New York: Viking Penguin, 1985), Part II, Introduction, 159. See also the comments by Leo Marx ("Patriotism," 20).

33. Amy Gutmann, *Democratic Education*, rev. ed. (Princeton, N.J.: Princeton University Press, 1999).

34. Beitz defends a "moderate cosmopolitanism" that embraces human rights education (as I indicated in the text) and that accommodates a 'patriotism based on loyalty to a just constitution and which acknowledges obligations to outsiders that could override obligations to compatriots" ("Patriotism," 23). It is this override that fits his patriotism within his cosmopolitanism.

35. Kok-Chor Tan, *Justice Without Borders: Cosmopolitanism, Nationalism and Patriotism* (Cambridge: Cambridge University Press, 2004).

36. It ratified the Genocide Convention in 1986, the Convention on the Political Rights of Women in 1967, the Supplemental Slavery Convention in 1967, the ILO Convention on Forced Labor in 1991, the Convention on Racial Discrimination in 1994, the Covenant on Civil and Political Rights in 1992, and the Torture Convention in 1990 and 1994, but it has not ratified the Optional Protocol to the ICCPR that allows for individual complainants to the oversight Committee, nor the Covenant on Economic and Social Rights, nor the American Convention on Human Rights, nor the Convention to Eliminate All Forms of Discrimination Against Women (CEDAW), nor, as I state in the text, the Convention on the Rights of the Child. For the paradox these ratifications and withholdings raise, see Andrew Moravcsik, "The Paradox of U.S. Human Rights Policy," in *American Exceptionalism and Human Rights*, ed. Michael Ignatieff (Princeton, N.J.: Princeton University Press, 2005), 147–97. For this list, see Moravcsik, 185.

37. See Michael Ignatieff, "Introduction: American Exceptionalism and Human Rights," in Ignatieff, *American Exceptionalism*.

38. See John Rawls, *Political Liberalism* (New York: Columbia University Press, 1993); Brian Barry, *Culture and Equality* (Cambridge, Mass.: Harvard University Press, 2001); Amy Gutmann, *Identity and Democracy* (Princeton, N.J.: Princeton University Press, 2003); and David Miller, *On Nationality* (Oxford: Clarendon Press, 1995).

39. Charles Taylor, *Multiculturalism: Examining the Politics of Recognition*, ed. Amy Gutmann (Princeton, N.J.: Princeton University Press, 1994); Will Kymlicka, *Liberalism, Community and Culture* (Oxford: Clarendon Press, 1989); Bhiku Parekh, *Rethinking Multiculturalism: Cultural Diversity and Political Theory* (Cambridge, Mass.: Harvard University Press, 2006); and Seyla Benhabib, *The Claims of Culture: Equality and Diversity in the Global Era* (Princeton, N.J.: Princeton University Press, 2002).

40. Miller, *On Nationality*, 27.

41. Yael Tamir, for instance, does not build a political component into his definition of nationalism. He adopts Seton-Watson's definition of the state as "a legal political organization with the power to require obedience and loyalty from its citizens" and of the nation as "a community of people whose members are bound together by a sense of solidarity, a common culture, a national consciousness." See Tamir, *Liberal Nationalism* (Princeton, N.J.: Princeton University Press, 1993), 59–60.

42. For an explanation of how this happened, see Johannes Morsink, "Cultural Genocide, the Universal Declaration, and Minority Rights," *Human Rights Quarterly* 21, 4 (November 1999): 1009–60.

43. United Nations Development Programme, *Human Development Report 2004: Cultural Liberty in Today's Diverse World* (Oxford: Oxford University Press, 2004).

44. The report points to the fact that "In Belgium citizens overwhelmingly replied when asked that they felt both Belgian and Flemish or Walloon, and in Spain that they felt Spanish as well as Catalan or Basque" (3), and to surveys showing that "Fears that if immigrants do not 'assimilate' they will fragment the country are unfounded" (3). It also refers to "cultural liberty" as "a human right and an important aspect of human development—and thus worthy of state action and attention" (6).

45. This crucial right of language did not end up in the text primarily because of French indecision about where in the Declaration support for minority language rights was best put. For this point, see Morsink, *Origins*, section 3.3, 105–9.

46. The websites for the treaties here are mentioned in the notes to section C of Chapter 1.

47. This was reversed in 2002–4.

48. UN DOC E/CN.4/57/Add. 1 (1947). Both the Second Session of the Commission and the Second Session of the Drafting Committee adopted the education article with this note attached. See UN DOCS E/CN.1/10/.13 and E/CN.4/SR.42/.2. See also E/600, Article 27.

49. Carrera Andrade of Ecuador said he had abstained because the Lebanese provisions that had been adopted as a third paragraph "were contrary to the system established in certain countries, especially Ecuador, where the State enjoyed certain prerogatives in the field of education" (606).

50. See the various entries of E/CN.4/Sub.2/4.

51. See the entries of E/CN.4/Sub.2/4–5.

52. The delegate from Chile argued that it "might not be altogether wise to adopt the Danish amendment. Many countries and particularly Chile had always tried to unify its heterogeneous population. By giving minorities the right to establish their own schools such work of unification which had been carried out so successfully by some governments, notably in the Americas, might be imperiled. For those reasons he could not support the Danish amendment" (GAOR Third, 588).

Chapter 5. The Charge of Unrealistic Utopianism

1. For a recent listing and discussion of figures like these, see Office of the UN Commissioner for Refugees, *The State of the World's Refugees: Human Displacement in the New Millennium* (Oxford: Oxford University Press, 2006).

2. Maurice Cranston, "Human Rights Real and Supposed," in *The Philosophy of Human Rights*, ed. Morton E. Winston (Belmont, Calif.: Wadsworth, 1989), 127.

3. These comments were made in the Third Session of the Human Rights Commission; Cisneros (877), Romulo (868).

4. See the comments in the Third Session of the Commission by Juliusz Katz-Suchy, the Polish delegate (904), and by Ljuba Radevanovic, his colleague from Yugoslavia (913).

5. It is scholarly custom to speak of three generations of human rights, the third kind comprising collective human rights of peoples and groups that (strictly speaking) are not present in the Declaration and therefore not discussed in this study of its roots.

6. For this use of Article 22, see Michael J. Dennis and David P. Stewart, "Justiciability of Economic, Social and Cultural Rights: Should There Be an International Complaints Mechanism to Adjudicate the Rights to Food, Water, Housing and Health?" *American Journal of International Law* 98, 3 (July 2004). My report here supports the authors' thesis (in far more detail than they give on 478) that the original objections to exactly equal implementation treatment for all human rights were of a practical and budgetary kind and not of an ideological or philosophical nature.

7. Since the specific elements of the right to social security are listed in Article 25, that opening right is not the main point of Article 22. Nor can it be the end right to the full and free development of our personality, for that right is mentioned only because it is the goal of the social, economic and cultural rights. Furthermore, that right is also mentioned in Articles 26 and 29.

8. The Egyptian delegation proposed to insert the clause "in accordance with economic and social possibilities" of each state, while the United States proposed the addition "or in collaboration with other States, in accordance with the social and economic system and political organization" (SR.71/3). Cassin defended the addition of the rights to social security to this particular article (rather than to Article 25) because "the welfare of workers had long since ceased to be a purely national concern; the mass unemployment of 1932 showed that action was needed on an international level. The clause referring to 'international co-operation' in the text of the article would satisfy that necessity" (SR.72/9).

9. René Cassin, *La Déclaration universelle des droits de l'homme de 1948* (Paris: Firmin-Didot, 1958), 7. By 10 votes to 6, the Third Session approved the general idea of a second covering article (SR.72/5), with the exact wording yet to be determined. Eleanor Roosevelt, Chairman and U.S. representative, incorporating suggestions from other delegations, proposed this wording: "Every person, as a member of society, is entitled to the realization of the economic, social and cultural rights enumerated below, through national effort and international co-operation, in accordance with the organization and resources of each State" (SR.72/7).

10. See Dennis and Stewart, "Justiciability," 478.

11. "The State and society shall undertake all necessary measures, including legislation, for ensuring to every person a real possibility of enjoying all the rights listed in this Declaration. In view of the particular significance which social, economic and cultural rights have, as listed in article 23 [22] to 30 [27] (particularly the right to social security) it is recognized desirable to have them implemented both through material national efforts and through international co-operation, taking into account the social and economic systems and resources of each State" (SR.72/9).

12. See Dennis and Stewart, "Justiciability," 478. Our account here conflicts with Cass Sunstein's contention that the United States had, through Eleanor Roosevelt, a formative influence upon the entry of social and economic rights into the international bill of rights. See his remarks in *The Second Bill of Rights* (New York: Free Press, 2004) 128, 178, 216. Roosevelt personally saw social and economic rights as a crucial part of the international bill, but the State Department, which kept a close eye on her, would not let her espouse her liberal views as part of her role as the U.S. representative on the Human Rights Commission. What she expresses here are the views of her government.

13. So as to avoid twice using the language of rights, the Third Session changed the opening phrase "has a right" to "is entitled" and then adopted the Article with six votes to three, with six abstentions (SR.78/11).

14. Nehmiah Robinson, *The Universal Declaration of Human Rights: Its Origin, Significance, Application, and Interpretation* (New York: Institute of Jewish Affairs, 1958), 40.

15. See the essays in Pablo de Greiff and Ciarin Cronin, eds., *Global Justice and Transnational Politics: Essays on the Moral and Political Challenges of Globalization* (Cambridge, Mass.: MIT Press, 2002), especially Thomas Pogge's contribution, "Human Rights and Human Responsibilities."

16. Cécile Fabre, *Social Rights Under the Constitution: Government and the Decent Life* (Oxford: Oxford University Press, 2000), 22. More specifically aimed at the case of the United States are the arguments in Sotirios A. Barber, *Welfare and the Constitution* (Princeton, N.J.: Princeton University Press, 2003).

17. Cass R. Sunstein, *The Second Bill of Rights: FDR's Unfinished Revolution and Why We Need It More Than Ever* (New York: Basic Books, 2004), chap. 3.

18. To "a useful and remunerative job"; to "earn enough to provide adequate food and clothing and recreation"; to raise and sell products so that one can give one's "family a decent living"; to be free from "unfair competition and domination by monopolies at home or abroad", "of every family to a decent home"; "to adequate medical care and the opportunity to achieve and enjoy good health"; to adequate protection from economic fears of old age, sickness, accident and unemployment"; and "to a good education" (Sunstein, *Second Bill*, ix)

19. Jeremy Waldron, "Homelessness and the Issue of Freedom," in Waldron, *Liberal Rights: Collected Papers 1981–1991* (Cambridge: Cambridge University Press, 1993), 11.

20. Charles Fried, *Right and Wrong* (Cambridge, Mass.: Harvard University Press, 1978), 110.

21. Cited from E. W. Vierdag, "The Legal Nature of the Rights Granted by the International Covenant on Economic, Social and Cultural Rights," *Netherlands Yearbook of International Law* 9, 69 (1978): 103, cited in Henry J. Steiner and Philip Alston, eds. *International Human Rights in Context: Law, Politics, Morals*, 2nd ed. (Oxford: Oxford University Press, 2000), 277.

22. See Office of the High Commissioner for Human Rights, Committee on Economic, Social and Cultural Rights, "The Domestic Application of the Covenant: .3/12/98. E/C.12/1998/24, CESCR General comment 9," "Justiciability," §10; http://www.unhchr.ch/tbs/doc.nsf/(Symbol)/4ceb75c5492497d9802566d500516036?Opendocument (accessed June 10, 2008).

23. Cited in Steiner and Alston, eds., *International Human Rights in Context*, 279.

24. See Henry Shue, *Basic Rights Subsistence, Affluence and U.S. Foreign Policy* (Princeton, N.J.: Princeton University Press, 1980), where he argues that a basic right needs to be met before or as part of the fulfillment of any other rights. Of Shue's three basic rights, two come from the classical civil and political side (security and liberty) and one, subsistence, from the social, economic, and cultural side of the ledger.

25. See Morsink, *Origins*, section 6.5.

26. See Michael Massing, "Amartya Sen's Famous Theory Is Being Tested in India," *New York Times*, March 1, 2003, B1, 9.

27. Unless otherwise noted, the figures in this and in the next paragraph are taken from *Human Development Report 2002: Deepening Democracy in a Fragmented World* (New York: Oxford University Press, 2002), 149ff.

28. Philip Alston, "Ships Passing in the Night: The Current State of the Human Rights and Development Debate Seen Through the Lens of the Millennium Goals," *Human Rights Quarterly* 27, 3 (August 2005): 756.

29. This is the title of a proposal adopted by ten UN agencies and other development agencies in 2003, which Alston discusses extensively throughout his indictment.

30. Philip Alston and Mary Robinson, *Human Rights and Development: Towards Mutual Reinforcement* (Oxford: Oxford University Press, 2005).

31. International Bank for Reconstruction and Development/World Bank, *World Development Report 2004* (Washington, D.C.: World Bank, 2003), 249.

32. See John Rawls, *LP*, where he phrases the international duty of assistance in terms of "peoples [that] have a duty to help other peoples living under unfa-

vorable conditions that prevent their having a just or decent political and social regime" (35).

33. Leif Wenar, "Contractualism and Global Economic Justice," in *Global Justice*, ed. Thomas Pogge (Oxford: Blackwell, 2001), 87.

34. Charles Beitz, "Does Global Inequality Matter?" in Pogge, *Global Justice*, 111.

35. Rainer Forst, "Towards a Critical Theory of Transnational Justice," in Pogge, *Global Justice*, 177.

36. Amartya Sen, *Inequality Reexamined* (Cambridge, Mass.: Harvard University Press, 1992), 109.

37. "That is where the idea of a threshold comes in: we say that beneath a certain level of a capability, in each area, a person has not been enabled to live in a truly human way" (*WHD*, 74). See also *Frontiers*, 381.

38. While the extreme deprivation we find in severe mental disabilities or senile dementia is, of course, important from the perspective of medical ethics, Nussbaum says her real focus is on "a higher threshold, the level at which a person's capability becomes what Marx called 'truly human,' that is *worthy* of a human being" (*WHD*, 73; emphasis original). It would seem that this observation goes beyond the initial minimalism of mere threshold fulfillment.

39. For the texts of all the documents mentioned in this and the next paragraph, see Ian Brownlie, ed., *Basic Documents on Human Rights* (Oxford: Oxford University Press, 2003).

40. These sites can be found at http://www.ohchr.org/english/bodies/treaty/index.htm.

41. For detailed descriptions of these regional activities, see Dinah Shelton, *Regional Protection of Human Rights* (Oxford: Oxford University Press, 2008).

42. Cited by Anne-Marie Slaughter in *A New World Order* (Princeton, N.J.: Princeton University Press, 2004), 75.

43. Justice Chaskalson, president of the African Constitutional Court, concluded a 1995 ruling in a capital case with the observation that the "rights to life and dignity are the most important of all human rights, and the source of all other personal rights" (Steiner and Alston, *International Human Rights*, 53 n.). He reached that decision by way of an exploration not just of the provisions in the new constitution of his own country, but also of the death penalty approaches of the United States and India (which do allow for the death penalty) and of Germany, Hungary, and Canada (which do not). He also investigated the rulings of the Human Rights Committee (ambivalent), and the European Court of Human Rights (against).

44. For a discussion of these provisions see Sunstein, *Second Bill*, 211–27, n. 19.

45. Cited in Paul Hunt, *Reclaiming Social Rights: International and Comparative Perspectives* (Aldershot: Ashgate, 1996), 227.

46. In another case, contractors who had "deducted" a 10 percent commission of their hired laborers' wages were held to have violated Article 23 of the Directive Principles, entitled "Prohibition of Traffic in Human Beings and Forced Labor." As part of the decision against the contractors, the Court noted that "there is indeed a close relationship between civil and political rights on the one hand and economic, social and cultural rights on the other" (P. Hunt, *Reclaiming Social Rights*, 162, n. 44).

47. For an update on the arguments in this section I recommend Sandra

Freedman, *Human Rights Transformed: Positive Rights and Positive Duties* (New York: Oxford University Press, 2008),

48. For an investigation of how the Human Rights Committee that monitors how the Covenant on Civil and Political Rights Covenant operates, see Ineke Boerefijn, *The Reporting Procedure Under the Covenant on Civil and Political Rights: Practice and Procedures of the Human Rights Committee* (Oxford. Intersentia Hart, 1999).

49. International Covenant on Economic, Social and Cultural Rights, Adopted and opened for signature, ratification and accession by General Assembly resolution 2200A (XXI) of 16 December 1966, http://www.unhchr.ch/html/menu3/b/a_cescr.htm

50. Matthew C. R. Craven, *The International Convention on Economic, Social and Cultural Rights: A Perspective on Its Development* (Oxford: Clarendon Press, 1995), 200.

51. For the influence and effectiveness of the International Labor Organization on the construction of work-related human rights, see the contributions to the Philip Alston, ed., *Labour Rights as Human Rights* (Oxford: Oxford University Press), 2005.

52. See Mary Bauer, *Close to Slavery: Guestworker Programs in the United States* (Montgomery, Ala.: Southern Poverty Law Center, April 2007), www.splcenter.org. For examples in a more popular venue of the roughly "27 million people worldwide who are bought and sold, held captive, brutalized, [and] exploited for profit," see Andrew Cockburn, photographs by Jodi Cobb, "21st Century Slaves," *National Geographic*, September 2003.

53. "The State Parties to the present Covenant recognize the right of everyone to the enjoyment of just and favourable conditions of work which ensures, in particular: (a) Remuneration which provides all workers with as a minimum with i) Fair wages and equal remuneration for work of equal value without distinction of any kind, in particular women being guaranteed conditions of work not inferior to those enjoyed by men, with equal pay for equal work; (ii) a decent living for themselves and their families . . . ; (b) Safe and healthy working conditions; (c) Equal opportunity for everyone to be promoted in his employment to an appropriate higher level, subject to no considerations other than those of seniority and competence; (d) rest, leisure and reasonable limitation of working hours and periodic holidays with pay, as well as remuneration for public holidays."

54. *New York Times*, March 29, 2007, C1, C10.

55. (1) Sweden, (2) Norway, (3) Netherlands, (4) Finland, (5) Denmark, (6) Germany, (7) Luxembourg, (8) France, (9) Japan, (10) Spain, (11) Italy, (12) Canada, (13) Belgium, (14) Australia, (15) United Kingdom, (16) Ireland, (17) United States, *UNDP 2000*, 161.

56. See Barbara Ehrenreich, *Nickel and Dimed: On (Not) Getting by in America* (New York: Metropolitan Books, 2001); Beth Shulman, *The Betrayal of Work* (New York: New Press, 2003); and the case histories in David Shipler, *The Working Poor: Invisible in America* (New York: Knopf, 2004).

57. See www.HRW.org.

58. See 23(4): "Everyone has the right to form and to join trade unions for the protection of his interests." For the influence of the union movement on the drafting of work related rights in the Universal Declaration, see chap. 5 ("The Socialist Shape of Work Related Rights") in Morsink, *Origins*.

59. See the Office of the UN High Commissioner for Human Rights, Committee on Economic, Social and Cultural Rights, General Comments,

http://www.unhchr.ch/tbs/doc.nsf/(Symbol)/94bdbaf59b43a424c12563ed 0052b664?Opendocument.

60. Human Rights Watch, *Unfair Advantage: Workers' Freedom of Association in the United States Under International Human Rights Standards* (New York: HRW, 2000).

61. While the original Wagner Act of 1935 that defined labor relations struck a fair balance between employee and employer, section 2 of the National Labor Relations Act of 1947 (also called the Taft-Hartley Act) determined that "The term employee shall not include any individual employed as an agricultural laborer, or in the domestic service of any family or person at his home, . . . or any individual having the status of an independent contractor or any individual employed as a supervisor" (cited in Bauer, *Close to Slavery*, 172).

62. For instance, "U.S. Labor Department studies in 1997 and 1998 indicated that nearly two-thirds of garment industry shops in New York violate minimum wage and overtime laws" (ibid., 132).

63. See Sunstein, *Second Bill*, 20ff., 85–88, 114ff.

64. See Steiner and Alston, *International Human Rights*.

65. International Bank for Reconstruction and Development/World Bank, *World Bank Atlas 2003* (Washington, D.C.: World Bank, 2003), 45.

66. Some of these statistics can be found in Shlomo Angel, *Housing Policy Matters: A Global Analysis* (Oxford: Oxford University Press, 2000). This book is based on the Global Survey of Housing Indicators.

67. Craven, *International Convention*, 378. This definition was given to it by the Commission on Human Settlements and the Global Strategy for Shelter to the Year 2000.

68. Cited by Brigit C. A. Toebes, *The Right to Health as a Human Right in International Law* (Antwerp: Intersentia, 1999), 48.

69. Toebes, *Right to Health*.

70. International Bank for Reconstruction and Development/World Bank, *03 World Bank Atlas*, 25.

71. Unless otherwise indicated the figures in these three paragraphs are taken from the tables in UN Development Program, *Human Development Report 2002* (New York,: Oxford University Press, 2002), 174–77.

72. See Sunstein, *Second Bill*, 103.

73. For the details of this see Morsink, *Origins*, chaps. 5 ("The Socialist Shape of Work Related Rights") and 6 ("Social Security, Education, and Culture").

74. Article 12 of the Convention on the Elimination of All Forms of Discrimination Against Women; Article 24 of the Convention on the Rights of the Child; Article 11 of the European Social Charter, Convention on Human Rights and Biomedicine (which focuses just on access to health care facilities); Article 10 of the 1988 Protocol of San Salvador, which elaborated the broad right to health in the American Convention on Human Rights (Article XI: "Everyone has the right to the preservation of his health through sanitary and social measures relating to food, clothing, housing and medical care to the extent permitted by public and community resources," which was drafted about the same time as UDHR Article 25. Article 16 of the African Charter on Human and Peoples' Rights repeats the Covenant's right to "the best attainable state of physical and mental health" and goes on to stipulate that the States Parties "shall take the necessary measures to protect the health of their people and to ensure that they receive medical attention when they are sick" (see Toebes, *Right to Health*, 52–73).

75 Dale Fuchs, "UNICEF Urges Countries to Improve Care of Indigenous Children, *New York Times*, February 26, 2004.

76. Web site of Office of the UN High Commissioner for Human Rights, Committee for Economic, Social and Cultural Rights. Section on Sessions by country and date: http://www2.ohchr.org/english/bodies/cescr/sessions.htm (accessed June 10, 2008).

Chapter 6. Human Rights and Democratic Participation

1. Jürgen Habermas, *Between Facts and Norms: Contributions to a Discourse Theory of Law and Democracy*, trans. William Rehn (Cambridge, Mass.: MIT Press, 1996), 101.

2. See Jean-Jacques Rousseau, *On the Social Contract*, trans. Donald A. Kress (Indianapolis: Hackett, 1987), 82.

3. Actually, it involves the interplay of the moral principle, the legal principle, and the democratic principle, with the discourse principle as the base of operation for all three. For facility of exposition I have left out the legal principle, which ends up being submerged into the democratic principle.

4. However, when it comes to "*ethical-political questions*, the form of life of the political community that is in each case our own constitutes the reference system for justifying decisions that are supposed to express an authentic, collective self-understanding" (Habermas, *Facts and Norms*, 108). "Here the totality of social or subcultural groups that are directly involved constitute the reference system for negotiating compromises. Insofar as these compromises come about under fair bargaining conditions they must be acceptable in principle to all parties, even if on the basis of respectively different reasons" (108).

5 Jürgen Habermas, *Moral Consciousness and Communicative Action*, trans. Christian Lenhardt and Sherry Weber Nicholsen (Cambridge, Mass.: MIT Press, 1990). The communicative presuppositions of argumentative speech are (1) "No speaker may contradict himself," (2) "Every speaker may assert only what he really believes," and (3) "Every subject with the competence to speak and act is allowed to take part in a discourse" (87–89).

6. Hilary Putnam, *The Collapse of the Fact: Value Dichotomy and Other Essays* (Cambridge, Mass.: Harvard University Press, 2002), 125. Putnam scans the discourse ethics rules as follows: "speaking honestly, trying one's best to say what is true, trying one's best to say what is justified, trying to win one another over by the force of argument and not by manipulation of any kind."

7. See Henry J. Steiner and Philip Alston, eds. *International Human Rights in Context: Law, Politics, Morals*, 2nd ed. (Oxford: Oxford University Press, 2000), 940.

8. The page references are to a copy Benhabib was so kind as to send to me just before she gave this address and before it was published in the Proceedings of the Society. Another example, to which Benhabib makes reference and which is quite similar to her own account, is Rainer Forst's "The Basic Right to Justification: Toward a Constructivist Conception of Human Rights," *Constellations* 6, 1 (1999). I believe Forst's account to have the same difficulties as Benhabib's.

9. For Hannah Arendt's account of what she sees as the demise of human rights, see her *The Origins of Totalitarianism* (New York: Harcourt Brace, 1951), chap. 9, pt. 2, "The Decline of the Nation-State and the End of the Rights of Man." The very title of this chapter suggests that in it Arendt commits what we have called the fallacy of implementation.

10. See Seyla Benhabib, *Situating the Self: Gender, Community and Postmodernism*

in Contemporary Ethics (New York: Routledge, 1992); *The Claims of Culture Equality and Diversity in the Global Era* (Princeton, N.J.: Princeton University Press, 2002); and *The Rights of Others: Aliens, Residents and Citizens* (Cambridge: Cambridge University Press, 2004).

11. Gregory H. Fox and Brad R. Roth, eds., *Democratic Governance and International Law* (Cambridge: Cambridge University Press, 2000).

12. Thomas M. Franck, "Legitimacy and the Democratic Entitlement," in Fox and Roth, *Democratic Governance*, 26.

13. Gregory H. Fox, "The Right to Political Participation in International Law," in Fox and Roth, *Democratic Governance*, 50.

14. Franck mentions Article 21 only in passing and instead briefly mentions the political implications of Articles 19 and 20. Fox begins his analysis of treaty law with a discussion of Article 25 of the ICCPR and also makes a passing reference to discussions by the drafters of the Universal Declaration as to whether "ballot secrecy was appropriate for States with a high percentage of illiterate voters, and the majority concluded that ballot secrecy was a fundamental aspect of a fair election and should be retained" (55). At this point Fox put in a note the observation that the Declaration does provide for "equivalent voting procedures," which option was dropped from Article 25 of the ICCPR.

15. See Morsink, *Origins*, 60.

16. See UN *Human Development Report 2000* (Oxford: Oxford University Press, 2000), 171.

17. See Morsink, *Origins*, section 2.4.

18. See Morsink, *Origins*, 69–72.

19. For more details and the references for the claims I make here, see Morsink, *Origins*, 87, 88.

20. See John Rawls, *A Theory of Justice* (Cambridge, Mass.: Harvard University Press, 1971), 218.

21. Amartya Sen, *Poverty and Famines: An Essay on Entitlement and Deprivation* (Oxford: Oxford University Press, 1982).

22. Thomas Pogge, *World Poverty and Human Rights* (Cambridge: Polity Press, 2002).

23. See Sen, "The Rich Get Hungrier," Op-Ed, *New York Times*, May 28, 2008, A21.

24. Joseph T. Siegel, Michael M. Weinstein, and Morton H. Halperin, "Why Democracies Excel," *Foreign Affairs* 83, 5 (September/October 2004): 57–71.

Index

234–35, 298n.46; and principle of non-discrimination in UDHR draft, 153, 156
Inequality Reexamined (Sen), 164–65
inherent human rights, *See* metaphysics of inherence
In Our Own Best Interest: How Defending Human Rights Benefits Us All (Schulz), 6
Inter-American Court of Human Rights, 133
International Convention Against Torture and Other Cruel, Inhuman or Degrading Treatment and Punishment (ICAT) (1984): Article 1 and definition of torture, 87–88, 286n.63; and metaphysics of inherence, 46; and signatory states' obligations, 231; state implementation, 192; U.S. ratification, 192, 294n.36; and U.S. interrogation practices, 86–88, 192–93; U.S. prosecutions of military "abuse," 87–88, 192–93
International Convention on the Elimination of All Forms of Racial Discrimination (ICERD) (1965), 45, 294n.36
International Convention on the Protection of the Rights of All Migrant Workers and Members of their Families (1990), 45–46, 231
International Court of Justice (ICJ), 131, 234
International Covenant on Civil and Political Rights (ICCPR), 45, 231; Article 27 and minority language rights, 199–200; Articles 13(3) and 13(4) and right to education, 199–200; monitoring committee, 232–33; state implementation, 192; U.S. ratification, 294n.36; and U.S. prosecution of military "abuse," 87
International Covenant on Economic, Social and Cultural Rights (ICESCR): debate on optional protocol (allowing quasi-juridical complaints), 210–11; and human rights thresholds, 231, 235–52; justiciability issue and language of positive rights, 219–20; monitoring committee, 232–33; and "progressive" realization/implementation, 240–41; thresholds for health-related rights, 247–52; thresholds for social security and housing rights, 242–47; thresholds for work-related rights, 236–42,

299n.53; U.S. ratification withheld, 239, 241, 246, 294n.36
International Criminal Court (ICC): creation, 95, 205; and defense for crimes committed pursuant to order of a Government or superior, 96–97; definition of "torture," 96; doctrine of manifest illegality, 77, 95–98; four categories of crimes, 96, 97; statute reference to " conscience of humanity," 95–96
International Human Rights Day, 19, 53
International Law Commission, 78–79
International Monetary Fund (IMF), 225
International Tribunal for Rwanda (ICTR). *See* Rwanda Tribunal (ICTR)
International Tribunal for the Territory of the Former Yugoslavia. *See* Yugoslav Tribunal (ICTY)
Inventing Human Rights: A History (Hunt), 59
Iran Constitution (1983), 160, 252
Islamic law (Shar'ia), 75–76, 115; and Golden Rule, 115; and adoption debates, 75–76
Islamic nations: abstentions from final UDHR vote, 75–76, 126; and Article 18, 75, 125–26; and health-related rights, 252; Rawls's imaginary "Kazanistan," 125–26, 129
Israel: Eichmann trial (1960–61), 82–83, 262; and test of manifest illegality in military law, 82–83, 262; Yesh Gvul (soldiers' movement), 106. See also *Kafr Kassem* case

Jefferson, Thomas, 21, 37, 100
Jiménez de Aréchaga, Eduardo, 31
Jones, Lieutenant General Anthony R., 85
justificatory approach, 58–59; and Golden Rule (reciprocity principle), 113–14

Kafr Kassem case in Israeli District Military Court of Appeal, 82–83
Kant, Immanuel, 33–34, 219
Katz-Suchy, Juliusz, 19, 71
Kayala, Abdul Rahman, 28–29, 152
Kayishema, Clement, 93, 288n.77
Kelsen, Hans, 79
King, Martin Luther, Jr., 151
Klevokin, Michael, 57
Koretsky, Vladimir, 28, 33, 151, 155

Acknowledgments

I want to thank David Forsythe of the University of Nebraska, Thomas Pogge of Columbia University, and Dinah Shelton of George Washington University Law School for reading a much longer version of this book and helping me see the need for more focus. I also thank the two anonymous readers for the University of Pennsylvania Press, whose comments on the present version were most helpful. Obviously, none of these readers should be blamed for any shortcomings and outright mistakes that this book may contain. I also thank Alison Anderson of Penn Press for using her superb editing talents in the production of the book. At Drew University, I thank the students in my human rights seminars for trusting me when I would say at the start that thinking very abstractly about real world problems can be fun. I thank John Cerone in Duplicating Services, Beth Patterson in the Library Reference Department, and Gamin Bartle, John Saul and Sarah Ashley in the Faculty Computer Lab for keeping me current and in touch with the outside world. Other colleagues deserve my many thanks for their generous support with sabbaticals and reduced teaching time grants. I also thank them for keeping the university going while I played at being a hermit. Such play involved needing big blocks of quiet time. I often found those times in the middle of the night or at the breaking of the dawn, which is when a great deal of this book was researched and written. That leads me to thank my wife Nancy for putting up with these owl-like habits of mine. In numerous other ways also, she created a wonderfully supportive environment in which to do the work for this book. I dedicate it to her, my loving partner in all things great and small.